LITURGY AND ARCHITECTURE

So frequently church buildings are treated as beautiful objects without appreciating why they vary from place to place and century to century, or how they were meant to function in the worship of God. Allan Doig is a sure guide to the drama of Christian liturgy and the ways in which it has shaped the spaces in which it is performed.

Diarmaid MacCulloch, University of Oxford, UK

The most important influences on the form of a building include functions, architectural traditions and innovations, availability of materials, and money. In the case of churches one of the chief functions is housing the liturgy, a subject which, to say the least, is difficult to pin down. Allan Doig's book performs the sterling service of synthesising – and analysing – great swathes of the disparate research on the subject, producing a clear overview of how the Christian liturgy interacts with architecture from the first century to the sixteenth. It will be greatly welcomed by architectural historians.

Eric Fernie, Courtauld Institute of Art, UK

This is a panoramic survey of Christian church architecture as viewed through the lens of liturgy. It commands both of these complex fields with ease and with welcome attention to political history as well. I know nothing of comparable range and readability.

Richard Pfaff, University of North Carolina, USA

In this book Allan Doig explores the interrelationship of liturgy and architecture from the Early Church to the close of the Middle Ages, taking into account social, economic, technical, theological and artistic factors. These are crucial to a proper understanding of ecclesiastical architecture of all periods, and together their study illuminates the study of liturgy. Buildings and their archaeology are standing indices of human activity, and the whole matrix of meaning they present is highly revealing of the larger meaning of ritual performance within, and movement through, their space. The excavation of the mid-third-century church at Dura Europos in the Syrian desert, the grandeur of Constantine's Imperial basilicas, the influence of the great pilgrimage sites, and the marvels of soaring Gothic cathedrals, all come alive in a new way when the space is animated by the liturgy for which they were built. Reviewing the most recent research in the area, and moving the debate forward, this study will be useful to liturgists, clergy, theologians, art and architectural historians, and those interested in the conservation of ecclesiastical structures built for the liturgy.

The Revd Dr Allan Doig is Fellow, Chaplain and Tutor for Graduates at Lady Margaret Hall, and a member of the Faculty of Theology in the University of Oxford.

D0705606

LITURGY, WORSHIP AND SOCIETY

SERIES EDITORS

Dave Leal, Brasenose College, Oxford, UK
Bryan Spinks, Yale Divinity School, USA
Paul Bradshaw, University of Notre Dame, UK and USA
Gregory Woolfenden, St Mary's Orthodox Church, USA
Phillip Tovey, Ripon College Cuddesdon, UK

The Ashgate *Liturgy, Worship and Society* series forms an important new 'library' on liturgical theory at a time of great change in the liturgy and much debate concerning traditional and new forms of worship, suitability and use of places of worship, and wider issues concerning interaction of liturgy, worship and contemporary society. Offering a thorough grounding in the historical and theological foundations of liturgy, this series explores and challenges many key issues of worship and liturgical theology, currently in hot debate within academe and within Christian churches worldwide - issues central to the future of the liturgy, to public and private worship, and set to make a significant impact on changing patterns of worship and the place of the church in contemporary society.

Other titles in the series:

LIBRARY
UNIVERSITY OF ST. FRANCIS
JOLIET, ILLINOIS

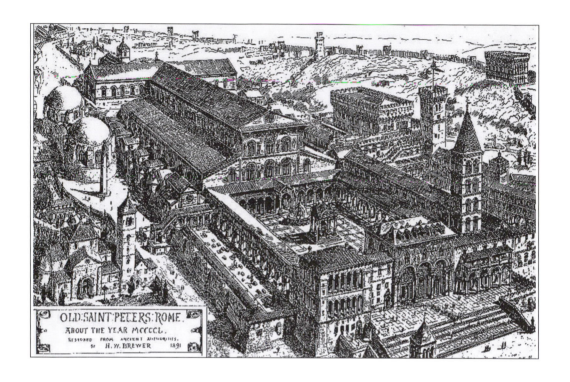

Frontispiece: Engraving of Old St Peter's Basilica, Rome, *c*. 1450; reconstruction by
H.W. Brewer, 1891.

Liturgy and Architecture
From the Early Church to the Middle Ages

ALLAN DOIG
Lady Margaret Hall, Oxford, UK

ASHGATE

© Allan Doig 2008

Reprinted 2009

All rights reserved. No part of this publication may be reproduced, stored in a retrieval system or transmitted in any form or by any means, electronic, mechanical, photocopying, recording or otherwise without the prior permission of the publisher.

Allan Doig has asserted his moral right under the Copyright, Designs and Patents Act, 1988, to be identified as the author of this work.

Published by
Ashgate Publishing Limited
Wey Court East
Union Road
Farnham
Surrey GU9 7PT
England

Ashgate Publishing Company
Suite 420
101 Cherry Street
Burlington, VT 05401-4405
USA

Ashgate website: http://www.ashgate.com

British Library Cataloguing in Publication Data
Doig, Allan
   Liturgy and architecture: from the early church to the Middle Ages. – (Liturgy, worship and society)
   1. Liturgy and architecture 2. Church architecture 3. Church history – Primitive and early church, ca. 30–600
   4. Church history – Middle Ages, 600–1500
   I. Title
   246.9'5

Library of Congress Cataloging-in-Publication Data
Doig, Allan.
   Liturgy and architecture: from the early church to the Middle Ages / Allan Doig.
      p. cm. – (Liturgy, worship, and society)
   ISBN 978-0-7546-5272-4 (hardcover : alk. paper) – ISBN 978-0-7546-5274-8 (pbk. : alk. paper)
   1. Liturgy and architecture. 2. Church architecture. I. Title.
   NA4605.D65 2008
   246'.909–dc22

                                                    2007036257

ISBN 978-0-7546-5272-4 (Hbk); 978-0-7546-5274-8 (Pbk)

Mixed Sources
Product group from well-managed forests and other controlled sources
www.fsc.org Cert no. SGS-COC-2482
© 1996 Forest Stewardship Council

Printed and bound in Great Britain by
TJ International Ltd, Padstow, Cornwall

For Belinda, John, Jamie, and Nick

Contents

List of Plates

The Plates are located between pages 114 and 115.

List of Figures

Preface

First as an architectural historian, then as a clergyman, I have long been searching for a book that outlines the history of the interaction of liturgy and architecture over the long centuries of the development of the Church. There is so much wonderful material out there produced by liturgists, Church historians, architectural historians, architects and archaeologists, but much of it is difficult to get your hands on unless you are fortunate enough to have access to very extensive library holdings. There are good thumbnail sketches, such as Peter Cobb's 'The Architectural Setting of the Liturgy' (1978), and Bouyer's *Liturgy and Architecture* (1967) was a polemical tract in the wake of Vatican II. Then there are the classic studies of aspects of the subject: J.G. Davies's *The Secular Use of Church Buildings* (1968), Addleshaw and Etchells' *The Architectural Setting of Anglican Worship* (1948) and Peter Hammond's studies on modern church architecture, *Liturgy and Architecture* (1960), and with others, *Towards a Church Architecture* (1962). These have all been valuable, and even groundbreaking, especially when they addressed and stimulated their contemporary situation.

Usually, writers on the liturgy will say something about how and where it is celebrated, and anyone writing about ecclesiastical architecture, or for that matter church archaeology, will have to say something about the liturgy, but it is not always appropriate for a detailed study in that specific context. When the study is extended, the results can be magnificent, for example Thomas Mathews' 'An Early Roman Chancel Arrangement and its Liturgical Functions' (1962), but not everyone has immediate access to the journal *Revista di Archeologia Cristiana*, though the article has recently been made more widely available in Ashgate's Variorum series. Another splendid, and accessible, example is Mainstone's integrative work on the liturgy and architecture of Hagia Sophia. For the most part, however, the material is specialist research in one of these specialized areas, restricted in its time span and geographical reach, and using material or making observations relevant to another specialist subject. What I have failed to discover is a work that synthesizes the most important of this vast amount of fascinating material into a single overarching narrative. It is a daunting task, and a work that begins as synthesis soon turns to new analytical work. What began as a new extended sketch revealed such rich material that I was drawn into a fuller study, culminating (for the time being) in the great rupture of the Reformation.

Acknowledgements

Resources for this growing project were provided in the form of a sabbatical from Lady Margaret Hall, Oxford, plus a generous research grant, a grant from the Faculty of Theology of the University of Oxford, and one from Education Services, an educational charity founded by the Cambridge Economist Jack Bellerby. For all this and for their confidence and friendship, I am very grateful.

Ranging over fifteen centuries and across a number of disciplines is a hazardous business, unless you are richly blessed in your colleagues, which I am. I want to offer them all my sincere thanks. Nothing can beat the college system for bringing you into direct contact with experts across the board. Colleagues have read earlier drafts of chapters: Simon Price, Kenneth Painter and Martin Henig were hugely generous with their time and advice about the Classical world, Mary Saunders about Classical languages, Henry Mayr-Harting on late Antiquity and Ottonian times, Hugh Wybrew was my guide to the Byzantine, Eric Fernie, John Blair and John Maddison scoured the Romanesque detail, and Gervase Rosser and Paul Binski the Gothic. Richard Pfaff, with his immense scholarship and familiarity with mediaeval manuscript material, has made invaluable interventions. Diarmaid MacCulloch, who is now working on a complete history of the Church (a feat few could or would dare to approach), Eric Fernie and Richard Pfaff have been kind enough to read the entire manuscript.

The general reader is also immensely important when dealing with a long narrative, and Peter Hainsworth and Jim Council have commented on the complete manuscript. Belinda Jack (my wife) has not only read the complete manuscript, she has throughout the project discussed almost every aspect with me, helping to shape, and absolutely essentially, to prune. She provided both the support and interest that was indispensable during the difficult times, and the hardest test of any when I had too easily made assumptions. With all this support (though naturally not always full agreement), there is no excuse for mistakes or infelicities that have crept in, inadvertently been allowed to remain (probably as a result of my limited computing skills), or that I have subsequently introduced; they are bound to be there somewhere, and they are entirely mine.

For making all this wonderful material available to me, my thanks go to Roberta Staples, Librarian of Lady Margaret Hall, and the librarians of St Catherine's College and All Souls College, Oxford, the Libraries of the Theology and History Faculties, the Sackler, and the Bodleian Libraries of the University of Oxford. Further afield, thanks go to Dumbarton Oaks, the Institute of Art, New York, the Bibliothèque nationale de France, the Metropolitan Museum of Art, the Conway Library of the Courtauld Institute of Art, the Courtauld Institute of Art Gallery, the University of Virginia Institute for Advanced Technology in the Humanities, J.J. Augustin, Professor L. Michael White, Wayne Boucher and Bill Storage for providing wonderful images, but the majority of illustrations have been most generously provided by Dr Allan T. Kohl of Art Images for College Teaching.

Dave Leal of Brasenose College, Oxford, as one of the general editors, kindly suggested to me that I write the volume for this series, and he, Sarah Lloyd, Barbara Pretty and Huw Jones, my editoral team at Ashgate, have been immensely helpful all along the way.

Finally, with the immortal phrase 'So where's the archaeology?' ringing in my ears, I dedicate this book to Belinda and my sons John, Jamie and Nick, who have been willing me on (despite knowing there is bound to be more to come).

Allan Doig
Lady Margaret Hall, Oxford
Epiphany, 2007

Introduction

Every act of worship must have a setting, whether in the open air, a domestic room, at a hospital bedside, in a prison, the parish church or the grandest cathedral. Aspects of the setting will seem more or less appropriate to the occasion, either detracting from, or by contrast intensifying, the meaning of the rite; Dietrich Bonhoeffer's deeply private communion in prison awaiting execution for his resistance against Hitler, without canonical means or text, is perhaps more moving (and surely as valid before a loving and merciful God) than the eucharist celebrated according to the most elaborate rubrics in a great cathedral, but the one simply could not be transferred to the other setting. It is like using the appropriate register of language in a given context; you know when it is right, and may be able to make some general rules. Likewise, there isn't a simple formula or necessarily a direct correspondence between given aspects of the register of the liturgical language and specific elements of its surroundings, which are almost always architectural. Still, the languages of the text, the gestures, the choreography of the movement within the space, and the specific details of setting all come together to interpret the rite to those present at that particular time. It should be fresh each time, but it is not new every time. Rites have histories, and each time we reflect on the grand narrative of salvation forms another layer of our understanding. It is part of the spiritual pilgrimage of the people of God.

So there is clearly some relationship between the liturgy and architecture. On the simplest level, there needs to be a table, vessels for the bread and wine, room for worshippers, often with offerings that have to be dealt with, and space for the celebrant and assistants to carry out the rite according to the given rubrics. The liturgy and its context (architectural and socio-political) shape one another. We have some idea how the earliest Christians worshipped through the biblical witness. They worshipped in the Temple of Jerusalem, in synagogues and in houses, different kinds of worship in different contexts and for different purposes. When Christians were excluded from Judaic worship, they had to make their own provision for the various aspects of worship. It wasn't long before the demands of worship required permanent changes to the house in which it took place. Of course, the earliest, unremodelled, houses actually used for worship cannot now be archaeologically identified, and the oldest identifiable place of Christian worship we know was discovered quite by chance at Dura Europos in modern Syria. The changes that were made to the house during the middle of the third century help us to reconstruct how worship would have unfolded within those spaces. For one thing, documents indicate that a higher theology of priesthood meant that priests were literally elevated to the level of a dais. Paintings and graffiti also help to reconstruct their theological outlook, their vision of the 'city of God' of the psalmist.

Changes outside both liturgy and architecture can also bring about profound changes in them both: developments in the socio-political context might trigger a change in the form of worship, which might in turn bring more changes to the building, or type of building, or technology being used. When Christianity found imperial favour with Constantine, the leader of the formerly oppressed cult was given magisterial status, an imperial palace and two huge basilicas were begun, one as the cathedral of Rome, the other over the tomb of St Peter. Needless to say, imperial ceremonial would have a very considerable impact on the form of worship in these great basilicas at the very least, though it would have little or no impact on worship in existing house-churches of Rome. Forms of worship would also differ between the two great basilicas, with *refrigeria*, or family picnics at the graves of relatives buried *ad sanctum*, close to the Apostle in St Peter's Basilica, where there were also ceremonies associated with the growing cult of the Martyr himself. Further developments of such cults will become a familiar thread running through the fabric of this story, until they come to a dramatic crisis.

Each situation will be found somewhat different from the last. Liturgy and architecture both have an internal logic, and their forms develop at different rates. Liturgical forms and texts were originally pretty fluid, with much being left to the ability of the presiding bishop to improvise, but through the centuries it became progressively fixed, becoming standardized in written form by about the sixth century. Even standard forms develop over time, and the rubrics, or red-letter glosses of the text giving the 'stage directions', can be highly individual to the 'Use' of the specific place, as at medieval Salisbury, Hereford or Durham. Those rubrics are very powerful liturgical engines for change in the architectural setting, since, for example, they detail the form and route of processions and interpret the theology of the architecture and the programme of the painting and sculpture, as will be found at Saint-Denis, Chartres and Wells.

The theological vision and imaginative world expressed in the liturgy in a private house, at a hospital bed, in a parish church or in different ages and climes in pilgrimage churches at Bethlehem and Golgotha, in an imperial basilica in Rome, in the basilicas of Gaul in the twilight of Empire, in the churches of Charlemagne's European Empire, or in the blaze of glory of high-windowed Gothic are all very different. That vision in its context brings the kingdom of God 'very near'. The liturgy seeks to join our worship with the heavenly worship, to bring us beyond imagery to reality itself in the presence of God. In his first letter to the Corinthians, Paul wrote: 'Like a skilled master builder I laid a foundation, and another man is building upon it. Let each man take care how he builds upon it. For no other foundation can anyone lay than is laid, which is Jesus Christ' (1 Cor. 4.10–11), and there is the vision of the heavenly city in the Revelation of St John (Rev. 21.10ff). Building the architecture of the church and edifying the Church by bringing its members closer to God through the liturgy became more than just parallel activities; one was a figure for the other, and would be used time and again by preachers and writers from Eusebius preaching at the consecration of the Cathedral at Tyre at the turn of the fourth century before the 'Peace of the Church' under Constantine, to the hymn for the rebuilding of the Cathedral at Byzantine Edessa in the middle of the sixth century, to Abbot Suger of Saint-Denis in the thirteenth. The great work of building the city of God was on the one hand architectural, because it was a physical interpretation of the theological and biblical vision, while on the other, the liturgical rehearsal and enactment of the biblical record of the events of salvation history brought the people into the very presence of those events in the dramatic presentation of the liturgy, and in the very presence of the Saviour himself through the transformative power of the sacrament:

> So then you are no longer strangers and sojourners, but you are fellow citizens with the saints and members of the household of God, built upon the foundation of the apostles and prophets, Jesus Christ himself being the cornerstone, in whom the whole structure is joined together and grows into a holy temple in the Lord; in whom you also are built into it for a dwelling place of God in the Spirit. (Eph. 3.19–22)

The interpretation and extrapolation of this scriptural image within liturgical fellowship and hard stone architecture together will vary endlessly from the Early Church to the close of the Middle Ages, but that variation is also endlessly rich and fascinating.

CHAPTER 1

The Earliest Christian Worship and its Setting

The New Testament gives us important clues, however fragmentary, about both the form and context of the worship offered by the earliest followers of Jesus. The disciples, like Jesus himself, were observant Jews, and though at first after the crucifixion they cowered behind locked doors, their subsequent visions of the risen Lord transformed their lives (John 20:19–20). In the very last verse of Luke (24:53), after the Ascension the apostles went up 'and were continually in the Temple blessing God'. The Temple of Jerusalem had been the centre of Jewish worship since the time of Solomon, then destroyed by Nebuchadrezzar in 587/586 BCE. It was rebuilt when the exiles returned from Babylon in 538 BCE, and extensively renewed by Herod from 20 BCE. In Acts (2:46), the three thousand who were baptized following Peter's sermon on Pentecost, 'day by day' spent much time together in the Temple. And it would be reasonable to assume that it was a return to their habitual pattern of worship when, after Pentecost, 'Peter and John were going up to the Temple at the hour of prayer, being the ninth hour'.

However, only about four decades after the crucifixion, in 70 CE, the Temple was destroyed by Titus, never to be rebuilt; then, with the exception of sacrifice, the social and religious functions of the Temple were taken over by the synagogue. Even by that time the Temple was only a distant image for the Jews of the diaspora, and its ways and worship were not known to them in any detail. Its lasting effect on Christian worship was as an image to be taken at different historical points and filled retrospectively with particular religious significance; examples of this will be seen later. Still, the power of such an image must not be underestimated, especially when the image usually emerges as a particular interpretation of the earthly reflection of a heavenly sanctuary.[1] Even when the contrast to, as opposed to the connection with, the Temple is emphasized, the image remains powerful, not to say controlling; for example, Gerd Theissen in his recent exploration of *A Theory of Primitive Christian Religion* argues:

> The objects present in the rite are removed from everyday, secular use – including the places and buildings in which the rites take place. A theory of primitive Christian religion has to deal with a great divide in the ritual forms of religious expression. At that time – in different ways in Judaism and Christianity (and also in philosophy) – the traditional ritual actions (bloody animal sacrifices) were replaced by new (bloodless) rites. Traditional holy objects like the temple lost their 'holiness'. But above all a paradoxical new relationship developed between ritual actions and their interpretations: the first Christians developed a religious sign system without temple, without priests, yet in contradiction to the facts they maintained these traditional elements of religious sign systems in their interpretations – often even in an archaic form what was already obsolete at that time. They may have ceased to sacrifice animals, but in their interpretations they reactivated a form of sacrifice which was already long obsolete, namely human sacrifice – as the atoning sacrifice of Jesus.[2]

This passage clearly demonstrates that the effects or influences of the Temple can be construed or presented in very different ways, and although in Theissen's sense the theological, architectural

---

1   Examples of this are given in Bijlsma (1990).
2   Theissen (1999), p. 3.

and even liturgical influence of the Temple was both considerable and complex (which will be further explored later), the inheritance by the early Church of specific patterns of liturgical worship was negligible.

On the other hand, the relationship with the synagogue was very different. When not in Jerusalem, the followers of Jesus, 'as his custom was' (Luke 4:16), would worship in the synagogue. St Paul too was clearly a strict and enthusiastic Jew who, even after his conversion, would go first to the synagogue on his arrival in a new city. When he and Barnabas journeyed to Cyprus, 'arriving at Salamis, they declared the word of God in the Jewish synagogues' (Acts 13:5), then in Pisidian Antioch they went to a service in the synagogue consisting of readings from the Law and the Prophets followed by a sermon from Paul himself. The following sabbath, the Apostles returned at the invitation of the congregation, but on that occasion there was conflict, as there was in the next town, Iconium (Acts 14). In the beginning, Christians were one non-normative Jewish sect among several, certainly in the diaspora; for example, on Delos from the second to the first century BCE there were two widely divergent Jewish groups, one Samaritan, and the other of a more orthodox cast.[3] Like Jesus before them, Jewish Christians soon met serious opposition in the synagogue, and were eventually banned from its gatherings.

Before the destruction of the Temple, these synagogue gatherings focused on readings from the Hebrew scriptures, and in the diaspora at least, on prayer, but there is little evidence of the use of prayer in the synagogues of Palestine itself apart from a few references such as Matthew 6:5: 'they love to stand and pray in the synagogues'. Although over a hundred sites have been identified as ancient synagogues in Palestine, only half a dozen can be securely dated before Constantine, and those are in the diaspora. The archaeological evidence indicates that the latter were all built for other uses, by and large domestic, and then adapted: 'In the Diaspora [the synagogue] functioned as a social as well as religious centre, and there was neither a fixed liturgy nor architecture in the pre-70 period.'[4] It was probably only in the second century, in association with the development of the Torah shrine as an architectural element, that a liturgy became more elaborated and fixed. The earliest known example is in the first synagogue at Dura-Europos on the right bank of the Euphrates in the Syrian Desert. The synagogue was adapted within a private house still in domestic use, towards the end of the second century.

Liturgical scholars had long maintained that Christians took some of their Jewish inheritance with them in the singing of hymns and psalms and the reading of scripture in the context of praise and prayer, but recently many have begun to question whether such a 'service of the word' existed as a separate entity before the third century.[5] The evidence of the Torah shrine at Dura may push that date back to the end of the second century, the same time that Tertullian described the content of Christian meetings: 'We meet together as an assembly and congregation, that, offering up prayer to God as with united force, we may wrestle with him in our supplications. ... We assemble to read our sacred writings, if any peculiarity of the times makes either forewarning or reminiscence needful.' In passing, Tertullian also mentions the setting of worship:

> You must get the accountants to tell you what the tenths of Hercules and the sacrificial banquets cost; the choicest cook is appointed for the Apaturia, the Dionysia, the Attic mysteries; the smoke from the banquet of Serapis will call out the firemen. Yet about the modest supper-room of the Christians alone is a great ado made. Our feast explains itself by its name. The Greeks call it agapè, i.e. affection. ... The participants, before reclining, taste first of prayer to God. As much is eaten as satisfies the cravings of hunger; as much is drunk as benefits the chaste. ... After manual ablution, and the bringing in of lights,

---

3   White (1990), p. 79.
4   White (2000), p. 702.
5   See the discussion in Bradshaw (2004), p. 70.

each is asked to stand forth and sing, as he can, a hymn to God, either one from the holy Scriptures, or one of his own composing, – a proof of the measure of our drinking. As the feast commenced with prayer, so with prayer it is closed.[6]

Since the *Apology* was written for a polemical purpose, Tertullian may have exaggerated the contrast, including the simplicity of the room, but it is useful to have a description of the structure and flavour of the occasion, with music as an important part. Scriptural 'hymns to God' doubtless included the psalms, a rich and wonderfully resilient element of Temple worship. The strength of the form is such that the musical chant has shown remarkable consistency for three thousand years from Temple to Gregorian to Anglican chant:

> Even in translation, the nature of the psalms have produced remarkably consistent patterns of musical setting over a period of nearly 3,000 years. Plainsong, Anglican chant, or the more recent settings of Joseph Gelineau all echo the patterns of the original Hebrew. ... This suggests that the structure and beauty of the Hebrew psalms are too strong to be neglected by musicians and will continue to enrich Jewish and Christian music. [7]

Tertullian tells us that every member of the community gave what they could for its use in these acts of worship, and for some that would mean hospitality and space in their houses for meetings of the assembly, and a private domestic setting was consistently the architectural setting of the earliest Christian liturgies. What he describes is entirely consistent with aspects of worship of the Apostolic age that can be gleaned from the Gospels, Acts and the Epistles.[8] Typically, the dining room of the house, or *triclinium*, was on the top floor, where it would be well lit and catch the breeze. The Last Supper itself had been celebrated in such an upper room of a house borrowed for the occasion (Matthew 26:18; Mark 14:14; Luke 22:11) and after Pentecost new Christians broke bread together in their homes (Acts 2:46) and here in Jerusalem, as later in Corinth (Acts 18), there would appear to have been a number of loosely associated house-churches.

Eventually, a part, or even the whole, of a house would be given over permanently to worship, when physical alterations would be carried out to accommodate changing practices. In the middle of the second century, Justin Martyr wrote what is the earliest surviving detailed description of the Sunday eucharistic breaking of bread. Because, as he says of the eucharist, 'no one is allowed to partake but the man who believes that the things which we teach are true, and who has been washed with the washing that is for the remission of sins',[9] there was a need for the exclusion of the uninitiated, and increasingly for a specially adapted built environment to accommodate the rite as it became gradually elaborated and more strictly codified as numbers grew:

> We afterwards [that is, after baptism and first eucharist] continually remind each other of these things. The wealthy among us help all those in need, and we always keep together. For everything we receive we praise the maker of all things through his Son Jesus Christ and the Holy Spirit. On the so-called Sunday everyone in town or countryside gathers together in one place, and the memoirs of the apostles or the writings of the prophets are read out, for as long as time permits. Next, when the reader has finished, the president in an address admonishes and exhorts us to imitate these good examples. Then we all stand up together and offer prayers; when we have finished praying, as I said before [in section 65], bread, wine and water are brought out, and the president offers prayers of thanks, to the best of his ability; the people assent, saying Amen, and each person receives and shares in that over which thanks have been given, and a portion is taken by the deacons to those not present. The wealthy and willing each gives what he wants

---

6   Tertullian, *Apology*, translated. S. Thelwall, in Roberts and Donaldson (1978), vol. III, pp. 46 and 47.
7   See Wilson-Dickson (1997), pp. 28–9.
8   See especially Meeks (1983), pp. 142–63.
9   Justin Martyr, *The First Apology*, in Roberts and Donaldson (1884), vol. I, p. 185.

as each sees fit, and what is collected is deposited with the president. He helps orphans and widows, and those in need through sickness or any other reason, those in prison, foreigners staying with us; in a word, he takes care of everyone in distress.

On Sunday we make our common gathering since it is the day on which God changed darkness and matter and made the world, and on which Jesus Christ our Saviour rose from the dead.[10]

Unlike Paul (1 Corinthians 11), Justin makes no mention of the *agape*, and in fact Tertullian is the only one to record a single community with celebrations of both the eucharist and a meal he refers to as an *agape*.[11] It used to be accepted that eucharist and meal became disengaged from one another very early in the history of the Church and that the meal finally ceased to be celebrated. Contemporary liturgical scholarship tends to draw a less rigid distinction between the two, seeing them as varieties of sacramental practice. The disappearance of the practice of taking a more extensive sacramental meal is intimately bound up with the architectural setting. The house in which hospitality was offered to the community would have to be reasonably large, with a dining room. In the ancient world a full meal would normally have been taken lying on couches, but this may have changed to sitting in order to be able to accommodate more people in the relatively small dining rooms of private houses. Alternatively, the meeting would convene in the relatively larger courtyard, or *atrium*.[12] With growth in the number of converts, the practice could no longer be accommodated domestically:

> That, at least as far as north Africa was concerned, seems to be the implication of a remark by Cyprian in the third century about the abandonment of the supper in larger congregations. Dining rooms even in substantial private houses would not normally have accommodated more than about a dozen persons, and it is unlikely that Christians would have wanted to rent out the dining spaces attached to pagan temples, which would have been the usual solution adopted by others to the problem of larger parties. On the other hand, if the atrium area of the home was also used for dining, up to forty or fifty people might have been accommodated, but greater numbers than that would have put an end to the older forms of the meal.[13]

At this point the pressure of numbers brought about both a permanent change of practice and architectural adaptation. Architectural historians use the technical term *domus ecclesiae* to describe the building specially adapted for Christian worship.[14] As the rite became more fixed and elaborated, the architecture changed too. It is clearly impossible to identify with any certainty buildings used for Christian worship before this point, at least on purely architectural grounds, since there were no features to distinguish them from buildings strictly in domestic use, or house-churches. If architectural historians are right that the change took place in the mid- to late second century,[15] then it is at least theoretically possible that one day such an early site of a *domus ecclesiae* may be identified where modifications to the fabric were both securely datable and clearly for use by a Christian congregation.

---

10   Translated in Beard, North and Price (1998), vol. II, p. 337.

11   Bradshaw (2004), pp. 29–30.

12   Aspects of hospitality and entertaining in the context of the private house are discussed in Smith (2003), particularly on pp. 176ff. He cites the example of I Corinthians 14, where the meeting is seated, but this is not specifically in the context of a meal.

13   Bradshaw (2004), p. 66.

14   See Krautheimer (1986), p. 27; White (1996–97), vol. II, pp. 25–6, and White (2000), p. 711.

15   White (1990), pp. 118–19.

House-church and *Domus Ecclesiae*

The oldest remains that are traditionally identified as house-churches are to be found in Rome under the so-called 'Title Churches' (*Tituli*), though subsequent changes and wholesale destruction have removed what would constitute archaeological proof for either a house-church or *domus ecclesiae*. A speculative historical reconstruction of the form of these house-churches, classically formulated by Georg Dehio in 1882 and championed in liturgical studies by Gregory Dix,[16] has now been discredited by archaeological evidence. It argues that Roman society was extremely conservative, and the public rooms of first- and second-century houses (particularly of the Campagna near Rome) of the Roman nobility preserved the general layout of the ancient houses of the original Latin settlements of at least a millennium earlier. Examples naturally vary, but schematically there was an entrance from the street into the vestibule and then into the *atrium*, which was a large pillared hall with a tank of water (*impluvium*) in the middle. The *atrium* was either open to the sky or lit by skylights. Continuing along the main axis, there was a room called the *tablinum*, which was generally up a step or two but entirely open to the *atrium*. The *tablinum* was a figure of the original family homestead, with the *atrium* being a vestige of the open yard with 'farm outbuildings' in the rooms either side. The *tablinum* had lean-to structures either side, separated by columns or low walls. At the entrance to the *tablinum* always stood a stone table. The *tablinum* housed the sacred fire, the household gods, and its side-rooms held the family trophies and memorials. Teachers of oratory saw the house as a 'storehouse of memories'. Andrew Wallace-Hadrill, in *Houses and Society in Pompeii and Herculaneum*, explains that 'what the rhetoricians systematized and turned into an art was already an intrinsic feature of the house. In its shapes and patterns, volumes and sequences, ornament and decoration, it stored away and encoded the conscious and unconscious memories of whole rhythms of social life' (p. xv).

A building type as rich in meaning as this could hardly have suited the growing Christian family better, and in the arrangement we are invited to see the nascent porch/narthex (for 'catechumens', those seeking baptism), the pillared nave with font for baptism (*atrium* with tank, or *impluvium*), the *tablinum* as a raised chancel with altar (stone table, or *cartibulum*), and the choir aisles (side-rooms, or *alae*). Just as the whole patrician family would meet in these inter-related spaces presided over by the *pater familias* in a large chair in the *tablinum*, the bishop would preside over his growing Christian family at the liturgy. It was a large urban family in a large urban house. The building with its particular arrangement of rooms was charged with meaning when the Roman patrician family gathered, and with an easy shift of religious context the meaning was transformed when the model was applied to the Christian family.

This theory provides a tempting image of early Christian worship that, not surprisingly, has been extremely persistent, most particularly in liturgical studies, but both the biblical witness and the archaeological evidence move the argument in a different direction. The Pauline epistles themselves emerged from very considerable activity within and between Christian groups which met in private houses, though Acts (19:9) also refers to the hall of Tyrannus at Ephesus. Acts 18 tells of Paul's first visit to Corinth, when he stayed with Priscilla and Aquila (verse 1) and then with Titus Justus (verse 8), whose house was next to the synagogue. Further, there were yet more houses available to the Christian community in Corinth, those of Stephanus (1 Cor. 1:16 and 16:15), Crispus and Chloe (1 Cor. 1:11), and nearby with Gaius (Rom. 16:23), and one near the seaport at Cenchreae under Phoebe, a deaconess (Rom. 16:1). Obviously, there was a good deal of coming and going amongst these house-churches, even if and when they did represent

---

16 Dehio (1882), pp. 301ff, and Dehio and von Bezold (1887), I, pp. 63ff.; Dix (1945), pp. 22–3.

different cells. The letter to Philemon sends greetings to 'the church in your house', and indicates that Paul was expecting him to 'prepare a guestroom for me' (verse 22).

Clearly, none of these house-churches, in their regional variety and relatively low social status, will have conformed to Dix's Campanian model, either physically or in terms of its social organization. Nor will the house of Priscilla and Aquila when they moved to Ephesus (Acts 18:2–4; 1 Cor. 16:19), nor even when they subsequently moved to Rome itself (Rom. 16:3–5).

Tituli or Title Churches

In Rome there are some twenty-five churches[17] which by tradition originated as such house-churches, handed over in whole or in part and adapted for the use of Christian communities. Only a few of these have provided hard archaeological evidence in support of the tradition. By the middle of the third century the Christian community had grown to become 'the largest "association" in the city' of Rome, with modern estimates from 10,000 up to 50,000, based on the large numbers of clergy serving the community and 1500 widows and poor supported by them.[18] Like Corinth, a large urban centre such as Rome certainly had a network of house-churches, and Christians there continued to meet in private domestic settings at least up to the martyrdom of Justin in 165, for when examined by Rusticus the Prefect, who asked 'Where do you assemble?', Justin said:

> 'Where each chooses and can. Perhaps you think we all meet in the same place?'
>   Rusticus the prefect said: 'Tell me, where do you meet, in what place?'
>   Justin said: 'I have been living above the baths of Myrtinos during the whole of this my second visit to Rome. [The text is corrupt.] I do not know any meeting place other than that. I would share with anyone who wanted to come to me the words of truth.'[19]

Justin gave just enough information to appear to be open with the Prefect, and to whet our appetites to search for an actual location.

Titulus Byzantis, SS. Giovanni e Paolo

It is tempting to associate Justin's meeting place 'above the Baths of Myrtinos'[20] with the *Titulus Byzantis*, which incorporated an *insula* complex, or mixed block of flats, of the second century, including baths on the lower floor and housing above. There is strong evidence to suggest that a Christian *titulus* was here as early as the second half of the third century, and clearly by the fourth century, and Krautheimer is more radical, suggesting that there was continuous Christian adaptation of the buildings here from the early third or even late second century. They met in a back shop, which they decorated with frescoes dated as early as 250; subsequently, in the second half of the third century or early fourth, a large staircase was built behind this room, the connecting door was enlarged (damaging the frescoes)[21] and the ground-floor walls were strengthened to carry a large hall, or *aula ecclesiae*, above, indicated by the seven equal and evenly spaced windows. In order to do this work, the Christian community would gradually have had to acquire the better part of the block and have the very considerable further financial resources to carry out the extensive

---

17 Krautheimer (1986), p. 28.

18 See Beard, North and Price (1998), vol. I, p. 267; Eusebius, *History*, VI, 43, in Louth (1989), p. 216.

19 Beard, North and Price (1998), vol. II, p. 345, taken from Masurillo (1972), no. 4, Recension A.

20 See White (1990), p. 110 (and related footnote 38 on pp. 190–91), where he regrets the corruption in the manuscript he has translated, 'as it might have provided evidence of a concrete locality in Rome'.

21 Illustrated in Snyder (2003), p. 146.

conversion. This could not have been a poor congregation. Their transformation of the *aula* continued later in the fourth century. They inserted a *confessio* in the form of a long shaft beside the stair rising from the ground to a *mensa* in the *aula* itself for the celebration of memorials or the eucharist. This caused the reorientation of the congregation towards the west, where the later apse is also found.

The archaeological evidence for Christian presence in the building appears to date from about a century after Justin's martyrdom, but the houses and baths existed already in the middle of the second century. Of course, none of this proves any connection with Justin, but it is tantalizing. Another candidate for the house-church 'above the baths' is the *titulus Pudentis*, of which Krautheimer writes that:

> At the same time [the late fourth century], a second-century thermae hall [public or private baths] was remodelled into the basilica of S. Pudenziana. Conclusive proof is lacking as to the previous use of these structures by Christian congregations, but the likelihood is undeniable. Notwithstanding uncertainty in specific cases, then, the domus ecclesiae of third-century Rome appear to have been installed in tenement houses and other utilitarian structures, only slightly adapted, along purely practical lines, to their new function.[22]

Conversion to a *domus ecclesiae* took place in all kinds of structures, including an *insula* at the *Titulus Byzantis*, a *thermae* hall at the *Titulus Pudentis*, and a private house and a factory hall, or *horreum*, at the *Titulus Clementis*.

Titulus Clementis, San Clemente

San Clemente is said by Dix to have been the palace of Titus Flavius Clemens, who was executed in 96 for 'superstition', and his wife Domitilla, who was exiled. Doubts remain whether the 'superstition' for which the Consul died was that he was a Christian, especially given that it is barely conceivable that such a high-ranking senator should be a convert to this Eastern mystery cult at this early date, however the claim persists. Long tradition connects the church of San Clemente with St Clement of Rome (perhaps a client of Titus Flavius Clemens), who died at the end of the first century. He has been identified as the author of a letter to Corinth dealing with a dispute concerning authority, and is thought to be the Clement mentioned by Paul in his epistle to the Philippians (4:3). In the middle of the nineteenth century, excavations below the twelfth-century church uncovered the previous fourth-century basilica (Figure 1.1), and in 1857 below that was discovered a house and a *horreum* or warehouse. Finally, in 1867 a *mithraeum* of the first half of the third century was discovered below the apse of the earlier basilica. If the tradition were accepted, then the *horreum* is to be associated with the house of Clement himself. The archaeological evidence will not support this, since there is no indication that any part of that building was in domestic use, but there is some evidence to suggest that the first- and second-century *horreum* was converted in the third century to provide a large hall, indicating the possibility of pre-Constantinian Christian activity not long before the first basilica was built incorporating the first floors of both buildings.

Wherever Clement performed his liturgy, it was already clearly ordered and the clerical and lay responsibilities differentiated. Around the year 95 he wrote to the Corinthians, presumably because they fell short of his ideal:

---

22 Krautheimer (1986), p. 29, my italics; see also discussions in Krautheimer, *Corpus*, 1, pp. 267–77, and Krautheimer (1986), p. 29; White (1990), pp. 114 and 146–7, and White (1996–97), vol. II, pp. 209–18; Snyder (2003), pp. 152–3.

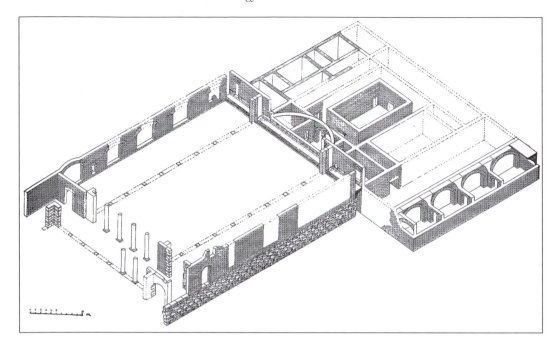

Figure 1.1   *Titulus Clementis*, San Clemente, axonometric of the fourth-century basilica; from the *Corpus Basilicarum Christianarum Romae*; courtesy of the Institute of Fine Arts, New York University.

> We are bound to perform in due order all that the master bade us to accomplish at their proper seasons. ... He ordered that the offerings and services should be performed at their appointed times and seasons, not at random and without order; and also by his own supreme will he himself appointed the place and the ministers of their performance. ... To the high priest are given his special ministrations, a special place is reserved for the priests, and special duties are imposed upon the levites, while the layman is bound by the ordinances concerning the laity.
>
> xli. Let each of you, brethren, in his own order give thanks to God with a good conscience, not transgressing the appointed rule of his service. For it is not in every place, brethren, that the perpetual sacrifices are offered, or the freewill offerings, the sin offerings and the guilt offerings, but in Jerusalem only; and even there the offering is not made in every place, but before the sanctuary at the altar.[23]

Clearly, Clement will have been aware that the Temple in Jerusalem had been destroyed a quarter of a century before he wrote, so his appeal to the model of Temple worship is particularly interesting. Using the present tense of its worship immediately allegorizes it and lifts it to a heavenly realm with an implied identification of high priest and master, and perhaps even bishop, since he goes on to trace the line of authority from the master to the Apostles, bishops and deacons. This strict ordering of Christian society and worship indicates that before the end of the first century, pressure already existed for the architectural ordering of the setting of the liturgy, at least in Rome under Clement's episcopate.

---

23   Translated in Bettenson (1943), pp. 62–3.

Titulus Equitii, San Martino ai Monti

The *Liber Pontificalis*, a chronicle of the Popes, describes how Pope Sylvester (314–34) established a church on the property of a presbyter called Equitius next to the baths of Domitian. Krautheimer identifies ancient remains to the south-west of the ninth-century basilica as entrance-chambers leading to an *aula ecclesiae* (Figure 1.2). The north-west corner of the hall is connected to an ancient *martyrium* under the old altar of the basilica:

> Krautheimer concludes, then, that the *titulus* associated with the property of Equitius must have been located [to the south-west of the basilica] just before and/or during the Constantinian donations, beginning in 314. It is not likely that this property would have been adapted for Christian use, probably as some sort of hall during the early to mid-fourth century.[24]

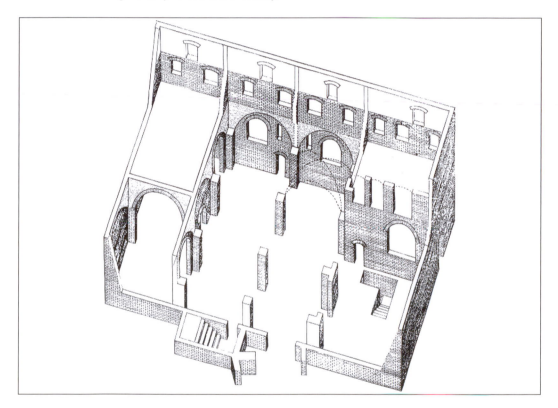

Figure 1.2   *Titulus Equitii*, San Martino ai Monti, the Roman Hall to the southwest of the church; from the *Corpus Basilicarum Christianarum Romae*, vol. I, fig. 81; courtesy of the Institute of Fine Arts, New York University.

Titulus Chrysogoni, San Crisogono

All of the preceding examples of either category of *domus* or *aula ecclesiae* were the result of the conversion of pre-existing buildings in response to the changing needs of the Christian community. There is considerable evidence that the fourth- to fifth-century basilica of San

---

24 White (1996–97), vol. II, p. 232.

Crisogono incorporates a pre-Constantinian hall, probably the earliest known, built *de novo* as a church building perhaps as early as 310.[25] It was a large building, about 35 metres long and over 19 metres at its widest. The portico at the east end had three great arches. Inside, the space was clear except for two discontinuous lateral partitions which Krautheimer considers to be a choir screen on a raised western *bema*. All this indicates a work of public architecture hierarchically arranged, setting apart clergy from people. Already between 251 and 253 Pope Cornelius wrote to Fabius, Bishop of Antioch, telling him of numerous clergy in Rome with diverse functions: 'there are forty-six presbyters, seven deacons, seven sub-deacons, forty-two acolytes, fifty-two exorcists, readers, and doorkeepers'.[26] Increasing diversification of function indicates formalization of the rite and growing pressure for the adaptation of the setting of the liturgy. It was against this more public architecture that Porphyry wrote in his accusation *Against the Christians* that they were now 'imitating the construction of temples, erecting great buildings in which they meet to pray, but there is nothing to prevent them from doing this in their own homes since, of course, their Lord hears them everywhere'.[27]

Other *tituli* include S. Cecilia in Trastevere, S. Prisca and more. These were brought together as the parish churches of Rome. The parish system was established by Bishop Dionysius (259–68), and it became common throughout the empire.[28] Dix maintains that it had been the ideal that the whole community should gather in one place as the *ecclesia* to perform the liturgy under the bishop of the city. In a great city like Rome, this had become impossible, and presbyters who were given charge of the title church would perform the liturgy 'under the bishop'.[29] For centuries in Rome, and as late as 1870, it was the practice to have representatives of all the clergy and laity of the 'titles' represented at the Pope's 'stational mass', from which a fragment of the consecrated bread would be sent to the title churches to be placed in the chalice at the local celebration. If modern estimates based on the letter of Cornelius are correct that by about 250 the number of Christians had grown to 10,000–50,000, it would clearly be difficult to maintain the direct link between a bishop and the whole of his *ecclesia* even before Christianity became a permitted religion.

What appear to have been house-churches are still to be seen in Rome, but they are not complete enough to see with any certainty how different rooms were used. If these are indeed the remains of house-churches, then confiscation of Christian property or the great success and expansion of the Church led to wholesale modification and destruction of early arrangements.

The Christian Building at Dura-Europos

One remarkably intact example of a house converted to a *domus ecclesiae* remains in the ruins of the frontier town and trading centre of Dura-Europos.[30] Dura was not just an isolated Roman garrison town on the extreme periphery of the empire. It held an important strategic position above the Euphrates River, protecting trade routes and facing the rival empire of the Parthians. It was a cosmopolitan town with a typical selection of places of worship. There was a military temple, temples of Zeus Theos, Zeus Megistos, Artemis, Atargatis, a Temple of the Gaddé, Azzanathkona, and along the western wall were ranged the Temple of Bel in the north-west corner, a Mithraeum,

---

25   Snyder (2003), p. 152.
26   Eusebius, *The History of the Church*, VI.43, translated in Louth (1989), p. 216.
27   Translated in White (1996–97), vol. II, p. 104; in the contested area of the visibility or invisibility of the cult, see also Beard, North and Price (1998), I, pp. 267–8, and Wharton (1995), pp. 32–3.
28   Krautheimer (1986), p.3.
29   St Ignatius, quoted in Dix (1945), p. 21.
30   For detailed discussion, see Kraeling (1967); see also White (1996–97), vol. II, and Perkins (1973).

the Temple of Adonis, the Synagogue, the Christian church, the Temple of Zeus Kyrios, and in the south-western corner the Temple of Aphlad. In 256, in preparation for an attack by the Sassanids, the buildings and the alleyway beside the wall were filled in with earth and rubble to strengthen the fortifications and as a precaution against mining. The walls were, however, mined and countermined. The tunnels collapsed, burying the soldiers, one of whom had his pay with him, including a coin dated 256. The level to which the Christian building was buried is the level to which it was standing after excavation, as indicated in the architectural drawings made at the time (Figure 1.3).

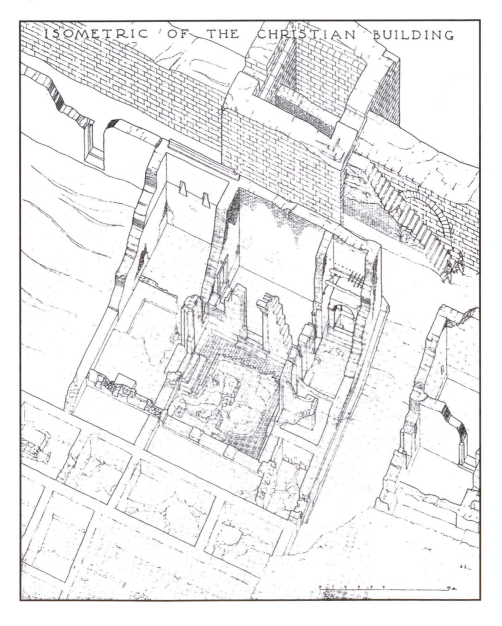

Figure 1.3   Dura Europos, the Christian Building, isonometric projection showing the remains as excavated; from Kraeling (1967), plan III; © J.J. Augustin Inc., by kind permission.

Had the church and the neighbouring synagogue not been amongst the buildings buried in this way, 'had they established their respective prayer-houses in some other houses of the city, we should have found only their foundations and probably a few scattered fragments of their wall-decorations. It is more likely that we should not have been able to identify these ruins and should have regarded them as those of private houses.'[31] Both the church and Synagogue had been established in a row of private houses that had subsequently been converted. Outwardly, the church retained its domestic character, and the Christian community here seems to have continued its worship unhindered during a time of severe persecution begun by the emperor Decius in 250. Origen himself perished in the Decian persecution, and in 257, contemporary with the fall of Dura, Cyprian was executed in Carthage in the Valerian persecution. Christians had every reason to be discreet about their worship. Still, the existence of the church can hardly have been a well-guarded secret, considering the major alterations that had taken place and the fact that a local artist appears to have been used, probably one who had worked on other places of worship of the town. The group of artists was distinctive enough to have been dubbed the Durene School. On the other hand the painting of the church is much cruder and the programme less elaborate than the Synagogue, which was also larger, presumably to accommodate a bigger, richer community. Certainly, they had been able to afford better artists in the 240s, who produced a magnificent scheme with three registers of scenes from scripture. It was a selected visual history of the Jewish people, and its narrative has been related to midrashic commentary. In the midst of this, on the west wall was the Torah shrine.

The Christian building was more modest in a number of ways. Though a relatively large house, it was a smaller structure than the synagogue, and was built earlier in the third century and probably converted to religious use in 232. Clark Hopkins, of the excavation team, noted:

> The most important graffito in the assembly room supplies the date 232. I noted that it was on an inner coat of plaster, and it was my impression, but this is extremely difficult to determine until the plaster breaks off and one can study it in cross section. It is not uncommon at Dura for a graffito to mark the erection of a building; it would have been equally appropriate to have had it mark a complete renovation and rededication. Kraeling [author of the Final Report on the Christian Building] believed the date 232 represented the erection of the earlier building. … If the Christian alterations were not made in 232, they were made shortly thereafter.[32]

The entrance to the house from the street was offset to the right in an arrangement that screened views into the house (Figure 1.3, bottom right of the building). The vestibule opened onto a typical domestic court around which were clustered a large rectangular room, a smaller square room with access to the courtyard as well as to the rectangular room to the south and to the north to a room that was smaller still, and finally onto a staircase rising to a room above the small room on the north side.

The large hall was opposite the entrance vestibule and through the largest and most impressive doorway. It was for assembly, and could accommodate a congregation of fifty to sixty. The room was plastered, but without any paintings, perhaps so that there could be no charge of idolatry. The only permanent fixture of the hall was a *bema* or platform with masonry foundations at the eastern end. There is one other example of such a structure in Dura at the Palace of the *Dux*, or military commander. In both contexts it was, of course, to set the speaker apart and in a position of authority. The *bema* literally conveyed authority; roughly contemporary with the conversion of the Dura Christian building, in 250, Cyprian ordained Celerinus as a Reader and placed him 'upon the

---

31   Rostovtzeff (1938), p. 102.
32   Hopkins (1984), p. 95.

pulpitum, that is upon the tribunal of the church'. The authority of the clergy and their teaching is also emphasized by the *Didache* (of Syrian origin, and dating most probably from the late first or early second century), where it says of the clergy, to 'receive him as the Lord'. This arrangement 'reflects the dominant function of such hall-like rooms, and in this connection suggests one possible answer to the question why the hall at Dura was left without mural decoration'.[33] In other words, the liturgical focus in the Hall was on the worship and readings conducted from the pulpitum, which gave authority both to the clergy and their teaching, without images around the dais which might suggest idolatrous practices.

A door at the western end of the hall gave access to the square room; to the right was a door to the court, and straight ahead another with 'a carefully moulded frame, suggesting that Room 5 [the smaller square room] is the formal means of access to Room 6 [the baptistery]'. This square room was prominently situated on the right-hand side of the courtyard as you entered. It has been speculated that this was a room for the *agape*, which seems unlikely considering that even when Justin wrote his *Apology* in the middle of the second century, the *agape* had completely disappeared from the celebration of the eucharist, at least in Rome. An appeal to a Roman example may seem rather attenuated in this far-flung border, but amongst the archaeological finds at Dura was a part of a manuscript (now Yale 0212) identified by Kraeling as a fragment of the *Diatessaron*, a harmony of the four Gospels in a continuous narrative compiled by Tatian *c.* 150–160, most probably at Rome.[34] The graffiti scratched into the walls of the square room point to another more likely use as a school for catechumens. After the service of the word (*missa catechumenorum*), they could conveniently retire here. And here they received further instruction, for 'it is not lawful for any man to partake of [the eucharist] but he who believes our teaching to be true, and has been washed with the washing which is for the forgiveness of sins and unto a new birth', according to Justin. Being for catechumens, the room also served as an anteroom to the baptistery. This supposition is supported by the fact that in the process of converting the building, the connecting door was given a new moulded plaster doorframe (highly unusual for an internal doorway) on the square room side, indicating the direction of formal movement.

This architectural arrangement suggests that the baptismal rite might begin in the assembly room with readings and teachings, perhaps with the singing of psalms and hymns. Then the candidate would be led from the hall into the catechumens' room, where they would presumably change, perhaps putting on a simple white robe. They would then enter the baptistery for 'the washing which is for the forgiveness of sins and unto a new birth', as Justin wrote in his *Apology*. They were now in a room facing its north wall with an elaborate canopied structure on their left and the whole room painted with a complicated cycle of frescoes with movement consistently indicated from right to left (counter-clockwise). The Syrian rite of baptism was described in the early third-century apocryphal *Acts of Thomas*, when Thomas prepares to baptize Siphor, his wife and daughter in their *diwan*. After teaching, 'he poured oil upon their heads and said, "Glory to you, the love of compassion. Glory to you, the name of Christ."' It is important to note that, unusually, the anointing comes first in the Syrian rite, as emphasized in the *Didascalia Apostolorum* and the *Apocryphal Acts of the Apostles*.[35]

The movement in the rite would naturally mirror the movement in the painted cycle, and turning to the right from the catechumens' door in the Dura baptistery is found a small arched aedicule (seen between the two doorways in the 'South Wall' drawing, Figure 1.4, top). Below

---

33   See White (1990), p. 124; *Didache* XI, translated in Bettenson (1943), p. 65; Kraeling (1967), p. 144.

34   Kraeling's identification of the fragment, made in *A Greek Fragment of Tatian's Diatesseron from Dura* (*c.* 1935), is disputed in Parker, Taylor and Goodacre (1999), pp. 225–8.

35   White (1996–97), vol. II, p. 131, begins the cycle from the door to the courtyard so that the baptism takes place before the anointing; but see also Johnson (2000), p. 479, and Bradshaw (2002), pp. 146–51.

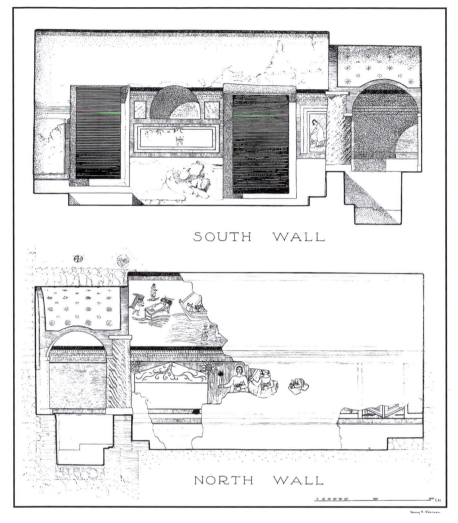

SOUTH WALL

NORTH WALL

Figure 1.4   Dura Europos, the Christian Building, the frescoes in the Baptistery; from Kraeling (1967), pl. XXXIII; © J.J. Augustin Inc., by kind permission.

that, and above a rebate for a table, is a painting of David bringing Goliath's sword down onto his neck. The scene is framed in coloured bands. There can be no doubt about the identification of the subject since the names are incised into the plaster. The young shepherd, recently anointed with oil by the prophet Samuel, has come out in the name of God and vanquished the enemy. The aedicule above the table will have contained the oil of baptism to prepare the candidate for the fight against 'the enemy of God': 'The main theme of this pre-baptismal anointing is the entry into the eschatological kingship of the Messiah, being in the true sense of the word assimilated to the Messiah-King through this anointing.'[36]

---

36   Winkler, 'The Original Meaning of the Prebaptismal Anointing and its Implications', *Worship* 52 (1978), p. 36, quoted in Bradshaw (2002), p. 150.

Continuing with the line of movement in the frescoes, the eastern wall is preserved only to the height of about a metre from floor level, with the result that only five pairs of feet and the lower hems of garments can be seen. This is evidently a procession, and corresponding figures of three women bearing bowls and black torches (with space for a possible further two figures) appear on the north wall on the other side of a design that has been reconstructed as open doors (Figure 1.4, bottom). The procession is approaching a sarcophagus with large stars at its corners. The only text this Christian community is known to have had which can act as an aid for us in the interpretation of the narrative cycle is the fragment now at Yale. Whether the *Diatessaron* or not, it was certainly from a similar sort of harmony: 'the text preserves an account of certain female disciples who witnessed Jesus' crucifixion, and an introduction to the story about Joseph of Arimathea'.[37] If Kraeling was right and it was the *Diatessaron*, that harmony of the Gospels is thought to have been originally in Greek but is now known only in a variety of translations, so the precise contents of the original are not known. The scenes on the east and north walls are closest to the Lucan version of the visit of 'Mary Magdalen and Joanna and Mary, the mother of James and the other women with them' (24:10): 'On the first day of the week at early dawn, they went to the tomb, taking the spices which they had prepared. And they found the stone rolled away from the tomb, but when they went in they did not find the body. While they were perplexed about this, behold two men stood by them in dazzling apparel; ... the men said to them "Why do you seek the living among the dead?"' (24:1–5). The east wall, then, would have shown the five women approaching the doors of the tomb, and the north wall (Figure 1.4, bottom) shows them inside the tomb with their torches appearing to be black because of the brightness of the two angels represented by the stars.

In the upper register of the north wall are two scenes of the miracles of Jesus, first Jesus and Peter walking on the water, and second the healing of the paralytic (again taken from right to left in progression towards the font). Walking on water is found in Mark 6:45–61 and Matthew 14:22–34. There is a ship with a group of Apostles, and below two figures meeting on a rough sea. Faith, and the presence of Christ with his followers, gives them miraculous power even against the violence of the powers of nature. The scenes of the healing of the paralytic progress from right to left, following Mark 2:1–12 and its parallels in the synoptic Gospels. On the right the paralytic is lying on his bed, on the left he is shown carrying it; above, at the apex of the composition, is Jesus with his hand outstretched: 'And when Jesus saw their faith, he said to the paralytic, "My son, your sins are forgiven."' Faith, healing and the forgiveness of sins come through the waters of baptism – as the apocryphal *Acts of Thomas* says:

> And he began to speak concerning baptism: 'This baptism is the forgiveness of sins. It regenerates light which flows all around. It regenerates the new man – mingling the spirit with men, renewing the soul, raising up the new man in threefold manner – and is a participant in the forgiveness of sins. Glory to you, the secret that is shared in baptism. Glory to you, the invisible power that is in baptism. Glory to you, the renewal through which those who are baptised, who take hold of you with (the proper) disposition, are renewed.'[38]

At first, some of the excavation team thought that the elaborate canopied structure at the west end of the room (seen to the right in the drawing of the 'South Wall' and to the left in the drawing of the 'North Wall' in Figure 1.4) near the door to the catechumen's room was an altar on a martyr's tomb because of its similarity to the arcosolium tombs in the Christian catacombs. The similarity of form is an interesting point, since the tomb depicted on the north wall is virtually the same size as the block of the structure, but weight of evidence has always pointed to it being a baptismal

---

37 Parker, Taylor and Goodacre (1999), p. 193.
38 Translated in White (1996–97), vol. II, p. 50.

font. Obviously, some considerable emphasis was placed on the death of the old Adam in baptism and resurrection to new life in Christ. Candidates would mount the step, sit on the edge and swing their feet over into the basin. With a depth of 95.5 cm and a length of 1.065 m, it is similar to the Roman baths at Dura, though not adequate for immersion. Still, the *Acts of Thomas* continue: 'He gave instructions that a basin (or tub) be brought in, and he baptized them in the name of the Father and the Son and the Holy Spirit.'[39] Syrian practice clearly didn't require full immersion. The main focus of the decorative scheme was naturally immediately under the starry canopy above the tank – it showed the Good Shepherd carrying a sheep (or rather a hefty ram!) behind his flock, the most familiar image of early Christian art. A later addition to the scheme on the wall to the left of this was a depiction of the Fall, to which the Shepherd (and the font) give the remedy, salvation through Christ. Both the *Acts of Thomas* and one of Narsai's *Liturgical Homilies* refer to the baptized as sheep. Narsai wrote:

> Lo, the King of the Height reaches out to him [the priest] the hand of the Spirit, and places in his hand the signet of his name, that he may seal his sheep. … Lo, he has brought him to visit the flock entrusted to him, and he lifts up his voice and calls the sheep by their names. Lo, the sheep are gathered together and the lambs and the ewes; and he sets upon them the stamp of life by the word of the Lord.[40]

The shepherd imagery here (and David dressed as a shepherd killing Goliath) connects the baptism with the earlier anointing as a single redemptive process, to remedy sin, fight against evil, and rise to new life. The stars at the corners of the sarcophagus were the angelic witnesses to the resurrection of Christ; the stars of the canopy likewise testify to the dying to sin and rising to new life of the Christian. Having emerged from the font, the newly baptized would turn right towards the door in the south wall to the square room or anteroom. To the right of the door before leaving, the last image presents itself – the Woman at the Well. The Gospel source is John 4, where Jesus said to her: 'If you knew the gift of God and who it is that is saying to you "Give me a drink," you would have asked him and he would have given you living water … whoever drinks of the water that I shall give him will never thirst; the water that I shall give him will become in him a spring of water welling up to eternal life."' This living water is also the water of baptism that has an effect once for all. In the anteroom, the newly baptized would have changed and returned to the hall for the eucharist. The text of *The Acts of Thomas* continues:

> And when they had been baptized and dressed, he placed bread upon the table and blessed it saying, 'Bread of life, of which those who eat remain incorruptible, bread which fills hungry souls with its blessing, you are the one worthy to receive the gift so that you might become forgiveness of sins for us and so that the ones eating you might become immortal.'

Strikingly, in the Dura church the permanent platform at the east end of the hall, being only 147 cm by 97 cm, was not large enough to accommodate both the president and a table. Being a permanent structure, the dais was of great significance, and lent that significance to whatever was placed upon it, and it was for the clergy – to be ordained was to be placed upon the pulpitum. Surely it was deliberate that the table for the eucharist was not placed on the dais. All the other places of worship available to the inhabitants of the town – except the synagogue – had their altars, and the Christians would want to distinguish themselves from pagan practice, but the letter of Clement to Corinth used the order and sacrifice of Temple worship as a strong analogy for what the Christian congregation was doing. No more than about fifteen years later, St Ignatius of Antioch (who died *c.* 110) wrote in his epistle to the Magnesians (ch. 7): 'Hasten all to come together as to one temple of

---

39 *Ibid.*
40 Homily XXII, quoted in Kraeling (1967), p. 181.

God, to one altar, to one Jesus Christ.' And he wrote to the Philadelphians: 'Be careful to use one Eucharist, for there is one flesh of our Lord Jesus Christ, and one cup for union with His blood, one altar, as there is one bishop with the presbytery and deacons.'[41] The Durene font was at first seen as an altar by some of the excavation team because the canopied structure resembled an arcosolium tomb from the Roman catacombs. It also resembled the tomb, in the fresco, from which Christ had risen; Christ was both priest and victim (Hebrews 9), and the newly baptized was about to die to sin, rise to new life offered up to God.

Theissen's theory of primitive Christian religion has some purchase here: 'traditional ritual actions (bloody animal sacrifices) were replaced by new (bloodless) rites. ... They may have ceased to sacrifice animals, but in their interpretations they reactivated a form of sacrifice which was already long obsolete, namely human sacrifice – as the atoning sacrifice of Jesus.'[42] What appeared to be an altar was not, though according to the *Acts of Thomas* it was 'for the forgiveness of sins. ... It regenerates the new man ... raising up the new man in threefold manner.' What appeared to be a table was an altar (seen to be of a different kind from the pagan altar), and the bread that was blessed on it was also 'for the forgiveness of sins'.[43] The piece of bread was both the body of the Lord, the sacrifice, and also the banquet, the *agape*. The ambiguities between the meanings of the ceremonies and the meanings of the objects were theologically rich; and the closeness of signs, conceptually, physically and temporally, in the rite were essential: that closeness required a correspondingly close architectural relationship.

Conclusion

The *Acts of Thomas* look back to an earlier time and a simpler rite that did not require a specially adapted architectural setting. Geographically, it would seem that we are dealing with the same tradition as at Dura. The *Acts* in that case would relate to the Durene Church as the *Apology* of Justin relates to the Roman. As Justin describes the progression from baptism to eucharist, it was clearly not always possible to link the two as closely as in the Christian church at Dura. He writes of catechumens:

> Those who are convinced and believe what we say and teach is the truth, and pledge themselves to be able to live accordingly, are taught in prayer and fasting to ask God to forgive their past sins, while we pray and fast with them. Then we lead them to a place where there is water, and they are regenerated in the same manner in which we ourselves were regenerated. In the name of God, the Father and Lord, and of our Saviour, Jesus Christ, and of the Holy Spirit, they then receive the washing with water. For Christ said, 'Unless you be born again, you shall not enter the kingdom of heaven' (John 3.5). ...
>
> After thus baptizing those who have believed and given their assent, we escort them to the place where are assembled those whom we call brothers and sisters, to offer up sincere prayers in common for ourselves, for the newly baptized, and for all other persons wherever they may be. ... At the conclusion of prayers we greet each other with a kiss. Then, bread and chalice containing wine mixed with water are presented to the one presiding over the brothers and sisters.[44]

For baptism, all that was needed was 'a place where there is water', and for some house churches like Justin's it would presumably have been possible to use neighbouring baths; there was no particular feeling that it would be better to bring a basin or tub, as in the *Acts of Thomas*, so that

---

41   Ignatius is translated in Pocknee (1963), pp. 34–5.
42   See above, page 1.
43   Translated in White (1996–97), vol. II, p. 50; see also the discussion in Kieckhefer (2004), pp. 70–75.
44   Translated in Whitaker (2003), p. 3.

baptism could be in the same place and united with the eucharist. Practice appears to have varied according to circumstance, resources, local tradition and theology. The contingencies included the local built forms, and the economic and social position of the congregation. The earliest existing 'church order', the *Didache*, already recognizes the variety in baptismal practice when it says: 'Baptize in the name of the Father and of the Son and of the Holy Spirit [Mt 28.19], in running water. 2. But if you have no running water, baptize in other water; and if you cannot in cold, then in warm. 3. But if you have neither, pour water on the head three times "in the name of the Father and of the Son and of the Holy Spirit".'[45]

What is striking about the evidence so far is not that a normative architectural prototype can be found at the end of a line of development from apostolic times, which was the goal of traditional scholarship as exemplified by Dix, but that there is a remarkable diversity of forms that served an equal diversity of communities over a vast geographical area. A similar picture of very early liturgical practice is emerging in modern scholarship:

> Whereas earlier generations of scholars were concerned to try to find the common core behind the variety, scholars today tend to be more interested in what the variety says about the particular theologies of the Eucharist that were espoused by the individual writers and their communities, even if they cannot always agree on the specific layers of meaning that exist in the New Testament texts or on the special emphasis being given to the material by a writer.[46]

Architecture, archaeology and texts all weigh in the balance against Dix's reconstruction of the development from the house-church to the basilica, the evidence provided by the house-church at Dura in particular. It also has much to say about the public aspect of Christianity even during the persecutions, since the community at Dura was carrying out its building works not long before the Decian persecution during which they appear to have continued to worship untroubled despite their growth in numbers being closely connected with the growth in the size of the local garrison.

The Public Aspect of Christianity

Persecution under Decius lasted between 249 and 251, and under Valerian between 253 and 260. Cyprian, who was soon to die, states in his Epistle LXXXI that there were many Romans of considerable rank, even of the Imperial Household itself, who were practising Christians, and that Valerian was determined to deal with this nuisance:

> There are many various and unauthenticated rumours going about, but the truth is as follows; Valerian sent a Rescript to the Senate ordering that bishops, priests and deacons should forthwith be punished; that senators, men of rank and Roman knights should be degraded and lose their property, and if, having been deprived of their possessions, they should still remain Christians, then they should also lose their heads; that matrons should be deprived of their property and banished; and that any members of Caesar's household who had confessed before, or should now confess, should lose their property and be sent in chains to forced labour on Caesar's farms.[47]

By the time of Diocletian's persecution at the turn of the fourth century, the Christian Church was neither hidden nor poor. Eusebius wrote in his *History of the Church* (VIII.2) that in March 303, 'an imperial decree was published everywhere, ordering the churches to be razed to the ground and the Scriptures destroyed by fire, and giving notice that those in places of honour would lose their

---

45   Translated in *ibid.*, p. 2.
46   See Bradshaw (2004), p. 2, where he cites a great range of studies.
47   Translated in Bettenson (1943), pp. 13–14.

places, and domestic staff, if they continued to profess Christianity, would be deprived of their liberty'.[48] The public visibility of the Christians was an affront to the Emperor, and his first act of persecution in 303, according to Lactantius, was to have their 'lofty temple' in Nicomedia, his eastern capital, razed as he watched from his palace.

The same year, detailed notes were made of the arrest of Paul, Bishop of Cirta, and his attendants and of the confiscation of Church property. His arrest had been ordered by Munatius Felix, 'high priest in perpetuity and mayor of the colony of Cirta' in Numidia.[49] The search and arrest took place on 19 May 303 'at the house in which the Christians would assemble'. The interrogation took place with Paul seated, flanked by four presbyters, two deacons, four sub-deacons and six named 'grave-diggers', amongst others. The inclusion of this last category in the record may indicate that, in official terms at least, the Christian congregation was viewed as a kind of funerary association. Religious and commercial associations of many kinds existed which owned and adapted properties. The congregation was not poor by any estimate; amongst the items confiscated were: '2 gold cups, 6 silver cups, 6 silver pitchers, a small silver kettle, 7 silver lamps' and other pieces of bronze and a considerable amount of clothing, presumably for distribution to the poor.

When asked for the copies of the scriptures, Paul replied: 'The readers have the scriptures but we will give you what we have here.' Felix the mayor pressed the point: 'Point out the readers or send for them.' Paul was naturally reluctant to betray any of his flock, but his reply is very interesting: 'You know them all.' They appear not to have been known to those immediately accompanying the mayor, because the text implies that one reader was betrayed by two of the deacons, but later in the text the public clerks did indeed offer to identify the rest. In the end, one exceedingly large volume, 30 large books and 6 smaller ones were confiscated. Together, they constituted a very significant library. The text specifically refers to a room set aside, and presumably modified, to serve as a library and the many books would normally have been kept there, but there must have been some expectation that there would be an attempt to seize them, so they were dispersed amongst the readers. The only other room in the house mentioned by name is the dining room. That implies either that the house was at least in part in domestic use, or that a more extended eucharist or *agape* was still held. The latter seems highly unlikely since there was not even room for the bishop's very large staff. As near as can be determined, this was another *domus ecclesiae* still partly in domestic use.

What was about to change under Constantine was not related to the hidden nature of the Church, nor that the Church was going to rise out of poverty, but that it was about to emerge into the imperial realm, taking on official and imperial forms in its architecture and in the performance of its liturgy. Half a century before, *c.* 265, Paul of Samosata, Bishop of Antioch, was censured by his congregation because in both architecture and ritual he surrounded himself with the trappings of a Roman magistrate. He occupied a throne on a platform, and also had an audience chamber. At the time it caused outrage, but under Constantine it would become the norm. With changed social circumstances and official position, the Church would develop a monumental public architecture which would dominate the Western tradition for the next one and a half millennia.

---

48   Eusebius, *History of the Church*, VIII, 2, translated in Louth (1989), pp. 258–9.
49   The Latin text and a translation are given in White (1996–97), vol. II, pp. 105–10.

CHAPTER 2

Constantine, Continuity and Change in the Fourth Century

The Conversion of Constantine

There were various routes for ambitious individuals to rise to imperial power during the Tetrarchy, or rule by two senior *Augusti* and two junior Caesars, established by Diocletian in 293.[1] On the death of Constantius I, Emperor of the West, the army proclaimed his son Constantine as his successor in York on 25 July 306. On the death of Severus, Augustus of the West, Constantine received that title from Maximian, who had previously elevated his father Constantius to the same dignity. There was only one man in the Western Empire who now stood between Constantine and total control, and that was the rebel Maxentius, who had taken the title *Princeps* and was safe behind the walls of Rome itself. When the senior Augustus, Galerius, died in May 311, overall control, such as it was, collapsed, and the Empire was effectively divided into four. In 312 Constantine marched on Rome. He met Maxentius and his army near Rome at the Milvian Bridge. What happened next is related by Lactantius in a contemporary history: 'Constantine was advised in a dream to mark the heavenly sign of God on the shields of his soldiers and then engage in battle. He did as he was commanded and by means of a slanted letter X with the top of its head bent round, he marked Christ on their shields.'[2] A quarter of a century later, Constantine's friend and biographer Eusebius recounts quite a different version of the vision:

> Who could hesitate to believe the [Emperor's own] account, especially when the time which followed provided evidence for the truth of what he said? About the time of the midday sun, when day was just turning, he said he saw with his own eyes, up in the sky and resting over the sun, a cross-shaped trophy formed from light, and a text attached to it which said, 'By this conquer'. Amazement at the spectacle seized both him and the whole company of soldiers which was then accompanying him on a campaign he was conducting somewhere, and witnessed the miracle.
>
> He was, he said, wondering to himself what the manifestation might mean; then while he meditated, and thought long and hard, night overtook him. Thereupon, as he slept, the Christ of God appeared to him with the sign which had appeared in the sky, and urged him to make himself a copy of the sign which had appeared in the sky, and to use this as protection against the attacks of the enemy.[3]

Within weeks of his victory at the Milvian Bridge, Constantine took the first steps towards building the Lateran Basilica, soon to be followed by St Peter's Basilica to commemorate the Prince of the Apostles, which some scholars say was on the very spot where the miraculous sign appeared above the site honoured as his tomb. Constantine's victory was Christ's victory – yet Eusebius'

---

1   Standard works treating the history and the architecture of this period include Krautheimer (1980 and 1965), Lane Fox (1986) and Elsner (1998); for important recent discussions of Constantine, see Leadbetter (2000), Curran (2000) and Holloway (2004).

2   Lactantius, *De Mortibus Persecutorum*, 44.5, translated in Creed (1984), p. 63.

3   Eusebius, *Vita Const.*, I, 28–9, translated in Cameron and Hall (1999), pp. 80–81.

protestations indicate that there were, even then, considerable doubts about the story.[4] There are, then, two attested witnesses to the vision, but both with the same vested interests, and there are, of course, other more cynical political interpretations of Constantine's conversion.

The reason Diocletian formed the Dyarchy (rule by a senior and a junior Emperor) and then expanded it to rule by a Tetrarchy (two Augusti and two Caesars), was the problem of unity – there were incursions by barbarians on the long borders of the Empire and dangerous fragmentation. Ethnic, regional and religious diversity created strong centrifugal forces which had to be resisted largely by the office and the person of the Emperor. When Diocletian divided the imperial office, he maintained his personal seniority and so was able to preserve unity in the office while sharing power with another Augustus, and each could depend on a deputy Caesar who would maintain the loyalty of the provinces and the integrity of the *limes*, or borders of the Empire. However, the succession became chaotic, and by the time Constantine shared the Tetrarchy, the Empire was effectively divided into four independent realms.

The Emperor cult had been a centripetal force as long as the imperial office was undivided. His image was to be found in all public basilicas. Contracts were validated before his image, justice could likewise only be dispensed in his 'presence', and at given times all had to sacrifice before his effigy. Whether the basilica was a market, an army drill-hall or the tribune of a governor, it was a religious building by virtue of the cult image of the Emperor in an apse on its end or even a side wall, and before it the swearing of oaths was religiously validated. Most of the great array of religions in the Roman world had no problem with this. But for Christians it was a different matter, and in refusing to sacrifice they were seen to question the guarantee of the integrity of the state. The traditional cults were all under imperial patronage: 'At the apex of the imperial organisation were the pontifices, who regulated the *sacra publica* as a whole. At the head of the pontifices was the *pontifex maximus*. Since the time of Augustus the emperor had been pontifex maximus, while the members of the great priesthoods owed their dignity to imperial favour.'[5] While Emperors had previously been unable to bring the Christians under their control, Constantine's adoption of the chi-rho monogram of Christ (known as the *labarum*) as the sign under which he would conquer, brought them into his fold. That does not necessarily mean that he gave up all his responsibilities as *pontifex maximus*. On the Arch of Constantine, erected by the Senate and completed by 315, he is shown very much in the image of his predecessors, with his features having been cut into relief panels originally showing Hadrian, and possibly Marcus Aurelius, carrying out the usual duties of the Emperor, including sacrifice. There is no reference to the miraculous sign in the iconography of the arch, and perhaps not surprisingly, all references to the divine are pagan. Above the frieze showing Constantine's triumphal entry into Rome is a tondo of Sol Invictus (east face of the arch), and his coinage continued this imagery until 320–21. This was an important imperial cult even before Constantine, and there is evidence for the assimilation of Sol Invictus by Christians as Christ Helios, for example in a mosaic in a mausoleum under St Peter's itself. There is, of course, a serious question about the nature of this assimilation, and whether it was syncretistic, or borrowing an established 'vocabulary', or meant to be a challenge.[6] In any event, the sculpture on the Arch of Constantine and the *Life of Constantine* by Eusebius have very different stories to tell about the completeness of Constantine's conversion.

---

4   For the connection with the siting of St Peter's Basilica, see Jongkees (1966), pp. 37–40; on the scale of the difficulties faced by Constantine and the building problems, see Toynbee and Ward Perkins (1956), pp. 12–17; concerning the two versions, see Cameron and Hall (1999), pp. 204–11.

5   Holloway (2004), p. 13.

6   Dunbabin (1999), pp. 249–51, illustrated on p. 250; Snyder (2003), pp. 120–22; Cameron (1993a), pp. 55–6; Jensen (2000), p. 42.

It may be that Constantine's mother, the Dowager Augusta Helena, was already a Christian by this time, or Constantine may have been accommodating himself to the Christians simply to bring them under his domination. Another possibility is that despite the existence of competing Christianities, he may have seen their intellectual vigour, their developing institutional organization, their universalism and drive towards unity of mind and purpose as having possibilities for the greater unification of the Empire. To the extent that this was a conscious policy, future developments would prove it to be pure genius. Whatever the motive, Constantine immediately issued an act of toleration that was to be observed everywhere in the Empire, and in 313 he and Licinius, at that time Emperor in the Balkan provinces, issued the 'Edict' of Milan (really only a policy agreed between them) in which freedom of worship was granted to all:

> And we have decide moreover with regard to the community of Christians that this should be ordained: if anyone is reported to have purchased in the past either from our Treasury or from anyone else at all those properties in which they used previously to gather, on which formerly a definite policy was laid out in a document sent to your office, they shall restore the said properties to the Christians without payment or any demand for money without any question of obstruction or equivocation ....
>
> And since the said Christians are known to have had other properties in addition to those in which they used to gather, belonging in law to their corporation, that is to the churches, not individual people, you will order all those properties, in accordance with the law expressed above, to be restored to the said Christians, that is their corporation and assemblies, without any equivocation or argument.[7]

Christians were both numerous and well off, owning considerable property individually and corporately. One of the panels on the Arch of Constantine shows the Emperor giving out the *liberalitas*, a support dole to Roman citizens, but where the state failed to supply the Roman populus, the Christians were succeeding with their charitable work.[8]

Maximinus, Emperor in Asia Minor, Syria and Egypt, half-heartedly complied with Constantine's act of toleration:

> Notwithstanding, to the people of Nicomedia and the other cities which with such enthusiasm have made the same request to me – that none of the Christians should live in their cities – I had no option but to give a friendly answer; for this very principle had been maintained by all my predecessors from the beginning, and the gods themselves, without whom all mankind and the whole administration of the Empire would perish, willed that such a request, put forward on behalf of the worship of their Deity, should be confirmed by me. ... If therefore anyone decides by his own choice that the worship of the gods must be acknowledged, such persons may appropriately be welcomed; but if some choose to follow their own worship, you will please leave them free to do so.[9]

The balance between the old gods and the exclusive demands of the God of the Christians was clearly a very delicate negotiation. Maximinus returned to persecution, giving Licinius a reason to eliminate his rival in the east. To avert war, Maximinus issued a decree of toleration as strongly worded as the 'Edict' of Milan, but too late, and the Christian issue had become a powerful token in the imperial power game.

Whatever the explanation for his conversion, Constantine became an active patron of the Church, giving grants of money, exempting the clergy from public duties, settling doctrinal disputes, guarding its unity and catholicity, and building on a magnificent scale. Within weeks of his triumphal entry into the city, he commissioned the vast Lateran basilica to be built on the site of

---

7   Lactantius, *De Mortibus Persecutorum,* 48, in Beard, North and Price (1998), 2, p. 284.
8   On the sculpture, see Holloway (2004), p. 28.
9   Eusebius, *The History of the Church*, 9a.8, in Louth (1989), pp. 295–6.

the barracks of Maxentius' guard, the *equites singulares*, on the Caelian hill beside the Sessorian Palace. It was to be 'an audience hall of Christ the King'.[10] The parallel between the Emperor of Heaven and the Emperor of Rome was not lost on Constantine's contemporaries; Eusebius described his eventual drive against Licinius for total control of the Empire in precisely those terms:

> The champion of the good set out with his son Crispus, that most humane emperor, by his side … then taking God the universal King, and God's Son the Saviour of all, as Guide and Ally, father and son together divided their battle array against God's enemies on every side, and easily carried off the victory: every detail of the encounter was made easy for them by God, in fulfilment of his purpose.[11]

To most of his subjects, the Emperor was divine; now even the Christians conceived the office in sacred terms and recognized Constantine as the instrument of God's purpose. For Eusebius, the Emperor was God's representative on earth, and just as Christ was God's instrument in Creation, so was the Emperor God's instrument in governing the peoples of the earth.

The Lateran Basilica or Basilica Constantiniana

The cathedral of the Bishop of Rome was to be a structure worthy of his performance of the liturgy before the 'universal King', to equal or surpass the basilicas where ceremonial was performed before the Emperor at his ceremonial entry or *adventus*. It was probably the first of the Constantinian Donations, dating from as early as 312–13, perhaps within two weeks of the battle at the Milvian Bridge, and was consecrated six years later, perhaps in November 318. Originally it was the only monumental building of the liturgy within the walls of Rome.[12] Only the foundations and parts of the walls of the original building survive, but the archaeological and documentary evidence is sufficient to give a clear picture of its vastness and magnificence (see Figure 2.1). It was 333 Roman feet long and 180 wide (100 m by 53 m), and despite its size it was built quickly and copied widely. The exterior was plain, with all expense concentrated on the interior. Entering on the longitudinal axis, there were long colonnades separating off the double aisles either side, the shafts and capitals being *spolia* (reused from elsewhere). During services there were probably hangings between the columns so that the catechumens in the aisles could hear, but not see, the eucharistic service. This would appear to have become widespread practice, since in a sermon at the dedication of the new Cathedral at Tyre built by the young, and very rich, Bishop Paulinus, Eusebius described the cathedral in terms of the membership of the Church, its 'living stones', saying: 'Others he [the Protector, the Word, the divinely bright and saving One] joined to the basilica along both sides, still under instruction and in process of advancing, but not very far removed from the divine vision that the faithful enjoy of what is innermost.'[13] This practice may also explain the unusual colonnades along either side at San Crisogono which were connected to the *aula* by doorways. The nave and possibly also the aisles of the new basilica were lit by a clerestory. The nave terminated in a great apse with the Bishop's throne canopied by the semi-dome, and the outer aisles ended in projecting rooms for the offerings at the eucharist. In line with these rooms was the chancel of about 65 feet to accommodate the Bishop's retinue, which by now was considerable. Bishop Paul of Samosata was condemned for arrogating to himself a dais and magistrate's chair – now, just more than half a century later, the Bishop of Rome was to have imperial honours that Paul could hardly have

---

10   Krautheimer (1980), p. 22.

11   Eusebius, 9.3, translated in Louth (1989), p. 332; see also p. xii.

12   For a very full discussion of the dating, see Curran (2000), pp. 94–5; see also Krautheimer (1983), p. 15, and De Blaauw (1987), p. 11.

13   Eusebius, 4.63, translated in Louth (1989), p. 320; and see below, pages 173–5.

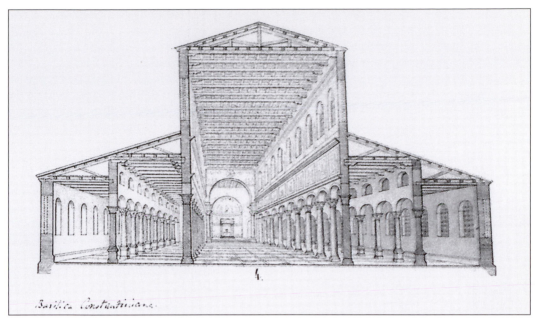

Figure 2.1   *Basilica Constantiniana*, Lateran, sectional perspective; reconstruction from Henri Hübsch (1866), *Monuments de l'Architecture Chrétienne depuis Constantin* (Paris, Morel), pl. IV, no. 4; Sackler Library, University of Oxford.

imagined. Like the Emperor, bishops were to be greeted by genuflection, and eventually (probably between the eighth and eleventh centuries), during the liturgy the honour was also accorded to the altar, relics and the crucifix.[14]

Only a few hundred yards away from the *Basilica Constantiniana* was the Sessorian Palace of Constantine's mother, the Augusta Helena. Performing the liturgy in such a grand context drew it irresistibly towards formal elaboration. The long naves encouraged processions, and bishops and clergy were vested according to their magisterial dignity.

Pressure of numbers had continuing effects on the liturgy too. The population of Rome in 312 has been estimated by Krautheimer at about 800,000, though others suggest that it had dropped drastically to nearer 250,000–500,000. Krautheimer maintains that as much as a third of the population were either sympathetic to, or were actually members of, the Church; Gibbon had been much more conservative, suggesting 50,000; Lane Fox considers even this too high.[15] Even if the numbers were only a third of that, they were served by only 25 known parish churches, or *tituli*, which continued to function socially and liturgically, for the most part little changed architecturally or functionally from the previous century. There are nine churches which may be connected to pre-Constantinian places of Christian worship, including San Clemente, SS. Giovanni e Paolo, San Martino ai Monti, San Crisogono, Santa Sabina and Santa Pudenziana. Those which had been confiscated during the persecution had been restored by Constantine; some were (further) renovated, but it is difficult to date much of the archaeological evidence precisely to either pre- or post-Constantinian activity. Some of these served as *domus* or *aulae ecclesiae* for generations before

---

14   Klauser (1979), pp. 114–15.

15   See Krautheimer (1980), pp. 4 and 18, and (1983), pp. 102–3, as opposed to Hodges and Whitehouse (1983), pp. 50–51; Lane Fox (1986), pp. 268–9, estimates that Christians were 'perhaps (at a guess) only 2 percent of the Empire's population by 250' (p. 317), making the number more than 20,000 sixty years earlier.

they were rebuilt or moved to new, more splendid basilicas. For example, the first basilica of San Clemente was not built until the late fourth century, between about 392 and 417; the *Titulus Equitii* shows first evidence of Christian use either just before or just after the Constantinian donations, then was renovated round about 500, and not reconstructed as the basilica of San Martino ai Monti until the ninth century; at the *Titulus Byzantis*, the *confessio* of St John and St Paul has been dated to the middle of the fourth century, and the basilica of SS. Giovanni e Paolo was not built on the site until the turn of the fifth century. This would indicate that at the *tituli*, worship continued in its less formal community gatherings, only gradually adapting to the new imperial Romanized way of doing things.

Although constant architectural adjustments were being carried out, the *tituli* would struggle to serve 20,000, and clearly could not cope with as many as a quarter of a million Christians. Even if these estimates are far too high, soon numbers would greatly increase – not always for the best of reasons. The favour shown by the Emperor (and the possibility of personal advancement under the new dispensation) played its part in the burgeoning of the catechumenate, which meant that the new Cathedral, for all its monumental scale, was simply a reflection of the size of the Christian community in Rome. The length of time under instruction was up to three years before baptism, and for many whose aim was simply to be regarded as Christians or who were waiting some while longer for the once-for-all remission of sins provided by baptism, a good deal of Christian teaching was still needed, perhaps even to bring about true conversion:

> Thus, the regular liturgies had to assume more of an instructional and formational role than heretofore. It was necessary to try to communicate through the style of liturgical celebration itself something of the majesty of God and the reality of Christ's sacramental presence, as well as of the appropriate attitude of reverence required before that divinity. Even the introduction of the narrative of institution into Eucharistic prayers at this period may well have been in order that it might serve a catechetical purpose.[16]

This state of affairs had powerful effects on both the liturgy and similarly on the architecture. The greatest magnificence was reserved for the interiors, and though little of the original *Basilica Constantiniana* is visible, paintings, drawings and documents come together to conjure a vivid and spectacular scene. The colonnade was of green marble, a *fastigium* of silver probably spanned above the chord of the apse or (more likely) somewhat forward of the altar, and the *Liber pontificalis* recounts the arrangement of great silver statues of Christ the Teacher and his Apostles facing the congregation while the clergy in the apse saw Christ enthroned: 'Like the Emperor, then, Christ revealed Himself in different but complementary aspects to the people and, as it were, to the high officials of His court.' The four bronze columns still in the Lateran are thought to have supported the *fastigium*, whether it took the form of a baldacchino or, more likely, a linear gable-end arrangement, and De Blaauw speculates that they may have belonged to the Temple treasure brought from Jerusalem and later given by Constantine.[17] The record in the *Liber pontificalis* continues, enumerating the coloured marble of the columns and revetment lining the walls, the gold of the half dome, seven silver altars (six were most likely to receive the offerings), and there were splendid gifts from the Emperor:

> A silver paten weighing twenty pounds.
> Two silver scyphi each weighing ten pounds.
> A gold chalice weighing two pounds.
> Five service chalices each weighing two pounds.

---

16   Bradshaw (2002), p. 219.
17   De Blaauw (1987), p. 54.

Two silver amae each weighing eight pounds.
A silver chrism paten, inlaid with gold, weighing five pounds.
Ten crown lights each weighing eight pounds.
Twenty bronze lights each weighing ten pounds.
Twelve bronze candlestick chandeliers each weighing thirty pounds.[18]

The interior was well lit by clerestories and glittered with candlelight glinting off the polished coloured marble and precious metals. The clergy were sumptuously clothed, and the plate that they handled during the liturgy was of heavy beaten silver and gold. The extant interior most evocative of such a magnificent space is the restored fifth-century church of Santa Sabina, with its similar polychrome revetment on the arcades, a timber roof, a large apse and light pouring in. All this could not fail to impress with the glorious majesty of God, and every detail of this had already been theologized in Eusebius (and most likely earlier still), via references to Solomon and the Temple, into an image of the universal Church, and a glimpse of the heavenly Jerusalem.

The Cathedral at Tyre: 'On Earth as it is in Heaven'

Only a very few years before the consecration of the Cathedral of Rome, Eusebius preached in 315/16 at the dedication of the new Cathedral at Tyre as Bishop of Caesarea and Metropolitan Bishop of Palestine.[19] The construction of the two cathedrals must have been contemporaneous, and presumably the theological justification for this new architectural magnificence was not fully developed by Eusebius himself, since in other matters he is enormously erudite but not often original. It is reasonable to suppose, then, that the theology he applied to the Cathedral at Tyre would have been used to justify the magnificence of the *Basilica Constantiniana* to avoid the disapproval directed at Paul of Samosata.

Eusebius begins his sermon by addressing the clergy and the young Bishop Paulinus, who commissioned and paid for the building: 'Friends of God, and priests clothed with the sacred vestment and the heavenly crown of glory, the divine unction and priestly garments of the Holy Spirit'. Everything, priests, vestments and the very stones themselves, is allegorized: 'Shall I call you a new Bezalel, the master builder of a divine tabernacle, or a Solomon, king of a new and far nobler Jerusalem, or a new Zerubbabel, who adorned the temple with the glory that was far greater than the old?' He laces his prose with heaped-up biblical references and quotations, exhorting all present to hymn and sing the praises of God. He maintains that the building of churches, and their being filled with beautiful votive offerings, is proof of the power of the King of Heaven, and it is important to be able to see their meaning, but that is less important in the sight of God, Eusebius reminds the congregation, than 'when He looks at the live temple consisting of us all, and views the house of living and immoveable stones, well and securely based on the foundation of the apostles and prophets, Jesus Christ Himself being the chief cornerstone.' He dwells at length on the architectural elements and their correspondence with various members of the Church. Eusebius presents a theology of worship in which the offering by the bishop in his cathedral is a direct parallel of that of Christ himself in the heavenly temple:

> In no respect is he inferior to the Bezalel whom God Himself filled with a spirit of wisdom and understanding and with technical and scientific knowledge, and close to the architect of the temples that

---

18   For details, see L. Duchesne (1886–92) *Le Liber Pontificalis*, vol. I, p. 172, Paris, Krautheimer (1983), pp. 16 and 20, and Krautheimer (1986), p. 48 (see also n. 24, p. 460); the translation is from Holloway (2004), p. 59.

19   Louth (1989), pp. xviii and xxx; the Williamson translation can be found on pp. 306–22.

symbolised the heavenly types. In the same way this man, having the whole Christ, the Word, the Wisdom, the Light, impressed upon his soul, has built this magnificent shrine for God Most High, resembling in its essence the patterns of the better one as the visible resembles the invisible.[20]

At this time Eusebius' theology was deeply tainted by subordinationism, which sees the second and third Persons of the Trinity as less exalted than the Father, and he wrote of the great triple entrance of the church as the supreme Father with 'the secondary beams of the light of Christ, and the Holy Ghost' on either side. For this tendency he would be branded as an Arian heretic at the Council of Antioch in 325, and would go on to the Council of Nicaea under this cloud, but there he joined the majority in condemning Arius. At that council he met Constantine, for whom this theology of worship, architectural magnificence, patronage and power was highly attractive.

St Peter's Basilica, Rome

The layout of the Cathedral at Tyre was very similar to Old St Peter's in Rome (Figure 2.2): an entrance led into a square colonnaded courtyard with a fountain or fountains on the axis. Numerous gateways opened into the aisled basilica with clerestories over the colonnade in the towering walls supporting a wooden ceiling. The floors were of marble laid in patterns. As at Tyre, the entrance of St Peter's faced the rising sun on the lower slope of the Vatican Hill. Climbing up to the gate and into a large atrium (a post-Constantinian addition not entirely complete until the early sixth century),[21] the axis led to a huge bronze pinecone fountain surmounted by a canopy, and then on via numerous doors to the gigantic basilica with a total internal measurement of about 391 by 208 Roman feet. A clear impression of the interior is given by a seventeenth-century fresco by Domenico Tasselli painted before the destruction of Old St Peter's to make way for the Renaissance rebuilding and there are many drawings of the period by Bramante, Peruzzi, Sangallo, Van Heemskerk and others. It was a funerary basilica, but unlike other funerary halls of Rome it was focused on the grave of the martyr. The site had been a large cemetery containing what was revered as the tomb of St Peter, and being considerably larger than the Lateran Basilica, vast crowds of pilgrims were clearly expected.[22]

Work was started probably some time between 319 and 322, and the structure was complete by 329. The 'Life of St Sylvester' in the *Liber Pontificalis* records that a golden cross weighing 150 pounds was given by Constantine and his mother Helena, so the basilica must have been completed before she died in 329 or 330.[23] St Peter's is the first basilica built in the form of a cross with transepts. Arguments have been put forward to connect this and its site to Constantine's vision at the Milvian Bridge – 'Constantine's army must have seen the phenomenon [caused by particular atmospheric conditions] south of W. S. W. (*before* sunset), that is, in the sky over the city, not much above the right river bank, just about the site of St Peter's.' Krautheimer originally considered that the plan had remained unchanged throughout its construction, saying that the foundations all belonged to a single building programme, but more recently he revised this view, noting that the eastern (interior) wall of the transept has a foundation of a size that indicates that it may originally have been an exterior wall. If that is the case, then the transept itself may have been the original building onto which the basilican nave was added.[24] This revised history of construction

---

20 *Ibid.*, p. 311.
21 See Beard, North and Price (1998), pp. 114–15.
22 See Jongkees (1966), where many of the drawings are reproduced and discussed.
23 *Ibid.*, pp. 31–5, addresses various aspects of dating.
24 See *ibid.*, pp. 37–9, for the argument concerning the vision of Constantine, and also Lane Fox (1986), p. 616, Krautheimer (1986), p. 56, for his original (and most generally accepted) analysis, and Holloway

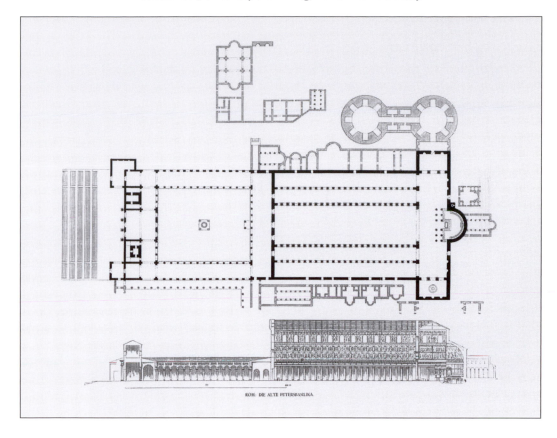

ROM: DIE ALTE PETERSBASILIKA

Figure 2.2   Plan and longitudinal section of Old St Peter's, Rome, from Georg Dehio, *Kirchliches Baukunst des Abendlandes*, Stuttgart, 1887, book I, ch. 3, pl. 18; (1736b.1&2) Bodleian Library, University of Oxford.

also suggests that the nave at first had only a single side-aisle north and south, both of which were subsequently doubled. The apostle's tomb was on the chord of the apse, enclosed in white marble with porphyry bands and sheltered by a baldacchino on four twisted columns. The baldacchino was linked to the apse by two architraved columns.

This basilica was an enormous covered cemetery and martyrium where the celebration of the eucharist was secondary to the memorial function. The altar was not part of the apostle's shrine, and was probably a moveable table standing under the triumphal arch at the entrance to the nave. The two distinct architectural sections, nave and transepts, served the dual functions of the building: the transept accommodated the rites associated with the martyr, veneration, the memorial eucharist and oblation tables; the nave and aisles were a covered cemetery where funeral banquets, or *refrigeria*, were held, a custom that continued until at least 397, when one was held for Paulina, wife of Pammachius.[25] The gold and silver furnishings and the rich endowment given by Constantine were even more lavish than at the Lateran. The size and richness indicate the level of regard for Peter by both the Emperor and the people. In life and in death, thousands wished to be near Peter's special sanctity and touched by his miraculous power.

(2004), p. 79, for a discussion of the most recent considerations.

    25   *Ibid.*, p. 84.

The New Jerusalem and Pilgrimage

St Peter's did not have its own regular services and congregation, it was a pilgrimage church, and as such played a part in the dissemination of an increasingly standardized liturgy that was developing in the fourth century, but it was above all the Holy Land and sites associated with the life of Christ that were of primary importance in this:

> The fourth century was a time when Christians travelled to other parts of the world much more than they had tended to do before, and consequently were more aware of other ways of worshipping than they formerly had been. There were pilgrims to the Holy Land, who not only saw what was done in that liturgical centre and carried the news back home, but also came into contact with the liturgical practices of other Christians arriving there from different parts of the world, as well as those through whose regions they passed on the way. One might say that Jerusalem became an important hub of the liturgical import-export business, a clearing-house for attractive ideas and practices.[26]

The liturgy was clearly transferable, and relics were portable, but above all architecture could re-create the holy places as at Santa Croce in Gerusalemme with the canopy over the relic of the True Cross imitating Constantine's *Anastasis*. Real connections were established with the people and events of salvation history, orthodoxy and theological allegiance were declared visually, and authority was established within the hierarchical architectural structure as a visual equivalent of ecclesial and imperial structures. Architecture was a powerful tool; after all, it shaped the spaces where heaven and earth met.

Even at the beginning of the fourth century, pilgrimage was by no means unknown. Then, as now, Palestine offered a spiritual geography which gave a tangible reality to the scriptures. Earlier in the third century, Origen wrote of Christians wanting 'to trace the footsteps of Jesus and of his disciples, and of the prophets'.[27] Some time after the death of Septimus Severus in 211 and the accession of Caracalla, Eusebius records that Alexander, Bishop of Cappadocia, was invited to share the Episcopal duties of the See of Jerusalem with its bishop Narcissus, who, he records, was 116. Alexander 'journeyed from Cappadocia, his original see, to Jerusalem, in order to worship there and to examine the historic sites'.[28]

The topography of Jerusalem had changed radically since the days of Jesus. For one thing, Golgotha, the site of the crucifixion, and the tomb too had been outside the city wall until 41–44, when Herod Agrippa built the Third Wall, extending the city in an arc to the north and north-west. In May 70, the city was destroyed as punishment for the revolt which had begun in 66, and Jews were forbidden to enter. In 130/31, on the ruins, Hadrian founded Aelia Capitolina, dedicated to Jupiter Capitolinus. Epiphanius, Bishop of Salamis and a native of Palestine, maintained that before that time there was little left 'except for a few houses and the little church of God. That was the upper room, where the disciples entered when they had returned from the Mount of Olives after the Ascension of the Redeemer. It was built there, namely on Zion.' It would appear that a Christian community had managed to survive, and in his record of martyrs of Palestine, Eusebius mentions Vales, a deacon in this community.[29]

Tons of rubble were used to level the area to the west of Temple Mount covering the traditional site of Golgotha and the tomb. Both on the Mount and on the levelled area, Hadrian built temples; the latter, Eusebius maintains, included a temple to Venus which would have been a particular

---

26   Bradshaw (2002), p. 222.
27   Origen, *Comm. Joann.* 1.28, quoted in Wilkinson (2002), p. 6.
28   Eusebius, *The History of the Church*, 6.11.2, translated in Louth (1989), p. 189.
29   See Wilkinson (2002), p. 10, where the quotation from Epiphanius is also translated.

abomination to Christians – though Eusebius may have supplied this detail for rhetorical reasons. In the 290s he described the site as 'Golgotha, "place of a skull", where Christ was crucified, which is pointed out in Aelia to the north of Mount Sion', so when Bishop Makarios of Jerusalem excavated here in 327, it would appear that was because there was a continuing tradition in the Jerusalem Church about the location of this most important site of the resurrection, as there was about the site of the nativity in Bethlehem, the Mount of Olives and the Oak of Mamre – just as the Jews preserved a sacred geography relating to scripture. All these traditional locations would become important pilgrimage sites for Christians under Constantine and his successors.[30] Constantine's mother, the Augusta Helena, made a pilgrimage to the Holy Land in 326 and was instrumental in the founding of great buildings at holy sites.

Buildings of the New Jerusalem

In 333 a nameless pilgrim from Bordeaux arrived in Jerusalem; the date can be firmly established because he mentions the consuls for that year. The record of the journey lists all the stopping-places to change horses, and indicates whether it is a milestone, fortress, palace or city. Interestingly, the traveller gives cumulative distances between the major centres: Rome, Milan, Constantinople and Jerusalem. Naturally, in the west Rome and Milan are most prominent, and in the east Constantinople and Jerusalem may not initially appear surprising, but Constantinople had only been founded three years before, in 330, and Jerusalem was only now being transformed from Hadrian's Aelia Capitolina to the Holy City of the biblical narratives. This was only nine years since Constantine's conquest of the East and already it was being reconceived within a Christian geography of Empire.[31] It is worth quoting his description at length since it is the fullest contemporary account of Constantine's New Jerusalem. This is what he found:

> Climbing Sion from there [as you leave Jerusalem] you can see the place where once the house of Caiaphas used to stand, and the column on which they fell on Christ and scourged him still remains there. ... As you leave there and pass through the wall of Sion towards the Gate of Neapolis, ... on your left is the hillock Golgotha where the Lord was crucified, and about a stone's throw from it the vault where they laid his body, and he rose again on the third day. By order of the Emperor Constantine there has now been built there a 'basilica' – I mean 'a place for the Lord' – which has beside it cisterns of remarkable beauty, and beside them a baptistery where children are baptized. ...
>
> On the Mount of Olives, where the Lord taught before his passion, a basilica has been built by command of Constantine. ... A mile and a half eastwards from there is the village called Bethany, and in it is the vault in which was laid Lazarus, whom the Lord raised. ...
>
> Four miles from Jerusalem, on the way to Bethlehem, on the right of the road, is the tomb in which was laid Jacob's wife Rachel. Two miles further on, on the left, is Bethlehem, where the Lord Jesus Christ was born, and where a basilica has been built by command of Constantine. ... It is nine miles to Terebinthus, where Abraham lived and dug a well beneath the terebinth tree, and spoke and ate with the angels. An exceptionally beautiful basilica has been built there by command of Constantine.[32]

Much earlier, Eusebius of Caesarea had mapped scripture onto the geography of Palestine in the *Onomasticon* of about 300, so the oral traditions had already been recorded locally and the terrain itself was already regarded as Holy. Within that geographical and theological matrix, places and

---

30 For the archaeological background for the tomb of Christ, see Biddle (1999), especially pp. 54–73; for the background to early Christian pilgrimage, see Wilkinson (2002), pp. 4–11.

31 See Elsner (2000), especially pp. 187–9.

32 Translated in Wilkinson (2002), pp. 30–34.

forms of worship would be constructed. The specific forms of architecture and liturgy developed here would exert a strong influence along the return journey of the pilgrim routes.

The Basilica at Mamre

In the *Life of Constantine* (3.53.3) Eusebius tells us that Constantine wished to honour the oak at Mamre where Abraham received 'the Saviour himself with the two angels'. There was already a walled courtyard and a well under the ancient oak that Josephus says was 'a huge terebinth-tree, which is said to have stood there ever since the creation'.[33] This tree had long been venerated by pagans, Jews and, some say, Christians, though that is disputed.[34] Whether or not the place was visited by Christians, Constantine considered it holy as the site of a theophany (the appearance of God to Abraham), and his mother-in-law Eutropia, a pilgrim to Palestine, told him of pagan sacrifice there. By building a church at the site, he presumably wished to prevent the defilement by pagan worship of the holy place where God himself appeared.

The plan of the church, built just before 330, is not very clear, but it appears that a portico replaced the eastern wall of the enclosure, giving access to a small basilica with an apse and side chambers. Its size indicates that it was not for congregational worship, but rather for personal pilgrimage, and that is confirmed by the way it is presented in early pilgrim accounts.[35]

The Lazarium

During the liturgical year, the bishop and his congregation in Jerusalem performed peripatetic services, most particularly during Lent and the Easter season. These itinerant liturgies survived in a truncated form in the great medieval processional liturgies of Eastertide. The original fourth-century liturgies are described in great detail by the pilgrim Egeria, who travelled from somewhere in Gaul via Constantinople to the Holy Land between 381 and 384 – an amazing feat for a woman under contemporary conditions.[36] Of course, the Empress Helena made the pilgrimage too, but she will have travelled in a style rather different from Egeria's, even if Egeria sometimes enjoyed the protection of guards. She describes how: 'In our part of the world we observe forty days before Easter, but here [in Jerusalem] they keep eight weeks.'[37] On the Saturday of the seventh week, the eve of Palm Sunday, the congregation would gather at the Lazarium to mark events leading up to the Passion:

> About half a mile before you get to the Lazarium from Jerusalem there is a church by the road. It is the spot where Lazarus' sister Mary met the Lord. All the monks meet the Bishop when he arrives there, and the people go into the church. They have one hymn and an antiphon, and a reading from the gospel about Lazarus' sister meeting the Lord. Then, after a prayer, everyone is blessed, and they go on with singing to the Lazarium.
>
> By the time they arrive there so many people have collected that they fill not only the Lazarium itself, but all the fields around. They have hymns and antiphons which – like all the readings – are suitable to the day and the place. Then at the dismissal a presbyter announces Easter. He mounts a platform, and reads

---

33   Josephus, *The Jewish War*, 4, 533, translated in Thackeray (1979), p. 159.

34   Taylor (1993), p. 94.

35   See Eusebius, *Vita Constantini*, 3. 51–3, in Cameron and Hall (1999), pp. 141–3; Lane Fox (1989), p. 674; Krautheimer (1986), p. 59, and Wilkinson (2002), pp. 22–3, and the translation from Egeria's *Travels* on p. 91.

36   For a description of contemporary travel conditions, see Leyerle (2000), and for detail of Egeria's journey, see Wilkinson (2002).

37   Egeria, 27.1, in Wilkinson (2002), p. 148.

the Gospel passage which begins 'When Jesus came to Bethany six days before the Passover'. After this reading, with its announcement of Easter, comes the dismissal. They do it on this day because the Gospel describes what took place in Bethany 'six days before the Passover' and it is six days from this Saturday to the Thursday night on which the Lord was arrested after the Supper. Thus they all return to the Anastasis [Church of the Holy Sepulchre] and have Lucernare in the usual way.[38]

Although not all would have such stamina, this pilgrim was living the liturgy, and the lectionary was arranged so that the worshipper was living the scriptures too. It is easy to see why pilgrims returned with a desire to re-create the liturgy and its setting, and with relics to create the immediacy of a physical connection to the sacred events and geography. Egeria tells of the lengths to which some were willing to go to collect a relic. On Good Friday at the veneration of the True Cross, the Bishop had to keep a hand on either end of the relic with the deacons all round him on guard, because 'all the people, catechumens as well as faithful, come up one by one to the table. They stoop down over it, kiss the Wood, and move on. But on one occasion (I don't know when) one of them bit off a piece of the holy Wood and stole it away.'[39]

There is a wonderful freshness and excitement to Egeria's account, and in quite lean prose she still pauses frequently to dwell on the sacred geography of the liturgical progression, punctuated by buildings commissioned by the Emperor of Rome for the Emperor of Heaven, which reveals the importance assumed by an increasingly formal architectural setting for an increasingly formal rite. It was clearly possible to participate in only some stages of this sequence, since many in the crowd seem to have joined the celebration at the Lazarium itself, but for those strong enough to sustain the lengthy participation, the sequence is seen as a coherent whole that fits into the run of daily offices, ending in 'Lucernare', the evening office at four. Another mention of the use of the Lazarium in a similar way by Egeria is on the fifth day of Epiphany, and all the Constantinian foundations in and near Jerusalem are used in sequence during the octave.[40]

The Church of the Nativity

The Church of the Nativity at Bethlehem was, not surprisingly, even more closely integrated into the celebrations of the liturgical year. At Epiphany, the festival continued for the whole of the octave. The church founded by Constantine's mother, Helena (a pilgrim at the great age of 80), at the cave of the nativity in Bethlehem was a large, almost square (28.3 m by 29 m), basilica consisting of nave and two aisles either side. Although the present building in Bethlehem is sixth-century, built on an even grander scale by the Emperor Justinian, the columns and capitals of the colonnades are consistent with fourth-century work, and may well have been reused from the original church. It was preceded by a forecourt (30 m) which led into a large atrium (45 m by 28 m) before entering the church on the axis. The culmination was an octagonal martyrium raised by three steps at the east end, focused on a platform raised a further three steps. A large opening in the middle of this platform gave a view of the grotto.

This church was by no means as large as the Lateran or St Peter's, but there were similarities to the latter in its axial planning which ran from the atrium, to the double-aisled basilica, which was rather loosely attached to an eastern martyrium where the congregation could circulate on either side during the service. Magnificent mosaic floors of the late fourth century have been excavated in the nave and the octagon, so these may have been seen by Egeria, but not the pilgrim of Bordeaux, who saw the church when it was very new and the decoration incomplete. By the end of the fourth

---

38   Egeria, 29.4–6, in Wilkinson (2002), pp. 150–51.
39   Egeria, 37.2, in Wilkinson (2002), p. 155.
40   Egeria, 25.11, in Wilkinson (2002), p. 147.

century, gold and silver were already so much associated with the most sacred focus of the church itself that what was widely believed (by both Origen and Jerome) to be the very mud cradle of Jesus had been replaced by one of silver.[41] In a church celebrating the first appearance of the Lord, it was of course breathtakingly arrayed for Epiphany, along with the other churches associated with the life and saving passion of Christ:

> And on this day in this church [on Golgotha] and at the Anastasis and the Cross and Bethlehem, the decorations really are too marvellous for words. All you can see is gold and jewels and silk; the hangings are entirely silk with gold stripes, the curtains are the same, and everything they use for services at the festival is made of gold and jewels. You simply cannot imagine the number, and the sheer weight of the candles and the tapers and lamps and everything else they use for the services.[42]

At Easter, the Church of the Nativity was again decorated like the great churches in Jerusalem, and on the eve of the fortieth day after Easter (Ascension) there was a vigil service there, followed by 'the usual service, with presbyters and the bishop preaching sermons suitable to the place and the day'. It is unclear from this whether 'the usual service' was eucharistic or not. Crowfoot thinks not: 'At the moment when these sanctuaries were planned evidential considerations were uppermost, as I read the texts of Eusebius and Cyril: the shrines were not built for liturgical worship but that all might see the places where Christ was born and buried and rose from the dead.'[43] To return to the services, curiously the fortieth day seems not to be described as the Ascension, nor does it take place at Eleona on the Mount of Olives in the Imbomon, 'the place from which the Lord ascended into heaven'.[44] The Ascension Egeria places on the fiftieth day (Pentecost), which is celebrated with a day-long peripatetic service beginning at the Great Church, the Martyrium on Golgotha.

The Great Church or Martyrium, Golgotha, and the Anastasis

Christian worship in Jerusalem was focused on Constantine's own foundation, the Great Church, which was also called the Martyrium, or 'witness' to the resurrection: 'New Jerusalem was built at the very Testimony to the Saviour, facing the famous Jerusalem of old.'[45] This description by Eusebius may point to a reason why no events in the life of Christ associated with the Temple, such as the Presentation, were celebrated on Temple Mount. Jesus' prophecy about the destruction of the Temple had been fulfilled that 'there will not be left here one stone upon another, that will not be thrown down' (Matthew 24:2). In fact, in the fourth century two pinnacles of the Temple appear still to have been in existence, but in surviving copies of Egeria's own text, at any rate, there is no mention of services or prayers of any kind being offered there by the Christian community.[46] Their new Holy of Holies was the Anastasis, or cave of the resurrection, 'where the bright angel once announced good news of a new birth, for all men, revealed through the Saviour' (*VC*, 34).

Eusebius' *Life of Constantine* may well have been a work of flattery, but the magnificence of the Constantinian buildings in Jerusalem described by him is amply confirmed by Egeria. Constantine

---

41 Crowfoot (1941), pp. 29–30.

42 Egeria, in Wilkinson (2002), p. 146.

43 Crowfoot (1941), p. 28.

44 See Egeria, 42 and 43.5, in Wilkinson (2002), pp. 159 and 160.

45 Eusebius, *Vita Constantini*, 3, 33, translated in Cameron and Hall (1999), p. 135; translation of Eusebius' description can also be found following on pp. 135–7; even Taylor (1993) concedes that 'this discussion suggests that the Jerusalem Church was able to preserve an accurate memory of where Golgotha was situated, but only up until the fourth century' (p. 140).

46 See especially *ibid.*, p. 88 where the twelfth-century text of Peter the Deacon, based heavily on Egeria, is translated.

himself had written to Bishop Macarius to build 'a basilica superior to all other places, but the other arrangements also, may be such that all the excellences of every city are surpassed by this foundation'. From the outset, Constantine had determined to construct a complex of buildings on the site of Golgotha and the cave of the resurrection. Macarius was instructed to request from Dracillianus, governor of the province, whatever labour or materials were necessary for the work to be as fine as possible: 'It is right that the world's most miraculous place should be worthily embellished.' What Bishop could resist an invitation like that from an Emperor? Work started in 325/26.

The entrance to the complex was from an ordinary street of shops, which must have presented an astonishing contrast. It was designed to allow a view into the colonnaded court and attract passers-by. The façade of the basilica faced the rising sun, and the entrance had gigantic heavily decorated columns between three doors, and unusually for a Constantinian church, Eusebius maintained that its exterior was also of polished stone 'by no means inferior to marble'. The basilica was again double-aisled with marble columns, coloured marble revetment and gilded coffered ceilings. Opposite the entrance was the apse (at the west end), which rose to the full height of the nave, 'the hemisphere attached to the highest part of the royal house, ringed with twelve columns to match the number of the Apostles of the Saviour, their tops decorated with great bowls made of silver which the Emperor himself had presented to his God as a superb offering'.[47] Krautheimer finds it difficult to reconcile this treatment with the apse of the basilica, and thinks the reference should be to the Aedicule in the Anastasis. Doors at the west end of the aisles of the basilica gave onto an open court with colonnades on three sides, a polished marble pavement, and in the south-east corner, the rock of Calvary. Further to the west was the Church of the Holy Sepulchre, a centrally planned martyrium, containing the holy Cave itself. The archaeology has broadly confirmed Eusebius' description of the plan. There is some scholarly disagreement concerning the dating of the Anastasis Rotunda, which Krautheimer considers to be after 336, or even the death of Constantine in 337, though Biddle dates it somewhat earlier, in 335.[48]

The buildings on Golgotha were central to the worship of the Christian community in Jerusalem throughout the year, even during the Great Week before Easter when the services geographically followed the movements of Jesus' passion. In the normal pattern there were daily services beginning before dawn, when the doors of the Anastasis itself were opened and the monks and nuns gathered with a few lay people. They sang antiphons and responses to hymns and psalms until first light, when the clergy arrived and the bishop would go directly into the cave. He began the service proper with a prayer for all and a blessing for the catechumens, then another prayer and a blessing for the faithful. Emerging from the sanctuary, he then laid his hand on each in turn as a blessing, and there was a dismissal. Very similar services took place at noon and at three in the afternoon. At four there was 'Lucernare', when all the lamps and candles were lit from a flame that was kept constantly burning in the cave. The bishop and presbyters then entered and took their seats, and the appointed hymns and antiphons continued. After these, the bishop rose and approached the sanctuary and a deacon offered the prayers for individuals, and after each name a large boys' choir would sing *kyrie eleison*. At the end, the bishop said a collect and the prayer for all. The deacon summoned the catechumens to bow their heads, and the bishop blessed them from his place. After another prayer, the same was done for the faithful. The dismissal was followed by the bishop laying his hand on each. With hymns and antiphons, all the faithful accompanied the bishop to the Cross. This does not mean the relic of the Cross, but rather the rock of Calvary, which makes sense geographically, since the relic could otherwise be incorporated into the service at the Anastasis as

---

47   Passages from Eusebius translated in Cameron and Hall (1999), pp. 134–5, 136.

48   Both references are to Krautheimer (1986), p. 60 n. 45, and p. 61; Biddle (1999), p. 67, at least in a preliminary way, seems to accept that it was 'dedicated in 335'.

on Good Friday – elsewhere Egeria refers to 'the Great Church built by Constantine on Golgotha Behind the Cross'.[49] Before the Cross there was a prayer, and blessings for the catechumens and for the faithful by the hand of the Bishop, and all this was repeated behind the Cross. By this time, dusk was beginning to fall.

On Sundays the people would gather in much the same way, but outside in the court in front of the Anastasis. According to Egeria, they gathered in very considerable numbers.[50] Again there were hymns and antiphons, and at cock-crow the bishop went directly into the Anastasis and the cave itself, 'already ablaze with lamps'. There were three psalms with responses alternating with three prayers, followed by the prayer for all, the cave was censed and the bishop read the gospel account of the resurrection. They went with singing to the Cross, where there was a psalm and a prayer, the blessing and dismissal. Then the bishop laid his hand on the people as they left. A time of rest followed, or for the strong there was a vigil until daybreak, when the people again assembled at the Great Church 'and they do what is everywhere the custom on the Lord's Day' (25.1). As always, Egeria gives no details concerning the holy mysteries, since they would be known to her readers on the one hand, and the profane might come to know their secrets on the other.

However, the bishop of whom Egeria wrote was St Cyril of Jerusalem, whose *Catechetical Lectures* (or *Mystagogical Catecheses*) to the newly baptized give both detail and the underlying sacramental theology. Interestingly, Cyril encourages the catechumens to 'imagine catechesis is a building'.[51] In his *Fifth Address on the Mysteries*, he begins: 'At our previous meetings you have, thanks to God's kindness, received instruction enough about baptism, anointing, and the communion of the body and blood of Christ. We must now move on to our next subject, for our intention today is to put the crowning piece on to the edifice of your spiritual equipment.'[52] He then proceeds to outline the communion, from the *lavabo* and then the kiss of peace, to the *anaphora* or offering. Within this, the eucharistic prayer 'makes mention of sky and earth and sea, of sun and moon and stars and of all creation, rational and irrational, visible and invisible' (5.6). Egeria refers to 'what is everywhere the custom', indicating to her 'sisters', for whom she wrote, that they, probably as far away as Gaul or Spain, would at least broadly recognize the rite as standard, but Cyril's description of the prayer of consecration indicates that there may have been variation at that point at least, or extemporization by the celebrant may even have continued to be the practice. This section ends with the 'Holy, holy, holy' of the Sanctus to join the prayer with that of the celestial host in the heavenly sanctuary. Next he describes the invocation of the Holy Spirit, or *epiclesis* (5.7), prayers 'for all who need aid that we, who also need it ourselves, offer this sacrifice' (5.8), those who have died (5.9 and 5.10), and the Lord's Prayer. There is an invitation to communion (5.19), and a cantor sings 'O taste and see that the Lord is good!' from Psalm 34, verse 8 (5.20). The faithful are told to cup their hands, making 'your left hand a throne for your right, which is about to receive your king. ... Carefully sanctify your eyes with a touch of the holy body and then consume it, taking care to lose none of it' (5.21). Similarly with the cup: 'and while the moisture is still on your lips, touch them with your hands and sanctify your eyes, your forehead and all your senses. Then wait for the prayer and give thanks to God for counting you worthy of such mysteries' (5.22). The prayer is at least as familiar to us as to Egeria's readers.

At this most important service of the week, it was customary for any presbyter present to preach, and finally for the bishop to deliver a sermon as well, so that the service would last from dawn to 10 or 11 p.m. Egeria found it necessary to add that 'the object of having this preaching

---

49   Egeria, 25.1, in Wilkinson (2002), p. 145; the discussion is based on Egeria's very full account.
50   Egeria 24.8, in Wilkinson (2002), p. 144.
51   Yarnold (2000), p. 36.
52   Cyril, *Fifth Address*, 1, translated in Wiles and Santer (1975), p. 190.

every Sunday is to make sure that the people will continually be learning about the Bible and the love of God', implying that preaching, or at least at such length, was not usual at home in Gaul.

After the dismissal, 'in the way that is usual everywhere', and therefore not described, all proceed with singing to the Anastasis, where only the faithful enter. The bishop enters the railed area by the cave, says a thanksgiving, the 'prayer for all' and the series of blessings. It is approaching noon by the time of the final dismissal. In the afternoon, as on every day of the year, there is *Lucernare*. However peripatetic, the festal services do not interrupt the regularity of the offices; however elaborated, the larger biblical narratives supplied by the readings and the preaching enhance the coherence and enlarge the new emphasis on the teaching function of the liturgy.

The New Perspective of the New Jerusalem

One of the aspects of worship in Jerusalem most admired by Egeria was the way readings, psalms and prayers were carefully selected according to both the occasion and place of the particular service. This suggests that the discipline at home amongst her sisters was to read the books of the Bible and the psalms straight through. The great joy of pilgrimage to the Holy Land was to connect with the life of Christ and biblical events. Services during the liturgical year and the movement between sites within or between services built up these larger narratives, and the architectural settings made their contribution to those narratives and controlled access to, and the experience of, the places and relics which provided the existential links with the sacred stories:

> The same concern for the emotive power of the liturgy can be seen in Cyril's exploitation of its celebration at the very places where each saving incident took place. In addition to the Martyrium, the Anastasis and the rock of Calvary, there were services at Sion, the Lazarium, the Eliona, the Imbomon, the place of the Agony, and that of the Arrest; there were also visits to Bethlehem.[53]

Although local practice in liturgy and architecture continued to dominate, especially in the countryside, the power of the Holy Places and relics could be transferred, transporting the sacred geography and the associated liturgical and architectural forms to major centres across the Empire. This contributed to a growing uniformity of liturgy, and to some extent, already at this early date, even of architecture in what was now becoming 'Christendom', strengthening the catholicity of the Church and the unity of the Empire.

Santa Pudenziana, Rome

Around the year 390 in Rome, only a few years after Egeria's return home, a large *thermae* bath was converted into the Church of Santa Pudenziana. Over the next fifteen years it was decorated with elaborate mosaics – in the apse, rather than pure gold, it had the first programme of figural mosaics executed in a church in Rome.[54] The apse mosaic (Cover illustration) shows Christ clothed in gold and purple below a jewelled Cross flanked by the Beasts of the Apocalypse, while he himself is flanked by the Apostles wearing Senatorial togas. They are accompanied by a woman representing the Church of the Jews on one side holding a wreath over the head of Peter, and one on the other holding a wreath over the head of Paul, standing for the Church of the Gentiles. One Apostle is missing from either side as a result of the mosaic being cut down in alterations of 1588. Egeria had

---

53   Yarnold (2000), p. 51.

54   Krautheimer (1980), p. 40; Beckwith (1970), p. 33, dates the mosaic to the papacy of Innocent I, 401–17; see also Jensen (2000), pp. 108–9.

described (37.1) a cross erected on Golgotha, and that it was also possible to place the Bishop's throne on the rock, both of which are presumably shown in the mosaic. In the background of the composition the scene is surrounded by the buildings of the courtyard on Golgotha, and beyond are seen the buildings of the New Jerusalem. In its style there is a new classicism after the fourth-century 'provincialism', or perhaps better, the hieratic emphasis of the art of the Tetrarchy.

The message of the apse mosaic is clear: Christ is the Emperor of Heaven, the Cross his throne, and the Apostles his heavenly court in the New Jerusalem. This reality of heaven is reflected on the earth beneath, in the worship of the Church, in the Christian Empire, and in the rebuilding of Jerusalem in the Holy Land and in the Churches of the Empire:

> Again and again, we find these two features in the pictures of the events of the Bible as they are seen on the walls of the basilicas. On the one hand, they are strictly historical, often, indeed an exact topographical record of the past: many of the Holy Places of Palestine, as of Egypt, Ur and Chaldaea, are included. In their picture of the Birth of Christ, the artists would never forget to show the grotto, which all pilgrims had seen in Bethlehem; and, in the scene of the Easter morning, they would never fail to place, behind the stone on which the man clad in white speaks to the three women, the *memoria* which stood beneath the dome of the Church of the Holy Sepulchre in Jerusalem, which contained the cave of the authentic grave. We even hear of a cycle of pictures which showed Abraham's Oak at Mamre, the Pillar of Salt (Lot's wife), the twelve stones in Jordan, the House of Rahab in Jericho, the burial cave of Lazarus, the Pinnacle of the Temple and many other of the sights of Palestine.[55]

Imperial imagery had been taken up in the decoration of churches; imperial forms dominated ecclesiastical architecture, and imperial ceremonial, dress and badges of office exerted a powerful influence over both the liturgy and liturgical dress. In 318 Constantine gave bishops jurisdiction over legal cases involving Christians, beginning a process of integration of the clergy into the legal, civic and social structures of the Empire. Bishops ranked with the *illustres*, amongst the highest dignitaries, and could claim the same rights, privileges and signs of rank: the *pallium* (a white woollen mantle), special shoes, headgear, ring and throne. Ceremonial attached to rank was to be performed in the presence of the bishop – he was to be greeted with a kiss of his hand and accompanied by candles and incense. As for the Bishop of Rome, he, like the Emperor himself, was to be greeted with genuflection, his foot kissed, and on arrival at a church he was met with singing, from which the *Introit* developed.[56]

Santa Croce in Gerusalemme

In the Sessorian Palace in Rome, the Empress Helena had a huge hall, which had originally been built *c.* 200, converted to a Palatine Chapel in 329, and endowed it with a relic of the True Cross, housed, it has been suggested, under a canopy which was a copy of Constantine's *Anastasis* over the Holy Sepulchre.[57] An apse was added, and two transverse walls supported by double columns separated it into three spaces – a narrow one at the apsidal end for the clergy, the wide central section for the imperial household, and a third narrow section at the back for retainers. The presence of the relic, and Helena's own pilgrimage to Jerusalem in 326–27, were reflected in the dedication of the building, and doubtless also in the way the liturgy was celebrated. Certainly, by the late fourth century, *c.* 382, Pope Damasus modelled the Roman daily office on that of Jerusalem. By the fifth century, papal 'stational masses' had developed to help cope with the crowds that engulfed the Lateran, especially on the great feast days. The pope would be led in solemn procession by a large

---

55 Van der Meer (1967), pp. 92–3.
56 Klauser (1979), pp. 34–5; for legal aspects, see also Lane Fox (1986), p. 667.
57 Krautheimer (1983), p. 129 n. 16, referring to Guarducci (1978), pp. 77ff.

entourage of clergy to Santa Croce in Gerusalemme on Good Friday, Santa Maria Maggiore for the first mass of Christmas, and Santo Stefano Rotondo on the next day, St Stephen's Day. Rome came to celebrate its own sacred geography through the liturgy in a way that had clear parallels with the Jerusalem of St Cyril.

The Architecture of Death, and of Rebirth

Centrally planned *memoriae*, as at Golgotha and Bethlehem, took their architectural form from the imperial mausoleum. 'The adaptation of central plan to temple architecture began in the second-century when Hadrian had the Pantheon rebuilt after it had long been favoured for imperial mausolea. … It was especially popular for martyria or churches built to memorialize key events in the biblical tradition and in the life of Christ, or to commemorate martyrs who had died for the faith.'[58] Just as the basilica, with its imperial associations, was thought appropriate for the worship of the Church, with Christ occupying the apse as Emperor of Heaven, so the imperial mausoleum was considered appropriate as the *memoria* of aspects of his life and death. The theology of baptism, the death of the sinfulness of the old Adam and rising to new life in Christ, made the centralized martyrium an eloquent architectural form for the baptistery.

Mausolea

Constantine probably prepared the circular imperial mausoleum (now the Tor Pignattara) on the Via Labicana, leading out of the city from Santa Croce in Gerusalemme, for himself before he moved the capital of the Empire to Constantinople. He had it built partly over a Christian catacomb along with its attached funerary Basilica of SS. Marcellino e Pietro, and partly over a portion of the cemetery used for the loathed *equites singulares*, who had been Maxentius' bodyguard at the Milvian Bridge. Constantine obliterated their camp by building the *Basilica Constantiniana*, and set aside the laws protecting burials to obliterate their cemetery, building this church and mausoleum, as a part of his *damnatio memoriae* of Maxentius.[59] The stamps on the bricks show them to be Constantinian, and the integration of the planning indicates that the mausoleum was never free-standing. Its interior was covered in coloured marble and porphyry, and a coin of 324–26 embedded in its mortar dates the addition of the revetment, or stone facing. The niches below the windows of the circular drum supporting the dome were covered in mosaic, still visible in the sixteenth century.[60] The mausoleum had a memorial, not a liturgical function, but its symbolic function and architectural form will be of importance when considering the development of the baptistery. The funerary Basilica of SS. Marcellino e Pietro will have functioned in a very similar way to St Peter's, as a covered cemetery. Architecturally, it differed in having its side walls continuous with the sweep of the apse, creating a complete ambulatory, rather than having an apse added to a square end wall as at St Peter's.

To get an impression of how the Tor Pignattara originally looked, it is necessary to go to Santa Costanza on the Via Nomentana (see Figure 2.3). This mausoleum was attached to another apse-ended funerary basilica dedicated to St Agnes. Excavations in the nineteenth century are said to have revealed a font in the church, which at the time was linked to the reference in the *Liber Pontificalis* to Constantine being prevailed upon by his daughter and his sister (both named Constantina, hence Santa Costanza) to build a church for Sant' Agnese and a baptistery, supposed by some to be this martyrium. All this has been much disputed, and some date the structure to

---

58   White (2000), p. 735.

59   Curran (2000), p. 101.

60   See Holloway (2004), pp. 90 and 87.

Figure 2.3   Santa Costanza, Rome, exterior view from the northwest; courtesy Allan T. Kohl/Art
                 Images for College Teaching (AICT).

337–57, when the younger Constantina was living in Rome, but what is important here is to note
the close formal connection between the martyrium and the baptistery because of the theology of
baptism: the dying to sin of the old Adam and rising to new life in Christ.[61]

Like the Tor Pignattara, Santa Costanza is another round mausoleum with a circular vaulted
ambulatory (Plate 1). The vault has a splendid mosaic, of which about thirty per cent is original; the
mid-nineteenth-century restoration was clearly very carefully done and faithful to the original. The
mosaic shows cupids, vines, flowers and greenery in a design consistent with pagan Roman art. The
iconographic status of the mosaic is problematical, encouraging some to connect the building with
Constantine's nephew, Julian the Apostate, who renounced Christianity on becoming Emperor.
Most, however, in the absence of further evidence, accept the claims of the *Liber Pontificalis*,
adding that at this early date, Christian art was content to use the earlier forms, invested with new
meanings in the new context. In this connection, it is interesting to note that the Mausoleum of
Centcelles near Tarragona is just about contemporary with Santa Costanza, and similarities in its
decorative programme suggest that it was built for Constantine's son Constans. Its dome mosaics
are in registers – the lowest with scenes of stag hunting, an allegory of the Christian soul based
on Psalm 42, and the next register up was of Old and New Testament themes.[62] Above that was a
further range showing 'enthroned figures in scenes of imperial ceremonial'. Were the lost upper
registers of Santa Costanza similarly reserved for biblical scenes? Around the years 1538–40, the

61   *Ibid.*, pp. 94–9, with Krautheimer (*Corpus*, 1.16, pp. 34–5), dates the building's dedication 'after she
[Constantina] was widowed in 337'; Claridge (1998), p. 375, dates it to 'about 337–57, when Constantina was
living in Rome, perhaps in a villa nearby'.

62   Dunbabin (1999), p. 251.

Portugese artist Francesco d'Ollanda produced a watercolour of the Santa Costanza dome mosaics as they then existed. It shows a register of Old Testament themes, including the Sacrifice of Cain and Abel, and in the upper register included the Miracle of the Centurion and presumably other New Testament themes.[63] The imperial tradition of mausolea continued with Constantine's astonishing Church of the Apostles in the New Rome (Constantinople), where he rested with the companions of the Lord himself, and there is also the Mausoleum of Theodoric in Ravenna.

Apse-ended Funerary Basilicas

In all there are six examples of Constantinian apse-ended funerary basilicas, including San Lorenzo on the Via Tiburtina, and the recent discovery in 1990 on the Via Ardeatina. Their remains are very fragmentary, making the Church of the Apostles (or San Sebastiano) in old Rome, very near the latter on the Via Appia, an extremely important, still extant, example of an apse-ended funerary basilica with ambulatory. The interior has been largely remodelled, and the early work can only be seen on the exterior. Interestingly, recent work has suggested that Maxentius may have begun the Church of the Apostles before his confrontation with Constantine:

> It is possible that the basilica is a genuine Constantinian building but was achieved by the same architect who constructed the tomb of Romulus which remained intact very close by. Alternatively, it is possible that Maxentius himself began the work on a Christian basilica employing the architect who had served him so well previously. This latter explanation would thus explain the failure of the *Liber Pontificalis* to attribute the foundation to Constantine.[64]

The basilica was built on or over a *memoria* commemorating St Peter and St Paul which had graffiti addressed to the Apostles dating from the middle of the third century. There also seems to have been an object of veneration in a small niche.[65] As at St Peter's, a very large number of Christians wished to be buried at this site, which had been sanctified by the presence of the Apostles and which still contained the grave of St Sebastian. Thousands of bodies were laid under the floor.

This type of covered cemetery was a short-lived phenomenon, and once filled with bodies, they probably tended to fall into disuse after a few generations. Recent ideas concerning the origin of the apse-ended basilica, if true, would throw an interesting light onto Constantine's religious position:

> Why did Constantine and his architects unite a basilica with the mausoleum and why did they give it its unusual form? The basilica extended burial within the walls of the imperial funeral structure to individuals not of the imperial family. This is not an act to be expected from a pagan. It is an act of Christian charity. As he opened his purse to the poor, orphaned children and women in distress, Constantine opened his door to his Christian brothers and sisters in a way unknown to the pagan, for whom the tomb and the household were inseparable. He housed them in the tomb complex intended for himself and occupied by his mother.[66]

It may have been a grand and pious gesture, but in the event, he would have rather different company in his final resting place in his new imperial capital. One puzzling aspect of this, however, is that the Tor Pignattara was added only in 324–26, possibly about a decade after the basilica itself was built, and Helena herself did not occupy the tomb until *c.* 330. A simpler interpretation has

---

63 See Beckwith (1979), p. 27.
64 Curran (2000), p. 99; but see also Holloway (2004), p. 108.
65 Krautheimer, *Corpus*, IV, pp. 112ff; also Snyder (2003), pp. 180–89.
66 Holloway (2004), p. 114.

also been offered: 'Constantine and his family transformed the gesture of linking the emperor's favoured dead (the most recent case being the *equites singulares*) with himself by providing funerary basilicas for the *milites christi*.'[67]

The iconography of the circular imperial mausoleum reached back through Diocletian's, built just at the turn of the fourth century at Spalato (Split), to Hadrian's in Rome (completed by 139), the Mausoleum of Augustus (end of the first century BCE), and may refer back to the tomb of Alexander himself.[68] They were not merely tombs, but also *heroa*, where 'heavenly honours' were offered to the individual commemorated.[69] Such a form was appropriate for the *martyria* at Bethlehem and the Holy Sepulchre, commemorating the birth and resurrection of Christ who had ascended into heaven. The unification of the circular mausoleum and the basilica in the form of the apse-ended basilica speaks of the hope of heaven for the Christian dead crowded under its floor. Furthermore, these structures were usually built over or near the graves of martyrs with memorials celebrated on their 'birthdays', that is to say the anniversaries of their martyrdom. Even the imperial family wanted to be near the sanctity of their presence or the place where they showed the way to heaven.

Baptisteries

The plan of Santa Costanza is found again with only minor, but significant, variation in the foundations of the Lateran Baptistery (see Figure 2.4). A baptistery was part of the Lateran scheme from the beginning, and archaeological excavations have revealed that the present octagonal brick structure stands on more substantial early fourth-century foundations which originally supported a round structure with eight engaged columns where the angles of the present octagon now stand. Formally, this is a martyrium, the clearest proof of a theology of baptism as a sharing in the death and risen life of Christ.[70]

The original entrance was on the opposite side of the building, that is, beside the Cathedral rather than onto the piazza as now. The present porch (which stands in the original position beside the Cathedral) is fifth-century, as are the present octagonal walls of the baptistery, but again the porch is on earlier foundations. There was, then, from the very time of Constantine's victory or within a very short time, a grand antechamber to accommodate the preliminary rites that must already have grown up around baptism itself. Many resemblances between the ceremonial elaborations of the Christian and pagan services of initiation have recently been traced:

> This accumulation of points of resemblance between Cyril's baptismal practice and the pagan initiation rites confirms Hugo Rahner's belief that there was here and elsewhere a conscious attempt to assimilate into Christian practice some of the liturgical techniques of the mystery-religions.
>
> If any one person is to be singled out as the original thinker behind this scheme, the most likely candidate is Constantine. Before his conversion the Emperor had been a devotee of the one god symbolised by the Unconquered Sun, and had been initiated into various mysteries.[71]

It is widely held that the rite became more dramatic, even awe-inspiring, in order to bring about an emotional conversion in those amongst the great number being baptized, who were doing

---

67   Curran (2000), p. 102.
68   Claridge (1998), p. 183.
69   Price (1987), especially pp. 77–80 and his discussion of the treatment of *divi*.
70   See the discussion of initiation in Johnson (2000), pp. 487–9.
71   The quotation is from Yarnold (2000), p. 54, where he also cites Rahner (1963), pp. 3–45, and Barnes (1981), p. 36.

Figure 2.4   Lateran Baptistery, plan, section and sectional perspective, from Dehio and von Bezold (1887–1901), vol. I, pl. 7, no. 3; (1736b.1&2)
Bodleian Library, University of Oxford.

so for less good reasons, given recent imperial favour expressed towards Christianity. Both the dramatic setting and the more elaborated rites would appear to have been in place earlier than would be expected if they simply developed in response to the gathering pace of conversions. This lends weight to Edward Yarnold's argument that the more pagan style of mysteries in the initiation rites was attributable to Constantine himself.[72] This certainly rings true in the light of a pagan and imperial architectural form being taken over directly as the new prototype baptistery.

Of course, we know nothing of the fourth-century decoration of the Lateran Baptistery, but some of the fifth-century work does survive, including a beautiful mosaic with gold and green tendrils on a deep blue ground in the north-east apse of the porch, and the overall scheme may have been not unlike that of S. Giovanni in Fonte, Naples (from *c.* 400) with its scenes from the New Testament, Christian symbolism including the Evangelists, figures of the Apostles, and in the centre the Christogram against a starry sky. High on the wall of the Lateran baptistery a section of green and red porphyry panelling with yellow scrollwork is still to be seen. Columns, capitals, bases, pilasters and lintels are *spolia* (architectural salvage) of the finest quality first-, second- and third-century work, and had probably been salvaged again from the fourth-century for the fifth-century building.

There were many ceremonies that made up the baptismal rite, and the architecture was planned to take these into account – with the progression from the dark apsidal porch and vaulted circular ambulatory, to its well-lit central domed space forming a monumental baldacchino over the font. Oratories to John the Baptist and St John the Evangelist were added in the fifth century. Not all churches used all the ceremonies, and the order could also vary, but these regional variations of the early part of the century diminished towards its end.[73]

The second, octagonal, structure (see Figure 2.4), which was possibly built by Sixtus III (432–40), was widely copied at the end of the fourth century, at Mariana, Corsica in the early fifth, and a simpler version with an arcade rather than an ambulatory at Fréjus, in Provence. The shape of the font varied, with a cross-shaped font at Mariana, but the octagon, as at Marseilles and Fréjus, became standard. The form has been attributed to St Ambrose's baptistery in Milan as early as 386 on the evidence of a poem attributed to him describing the symbolism of the eight sides as a reference to the eighth day – the seven days of creation, and the eighth is the resurrection and new creation – but in *De Sacramentis* he speaks of fonts in the shape of tombs, as at Dura. The actual shape of the Milan font is in doubt, but not its symbolism. Even a hexagonal font could be understood in terms of the sixth day, when Christ was crucified.[74] In Ravenna, both the Baptistery of the Arians (of the late fifth century; see Figure 2.5) and the Baptistery of the Orthodox (the lower part of the early, and the dome of the mid-fifth century; see Figure 2.6)) are octagonal. The latter preserves the most complete impression of a contemporary baptistery in its fabric and its wonderful decorative programme. Rising through the zones, the gaze meets the prophets, then 16 Minor Prophets, and in the mosaic of the dome is a band of empty thrones and altars, Apostles, and finally the central roundel of the Baptism of Christ.

---

72   Bradshaw (1996), p. 22; Bradshaw (2002), pp. 213–17; Yarnold (2000), pp. 247–67.

73   A detailed analysis of the sequence of the baptismal rite is given in Yarnold (1978), pp. 97–105; a comparative table is found in Bradshaw (1996), p. 24.

74   See Barral I Altet (2002), pp. 58–61; Yarnold (1978), p. 103; Whitaker (1970), p. 130; Davies (1962), pp. 1–42, and Davies (1982), pp. 101–2.

Figure 2.5   Baptistery of the Arians, Ravenna, exterior view from the east; courtesy Allan T. Kohl/Art Images for College Teaching (AICT).

Figure 2.6   Baptistery of the Orthodox, Ravenna, exterior; courtesy Allan T. Kohl/Art Images for College Teaching (AICT).

Aquileia

The Cathedral at Aquileia in northern Italy was in a minor place, but set over a major see. Three buildings of the complex, consisting of double cathedral and episcopal residence, may have been 'completed prior to 319 and perhaps as early as 313', that is, during the episcopate of Bishop Theodore, who is commemorated in an inscription saying that he 'made everything happily and dedicated it gloriously'. However, an eyewitness, Athanasius, refers to the church as 'under construction' between 336 and 345. He had been expelled by the Eastern Bishops, and was present at the Easter service in the Cathedral of Aquileia in 345, from where he addressed that year's Festal Letter. In his Apology to Constantius in the mid-350s, in which he was defending himself against charges including the celebration of the liturgy in an unconsecrated church, he defends himself by referring to the Easter Service at Aquileia attended by Constantius' own brother Constans, which was also held in an unfinished, and similarly unconsecrated, church.[75]

The double churches (see the plan, Figure 2.7) are actually *aulae ecclesiae*, and are built over a structure supposed by Krautheimer to be a *domus ecclesiae*, a notion not entirely compatible with the archaeological evidence.[76] The two halls were painted with garden scenes, and the floors were covered with splendid mosaics. These were arranged in panels showing animals and birds in the northern hall, as might be used in secular contexts, but in the southern hall, the east end (nearest the entrance) was entirely covered with a single panel showing fish and fishermen and three scenes from the story of Jonah, swallowed by the whale, regurgitated, and reclining under the gourd. It is a neat allegory of Christian salvation through the waters of baptism. Other panels further west showed a Good Shepherd, and another a 'Victory between probable symbols of the eucharist'.[77] The twin halls were linked by a transverse section which provided for baptism, suggesting the possibility that one hall was for the catechumens, the other (the northern hall) for the celebration of the liturgy. The complex was contemporary with the Lateran, but its architecture and even the constructional details are more closely related to the Rhineland and the double cathedral at Trier.[78] The continuing strength of the connection between northern Italy and the Rhineland is demonstrated by the fact that Ambrose of Milan himself was born at Trier *c.* 339.

During the second half of the fourth century, the northern hall was rebuilt, doubling its dimensions in both directions, and it was possibly this rebuilding that was witnessed by Athanasius. It is very likely that the differences between the episcopal architecture of Rome and the double cathedral at Aquileia can be accounted for by reference to differences in liturgical practice. The main differences are described by Ambrose. In the first place, in Aquileia there was a longer preparation period, running from enrolment at Epiphany to Easter, rather than from the beginning of Lent. The day before baptism, the *apertio*, or touching of the nostrils and ears of the candidate by the bishop, took place. This has most recently been interpreted as 'the remnant of a transition to a period of "restricted" teaching'. There was a pre-baptismal anointing, described by Ambrose as an athlete preparing for combat, and finally (a departure which Ambrose found simply embarrassing) there was the washing of feet, which took place before baptism in Aquileia. The authority of Ambrose

---

75   McLynn (2004), p. 243.

76   Krautheimer (1986), p. 43; inscription noted in White (1996–97), vol. II, pp. 207–8; eyewitness report mentioned in *ibid.* p. 202, where a plan is reproduced. The late fourth-century plan is reproduced in Krautheimer (1986), p. 44. For arguments relating to the *domus ecclesiae*, see especially *ibid.*, pp. 204–7; see also Snyder (1985), pp. 137–40, who is more positive about the possibility of the *aula* being pre-Constantinian.

77   Dunbabin (1999), p. 71.

78   See Krautheimer (1986), pp. 85–7.

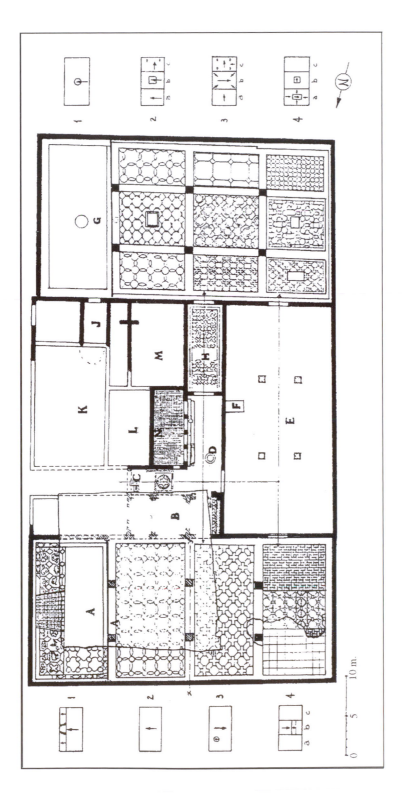

Figure 2.7   Aquileia, Istria, church of Bishop Theodore, early fourth century. Plan with schematic representation of mosaic orientation; from White (1996–97), vol. II, *Texts and Monuments of the Christian Domus Ecclesiae in its Environment*, p. 201; used by kind permission of L. Michael White.

and his See of Milan, especially in liturgical matters, was second only to Rome in the West, and exercised considerable influence in the East as well.[79]

In Rome, pre-baptismal ceremonies took place as the candidate progressed through the architectural spaces on the way to the font in the light under the 'monumental baldacchino' of the dome with its drum resting on eight columns; in Aquileia, it is tempting to speculate that the pre-baptismal ceremonies took place as the candidates entered through the south-eastern door (with the *apertio* perhaps taking place here?), via a small room previously associated with baptism, which may have been for undressing the candidate, with full anointing of the body perhaps taking place in the first bay of the southern hall. The renunciation of the devil in the Eastern rite was performed facing west, reflected in the orientation of the mosaic in the next bay, if the orientation is as for the officiant. The candidate then turned back towards the east in the next bay to undertake the 'contract with Christ' implied in Ambrose's description.

The precise unfolding of the rite in time is easier to reconstruct than in space, since each locality will differ in layout; however, in broad terms, the complex mosaics and their orientations would appear to define the processional route and its stations for the various ceremonies of the pre-baptismal rite, taking the candidate gradually deeper into the architectural complex until reaching the font in the transverse hall:

> Mosaics might be designed to mark on the floor the patterns of use of a room: the habitual location of furniture, the division into parts serving different purposes, or the desired flow of movement. They could establish … a hierarchy of use between different spaces, … and could link areas connected in function. The choice of themes could convey a message about the function of the room, or about the significance of the activities that went on there.[80]

By the middle of the fourth century, and almost universally by the time of Egeria, detail concerning the mysteries was withheld, often until after the candidates had been initiated, so they would certainly not be made entirely obvious in the detail of the mosaic, but the complexities of the pattern and its directionality must correspond to the complexity of the movement of the participants.

Lullingstone Villa, Britannia

In the middle of the fourth century, in faraway Britannia, where circumstances were different and the influence of the Bishop of Rome weaker, the north wing of a large villa was converted to a church. In Gaul, founders of early monasteries tended to come from wealthy landed families, or frequently built within or on the site of Roman villas, as Gregory of Tours tells us of St Aredius (see below, pages 137–8). If these practices had reached Britain, then Lullingstone presents the right circumstances.[81] Evidence suggests that there was farming activity here beside the river even before the Roman occupation, and a house on the site by the end of the first century. The north wing originally had the form of a 'Romano-British Temple'. By the turn of the third century the house was partly destroyed, abandoned, and reoccupied at the end of the century. Early in the fourth century a young man and woman were buried in this part of the villa, and though there were some similarities to Christian burial (for example, the bodies were covered with gypsum), other details suggest that it was pagan.[82] By the 330s the villa had been decorated with good-quality (if

---

79   See also in this connection Duchesne (1903), pp. 32ff.
80   Dunbabin (1999), p. 304, the conclusion of the study.
81   Morris (1989), p. 97; see also Percival (1976), pp. 182–99, and Dunn (2000), p. 139.
82   White (1996–97), vol. II, pp. 248 and 249.

provincial) mosaics with elegant Latin and sophisticated pagan literary references, and two large antique portrait busts. By the mid- to late fourth century, a room with Christian decoration had been added, most probably in Christian use from *c.* 350/60 until after 383:[83]

> The renovation of the chapel room is the only clear indication of Christian presence. Yet, insofar as the proclivities of the owner and his/her family were likely part of the change, it may suggest an earlier Christian presence. On the other hand, it is clear that the nymphaeum and pagan shrine … continued in use throughout much of the fourth century, even after the Christian chapel was installed above.[84]

In the next stage of renovation, the chapel wing was given an independent entrance and the internal connection to the rest of the house was sealed, so the wing was used by those outside as well as within the household. On the west wall of the chapel was a frieze of six panels separated by painted columns, each containing a praying figure. These figures were of both sexes and of different ages, perhaps representing a family, possibly the patron's. The south wall had chi-rho monograms and a landscape showing what may be the villa, or alternatively a scriptural scene.[85] The chapel remained in use up to the early fifth century, when it was destroyed again by fire.

There were other contemporary churches in Britannia, though there are no other securely identifiable sites; for instance, even the examples at Silchester, Colchester, Lincoln and Richborough have been disputed. It is possible, though unlikely, that a church was in the villa at Hinton St Mary, Dorset, with its pavement displaying a roundel containing a head with a chi-rho behind it, almost certainly a head of Christ, though it is conceivably an imperial portrait (now in the British Museum). Not far away, at Frampton, was found a room with an apse and a cruciform mosaic floor with a chi-rho. The anteroom to this has mosaic floors with pagan imagery, like Hinton St Mary and Lullingstone showing Bellerophon. Of course, there may have been a complicated situation where both pagan and Christian worship was happening concurrently (as appears to have been the case at Lullingstone), but the possibility seems very remote here.[86] On the other hand, the pagan motifs may have been 'baptized', so to speak, and used allegorically for Christian purposes, for example with Bellerophon referring to an active fight against evil, and the hounds and deer possibly referring to 'hunted' Christians, though a precise reading is difficult to reconstruct. Most would say the design is Christian, and even that the rooms 'were, from time to time used for Christian worship', but some have gone so far as to suggest that the floors are 'explicitly Christian' and must belong to chapels or house-churches.[87]

There is a growing body of evidence relating to Roman Britain, and Martin Henig maintains that: 'Two conclusions seem inescapable from a reading of the evidence: congregations of Christians were actually growing in the fifth and sixth centuries, not declining, and to be Christian was coming to be seen as the same thing as being Roman, as, indeed, it was almost everywhere else in Europe.'[88]

---

83   Elsner (1998), pp. 136–38, dates the work cautiously to the 'later fourth'; White (1996–97), vol. II, p. 254, dates the work by numismatic evidence to 360, along with Meates, Greenfield and Birchenough (1952), pp. 35–8, the original excavator, somewhat earlier to *c.* 350–60; Dunbabin (1999) p. 97 dates the mosaics to the mid-fourth century.

84   White (1996–97), vol. II, p. 254.

85   Thomas (1981), pp. 94 and 180–81; see also Petts (2003), pp. 80–81, where the figures and monogram are reproduced.

86   For other possibilities, see *ibid.*, pp. 83–6, including fonts, pp. 90–99; see also Thomas (1981), pp. 214ff.

87   I am grateful to Martin Henig for this suggestion concerning Bellerophon; see Dunbabin (1999), pp. 95–6; but the Christian design is accepted by Thomas (1981), p. 182, and even its use for worship, p. 183; the stronger position is presented by Black (1986), p. 150.

88   Henig (2004), p. 18.

Recent excavations at Bradford on Avon have been interpreted in support of this view, with the suggestion that during the fifth to sixth centuries a baptistery was created within a villa complex by laying a circular curb on, and partially cutting through, a fourth-century mosaic. The font, either of stone or perhaps a lead tank (of which many exist with chi-rho monograms), would have stood within this walled enclosure.[89] An interesting illustration, possibly of the baptismal liturgy in an architectural setting, is shown in the Walesby tank, a fragment of a lead tank ploughed up at Walesby, near Market Rasen, Lincolnshire. Though only a fragment, above a chi-rho it appears to show a short frieze of three panels separated by columns. The central panel shows a naked female candidate for baptism between two other women; the panel to the right shows three male figures, and there appears to have been a like panel to the left. If contemporary pictorial conventions are applied, the architectural setting may be reconstructed as a baptistery or a columned ciborium related to the Richborough type of font, but apparently with four rather than six columns, though such a schematic convention cannot be expected to provide that level of detail. Excavations at Richborough have suggested that its baptistery was a wooden construction.[90]

These lead tanks could have been for baptism or footwashing. Perhaps their 'afterlife' can throw some light on how they were originally used. Some of the lead tanks that have been excavated seem to have been deliberately cut into pieces before being buried (quite apart from any damage since sustained in the course of ploughing). Such treatment is not likely to have been given by invaders, but as now, being an object used in a sacrament, a redundant font should be buried and/or broken up, rather than re-used for another purpose. This argues for their having been portable fonts, taken on carts to baptisms by the bishop in much the same way that clergy went out from minster churches to administer the sacraments.

The Water Newton Liturgical Silver[91]

Although we know that there were many Christian churches in Roman Britain, only Lullingstone has been identified with certainty. But there are numerous other possibilities. Still less has been established about the liturgical use of such settings on the periphery of the Empire. Lullingstone itself was clearly used for prayer, as attested by the decoration of the chapel, but the architecture tells us very little else except the broad timescale, the possible makeup of the congregation, and that pagan worship continued. There is, however, other evidence to consider. In 1975 a hoard of Christian silver was unearthed at Water Newton, Cambridgeshire, within the Roman town of *Durobrivae*. Some of the objects were clearly votive, unique examples of Christian silver plaques similar to pagan ones dedicated as thank-offerings. Two of the cups, potentially for liturgical use, have dedicatory inscriptions, so we can deduce a little more about their use. On the deeper cup 'there is also an inscription …. It is a line of verse, a dactylic hexameter, which reads, "sanctum altare tuum, Domine, subnixus honoro" ["I honour your sacred altar, Lord"].' Because of the inscriptions, and for formal reasons, the hoard has been dated to the second half of the fourth century; secondly, 'if … the inscription on the deep cup incorporates reminiscences of the Old Latin Bible and of the Mass, particularly that for the newly baptized in Milan, which St Ambrose describes, the inscription must be from the last decades of the fourth century'.[92] The most recent study of the hoard proceeds

---

89   See Corney (2004), pp. 11–13.

90   See Thomas (1981), pp. 221–4, reconstruction on p. 222, Richborough discussed pp. 216–17; see also Petts (2003), p. 91.

91   The argument in Painter (1999) is worth summarizing in some detail; it answers in detail the criticism of Thomas (1981) and also Frend (1997).

92   *Ibid.*, p. 3.

meticulously and cautiously to establish that this is the earliest surviving liturgical service, 'but, it has to be remembered that the concept of exclusively liturgical silver had not been formed clearly in the fourth century. [The vessels] acquired their character from the authority of the person using them' (p. 10). It is the inscriptions that set certain of these pieces apart as liturgical plate used at specific points in the service. The hinge of the ingenious argument is this: 'As regards what follows it must be remembered first that in late antiquity books were expensive and rare, that memory played a far greater role in all culture than nowadays, that much literature, including large parts of the Bible, was known by heart, and consequently the use of a single word would act as the reminder of whole swathes of scripture and the liturgy' (p. 13). The phrase 'sacred altar' is traced to Ambrose of Milan and the Easter acclamation by the newly baptized:

> The people who have been purified and enriched with wonderful gifts [Baptism and Confirmation] begin to walk in procession towards the altar, saying: 'Introibo ad altare Dei, ad Deum qui laetificat iuventutem meam.' Having stripped themselves of the last traces of the ancient error, renewed in the youth of the eagle, they hasten to the heavenly banquet. They enter then, and, seeing the holy altar prepared, they cry out: 'You have prepared a table before me.'

There is a strong suggestion here that Publianus, who dedicated this cup, did so to celebrate his own Easter baptism. The echoes of Milan imply that it was either Ambrose's liturgy or one very like it that was used along with the cup itself at this very point. Moreover, the inscription may have been the prompt for the next section of the service. Another possibility is that this cup was a reliquary which would have been illuminating of quite other Christian practices, but the evidence is attenuated and unconvincing. If the argument is correct that these objects constitute a liturgical set, then it gives a peculiarly personal, even intimate, insight into the celebration of the contemporary form of the celebration of the mass.

Conclusion

Perhaps at Aquileia, and certainly at Lullingstone, the setting of worship had developed according to the earlier model of architectural adaptation in a way that characterized second- and third-century Christianity. The liturgy celebrated, certainly at Aquileia, and probably at Lullingstone, in the late fourth century (unless remarkably independent of the Milan-inspired mass at *Durobrivae*) was much more highly elaborated and universally recognizable than the liturgy of those early centuries. The inscription is evidence of just how fixed the liturgy had become by this point, even in this northern diocese. The evidence suggests that were Egeria even to have travelled north as far as Britannia on the edge of empire, she would have recognized most of what she saw and heard as 'the way it is done everywhere' – barring a few strongly rooted local variations about which she would doubtless have written at length to her sisters.

The liturgy was becoming standardized, though a good deal of local variation continued. It was seen as the outworking, in the time and the place of the participants, of the universal worship of God – joining the worship of heaven with worship on earth. The hallowed time of worship would naturally unfold most effectively in holy space, which was quintessentially provided by the cult of martyrs and places of witness associated with the life of Christ, or other theophanies, as at Mamre. So the identification of these sites (often said to be by direct revelation) was exceedingly important, as was their architectural articulation. Once authenticated and framed architecturally and liturgically, the place, as a point of connection with the worship of heaven, could paradoxically become highly portable, in images on ivories,[93] through repeated references to their particular architectural form, or if a physical connection could be made by means of a relic. This phenomenon was to be seen at the Holy Places of Jerusalem, transported to Rome at Santa Croce in Gerusalemme, with its relic of the True Cross. Proximity to the graves of the martyrs in Rome, particularly at St Peter's, allowed others buried there to share the protection of the martyr's sanctity. Constantine would share the holiness of the collected relics of the Apostles themselves, and be interred as the 'thirteenth Apostle' in Constantinople. By these means, sacred geography would continue to spread across the Holy Roman Empire through architectural references to St Peter's, the Baptistery of the Lateran, and the Holy Sepulchre. Observing these phenomena demonstrates that there is both a liturgical and an architectural dimension to the worshipper's entry into the presence of God, participation in the worship of heaven, and understanding of salvation history.

The ceremonial of the liturgy was becoming highly elaborate, and in the case of baptism, highly dramatic; but it was not mere theatre, it was the articulation of the fundamental truths of heaven and earth – spiritual, religious and political. Constantine worshipped in the palace, only once having been recorded attending a cathedral service. That was the Cathedral of Holy Peace in Constantinople for the Easter Vigil in 337, only weeks before his death. The Emperor was a ceremonial figure and always its focus, so it would have been difficult to know what to do with an emperor at the liturgy.[94] In that sense, Constantine was an emperor of the old mould, keeping the Church at arm's length, presiding over its Councils and brokering unity, but not himself becoming embroiled. It was different with his sons, who by their participation in the liturgy became implicated in factional controversies, as happened to Constans at Aquileia. Ceremonial and architecture were powerful in shaping realities – they bestowed authority, even sanctity, and created power relationships. Old Rome had proved resistant to Constantine; in founding Constantinople, 'New Rome', he would be able to shape authority, sanctity and power to suit his own taste.

---

93   Such as 'The Maries at the Sepulchre' preserved in the Castello Sforzesco in Milan and 'The Maries at the Sepulchre and the Ascension' at the Bayerisches Nationalmuseum in Munich, the ivory buckle of St Caesarius (470–542 from his tomb at Arles) and examples at the Victoria and Albert Museum including 'Three Maries at the Sepulchre' (no. 380-1871), a Crucifixion from Metz of *c.* 860 (no. 251-1867) showing two round sepulchres below with faces three high in the two doors of each, all looking towards the crucified Christ, and a Crucifixion with other scenes (again from Metz, *c.* 880–900, no. 266-1867) showing the three Maries, one with a censer, at a round Sepulchre very reminiscent of one of the towers at Saint-Riquier. On the reverse of this last example is a carving which shows that it had been the upper half of a Consular diptych of *c.* 520–30.

94   See McLynn (2004), pp. 236ff.

CHAPTER 3

The Emergence of the Byzantine Rite and the Church Building as Sacrament

The Founding of Constantinople

After the defeat of Licinius, Emperor of the East, in 324, Constantine visited Byzantium repeatedly, formally marking out its walls on 8 November. He built a palace, erected a statue of himself with rays around his head, and according to the *Chronicon Paschale* dedicated the city with what appears to have been pagan sacrifice. Later he plundered pagan shrines of the Empire, transferring statues to decorate his new city. In 330 he named it Constantinople with feasting and the celebration of the first games. Eusebius paints a very different picture:

> Honouring with special favour the city which is called after his own name, he [Constantine] adorned it with many places of worship and martyrs' shrines of great size and beauty, some in the suburbs and some in the city itself; by which he both honoured the memory of the martyrs and consecrated the city to the martyrs' God. Being altogether inspired with the divine wisdom, he determined to cleanse of all idolatry the city which he had decreed should bear his own name; so that there should nowhere appear in it statues of the supposed gods worshipped in temples, nor altars defiled by pollutions of blood, nor sacrifices burnt by fire, nor demonic festivals, nor anything else that is customary among the superstitious.[1]

The statue of Constantine was itself a deeply ambiguous figure. It is reputed to have originally been a statue of Apollo with a portrait head of Constantine replacing that of Apollo, and the rays were said to have been the nails from Christ's Passion. So is this the Emperor, and is he to be associated with Apollo, the Invincible Sun, or Christ-Helios? The statue was placed on top of a huge porphyry column in the Forum of Constantine, and beneath the base were relics and the palladium brought by Aeneas from Troy to Italy. On the base was the inscription: 'O Christ, Ruler and Master of the World, to You now I dedicate this subject City, and these sceptres, and the Might of Rome, Protector, save her from all harm.' While all this has led some to conclude that we have no reason to doubt Eusebius' Christian interpretation, others argue that Constantine 'did not build a conspicuously Christian city'.[2] It is entirely possible that interpretation of his position was as wide open for his contemporaries as it remains for us, and it is easy to see why Constantine might have wanted it that way, ruling an Empire of diverse religious allegiances. Churches were undeniably prominent in Constantine's building programme in his new capital, but even these are not unproblematic.

---

1   Eusebius, *Vita Constantini*, III, 48, translated in Mango (1986), pp. 10–11; for confiscations, see Barnes (1981), p. 247; for the transfer of pagan cult images, see Kartsonis (1998), pp. 67–8.

2   Beckwith (1979), pp. 75–6, quoting Sherrard (1965), pp. 8ff., accepts Eusebius; Lowden (1997) does not, see pp. 33–4.

The First Hagia Sophia and Hagia Irene

Hagia Sophia, originally called the Great Church, was the Cathedral of Constantinople, begun by Constantine himself, but not completed until 360 by Constantius:

> At the time of this council of Bishops [which condemned Bishop Macedonius of Constantinople as a heretic], a few days after Eudoxius had been consecrated bishop of Constantinople, was celebrated the dedication of the Great Church of that city, more or less 34 years after its foundations had been laid by Constantine, the Victorious Augustus. This dedication was carried out … the 16th day before the Kalends of March [14 February] … . At the dedication the Emperor Constantius Augustus presented many offerings, namely vessels of gold and silver of great size and many covers for the holy altar woven with gold and precious stones, and furthermore, various golden curtains (*amphithura*) for the doors of the church and others of gold cloth for the outer doorways.[3]

The Great Church was subsequently dedicated to the Holy Wisdom of God, and in form (and liturgical use) was probably closely related to the Great Church at Jerusalem, another double-aisled basilica preceded by an atrium – built, significantly, between 325/26 and 335 by Zenobius and by Eustathios, 'a presbyter from Constantinople'. It was to this Great Church in Constantinople that the 'golden-tongued' John Chrysostom was brought under protest from Antioch to be Bishop of Constantinople in 398. He was a charismatic preacher who might hold forth for two hours, not (as was customary) from his *cathedra* in the apse which was the symbol of his teaching and governing authority, but from a second throne placed on the *ambo*.[4] He famously and frequently complained of the unruly and noisy congregations who would talk and laugh during the readings, and worse still, even during his sermons.

All that remains of the whole Constantinian complex is the treasure-house or *diaconicon* to the north-east. Besides being the sacristy, it may also have functioned as the place where the people left their gifts before the service, with doors on either side allowing an orderly passage of the faithful. The gifts would be prepared here, and when they were brought in to the Great Church, it was done simply and with silence. There appears not to have been any singing, and it was performed with so little ceremony that John Chrysostom never mentions the offering in his sermons, which is most remarkable considering later elaborations of the rite. The contemporary *Mystagogical Catecheses* of Theodore of Mopsuestia in southern Asia Minor, written after 392, do mention the entrance of the gifts:

> It is the deacons who bring out this oblation … which they arrange and place on the awe-inspiring altar … by means of the symbols we must see Christ, who is now being led out and going forth to his passion, and who, in another moment, is laid out for us on the altar. ... And when the offering that is about to be presented is brought out in the sacred vessels, the patens and chalices, you must think that Christ the Lord, is coming out, led to his passion … by the invisible host of ministers … who were also present when the passion of salvation was being accomplished.[5]

Theodore goes on to say that it was appropriate for such a fearful moment to be met with complete silence when the very Body of the Lord will undergo the passion and resurrection, and at this point the deacons begin to wave their fans so that nothing will fall on the glorious Body. At some later time, the gravity of the moment began to be marked with singing and greater ceremony.

---

3   *Chronicon Paschale*, I, 544, translated in Mango (1986), p. 26.
4   Mathews (1971), pp. 13 and 150–51, referring to Sozomen, Socrates, Van de Paverd and Taft.
5   Theodore of Mopsuestia, quoted in Wybrew (1989), p. 53.

Chrysostom was deposed in 404 through the influence of the Empress Eudoxia, and in the ensuing disturbances Hagia Sophia was disastrously damaged by a fire which started near his throne on the ambo. From there it quickly spread up the hanging lamps to the wooden roof. Along with what would appear to be a large part of the church, the baptistery near this central section towards the east end of the church was also destroyed. The restored church was not re-dedicated until 10 October 415 under Theodosius II.

Alongside the Hagia Sophia, about a hundred metres north, was Hagia Irene, Church of the Holy Peace, where Constantine made his one recorded appearance at a public liturgy, at the Easter Vigil in 337, shortly before his death. These two major churches shared a common precinct, and together they may have functioned as a double cathedral:[6] for example after the fire in the Great Church in 404, Hagia Irene took over its functions until its reopening in 415. Both were destroyed in the Nika riot of 532.

The Church of the Holy Apostles

Nothing remains of Constantine's *Apostoleion*, or Church of the Holy Apostles, with the possible exception of the monolithic columns of what became the Mosque of Mehmet the Conqueror, or Fatih Camii, now standing on the site. Eusebius describes the church as taking the form of a cross in the centre of a large courtyard surrounded by halls and baths. Over the crossing was a large drum, well lit by grilled windows and topped by a conical roof. As with so many other Constantinian buildings, the walls shone with polished marble revetment and the coffered ceilings with gold. Only somewhat later, Gregory of Nyssa, in the 'Laudatio S. Theodori', gives an impression of what it was like to enter even the relatively obscure Martyrium of S. Theodore at Euchaita, near Amaseia in the Pontus:

> When a man comes to a place like the one where we are gathered today, wherein are the memorial and the holy relic of the Just one, he is at once inspired by the magnificence of the spectacle, seeing, as he does, a building splendidly wrought both with regard to size and the beauty of its adornment, as befits God's temple, a building in which the carpenter has shaped wood into the likeness of animals, and the mason has polished slabs to the smoothness of silver. The painter, too, has spread out the blooms of his art, having depicted on an image (*en eikoni*) the martyr's brave deeds, his resistance, his torments, the ferocious faces of the tyrants, the insults, that fiery furnace, the martyr's most blessed death and the representation in human form of Christ who presides over the contest – all of these he wrought by means of colors as if it were a book that uttered speech, and so he both represented the martyr's feats with all clarity and adorned the church like a beautiful meadow; for painting, even if it is silent, is capable of speaking from the wall and being of the greatest benefit. As for the mosaicist, he made a noteworthy floor to tread upon.[7]

The natural quality of these images was valued because it brought the observer into the presence of the action like a particularly vivid form of preaching. The interior, even of a more minor church like this, was intended to be memorably impressive by its size, beauty and costliness. An imperial foundation like the *Apostoleion* would seek to be utterly breathtaking as a setting for the awe-inspiring holy mysteries.

The focus of the *Apostoleion* at the crossing, bathed in light, was the sanctuary containing the porphyry sarcophagus of Constantine himself, of which a probable fragment remains.[8] Surrounding the sarcophagus were cenotaphs to the Apostles, companions of the Saviour himself, and in 356/57 Constantius translated the bodies of the Apostles Andrew, Luke and Timothy to the *Apostoleion*,

---

6   Krautheimer (1986), p. 460 n. 27.
7   Mango (1986), pp. 36–7.
8   Beckwith (1979), p. 76; Vasiliev (1948), pp. 1ff.; Grierson (1962), pp. 3ff.

placing them below the altar and enhancing the presentation of Constantine as the thirteenth Apostle. This was an early translation of relics (the first recorded ceremonial movement of relics being of St Babylus to Daphne between 351– and 354), and its imperial sponsorship ensured its emulation. An ivory, dating from the sixth century or earlier and preserved in the cathedral treasury at Trier, shows just such a translation of relics at Constantinople, with prelates in a carriage bearing a reliquary, and the Emperor preceding the horses on foot to the entrance to the church. Jaś Elsner has pointed out the similarity between this image and the description by Herodian of the triumphal arrival of the Baal borne on a chariot to the temple, preceded by the pagan Emperor Elagabalus. During this period of very rapid transition, these two images are both to be read (perhaps worryingly) within the same ambiguous imperial conceptual framework, as are architectural forms and aspects of the ceremonial of the liturgy. Christian processions with relics functioned in ways very similar to the arrival, progress and departure of the statue of a pagan god in civic celebrations. In Byzantium, a similar function would be performed by icons, most particularly of the Virgin, carried in procession for the protection of the city.[9]

The literary evidence provided by Eusebius and later by Procopius concerning the building of the *Apostoleion* is at odds, with the former maintaining that Constantine himself built the *Apostoleion* to house his own tomb, and the latter believing that it was built by his son and successor Constantius. If the section in Eusebius is genuine (which some doubt), then it must have been written between the death of Constantine in 337 and Eusebius' own death by 340. What pleads for the earlier date of construction by Constantine, and acceptance of Eusebius' record, is that though it may not have seemed odd to Constantine himself that he should be at the centre of the cult – after all, that had for generations been one of the Emperor's (albeit pagan) functions – for a Church that was maturing as an institution, such a potentially syncretistic juxtaposition was becoming intolerable.[10] For Constantius to have conceived such a problematic liturgical setting and carried it out at a later date against growing opposition seems increasingly unlikely.

Constantine's death in 337 posed a problem: until now, Emperors had been cremated on an elaborate pyre, aggrandized by an apotheosis, and latterly at least, deified. This was clearly impossible with the first Christian Emperor. The Roman Senate wanted his body returned to Rome, presumably for the traditional pagan ceremonial of *consecratio*, but the request was refused. In the *Life of Constantine* (4.64.2), Eusebius used vocabulary that would have been familiar to them, saying that on 'the Feast of Feasts [Pentecost], about the time of the midday sun the Emperor was taken up to his God' (4.65.1). The notion that Constantine was the earthly representative of his Lord continued: 'Tribunes and centurions wept aloud for their Saviour, Protector and Benefactor, and the rest of the troops suitably mourned like flocks for their Good Shepherd' (4.65.2). The commanders, the ruling class and Senate of New Rome all came in their customary order of precedence to his glittering lying-in-state 'and saluted the Emperor on the bier with genuflections after his death in the same way as when he was alive … and it is right that he alone enjoyed these things, as the God over all allowed his mortal part to reign among mankind, thus demonstrating the ageless and deathless reign of his soul to those with minds not stony-hard' (4.67.1 and 4.67.3). The Emperor was taken in procession, led by his second son, Constantius, along with his brothers recently declared Augusti, Eusebius says, although this did not actually occur until 9 September 337.[11] There was a military escort, and crowds followed. Constantine was laid to rest in the *Apostoleion*, where his 'soul shares the honour of the invocation of the Apostles and is numbered among the people

---

9   See Elsner (1998), pp. 202 and 231; Lane Fox (1986), pp. 678–9.

10   See Ward-Perkins (1966), p. 36; see also Krautheimer (1983) on Constantine as the 'earthly double of Christ'.

11   Cameron and Hall (1999), p. 345.

of God, having divine rites and mystic liturgies bestowed upon it, and enjoying participation in sacred prayers, he himself even after death holding on to empire' (4.71.2). This was by no means a radical departure from tradition, but it was a new idiom which could be read by both Christian and pagan subjects, satisfying the Senates of both New and old Rome. Consecration coins struck in his honour, Eusebius records, showed the 'Blessed One' (Constantine) in a veiled portrait on the obverse, and driving a chariot on the reverse, 'being taken up by a right hand stretched out to him from above' (4.73). The image could easily be read as the traditional charioteer in the race of life with the hand of Jupiter, or 'the chariot might evoke the chariot which bore Elijah up to heaven, where the hand could be the hand of God. Surely the imagery is neatly ambiguous, designed to be understood in different ways by the pagan and Christian subjects of the empire.'[12] Constantine was granted the title of *divus*, a title given to deceased Byzantine emperors until the early sixth century; early ambiguities left deep marks on Christianity, some becoming embedded in the ceremonial and in the architecture, as at the *Apostoleion*.

There were even more extraordinary ceremonies at Constantine's column in the forum, where mass was celebrated inside the tetrapylon of the base and prayer was offered 'to Constantine's image on the column … as if to a god to avert disasters'.[13]

In his life there had been some difficulty integrating the ceremonial person of the Emperor into the liturgy of the Church; in his death it hardly became less acute. With the celebration of the eucharist, which was liturgically focused on the Emperor of Heaven, in the sanctuary of the *Apostoleion*, which was architecturally focused on the Emperor of Rome, the long association between the two Emperors, as in Eusebius' *Life of Constantine*, became all too real, and bordered on the blasphemous – approaching a Christianized deification of the Emperor. All this constitutes a renegotiation of the relationship between the Church and the world, between the kingdom of this world and the Kingdom of God, between the Emperor of Rome and the Emperor of Heaven. With the absence of the Emperor from Rome since 326, the Bishop of Rome, unlike his brother in Constantinople, was free to concentrate on congregational and pastoral matters. At this point, before a canon has developed, an enormous number of architectural and ceremonial forms were available to be reinvested with the newly negotiated orthodoxy, but the visual, the ceremonial and the doctrinal all had to conform to the same internal logic, which was not at all obvious in the arrangement of the *Apostoleion*.

The inevitable solution was soon reached with the removal of Constantine from the sanctuary of the *Apostoleion* to a nearby traditional circular mausoleum and the re-dedication of the whole complex, probably in 370. Enormous trouble had been taken at St Peter's to overcome the difficulties of the site on the Vatican Hill in order to have the architectural focus on the altar above the tomb of the Prince of the Apostles, but the tomb itself was below floor-level in a *confessio*. It was only the tomb of the Saviour himself in Jerusalem that was both the architectural and liturgical focus of a great church complex, and its place in the liturgy was carefully controlled by the progression of the service through the architectural spaces. Now the three Apostles together occupied this focal position (again below the altar) at the *Apostoleion* and many other churches would follow this pattern during the next century, with the plan in the form of the Cross and its dedication to the Apostles, or some other saint as a local apostle.[14] For example, as early as 379 work was begun on the Church of St Babylus in Antioch, clearly modelled on Constantine's *Apostoleion*. The square martyrium contained the altar, the grave of the saint and two of his successors as Bishop of Antioch,

---

12   For an analysis of imperial funerals, see Price (1987); the quotation is on p. 101. See also Cameron and Hall (1999), pp. 347–50.

13   Krautheimer (1983), p. 67.

14   Krautheimer (1986), p. 70.

and from it radiated four long arms with colourful mosaic floors. Around the year 380, Gregory of Nyssa in a letter to Amphilochius, Bishop of Iconium, described in great detail a martyrium he was building in his native city which was to be an octagon with four conches alternating with arms 'coming together in a manner that is inherent in the cruciform shape'.[15] The octagonal crossing probably relates to the Golden Octagon, Constantine's court church in Antioch. At the turn of the fifth century at Ephesus, a cross-shaped church was built over the grave of St John.[16] At about the same time, Mark the Deacon in the 'Life of Porphyry' (75) records how the Empress Eudoxia gave money to Bishop Porphyry when he was in Constantinople to build the Cathedral of Gaza, and later sent letters and 'on another sheet enclosed in the letter was the plan (*skariphos*) of the holy church in the form of a cross, such as it appears today by the help of God; and the letter contained instructions that the holy church be built according to this plan. ... Furthermore, the letter announced the despatch of costly columns and marbles.'[17] Imperial patronage and travel between imperial capitals ensured the dissemination of both architectural and liturgical ideas. In the West, St Ambrose, in the dedicatory verses for his Church of the Apostles, Milan in 382, emphasizes the symbolism of the plan:

> Forma crucis templum est, templum victoria Christi
> Sacra, triumphalis, signat imago locum.[18]

> (The form of the cross is a temple, the temple of Christ's victory
> The sacred, triumphal symbol marks the place.)

Eastern Influence: Milan

Milan, as the main capital of the Emperor of the West, was strongly linked to the other imperial capitals at this period, and competed with Constantinople. That Milan was a very credible competitor is amply demonstrated by surviving fourth-century churches, including San Lorenzo (built before 378; see Figure 3.1), a centralized plan resembling a huge baldacchino indicating that it may have served originally as a chapel for the nearby palace. Ambrose's Church of the Apostles was a copy of, and a challenge to, its prototype, the *Apostoleion*: it was a full 200 Roman feet long with arms 50 Roman feet wide. Its walls still exist virtually to their full height within the present S. Nazaro. Here, as in the *Apostoleion*, the sanctuary and altar were at the crossing, and below the altar Ambrose placed relics of the Apostles in a silver casket. The *Martyrologium Hieronymianum* records a ceremony on 9 May 386, when the relics of the Apostles John, Andrew and Thomas were brought into the *Basilica Apostolorum*. Since Andrew's body had been in the *Apostoleion* in Constantinople since 356/57, it suggests that the relics may well have been the gift of Theodosius, Emperor in Constantinople. The gift would certainly have had a political dimension considering Ambrose was in 385/86 in conflict with Valentinian, Emperor of the West, and his court based in Milan. The issue at the centre of this conflict was that Valentinian, and his heretical Arian clergy, wished to use one of Ambrose's churches as a Palatine Chapel. At one point the purple hangings that always accompanied an imperial celebration were damaged in the Portian Basilica. This amounted to a direct assault on the Emperor's person, which placed Ambrose and his people in very real danger of imperial retribution. What followed was a visionary use of liturgy

---

15   The letter is translated in Mango (1986), pp. 27–9.
16   See Krautheimer (1986), p. 106, but Peeters (1969), p. 152, maintains that 'it is more likely, that Ephesus had been the example for the Apostoleion'.
17   Translated in Mango (1986), pp. 30–32, 31.
18   Quoted in Ward-Perkins (1966), p. 34.

Figure 3.1   San Lorenzo Maggiore, Milan, exterior view from the east; courtesy Allan T. Kohl/ Art Images for College Teaching (AICT).

to strengthen community and defend their church building. Ambrose was blockaded with his congregation in his church. To pass the time and to boost sagging morale, Ambrose divided the congregation into two choirs to chant the psalms antiphonally. The success of the improvisation was built upon in a further encounter, and congregational singing became a distinguishing mark of the Ambrosian liturgy.[19]

Ambrose won the confrontation with the Emperor over the use of church buildings, the blockade was lifted, and Valentinian appears to have celebrated Easter on the road to Aquileia. When the conflict flared up again, Ambrose and his embattled congregation returned to the singing of psalms, reinforcing their sense of oppression. He also composed rallying hymns which declared their orthodox faith in the Trinity. The hymns were appropriate to different times of the day: 'a round-the-clock liturgy was thus improvised, each day and night being punctuated by services and song', at cock-crow, morning, noon and evening, and on special occasions with an all-night vigil. This round of sung services became a characteristic of the Milanese liturgy.[20] Typically, Ambrose wrote: 'What human being would not be ashamed to end the day without the festal recital of psalms, when even the tiniest birds observe the beginning of day and night with solemn devotion and sweet song.'[21] Even St Augustine, normally rather austere in these matters, conceded how profoundly moved he had been by the singing of Ambrose's choirs.[22]

---

19   See McLynn (1994), pp. 194–5; the relics at the *Basilica Apostolorum* may have included Peter and Paul, see pp. 230–31.

20   See Homes Dudden (1935), vol. II, p. 442; McLynn (1994), pp. 201 and 223.

21   Quoted in Homes Dudden (1935), vol. II, p. 444.

22   *Confessions*, 9.16.14, translated in Chadwick (1991), p. 166.

The shorter vigil appears to have originated during the confrontation with the Imperial court, but on the eve of a festival the vigil would last throughout the night. The midday service preceded the celebration of the eucharist. On days of fasting, the eucharist was delayed until the end of the fast. As at Cyril's Jerusalem the service consisted of the Liturgy of the Catechumens, after which they were dismissed for the Liturgy of the Faithful. While the catechumens were present, perhaps understandably, but also tellingly, Ambrose describes how difficult it was to maintain order: 'What a work there is in church to procure silence when the lessons are read!'[23] Those lessons were from the Prophets, the Epistles, then the Gospels, interspersed by the singing of psalms. By this time, the lessons for special days at least appear to have been fixed, following the practice of Jerusalem. The sermon followed, and then the catechumens were dismissed. As usual, a degree of reticence is shown by Ambrose concerning the mysteries, which were 'sealed'. Those details which he does mention concur with the use in Jerusalem, but in addition there are now the words of institution: 'This is my body … this is my blood …'. At the altar, the celebrant stretched out his arms in the form of the cross, emphasizing the identification between the priest and Christ.

Ambrose had been a governor before his election to the See of Milan, but his political manoeuvrings in relation to the imperial court were now staged in a liturgical context, including preaching in which he condemned his Arian opponents for their practice of re-baptizing converts from orthodoxy. Having won in his confrontation with the Emperor of the West, he consolidated his powerful position architecturally by completing the *Basilica Ambrosiana* in which he was to be buried under the altar – it was to be his own martyrium, which was a daring gesture in the arrangement of the liturgical setting, further enhancing his prestige; should he be killed for his opposition, the Emperor would have a martyr on his hands. The liturgical gesture was also a political statement – burial under the altar, or nearby, had been unacceptable even for Constantine, but it was appropriate for a bishop. Ambrose was making the authority and independence of the Church abundantly clear.

Within a very short time, the cruciform plan of Ambrose's *Basilica Apostolorum*, however conceptually and symbolically appropriate, was proving problematical. The function of the church was multi-layered. It had not been built on the site of a martyr's grave nor of a martyrdom; its relics were brought into a completed church on the main ceremonial entrance to the city. The church provided the stage for the initial encounter between the Bishop and the Emperor at his *adventus*, or ceremonial arrival in his capital. The building functioned politically, both in relation to the Emperor of the West and the Emperor of the East (in rivalling its Eastern prototype and in the gift of relics); it announced the equivalence of Milan, as effective capital of the West, with the prestige of Constantinople, capital of the East. Primarily, however, it was a congregational church for the regular celebration of the liturgy, but during the celebration of the liturgy, the headpiece of the cruciform plan became redundant. Still, the presence of the relics of the Apostles made it a very desirable place for the burial of local dignitaries, which duly took place in the apsidal structures in the arms near the crossing. A centralized altar was clearly an unsatisfactory arrangement for a congregational church, and in 395, with the discovery of the remains of a new martyr, Nazaro, close to the church, Ambrose translated him and interred him below a newly relocated high altar at the east end, removing the sanctuary from the crossing. All this took some explaining, and in a poem incised in stone in his newly re-ordered church, he presents the cruciform plan as an appropriate symbol of the victory of the martyr: 'he whose palm was once a cross now has a cross as his resting place'.[24] The relics of the Apostles were there to enhance the prestige of the local saint, and Ambrose was able to transform the *Basilica Apostolorum* to the liturgically more suitable

---

23   Homes Dudden (1935), vol. II, p. 447 n. 6.
24   McLynn (1994), p. 235.

S. Nazaro through a combination of poetic agility and simply moving the altar into the eastern headpiece of the church over the tomb of his newly discovered martyr.

This type of plan was repeated on a grand scale by Ambrose in Milan in the late fourth century in the still extant (though remodelled) S. Simpliciano. Its basic structure and brickwork with blind arches and buttressing still give a very clear idea of its original appearance. The influence of Milan throughout northern Italy ensured the spread of this new plan, and it is to be found in Como, Ravenna and Verona. Ambrose's political influence had an even greater reach: in 390, Theodosius I massacred the inhabitants of Thessalonica as punishment for an insurrection. Ambrose demanded that he do penance for the crime, and the Emperor of the East obeyed. The independence of the Church had been asserted.

Liturgically, the Cathedral of Milan, St Tecla's, built in the mid-fourth century, is revealing of prevailing practice. It was a double-aisled basilica with a deep sanctuary raised above the level of the nave. The chancel had wings on either side reached through colonnades, and used probably for the offerings of the people. In front of the *bema*, or raised chancel, was a *solea*, or long pathway, projecting well down the nave. The arrangement was similar to Constantine's Lateran Basilica, and will be seen to develop further into an array of variations in the Eastern Empire. A good extant comparative example of this arrangement (though with single aisles, and some of the liturgical furnishings have disappeared) is the *Acheiropoietos* Church in Salonica (*c.* 450–70), another is the reconstructed H. Demetrios, Salonica, built in the late fifth century. These arrangements would be formative for the emergence of the new Byzantine architecture, though the sheer size of the Empire and diversity of local culture and building traditions would result in a wide variety of artistic and architectural styles.

Constantinople in the Fifth and Sixth Centuries

In the late fourth century, Constantinople had grown in importance until, in 381, the Ecumenical Council held in the city by Theodosius I pronounced that: 'the Bishop of Constantinople shall have the precedence of honour after the Bishop of Rome, because Constantinople is New Rome'. Of the glories of his New Rome, almost nothing is left. Hagia Sophia was seriously damaged in the fire of 404 which followed the deposition of John Chrysostom, and rebuilding continued until 415. Only elements of the decorative detail of this structure survive, and the very success and wealth of Constantinople in the fifth century has meant that building and rebuilding activities have obliterated all other churches of the period with the exception of the Basilica of St John Studios, which was built in the 450s and survives only as a ruin. Its revetment and fine marble columns are now familiar elements, and its squat proportions, galleries and plan recall the Church of the Holy Sepulchre, but its decoration, plan and liturgical furnishings have developed a more recognizably Byzantine quality. There is a *synthronon*, or bench for the clergy, wrapped round the inside of the apse, the *bema*, or raised platform, projected 5.45 metres into the nave with parapets and doors placed centrally on the north, south and western or nave side. Here it probably extended down the nave as a raised *solea*, or pathway, leading to the pulpit, though the *solea* and *ambo* are now completely lost. Below the altar was a small crypt in the shape of a cross, which was a deposit for relics. Steps descended from the chord of the apse into the small space only 1.45 metres high. Since the steps descend immediately behind the altar, this is a good indication that, here at least, the celebrant must have faced east.[25] A very similar arrangement is indicated in what little remains of the Church of the Theotokos, Chalkoprateia, near the Great Church.[26]

The liturgy celebrated here may have emerged from the tradition described in the eighth book of the *Apostolic Constitutions*. Though it claims to be the Apostolic tradition transmitted to the Church of Rome by St Clement, it is generally accepted to reflect the use of Antioch at the end of the fourth century.[27] The text speaks of readings from the Law, the Prophets, the Epistles, the Acts and the Gospels, but it is not clear how many readings were expected. They were to be read from an elevated place in the centre, presumably the *ambo*, or raised pulpitum. Very similar, roughly contemporary, arrangements of basilicas with galleries were to be found (with the addition of round martyria) at St Mary Chalkoprateia, at Hagia Euphemia in nearby Chalcedon, and St Mary Blachernai.

Justinian came to the Imperial throne in 527. He was an autocrat of the first order, and his rule met significant resistance. Most of Constantinople was destroyed in the fire following the popular Nika Riots of 532 which very nearly toppled Justinian, but he rebuilt the city with astonishing speed, completing SS. Sergius and Bacchus, and replacing Hagia Irene, the *Apostoleion* and Hagia Sophia. The new imperial architecture was to play its part in Justinian's project of unification, and his official historian, Procopius, dedicated a whole book to these four buildings. Doctrinal disputes over the nature of Christ – human or divine – had fragmented the Church, especially in the East. However, doctrine seemed to intrude surprisingly little into the celebration of the liturgy, with the exception of the use of Trinitarian doxologies by the orthodox, and it was the liturgy that was the determining factor in the new architectural developments under Justinian. The most radical architectural change was to be the increasing centralization of church planning, partly as the result of the increasing fear and awe in the presence of the sacrifice.

The Centralized Church: SS. Sergius and Bacchus

Very early in his reign, Justinian began work on SS. Sergius and Bacchus which was completed by 536 (Figure 3.2). It was fitted into a small site between his former Hormisdas Palace and the Basilica of SS. Peter and Paul, becoming the focus of the whole complex. The structure is supported on eight piers with alternating rectangular and semicircular bays, forming on plan an octagon surmounted by a dome within an irregular square. The centralized plan appears to be relatively simple, but viewed from the ambulatories or the galleries – that is, from the point of view of the congregation – it is difficult to make sense of the complicated space that appears to billow out from the area in which the liturgy is performed. The decoration is superb and finely wrought, mass and void are powerfully handled, light and shade are beautifully modulated, but the irregularities of the site produce unfortunate distortions. Despite this, the little church signals an extremely significant departure and a touchstone of Byzantine architecture. All the elements can be traced historically, and the planning is not without precedent, with roots that go back presumably to the rather enigmatic San Lorenzo built before 378 near the Imperial Palace in Milan and the Golden Octagon begun in 327. That was Constantine's palatine church and cathedral in Antioch, though it was not completed until 341. Influence from Antioch had certainly been strong during the fourth and fifth centuries, when it was effectively capital of the East under Constantius II. Antioch had previously had ecclesiastical jurisdiction over Byzantium, and since the time of Constantine, the

---

25 See Peeters (1969), pp. 134–5, with measured drawings; Wybrew (1989), p. 55, and Mathews (1971), pp. 19–27.

26 *Ibid.*, pp. 32–3.

27 Bradshaw (2002), p. 84.

Figure 3.2   Church of SS. Sergius and Bacchus, interior; Conway Library, Courtauld Institute of Art.

connection had continued to be strong with a number of Bishops of Constantinople coming from Antioch, including St John Chrysostom.[28]

Here, it is neither the stylistic nor the structural antecedents and refinements that are of greatest significance, but the fact that with the liturgical focus moving between the eastern apse and along the *solea* to the pulpit in the centre of the nave, the basilica had effectively been wrapped round the action as in centralized palace audience halls. When liturgical patterns change, the architectural setting responds, often drawing from, and reinterpreting if necessary, a wide variety of its historical stock of forms. The galleried basilica was clearly a lineal antecedent, and since SS. Sergius and Bacchus housed relics, perhaps the martyrium was reinterpreted with a poetic dexterity akin to Ambrose's simple, but skilful, transformation of his *Basilica Apostolorum* into S. Nazaro. The basilica had been transformed from an imperial audience hall to audience hall for the Emperor of Heaven, and Krautheimer also traces the centralized church to the palace audience hall:

> The design of centrally-planned audience halls is transposed from palace architecture into church building, and is thus adapted to the requirements of the sixth-century liturgy of Constantinople. Construction and design, ecclesiastical and Imperial ceremonial interlock. The traditional forms are a source to be tapped, placed into new contexts, adapted to new demands, transformed, and imbued with new life. Such revitalization of a living tradition is a basic trait of Justinian's architecture as it is of his policies.[29]

---

28 Wybrew (1989), pp. 29 and 47.

29 Krautheimer (1986), p. 232; see also p. 230.

As far back as St Cyril of Jerusalem's *Catechetical Lectures* (or more properly *Mystagogical Catecheses*), there had been an emphasis in the East on awe and fear in the presence of the sacrifice of the mass. By their ordination to the service of the altar, the clergy occupied the sanctuary, but as churches became more centralized, the people withdrew increasingly to the aisles and galleries. The *bema* had long been screened by parapets, as would the emperor or a magistrate in his basilica, but now the aisles were often similarly marked by a change in the level of the floor, or even by low parapets, as for the *bema*. Only Justinian and his immediate entourage would occupy the nave in SS. Sergius and Bacchus – the earthly image of the court of Heaven.

SS. Sergius and Bacchus was a highly sophisticated combination of spaces for a highly developed rite, and the conceptual apparatus unfolding the one into the other would need to be theologically and symbolically as subtle and sophisticated. Procopius wrote primarily as a historian, but like Eusebius before him, he also gave anagogical commentary on the structure of the building. Early in his book *On Buildings* (*De Aedeficiis*), Procopius writes of Hagia Sophia itself how it was impossible to comprehend the whole of it at once, just as in the liturgy. Similarly, in the spaces of SS. Sergius and Bacchus: 'Even they who are accustomed to exercise their ingenuity on everything are unable to comprehend this work of art but always depart from there perplexed at the shortcomings of eye and mind.'

These churches required long contemplation and reflection, and the ultimate goal was a better understanding of God: 'And whenever anyone enters this church to pray, he understands at once that it is not by any human power or skill, but by the influence of God that this work has been so finely turned. And so his mind is lifted up toward God and exalted, feeling that he cannot be far away, but must especially love to dwell in this place which He has chosen.'[30]

Such commentary was not at all unusual, and an important contemporary example with a Justinian connection is found in the Syrian context. The Cathedral, or 'Great Church' at Edessa was built in 313 according to the *Chronicle of Edessa* and completed between 325 and 328. It was destroyed in a flood in 525, and Procopius relates how rebuilding began almost immediately with Justinian's help. The new building was re-dedicated in about the middle of the sixth century, and a hymn exists that appears to have been written for the service. The reconstruction from the sparse details given in the hymn suggests that the church was of the cross-in-square type, with a dome covering almost the entire church[31] – a plan similar to SS. Sergius and Bacchus:

> In a broader sense the hymn on the Church of Edessa may be appropriately characterised as architectural *theoria*, a contemplation of the church building. The fundamental theological postulate underlying the hymn is that God is a mystery, who is both revealed and hidden (str. 3). Although beyond the comprehension of creatures, God may be truly known if approached through three modes of contemplation: (1) theological: the Godhead in Itself, the Trinity (strs. 12–13); (2) Scriptural: God as Savior revealed in the Bible (strs. 11, 14–19); (3) cosmological: God as Creator revealed through the creation (str. 4–8). Each of these three ways of contemplating the mysterious God is accessible through the contemplation of the church building (strs. 3, 20–21). Consideration of each of the architectural features of the building – the structural components as well as the major liturgical furnishings – leads to one of the three essential ways of knowing God. So the building is a prefatory means of contemplation, which leads to the three major routes to the mystery of the Godhead Itself.[32]

Contemplation could be focused on the architecture, on scripture and the liturgy. When focused on the liturgy, this contemplation was called *mystagogia*, as in Cyril's *Mystagogical Catecheses*. Those lectures explained the rite to the newly baptized as an aid to their contemplation of the action

---

30   Quotations from Wybrew (1989), p. 74, and McVey (1984), p. 98.
31   *Ibid.*, p. 106, referring to Grabar (1947), pp. 29–67.
32   McVey (1984), p. 110.

of the liturgy. Within the liturgy, scripture would be read and a sermon given as explication to aid contemplation. Finally, the hymn as architectural *theoria* was an aid to the contemplation of the setting, and the instruments of the action of the liturgy.

The tradition of liturgical *theoria* represented by Gregory of Nyssa reflected on the Jewish Tabernacle, and the tradition in Antioch similarly followed this line of thought, through the ceremonial of the Tabernacle, towards an understanding of the Christian liturgy as the earthly image of the angelic liturgy where Christ is both priest and victim. This is made explicit in the later prayer at the Great Entrance (of the bread and wine), where in its address to Christ it says: 'for it is you who offer and are offered'. These are all examples of the transposition of meanings: 'That is, in its more developed phase the contemplation might proceed from Christian temporal reality (the church building) to heavenly reality (the pre-existent Church), or it would clearly subordinate the Jewish antitype (the Tabernacle) to its type (the Church).'[33] Not surprisingly, there was another strand that explored the Temple as antitype. Within these integrated layers of contemplation of the divine, the architecture becomes sacramental space, the permanent manifestation of the liturgy, and more than that, heaven on earth.

A gilded image of the heavenly liturgy showing Christ administering communion is seen on the silver paten found near Riha (Plate 2), about 55 kilometres south-east of Antioch, and dated by its stamps to the time of Justin II (565–78). In front of a silver revetment, or fastigium, Christ administers bread to the right and chalice to the left. In the *Apostolic Constitutions*, just after the *anaphora*, or eucharistic prayer, the deacon made a series of petitions, the first of which was: 'Let us pray for the gift which is offered to the Lord God, that the good God may, through the mediation of his Christ, receive it upon his heavenly altar for a sweet-smelling savour.'[34] 'The gift' at the altar of the Church was in this petition identified with the offering in Heaven. The dedicatory inscription round the rim of the paten reads: 'For the repose of the souls of Sergia, [daughter] of Ioannes, and of Theodosios and the salvation of Megas and Nonnous and of their children'. It has been speculated that, as donor, Megas may also have given a similar silver fastigium and other silver vessels depicted on the paten to the church.[35] In this way, the paten acts as a point of intersection for the action of the liturgy in which it is used, the architectural setting which it depicts, and scripture to which it refers (the Last Supper in Matthew 26:26–8). Within the liturgy, these offerings would be made and dedicated, and in the prayers that took place between the dismissal of the catechumens and the sacrament itself, the donor would be mentioned along with those whose names appear in the inscription. In this way, it can be seen as the physical equivalent of the Edessa Hymn, reflecting on the Godhead, the liturgy, the architecture, and placing the individual within the whole, through a finely wrought work of art.

The Second Hagia Irene

Hagia Irene was also destroyed in the fire following the Nika riots, and was rebuilt between 532 and 548. In 564 this new building was again damaged by a fire which destroyed the atrium and narthex, and *c.* 570 there was further damage from an earthquake. The church as seen today is as remodelled after 740, but the main fabric and layout all appear to have survived from the rebuilding of 532 and still gives a remarkably clear impression of the liturgical space of a 'domed basilica', with the central dome supported here on transverse barrel vaults (Figure 3.3). There are two barrel-vaulted

---

33 The *Apostolic Constitutions* is quoted in Wybrew (1989), p. 44; the second quotation is from McVey (1984), p. 111.

34 *Apostolic Constitutions*, quoted in Wybrew (1989), p. 43.

35 Lowden (1997), pp. 80–81; for the dating of the paten, see also Beckwith (1979), p. 98.

Figure 3.3   Hagia Irene, longitudinal cross-section; from Van Millingen (1912), fig. 33; Sackler Library, University of Oxford.

bays in the nave providing large arched galleries supported on colonnaded aisles. The aisles end in square chambers which may have been for the offerings of the people, though at one time the arrangement was interpreted as a 'triple sanctuary'. More recently, these have been demonstrated to be entrance bays, a significant characteristic of church planning in Constantinople itself.[36] Between these at the east end is a sanctuary with a stepped *bema*, as at Hagia Sophia and SS. Sergius and Bacchus, and a magnificent *synthronon* with six levels of seating below the protective sweep of the semi-dome of the apse. The third level of the *synthonon* is divided into eight seats, with the gaps between providing light for a semi-circular corridor beneath, an arrangement that may well have existed at the Hagia Sophia, although at the time of Justinian there was apparently a seventh level. In front of the chord of the apse the stones in the floor indicate the position of the altar.

Although the rest of the liturgical furnishings have been lost, from what is left it is clear that despite the remarkable architectural development under Justinian, the liturgical arrangement remained very much the same as it was a century earlier in 463 at St John Studios. It is worth noting in passing that the Cross decorating the semi-dome of the apse dates from after the remodelling of 740, and was placed there by the iconoclast Emperor Constantine V.

The Second Apostoleion

After the Nika riots, it seems to have taken a few years before the rebuilding of the *Apostoleion* and it was finally re-dedicated on the eve of the Feast of the Prince of the Apostles, 28 June 550.

---

36   Mathews (1971), pp. 84 and 105.

The plan was modified, but unlike Ambrose's *Basilica Apostolorum* in the Western context, there was no need to remove the altar to an eastern apse since a centralized plan, with two tiers of aisles and galleries in all four arms, was well suited to recent developments in the Byzantine rite. It was rebuilt with a well-lit dome over the sanctuary at the crossing, 'and the dome that curves above seems to be somehow hovering in the air and not standing on solid masonry, although it is perfectly secure'.[37] Each of the arms was covered by another unlit dome. Though there is some debate about the precise arrangement,[38] the sanctuary itself appears to have been square with a semicircular *synthronon* containing the cathedra on the eastern side. The usual parapet enclosed the other three sides. The silver altar over the graves of the three Apostles was probably central under the dome, and was sheltered by a ciborium with a pyramidal roof: 'John Chrysostomos, referring to the rebuilding which made the family mausoleum where the emperors were buried into an annex of the church which housed the relics of the apostles, pretended to see this as proof of the humility of the sovereigns, who "considered that they should be content to be buried not next to the apostles [that is, inside the church] but in their 'external antechamber', so becoming 'their doorkeepers'."'[39] On the north side of the altar was the grave of St John Chrysostom, and on the south that of St Gregory Nazianzus. Like Ambrose's *Basilica Apostolorum*, 'the incomparable church of the Holy Apostles' became a highly desirable place for burial, 'wherein emperors and priests are given the burial that is due to them'.[40]

The influence of the domed cross pattern was immense, becoming a standard throughout Justinian's dominions from St John Ephesus (which was focused on the shrine of the saint), to St Mark's Venice (see Figure 3.4).[41] Entry was via a colonnaded atrium and western narthex into a space that was much simpler and more easily comprehended than SS. Sergius and Bacchus. The *Apostoleion* was a much more sober, standardized structure lacking the refined decoration.

Figure 3.4   Basilica San Marco, Venice, aerial view showing five domes in a cruciform pattern; courtesy Allan T. Kohl/Art Images for College Teaching (AICT).

---

37 Procopius, *De Aedeficiis*, I, iv, translated in Mango (1986), p.103
38 Peeters (1969), p. 151.
39 Dagron (2003), pp. 142–3, quoting *Contra Judaeos et Gentiles*, 9.
40 Evagrius, *Hist. Eccles.*, IV, 31, translated in Mango (1986), p. 80.
41 See the discussions in Peeters (1969), pp. 150–53, and Krautheimer (1986), pp. 106–7 and 242–5.

Justinian's Hagia Sophia

The masterpiece of all Justinian's churches was undoubtedly Hagia Sophia, which became the mother church and touchstone of all orthodoxy (Figure 3.5 and Plate 3). By this point it was a commonplace that the church building was seen as an allegory, even a sacrament, of the union of the people of God and of the Kingdom of God, but the potency of the image created here was truly astonishing in both size and richness. On the day of the church's consecration, Justinian is reputed to have said: 'Solomon, I have vanquished thee!'[42] The church is almost square (71 m by 77 m), with the spaces billowing both outwards and upwards and the great dome seemingly free-floating in the air above the whole (see Figure 3.6). The relationship of this magnificent interior with the spatial complexity of SS. Sergius and Bacchus is apparent in the inability of the observer to comprehend the entirety, but the gradual unfolding to the mind of the interlocking spaces, together with the ingenuity of revolutionary structural design on such an immense scale, is like an encounter with the Architect of the universe himself. If those relegated to the galleries and aisles, separated as they were by columns from the nave, were further screened by curtains as suggested by Krautheimer, then the space, and the liturgy too, would have been impossible to comprehend.[43] The Empress herself watched from one of the side galleries, and scholars generally understand Procopius as saying that the galleries were reserved for women, but Mathews in particular points to Evagrius, who refers to those in the galleries in a masculine grammatical form.[44]

Contemporary writers recorded with amazement the details of this new architectural system and their further significance. Columns, marble, silver, gold and craftsmen were collected from throughout the Empire, and within five years of the riots the structure itself could be consecrated on 27 December 537, a staggering feat accomplished by the engineers Isidorus of Miletus and Anthemios of Tralles:

> Indeed, our emperor, who has gathered all manner of wealth from the whole earth, from barbarians and Ausonians [subjects of Rome] alike, did not deem a stone adornment sufficient for this divine, immortal temple in which Rome has placed all its proud hopes of joy. He has not spared, too, an abundant enrichment of silver. The ridge of Pangaeus and the cape of Sunium have opened all their silver veins, and many a treasure-house of our lords has yielded its stores.[45]

The church was an embodiment of the Empire, and the end of the south aisle (or, some maintain, at the eastern end of its central colonnade;[46] see Figure 3.7) 'contains a space separated by a wall, reserved for the Ausonian emperor on solemn festivals. Here my sceptered king, seated on his customary throne, lends his ear to [the reading of] the sacred books'.[47] The sacred books were read from the *ambo*, which in reconstructions stretched out from the *solea* almost to the middle of the central domed space. It is from this spot that both the liturgy and the architecture unfold.

Paul the Silentiary described the *ambo* in great detail, including its position, shape and materials: 'In the centre of the wide church, yet tending rather towards the east, is a kind of tower, fair to look upon, set apart as the abode of the sacred books.' Like the sanctuary, the oval platform was set about with marble parapets sheathed in silver. The whole was supported on columns with gilded capitals which sheltered 'as it were, another chamber, wherein the sacred song is raised by fair

---

42   Krautheimer (1986), p. 206.
43   *Ibid.*, p. 216.
44   Mathews (1971), pp. 130–32, especially p. 131.
45   Paulus Silentiarius, *Descr. S. Sophiae*, 682, translated in Mango (1986), pp. 86–7.
46   See Mathews (1971), p. 134.
47   Paulus Silentiarius, *Descr. S. Sophiae*, 682, translated in Mango (1986), p. 85.

Figure 3.5   Hagia Sophia, perspective; from Henri Hübsch (1866), *Monuments de l'Architecture Chrétienne depuis Constantin* (Paris, Morel), pl. XXXIV, no. 1; Sackler Library, University of Oxford.

Figure 3.6 Hagia Sophia, sectional perspective; from Henri Hübsch (1866), *Monuments de l'Architecture Chrétienne depuis Constantin* (Paris, Morel), pl. V, no. 7; Sackler Library, University of Oxford.

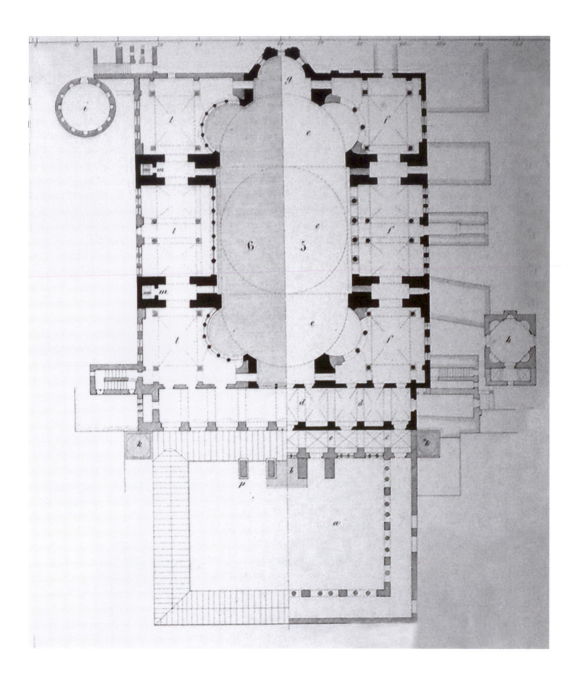

Figure 3.7   Hagia Sophia, plan; from Henri Hübsch (1866), *Monuments de l'Architecture Chrétienne depuis Constantin* (Paris, Morel), pl. V, nos 6 and 5; Sackler Library, University of Oxford.

children, heralds of wisdom'. Flights of steps rose to west and east, the latter leading via the *solea* to the sanctuary. Judging by the amount of text Paul lavished on the colour and detail of the various marbles, the materials and their qualities were of immense importance. The use of materials and the architectural arrangement gave word and sacrament equal prominence, and Paul presents a lively impression of the spatial unfolding of the rite that gives the idea that usually the nave was also occupied by the congregation:

> And as an island rises amidst the waves of the sea, adorned with cornfields, and vineyards, and blossoming meadows, and wooded heights, while the travellers who sail by are gladdened by it and are soothed of the anxieties and exertions of the sea; so in the midst of the boundless temple rises upright the tower-like ambo of stone adorned with its meadows of marble, wrought with the beauty of the craftsman's art. Yet it does not stand altogether cut off in the central space, like a sea-girt island, but it rather resembles some wave-washed land, extended through the white-capped billows by an isthmus into the middle of the sea. ...
>
> Such, then is the aspect of this place; for, starting at the last step to the east, there extends a long strait (*aulon* [or *solea*]) until it comes near the silver doors and strikes with its lengthy plinth the sacred precinct. On either side it is bounded by walls. They have not used lofty slabs for this fence-wall, but of such a height as to reach the girdle of a man standing by. Here the priest who brings the good tidings passes on along on the return from the ambo, holding aloft the golden book; and while the crowd strives in honour of the immaculate God to touch the sacred book with their lips and hands, the countless waves of the surging people break around. ...
>
> Such works as these our bountiful Emperor built for God the King ... to the Governor of the world, Christ the universal King.[48]

The Liturgical Furnishings

When it came to the sanctuary with its vessels and treasures, Justinian's historian Procopius was satisfied simply to relate in his book *On Buildings* (I, i) that it 'exhibits forty thousand pounds of silver'. Paul the Silentiary adds more detail (682):

> For as much of the great church by the eastern arch as was set apart for the bloodless sacrifice is bounded not with ivory or cut stone or bronze, but it is all fenced under a cover of silver. Not only upon the walls which separate the priest from the choir of singers has he set plates of naked silver, but the columns too ... . Elsewhere it [the tool wielded by a skilled hand] has carved the host of winged angels bowing down their necks, for they are unable to gaze upon the glory of God, though hidden under a veil of human form – He is still God, even if He has put on the flesh that removes sin. Elsewhere the sharp steel has fashioned those former heralds of God by whose words, before God had taken on flesh, the divine tidings of Christ's coming spread abroad. Nor has the artist forgotten the images of those who abandoned the mean labours of their life – the fishing basket and the net – and those evil cares in order to follow the command of the heavenly King, fishing even for men and, instead of casting for fish, spread out the nets of eternal life. And elsewhere art has depicted the Mother of Christ, the vessel of eternal life, whose holy womb did nourish its own Maker. ... And the screen gives access to the priests through three doors. ...
>
> And above the all-pure table of gold rises into the ample air an indescribable tower, reared on four arches of silver. ... And on columns of gold is raised the all-gold slab of the holy table, standing on gold foundations, and bright with the glitter of precious stones.

Not surprisingly, none of this vast amount of silver, gold and precious stones survives, but an impression of what an altar covered with revetment of precious metal would be like is given by a single remarkable survival in the Sion Treasure, now in the Dumbarton Oaks Collection in Washington, DC. The treasure is an almost complete set of liturgical silver (including an interesting

---

48   Paul the Silentiary, *Descr. ambonis*, 224 and 240, translated in *ibid.*, pp. 95–6.

flabellum worked with a seraph and peacock feathers in gold; Figure 3.8) produced during the reign of Justinian, giving a very clear idea of what the even grander altar-plate of Hagia Sophia would have been like. Silver and precious materials had long been invested with theological importance and used to provide liturgical emphasis, and this reaches its definitive statement at Justinian's Hagia Sophia.

Procopius' description continues with the silk, gold and purple embroidered altar-cloth, the lamps and candles lit via catwalks above the columns. Examples of silver lamps in open work, standing lamps in the shape of cups, and various shapes of *polycandelion* each to hold 12–16 glass lamps. These were elaborately pierced discs and crosses, as Paul the Silentiary wrote of Hagia Sophia: 'Yet not from discs alone does the light shine at night, for in the circle you will see, next to the discs, the shape of the lofty cross with many eyes upon it, and in its pierced back it holds many luminous vessels.'[49]

The Liturgy

The spectacle, for spectacle it surely was, viewed from the galleries or the aisles, or evidently from the nave amongst the waves of humanity, or even the Emperor's own area (the imperial *metatorion*) in the south aisle, must have been stirring in the extreme, with the glittering light reflecting off polished marble, the movement, the incense, and the whole of society ranged in its hierarchical

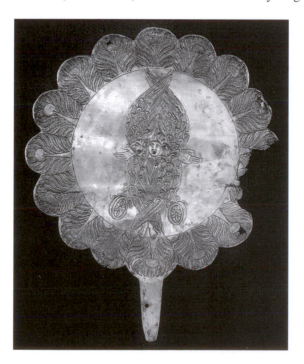

Figure 3.8   The 'Riha' Flabellum, silver with gilding, 30.9 cm. Early Byzantine, Constantinople (565–78), from the Kaper Koroan Treasure, found in Syria; © Dumbarton Oaks, Byzantine Collection, Washington, DC.

---

49   Detailed discussion and many illustrations of Byzantine silver are found in Boyd (1998), pp. 152–83; the quotation is from p. 170; see also Leader-Newby (2004), p. 71.

stratification. According to the *Book of Ceremonies* of Constantine VII Porphyrogenetus in the tenth century, the Emperor himself participated in the liturgy 17 times a year (four of which are post-Justinian). On these occasions he would have processed in with the Bishop and then appeared again at the offering of the gifts at the Great Entrance, and the second-ranking bishop of Christendom would preside from his throne on the silver-covered *synthronon*, very like the structure still in position in the apse of Hagia Irene. None of this arrangement was radically new by any means, but here the pattern received its definitive statement.

What does appear to have developed considerably by this time (though it may also have been true of the liturgy celebrated in the Theodosian church) is the way the symbolic figure of the Emperor has been absorbed into the ceremonial of the liturgy on those relatively rare occasions when he was present. What had been incipient with Constantine, and was now more fully developed, was the quasi-priestly status of the Emperor. Constantine's rule and the advent of a Christian Empire was seen as providential; he was chosen by God, and the ceremonial acclamations for a new Emperor became 'a New David' and 'a New Constantine', and though there appears not to have been an anointing even as late as the *Book of Ceremonies*, it records that the Patriarch prayed that God himself might 'deign to anoint with the oil of gladness your faithful servant'.[50] It had been difficult for Constantine to be present at the liturgy, but by Justinian's day, the Emperor's presence, in his new Hagia Sophia, had been structurally integrated, to some extent by this quasi-priestly status, but to an even greater extent by the architectural and ceremonial arrangement by which his appearances and access to the chancel were very closely controlled. By the tenth century, the *Book of Ceremonies* records the elaborate approach of the Emperor to the Great Church across the political landscape, being met at different points by the 'democrats' of the political parties and court officials as a way of displaying the balance of temporal power. The Emperor, the people and the clergy all had their allotted place within the significance of the ceremonial topography. There were secret, sudden and ceremonial means for the Emperor to arrive in his private apartments, or mini-palace, in the east end of the south aisle and the gallery above: 'In fact, he was leaving a place [the palace] where the emperor was both a soldier and high priest, directly delegated by Christ to the government of men, to a place where all power belonged to Christ through the intermediary of the clergy and where the cross was not that of imperial victory [as in Constantine's vision] ... but a replica of that of Jerusalem.'[51]

At the Great Church itself, the ceremonial appears to have varied according to season and specific occasion, but the general pattern was this. The congregation would throng the atrium in anticipation. The Emperor arrived in the south vestibule of the narthex and removed his crown in a screened-off area, then entered the narthex proper, where the Patriarch was waiting.[52] The Emperor would first bow to the Gospel Book, then greet the Patriarch. They proceeded to the Imperial Doors and prostrated themselves three times, giving thanks to God. The Patriarch repeated the prayer of entry, which in the Liturgy of St John Chrysostom in the *Codex Barberini*, reads:

> Benefactor and Creator of all Creation, receive the Church which is advancing, accomplish what is good for each one: bring all to perfection, make us worthy of your Kingdom; by the grace and mercy and love for men of your only-begotten Son, with whom you are blessed, together with your holy and good and life-giving Spirit, now and always ...[53]

---

50   Dagron (2003), p. 50; on anointing, see p. 58 and n. 17.
51   *Ibid.*, p. 97.
52   *Ibid.*, p. 92.
53   Translated in Wybrew (1989), p. 77; Mathews (1971), p. 141.

In the later eighth-century text of the liturgy, this is found at the Little Entrance (of the Gospel); Wybrew points out that it perfectly describes the first entrance of the whole congregation to the church.

After the prayer of entry by the Patriarch, he would accompany the Emperor through the central imperial door. In contrast to Western practice, preceded only by the Gospel book and its attendants, they would lead the procession and the people into the church during the introit psalm, with a *troparion*, or refrain, sung by the congregation. At this date the *trisagion*, 'Holy God, holy and strong, holy and immortal! Have mercy on us', was used as the *troparion*. Not surprisingly, the Trinitarian formulation of the *trisagion* became a point of doctrinal controversy.[54] On entry, Emperor and Patriarch were preceded by a deacon bearing the jewelled Gospel book, representing Christ himself, accompanied by candles and a thurifer with incense. The procession followed the axis of the church past the *ambo* and entering the *solea*. On reaching the sanctuary, the Patriarch entered, leaving the Emperor before the entrance, praying with a lighted candle. The Gospels were placed reverently on the altar, the Emperor prostrated himself three times, entered the chancel, prostrated himself before the Patriarch, and kissed the altar-cloth. He left his offering of gold, or on occasion a liturgical vessel (as shown in the San Vitale mosaic in Plate 4; note also how Hagia Sophia itself and even the city are portrayed as such offerings in Plate 3). He was then led behind the altar to venerate, then cense, the great golden cross before retiring to his *metatorion*, or area screened off for his throne. The Patriarch mounted the *synthronon* and greeted the people with the words: 'Peace be with you all.' In his *Ecclesiastical History and Mystical Contemplation*, Germanos (Patriarch 715–30) invested this action with spiritual meaning: 'That the celebrant ascends into the *synthronon* and blesses the people, this is the Son of God [who], when he fulfilled the work of salvation, lifted up his hands, and blessed his holy disciples telling them, "Peace I leave you," meaning that Christ gave the same peace and blessing to the world through his apostles.'[55] The whole action so far is seen as the coming of salvation in Christ and his enthronement at the right hand of God.

After two readings by lectors in sequence, the Gospel procession, with its candles and incense, bore the Gospels (which looked and was treated very much like a reliquary or an icon of Christ) from the altar along the *solea* to the *ambo*. The Gospel proclaimed, the procession returned along the *solea* through the surging crowd to replace the Gospel book on the altar; then the Patriarch would preach, customarily from his throne, though it is difficult to imagine that he could make himself heard from the *synthronon* of the Hagia Sophia, and even Chrysostom is recorded preaching from the pulpitum. After this, the catechumens would be formally dismissed before the beginning of the sacrament itself, though there is some doubt that the catechumenate continued even by Justinian's time, in which case these prayers and the dismissal became a mere formality.[56]

The Patriarch now descended from the *synthronon* to prepare the altar, and the Emperor emerged for the entrance of the eucharistic elements – bread and wine – and took up a place just west of the *ambo* along with his chamberlains, ministers and senators. The Emperor took a lamp and accompanied the gifts via the *solea* as far as the Holy Door of the sanctuary, then retired to his place in the south aisle. The gifts had been brought by the deacons along with *flabella* (ritual fans; see Figure 3.8) and the great veil from the *skeuophylakion*, or sacristy – the only surviving part of Constantine's Great Church. On great occasions the procession would necessarily be very large, considering the number of vessels needed for adequate bread and wine for the number of communicants. All this was again accompanied by chant, probably Psalm 24 with the verse 'Lift

---

54 See Wybrew (1989), pp. 77–80, for a fuller discussion.
55 Germanos, *Hist. eccl.*, ch. 26, translated in Mathews (1971), p. 143.
56 See Mainstone (1988), p.230; Wybrew (1989), p. 81; Mathews (1971), p. 127.

up your heads, O ye gates, and be ye lift up, ye everlasting doors: and the King of Glory shall come in.'[57] In the later sixth century, the Cherubic Hymn was introduced here.

The Cherubic Hymn became a hinge to the celebration of the sacrament, emphasizing the parallel worship in heaven and on earth as the congregation sang: 'We who mystically represent the Cherubim and sing the thrice holy hymn to the life-giving Trinity, let us lay aside all worldly care to receive the King of All, escorted unseen by the angelic hosts. Alleluia.'[58] After the *proskomide*, or preparatory prayer, the Patriarch greeted the people with 'Peace be with you all' and met the Emperor again at the chancel barrier for the kiss of peace. The singing of the Nicene Creed followed as a sign of orthodoxy. Then followed the mysteries. On the Riha chalice, also mid-sixth-century and thought to have been from the same hoard as the Sion Treasure, there is an unusual inscription: 'Thine own, of Thine own, we offer unto Thee, O Lord' – the very words the celebrant would use at the offering of the gifts. The Chalice of Antioch, which appears to be roughly contemporary, emphasizes the theological importance of the ensuing section of the service by showing two images of Christ, once enthroned on earth giving the Law, and once enthroned above an eagle, clearly in heaven. The consecration united these two 'moments'.[59]

Finally, at the culmination of the mysteries, the Patriarch would process to the Emperor, who by now was at the entrance to the sanctuary, to administer communion. During processions, the ceremonial and the mysteries (with an indication that even at this time many of the prayers and much of the *anaphora* were said quietly by the celebrant), hymns, chants, antiphons and psalms would be sung by choirs and congregation, giving the rite a high degree of simultaneity and movement. The ceremonial continued to be the earthly reflection of the angelic, heavenly worship, knit together in the various carefully controlled encounters between the Emperor and the Patriarch:

> Similarly, the Emperor, one wants to recall, had his assigned place in the celestial hierarchy as mirrored on Earth. Since Constantine's time he had been considered equal to the apostles, and perhaps more than equal. Certainly in the tenth century he acted the part of Christ on solemn occasions – breaking and blessing the bread and raising the cup of wine to his lips after state dinners; swathed in white bands as Christ resurrected and surrounded by twelve apostles on Easter Sunday Emperor and Patriarch were the 'two halves of God'.[60]

The unity of the Empire sought by Constantine in and through the Church was enacted in this liturgical ceremonial, for example at the exchange of the peace first between Patriarch and Emperor, then between the Emperor and key members of the court in turn. It could well be seen as the fulfilment of prophecy: 'The kingdom of the world has become the Kingdom of our Lord, and of his Christ' (Rev. 11:15). The hymn written for the dedication of the Cathedral of Edessa is almost contemporary (perhaps a decade or two later), and with the building of Justinian's Hagia Sophia, is only a small step away from its liturgical and ceremonial reality. Such displays of power and unity present risks as well, as in 390, when Theodosius I was refused entry to the church in Milan by St Ambrose because the Emperor had abused his power against the people. The pious Emperor was brought to public repentance, and this became a model for potential, and actual, future confrontations. Ecclesiastical power over the sovereign's 'entry' into the church building to perform his ceremonial duty during the liturgy was the single 'constitutional' constraint on imperial power.

---

57   See Taft (1975), p. 84.
58   Translated in Mainstone (1988), p. 228; see also Wybrew (1989), pp. 83–4.
59   The Chalice is reproduced, with commentary, in Peña (1997), pp. 81–2.
60   Krautheimer (1986), p. 218.

The flip side of the ceremonial was that behind the scenes, the management of ritual, and crowds, on this scale took a huge clerical establishment, and 'Justinian found it necessary to limit the establishment of the Great Church to not more than 60 presbyters or priests, 100 deacons, 40 deaconesses, 90 sub-deacons, 110 lectors, 25 psalmists [singers] and no less than 100 *ostiarii* or doorkeepers.'[61] Finally, except on those relatively few occasions when the Emperor was expected to take a very visible part in the service, he might choose to worship privately from the south gallery, which was reserved for imperial use.

The Liturgy and its Setting

Some generalizations can now be made about the relationship between the liturgy and the architecture. The atrium was for the gathering of the congregation before worship, and its colonnades provided a degree of shelter. The narthex provided for the hierarchical forming up of the procession for the Entrance, and the double narthex at Hagia Sophia attests to both the size of the processions and their elaborate protocol. The many doors were necessary to allow the large congregation to flood in and be in their places by the time the Patriarch reached the *synthronon* for the blessing.

The longitudinal axis remained dominant as long as the entrance began in the narthex, while the dome and centralized space dominated when, during the Middle Byzantine period, the Little Entrance began in the sanctuary, circling round through the north door of the sanctuary and returning via the Holy Doors back to the altar. By that time it was also necessary to have auxiliary spaces at the east end for the clergy to robe (the *diaconicon*), and for the *prothesis* ceremony or preparation of the gifts – which resulted in a tripartite east end (though the specific arrangement differed between Constantinople and the provinces[62]). The readings by the lectors took place on the *ambo*, and cantors also led the singing from there. The *solea* with its parapets provided protection for the Gospel procession, and the semicircular *synthronon* represented the teaching and magisterial authority of the celebrant, standing in the place of Christ: 'The repeated representations in Early Christian Art of Christ teaching, seated in the semi-circle of his disciples, contained for the faithful a very specific point of comparison with the view they had every Sunday of the bishop teaching, seated in the semi-circle of his clergy.'[63]

The Great Entrance of the gifts required a *skeuophylakion*, or a separate area to the north of the sanctuary for the liturgical vessels and the preparation of the gifts. The 'bloodless sacrifice' needed an altar and protective ciborium, and deacons had fans with which they ensured nothing fell on the elements. These were associated with angels hovering about the throne, and silver hoards have contained superb examples of silver fans, or *flabella*, engraved with cherubim, but by the time those were made they had probably become purely symbolic and decorative items.

In manuscripts, the *templon* (*fastigium*, or superstructure of the sanctuary screen) was sometimes shown with curtains, as were ciboria (though rarely and with only very short hangings) over the altar, and Krautheimer also supposes that the aisles and galleries were also curtained. There is little firm evidence that any of these were used during the early or middle Byzantine periods to screen the mysteries, but their use at some point would of course be consistent with the transition from open *templon* to closed iconostasis, and the shutting of such curtains after the creed is specifically attested by Nicholas of Andida in the eleventh century.[64] On the other hand, the low type of sanctuary parapet without superstructure continued to exist at Chalkoprateia into the sixth

---

61 Mainstone (1988), p. 229.
62 See Mathews (1971), pp. 105–7.
63 *Ibid.*, p. 150.
64 Translated in *ibid.*, p. 171; see also Cormack (2000), pp. 150–52.

century at least. If curtains in the *templon* were so little attested, then they can hardly have been of great importance, and then only at a late date. It was the medieval orthodox liturgy that closed the screen.[65]

Ravenna and the Provinces

The most vivid portrayal of imperial liturgical ceremonial is to be seen in the mosaic in the apse of San Vitale in Ravenna (Plate 4), built by Julianus, a wealthy local banker, soon after the re-conquest of the area by Justinian. On the north side of the apse (the Gospel side), Justinian appears holding a magnificent golden paten in procession with Bishop Maximian on his left wearing a pallium and bearing a cross. They are preceded by two deacons, one bearing a jewelled Gospel book and the other with a thurible, or censer. They are followed by two members of the court and a guard of honour, just as they would be ranged for entering the church and processing to the sanctuary, where indeed they now stand. Opposite is a mosaic showing the Empress Theodora bearing a large golden chalice and wearing a *chlamys* with the hem embroidered with the three magi (Plate 5). She and her attendants are in a very clearly architectural setting walking past a fountain about to enter a curtained doorway.

The identities of the main figures are not in doubt, and the objects and dress are clearly liturgical and would appear to relate to the dedication of the church, but Justinian and Theodora never went to Ravenna, and the two panels cannot refer to a single procession, for the Empress would have remained hidden in the gallery. The interpretation is fraught with controversy, centring primarily on the date when the grand entry of the Emperor at the liturgy was first introduced – some maintaining that it was only under Justin II, who succeeded Justinian.[66] Even the Justinian panel may not be of a single procession, since it contains the Gospel book, the offering and the guard of honour, and so can refer to the entrance into the church and perhaps the gospel procession too.

It may be that the book, the paten (or dish for bread) and the chalice are dedicatory tokens sent by the imperial couple to show their favour and symbolic presence. The Augusta Theodora died in 548, so the mosaic was presumably completed for the dedication of the church by Maximian in 547. Despite both processions moving clearly towards the east, indicated by their feet, the fall of various garments and the courtier pulling the curtain aside for the Augusta to pass, the main figures turn to fix the viewer with their gaze, emphasizing their presence. Bishop Maximian was an imperial nominee against the wishes of the people of Ravenna, and these images confirmed his imperial authority. The sign of a bishop's authority was his throne, and remarkably, Maximian's throne, thought to be Justinian's gift, still exists (see Figure 3.9). It has a wooden frame, originally entirely covered in ivory, and still largely intact. The panels are in two sets, the Old Testament one of the life of Joseph, and the New of the life of Christ. It was not designed to be sat on, and so remains a symbolic object, probably used as a throne for the Gospels. An attempted interpretation of its symbolism has suggested that 'perhaps the parallel to be drawn from these scenes is that

---

65   The traditional view, presented by Maxwell (1936), pp. 38–9, is that 'after the fourth century this curtain became a screen, and, except in Egypt and Cappadocia, this screen became solid'. This implies that the process was relatively swiftly completed. Though the clergy were separated off from the nave in the middle of the sixth century at Hagia Sophia, perhaps by a curtain during parts of the service which was known by the second half of the eleventh century, there was certainly no solid screen. The more recent view places the completion of this tendency around 1100 (Lowden, 1997, p. 366) or even as much as a thousand years later than Maxwell maintains, in the fourteenth century, for which see, for example, Wybrew (1989), p. 147.

66   Beckwith (1979), p. 116; also Mainstone (1988), p. 234 and Mathews (1971), pp. 146–7.

Figure 3.9   Throne of Archbishop Maximian, ivory panels on a wooden frame, Byzantine, Constantinople; courtesy Allan T. Kohl/Art Images for College Teaching (AICT).

Maximian was expected to be to Justinian what Joseph was to Pharaoh'.[67] Just as Joseph engineered a reconciliation with his brothers, the same was expected of Maximian and the brethren of his flock. Furthermore, if the throne was actually to be a throne for the gospels, then it fittingly had Eucharistic imagery in the scenes of changing water into wine at the marriage in Cana, and also the feeding of the multitude.

Notably, St Vitalis, to whom the church was dedicated, was not an early martyr, but one of those saints discovered by St Ambrose in Bologna in 395 and reputed to be the father of SS. Gervasius and Protasius, whose cults were prominent in Milan. This would have been important in establishing the relationship of Ravenna with Milan. The other major dedication in the city was to S. Apollinare in Classe, the port of Ravenna. The marble for these churches came from the quarries on Prokonnesos in the Sea of Marmara near Constantinople, and the imperial workshops carved the major architectural features, including capitals, bases, the columns themselves, as well

---

67   Beckwith (1979), p. 116.

as the liturgical furnishings, including parapets, *ambo* and altars. If the liturgical furnishings were imported, not just imitated, then the liturgy was likely to have been as well. In the apse mosaic (Plate 6), S. Apollinaris himself is shown in the 'orant' position for liturgical prayer, and on either side of the apse are mosaics of archangels bearing banners inscribed with the Sanctus 'Holy, Holy, Holy' in Greek.

During his reign in the seventh century between 668 and 685, Constantine IV Pogonatus recorded his bestowal of privileges on the church with a mosaic closely paralleled with that of Justinian and Maximian. In it, however, not only the Emperor, but also his brothers, his son Justinian II and the Archbishop Reparatus have haloes. They too are led by two deacons, one with the elements and another with a thurible, which places the scene in a liturgical setting, specifically the eucharist at which those privileges were granted, but it is more clearly a *laurata*, or (composite) memorial to the occasion, than any possible moment within the liturgy. The net result is the same: it gives imperial authority to the relevant claims.

In the sixth century, from the Monastery of St Catherine on Mt Sinai to Rome itself at the Church of SS. Cosmas and Damian, there was a controlling influence by Constantinople to the extent that the liturgical furnishings and decorative architectural elements for some churches were 'pre-fabricated' in the imperial workshops.[68] This religious, architectural and liturgical dominance conquered what would become another eastern empire when, as famously recorded in the *Primary Russian Chronicle*, the emissaries of Prince Vladimir of Kiev attended a service in Hagia Sophia in 987:

> We knew not whether we were in heaven or on earth. For on earth there is no such splendour or such beauty, and we are at a loss how to describe it. We only know that God dwells there among men, and their service is fairer than the ceremonies of other nations. For we cannot forget that beauty.[69]

However much this may have been exaggerated, it none the less points to the power of liturgy and architecture together, and attributes to them the evangelization of Russia, and bringing that vast empire into the fold of orthodoxy.

Conclusion

No other orthodox church would ever rival Hagia Sophia in its vast scale – either during Justinian's reign or afterwards – but many of its characteristics would be used again and again. Most churches, for instance, would be vaulted with a centralized dome. Though the clergy continued to occupy the apse, the *synthronon* disappeared. The *bema* housed the altar centrally at the east end, but in addition, in later churches there were two apsed chapels: the one to the south was the *diakonikon* for the vestments and books, the one to the north being the *prothesis* where the communion vessels were kept and where the bread and wine were prepared for communion. Liturgically, they correspond respectively to the Little and Great Entrances, which already by the tenth century had been very considerably reduced in scale, and this in turn was paralleled in architecture, with its increased centralization.[70] A screen, which developed into the *iconostasis*, separated the three spaces from the body of the church, though each was provided with a door. The sacred mysteries were increasingly protected from view, and the iconographic programme that came to cover the *iconostasis* and the whole of the interior emphasized the heavenly nature of the rite. By the fourteenth century the

---

68 *Ibid.*, pp. 104–5.
69 Translated in Mainstone (1988), p. 11.
70 See the discussion in Mathews (1982), p. 126.

iconostasis became totally closed. This had gradually created two separate worship spaces: one for the clergy, and the nave for the people. The *solea* and *ambo* disappeared, the readings took place below the dome, and processions would emerge from one of the doors in the screen and return by the central Royal Doors; even the beginning of the service was marked by the singing of antiphons rather than by a procession into the church. All this was in response to an increasingly centralizing tendency in the liturgy recognized in a less axial and increasingly centralized architecture, perfectly reflected in the cross-in-square which made its initial appearance immediately before Justinian's magnificent building projects.[71] The exterior could be seen as the outward manifestation of the internal arrangement and function. In the fully developed iconographic scheme, in the space and in the massing of the building, the structure of the liturgy was visible, reinforcing the old symbolic interpretation of both as heaven on earth. In the *Historia Mystagogica* attributed to Germanos, every element of the liturgy, vestments, liturgical furnishings and the architecture were interpreted theologically:

> The church is heaven on earth wherein the heavenly God 'dwells and walks' [2 Cor. 6:16 and Lev. 26:12]. It typifies the Crucifixion, the Burial and the Resurrection of Christ. ... The conch is after the manner of the cave of Bethlehem where Christ was born, and that of the Cave where He was buried as the Evangelist saith, that there was a cave 'hewn out of the rock, and there laid they Jesus' [Mk 15:46; Jn 19:42]. The holy table is the place where Christ was buried, and on which is set forth the true bread from heaven, the mystic and bloodless sacrifice, i.e. Christ. ... It is also the throne on which God, who is borne up by the cherubim, has rested. At this table, too, He sat down at His last supper ... . The ciborium stands for the place where Christ was crucified. ... The place of sacrifice is after the manner of Christ's tomb where Christ has given Himself in sacrifice to God the Father by the offering of His body, as a sacrificial lamb, but also as a high priest and as the Son of Man who offers Himself and is offered. ... The place of sacrifice is so named after the spiritual one in heaven, and the spiritual and immaterial hierarchies of the heavenly host are represented by the material priests on earth who stand by and worship the Lord continually. ... The *bema* is a place like a footstool and like a throne in which Christ, the universal King, presides together with his apostles. ... The *cancelli* denote the place of prayer, and signify that the space outside them may be entered by the people, while inside is the holy of holies which is accessible only to the priests.[72]

At the end of Germanos' patriarchate, iconoclasm became the official doctrine of the Empire under Leo III, who replaced the iconophile Germanos with the iconoclast Anastasios. Leo's edict requiring the removal of images from churches was most seriously enforced under Constantine V until it was rescinded in 787. A second period of iconoclasm lasted between 814 and 843, when the making and venerating of icons was restored – the Triumph of Orthodoxy which continues to be celebrated in a special liturgy on the first Sunday of Lent. St John Damascene stated the orthodox position in his *De Fide Orthodoxa*:

> Inasmuch as some people blame us for reverencing and honouring the images of the Saviour, of our Lady and furthermore of the other saints and servants of Christ, they should hearken to [the statement] that in the beginning God made man in his own image. Why is it indeed that we revere each other, if we had not been made in God's image? As the God-inspired Basil, who was learned in things divine, says, 'the honour [shown] to the image is conveyed to its prototype.'[73]

---

71   For a detailed discussion of the origins and development of the cross-domed church, see Krautheimer (1986), pp. 296–9.

72   Brightman (1908), pp. 257–9; for a discussion of the symbolism of the liturgy and vestments, see Wybrew (1989), pp. 123–8.

73   Translated in Mango (1986), p. 169.

The orthodox position is very careful to insist that there is nothing novel either in the doctrine or in the images themselves – all is compatible with received tradition, though elaborated. The tradition was increasingly elaborated and fixed in the distribution of the programme of images, with the dome covered by Christ as *Pantocrator*, the eastern apse by Mary as Mother of God, the upper range showed the life of Christ with Nativity, Baptism, Crucifixion and Ascension in the pendentives of the dome, and the lower range of icons portrayed the saints.

Just as imperial and secular ceremonial were intertwined, so too the iconographic scheme of Hagia Sophia has its parallel in the iconographic scheme of the palace. After the end of Iconoclasm in 843, a poem celebrated their return:

> Behold, once again the image of Christ shines above the imperial throne and confounds the murky heresies; while above the entrance is represented the Virgin as divine gate and guardian. The emperor [Michael III] and Bishop [Photius] are depicted close by, along with their collaborators inasmuch as they have driven away error, and all round the building, like guards [stand] angels, apostles, martyrs, priests. Hence we call 'the new Christotriklinos' that which aforetime had been given a golden name [a pun on Chrysotriklinios or 'Golden Hall' and Christotriklinios or Christ's Hall], since it contains the throne of Christ our Lord, the forms of Christ's Mother and Christ's heralds, and the image of Michael, whose deeds are filled with wisdom.[74]

These twin tendencies of fixed tradition and elaboration characterize both the architecture and the liturgy of the Orthodox Church, producing a very clear lineage from Byzantium to the present while allowing variety and considerable development of core themes. Across the Empire, local liturgical and architectural traditions produced widely divergent results. One intriguing example of this is the variety of rock-cut churches in Cappadocia dating from the fifth or sixth century onwards. The forms, carved from the 'living rock', use the whole Byzantine architectural vocabulary, and the liturgical arrangements combine the familiar Byzantine elements in surprising combinations, and even multiplications – double, triple and transverse naves, and multiple sanctuaries, even in single naves. The explanation offered for this multiplication of altars is that at the time there was a prohibition on celebrating the liturgy more than once a day on an altar, many of these were mortuary chapels, and 'besides funeral services, there were a variety of other liturgical services for various occasions'. Another explanation for this multiplication of altars and chapels, also found at Constantinople, Alexandria, Lips and St Catherine's Sinai, concerns the 'privatization' of the liturgy (in a variety of forms, including baptism), particularly within the monastic and domestic contexts.[75]

A contrasting example of this diversity comes from the centre of Empire in the intertwining of imperial and religious ceremonial and the identification of the Emperor as Christ's representative on earth. In the *Book of Ceremonies* of the Emperor Constantine VII Porphyrogenitus (913–59), he recounts the form of court and religious ceremony for Palm Sunday, which began in the Golden Chamber of the palace. The court assembled before the enthroned Emperor, above whom always hung an icon of Christ. Each official bore in his hand the cross given by the Emperor the night before in the Church of St Demetrius, and in order of precedence they saluted the Emperor. Other groups presented crosses to the Emperor and prostrated themselves before him. The Emperor descended from his throne and took up his place. What happened next reinforces the identification of his authority and Christ's:

---

74   Mango (1986), p. 184; see also the commentary in Cameron (1987), pp. 133–4.
75   The first explanation is offered by Teteriatnikov (1996), see especially pp. 27, 33–5 and 42–5; on multiple altars, see pp. 72–3; the second by Mathews (1982), pp. 127–37.

The deacon places the Gospels on the imperial throne and the usual litany is recited. The emperor goes with the people of his Bedchamber to the Church of the Holy Virgin in Pharos, and the patricians leave after acclaiming the emperor. Then if the emperor so orders, they summon the patricians and they take part with the emperor in the liturgy at the church of the all-holy Virgin: if not, they celebrate the liturgy outside at the church of St Stephen in the Hippodrome.[76]

The Emperor's purpose in writing the book, he claimed, was to record and revive ritual, to reinforce and to develop traditional ceremonial. As in other areas, however, the visibly rigid, glittering and unified structure was required, in part at least, to mask the divisions and instability beneath the surface. Then, as earlier, the imperial liturgy and the architecture were designed to 'put people in their place' – and, it was hoped, to keep them there.

The one instance of a deliberate, obvious and violent break with historic continuity of architectural forms is in the conversion of pagan temples to churches. This was not easily done, and provision of appropriate space for Christian worship could have been more satisfactorily accomplished, at least in a practical sense, by starting afresh. However, some of the most famous ancient pagan temples, including the Parthenon at Athens, the Temple of Apollo at Didyma and the Temple of Athena at Syracuse, were converted, often with great difficulty, for Christian worship. The Parthenon was visibly still a classical and pagan building with the limited Christian alterations left in stark contrast. The Temple of Apollo at Didyma was virtually unchanged on the exterior, with a complete basilican church built within. In the seventh century, what had been the Temple of Athena at Syracuse became the Cathedral. The conversion wholly encased the ancient temple, leaving very few architectural features still visible, half buried, in the new structure. Clearly, this was to demonstrate the triumph of Christianity: 'Probably no Christian worshipper in the fifth, sixth, and seventh centuries could have experienced the interior of a temple converted into a church without a feeling of deep satisfaction: the pagan cult statue had been removed, abhorrent practices had been discontinued, and the pagan site had been sanctified by its conversion into a church.'[77]

However, since the sixth century Arabs had been pressing at the borders of the Eastern Empire. The fact that from the seventh century the Muslims were militarily so successful and strictly against the use of images was part of the reason that Emperor `Leo III thought that God was displeased with the iconophile tendencies of orthodoxy. By the end of the century, the Byzantines were no longer the dominant power in Christendom, and in 800 Pope Leo III crowned Charlemagne Emperor in Rome. The coronation was contemporary with the production of the *Codex* Barberini, the earliest surviving text of the Byzantine rites of SS. Chrysostom and Basil. The fiction of seamless continuity with the greatness of the past is exemplified by the early tenth-century mosaic in the south-west vestibule of Hagia Sophia, which shows Constantine offering a model of Constantinople itself, and Justinian offering a model of the church to the Virgin and Child (Plate 3). The response of acceptance and blessing of the Christ child is either hopeful of a return to past glory, or simply a denial of the reality which by now was closing in on 'the New Rome'. But however diminished the political power of Constantinople, it was still the liturgy of the Great Church that was the standard of orthodoxy in the ancient patriarchates of Alexandria, Antioch and Jerusalem, as well as the new Slav Churches.

---

76 See Cameron (1987), p. 116, where the text is also quoted.
77 Buchwald (1999), p. 9; see also Cormack (1990).

CHAPTER 4

Late Antiquity in the West
and the Gallican Rite

The Fifth Century in the West

From 401/2, the Emperor of the West, Flavius Honorius, was resident in Ravenna for both strategic and defensive reasons. Under his half-sister Galla Placidia, Regent during the minority of Valentinian III (425–50), Ravenna was adorned with some of its finest buildings, including her mausoleum and San Giovanni Evangelista. Barbarians had made deep incursions, be it either as migrants or invaders, into many areas of the Empire, and over a period of three days in August 410, Alaric the Goth sacked Rome itself. It was a profound shock that the Imperial and religious capital of the world should fall to heretic barbarians. St Augustine, who wrote his *City of God* in response to the sack of Rome, said elsewhere: 'Universum regnum in tot civitatibus constitutum dicitur Romana civitas'[1] ('The universal empire, established in so many cities, is called the Roman city'). Of course, Rome had, as a consequence of the emperor's long absence, declined in its administrative importance since it was no longer the imperial residence, but in the East as well as in the West, people saw themselves as Roman citizens, and the Bishop of Rome was recognized as first in precedence and authority. He took precedence even over the Bishop of Constantinople, or 'New Rome', who had been recognized as second in authority at the Council of Constantinople of 381, though 'New Rome' would challenge old Rome during the papacy of Gregory the Great. Both the Roman Empire and the Church saw themselves as having a universal calling, so the brief sack of Rome and its permanent occupation by barbarians in 476 on the deposition of Romulus Augustulus, the last Western Emperor, struck at the heart of Western cultural identity.

These Germanic tribes had been evangelized in the fourth century by Ulfila (*c.* 311–83), who had been consecrated bishop in 341 by the Arian Bishop Eusebius of Nicomedia. Ulfila's exile effectively exported Arianism to the Goths; he translated the Bible into Gothic, and the liturgy was also in the vernacular. Yet, although these barbarians were for the most part heretical Arians, they were still Christian, and the ideal of a universal Christian empire was still, even after the fall of Rome, deeply embedded in contemporary culture. Their relations with the emperor in Constantinople were complex and tense, but generally positive. He granted them Roman titles, and they in turn recognized the authority of the emperor of the West in Ravenna. Ricimer, the Ostrogothic ruler of Italy, was given the rank of patrician, while at the same time making and removing a sequence of puppet emperors. Odoacer, because he finally deposed the last Western emperor in 476, was, perhaps not surprisingly, refused the title of Patrician by the emperor of the East. The barbarian conquerors adopted Roman law, art and, gradually, language. The Arian Ostrogothic ruler Theodoric (490–526), from his capital in Ravenna, treated the Western Church with great respect, and with the secular administration dismantled, the Church, the clergy, and ultimately the Bishop of Rome assumed the central role as both guardians and purveyors of *Romanitas*, enhancing their prestige and power.

---

1   Augustine, *De Consensu Evang.*, II, 58, quoted in Dix (1945), p. 385.

The Sack of Rome may not have been as destructive or violent as generally imagined, but the stories contained in various documents are difficult to reconcile, which means that in widely varying historical situations they have been used to equally diverse ends. Zosimus, in his *New History* (V.39), tells of starvation followed by plague as the siege progressed. On the other hand, Orosius, in his *History against the Pagans*, written in 417–18, a few years after the events, was trying to show that the pagan past was even worse than the Christian present, and in trying to explain away the disaster that had struck at the heart of the Church, maintained that few were killed, as there was little resistance and the Visigoths, though barbarians, were under instruction not to loot the churches and showed great respect towards them and the shrines of the saints (VII.39). Augustine speaks of the clemency of the Goths towards those who sought sanctuary in 'the sacred places of the martyrs and the basilicas of the Apostles'.[2]

Financially, it was a setback for the Church because of the loss of Italian estates, but the pope had other enormous estates, especially in North Africa, and revenues from those provided the means for the Church to support the poor of Rome. Soon the Church was also able to build, including the basilica of Santa Sabina little more than a decade after the Sack, Santa Maria Maggiore from *c.* 430, and S. Pietro in Vincoli, dedicated in 439/40. Between *c.* 380 and 440, about half the *domus ecclesiae* were being replaced by large basilicas.[3] These churches were less complex and more standardized than the great diversity of the Constantinian period. Norms were established for different liturgical functions, including congregational worship, baptism, the cult of the martyrs, and private devotion. Traditional practices continued, especially in the depths of the provinces, but great basilicas and village churches throughout the West took on a simple familiar shape with nave, apse and aisles, with local needs and customs (both architectural and liturgical) dictating variations.

Santa Sabina

Santa Sabina is the best surviving example of a fifth-century basilican church (Plate 7). It was built between 422 and 432, just prefiguring the great burst of building under Sixtus III. Like the columns of San Clemente, those at Santa Sabina are *spolia*, probably salvaged from a single older source, since in this case they are perfectly matched and probably of the second century. Emile Mâle is lyrical about their perfection, praising the beauty of the Parian marble, Corinthian order and Classical proportions:

> they do not at all resemble those rows of dissimilar columns, taken from collapsed temples and arcades which the later architects of temples were content to use. All equal and all perfect, they belong to a time when art was still faithful to its laws. Did they come from a temple or from some rich mansion destroyed by the Goths under Alaric? We do not know.[4]

He continues his praise of its proportions and 'all this perfection in the service of the Gospel'. Most interestingly, he concludes this section by saying: 'At the time Santa Sabina was built St Augustine was still alive; and how often, when reading St Augustine, are we reminded of Plato! Thus do the pagan columns of Santa Sabina lead us on towards the Christian altar.' What is important here is the appeal to the perfection of Classical Antiquity – that is, an appeal to the cultural, in the absence of political, authority of Classical Rome as the inheritor of the mantle of Greece.

---

2   See Cameron (1993b), p. 38, and Ward-Perkins (2005), pp. 21–2; *City of God*, I.1.
3   Krautheimer (1983), p. 94.
4   Mâle (1960), p. 52, continuing his argument to p. 53.

The interior shines with light admitted by 26 windows in the nave and apse, reflected by mosaics, still visible on the interior of the entrance façade below the windows. The inscription in the mosaic says that the church was built under Pope Celestine I (422–32) by Peter from Illyria, and the *Liber Pontificalis* tells us that it was consecrated by Sixtus III. Here the chancel, with barriers and an *ambo* either side, extends five bays into the body of the church, but in this case there is no *solea* extending further down the nave. The arrangement is one of simplicity, clarity, authority and order, in the face of a chaotic world.

The wooden doors themselves are magnificent contemporary survivals (a full 18 of the original 28 panels) which show Old and New Testament scenes in parallel. One extremely interesting panel shows a man and an angel in a church surmounted by a cross with clergy ranked below (see Figure 4.1). Their gestures are ambiguous. If, like the other scenes, this has a biblical source, then it

Figure 4.1   Santa Sabina, Rome, panel from the doors, perhaps showing a bishop and his clergy in ranks and an angel interceding on their behalf; photograph Bill Storage.

may be Zecharias (who was to be father of John the Baptist) having been struck dumb during his encounter with the angel, being unable to respond to others as he emerged from the Temple. If so, then why is there a cross above the building? The angel seems either to be commending the man (perhaps Peter of Illyria, or even Theodosius II?) to the assembled clergy, or all of them, and their prayers, to God. The man is either greeting the clergy, or possibly offering prayers on their behalf. Could this be a bishop[5] (even Pope Sixtus III at the consecration of Santa Sabina?) and his clergy during the liturgy, with an angel connecting their worship with the worship of heaven?

Santa Maria Maggiore

In 431, the Council of Ephesus proclaimed the Virgin Mary 'Mother of God', and it was perhaps the following year when Pope Sixtus III (432–40) began building Santa Maria Maggiore. Even after the loss of vast Italian estates, he was still able to provide the church with a silver altar and silver and gold altar-plate.[6] It has been convincingly argued by Emile Mâle that the wonderful mosaics of the church (which though they are of the life of the Virgin, are focused on the person of Christ) are an answer to the 'adoptianist' heresy of Nestorius, Patriarch of Constantinople, who considered that Christ was not born divine, but became divine through a sinless life. The Christological controversies left subtle marks on art, architecture and liturgy. The Virgin appears as a Byzantine empress, but is placed to the side, while Christ, as a young child rather than a baby, is seated on a jewelled throne attended by angels and adored by the Magi. It is the image of a child who was born the Son of God – a clear statement of orthodoxy.

The artistic history of Santa Maria Maggiore reveals the way other doctrinal disputes were played out and had consequences for the liturgy, not in terms of its texts, but rather in its performance. In the eighth century, Pope Stephen (752–57) installed two remarkable images in the church: one was an icon of Christ said to have been painted by St Luke and completed by angels. According to legend, it had been saved from destruction by the iconophile Patriarch Germanos, who was deposed in 730 and replaced by the emperor with an iconoclast, Anastasius. In 731, Gregory III succeeded to the papacy and held a synod which declared excommunicate anyone who destroyed or dishonoured any likeness of Christ, the Virgin or the saints.[7] Patriarch Germanos is said to have set the icon adrift in a boat which miraculously carried it across the sea and up the Tiber into the hands of the pope, to whom its advent had been revealed. To install it in Santa Maria Maggiore was an act of defiance to the iconoclast Emperor Constantine V Copronymus (741–75). In 753, Constantine V called the Synod of Hieria, not attended by Pope Stephen, nor the Patriarchs of Antioch, Jerusalem or Alexandria. The Synod declared icons of the Virgin Mary and the saints to be idols, and ordered their destruction. Pope Stephen had also had another majestic icon made for the church. It is unclear whether it was just encased in or even entirely made of gold, but either way it emphatically declared his iconophile orthodoxy. In 753, it was Stephen who, with Rome threatened by the Lombards and without hope of support from Constantinople, crossed the Alps with a Frankish escort in mid-winter to solicit help from the King of the Franks, Pepin the Short. Pepin sent his son Charles to meet the pope in present-day Switzerland and accompany him through the Frankish realms. In 755, Pepin agreed to help, then went on to defeat the Lombards and establish a papal state. The pope now fell increasingly under the protection of the Franks, and saw the emperor in Constantinople as an enemy. If the iconoclastic emperor of the East, who had caused

---

5   Bill Storage thinks it highly unlikely that this is a bishop, because of what appear to him to be riding boots.

6   Mâle (1960), p. 63.

7   Duckett (1951), pp. 51–2.

such widespread destruction of icons and relics, had come to Rome's aid rather than the King of the Franks, and consequently, if iconoclasm had struck at the heart of the Western Church, then it would be difficult to imagine how radically this might have changed Western religious practice as a whole, including the liturgy and its setting, since the cult of saints, relics and pilgrimage was becoming fundamental to Western development. Exiles from the violent iconoclastic purges in the East hugely enriched the art, architecture and liturgy of the West.

Relics became simultaneously the focus of the liturgy and architecture, and as early as 401, at the Council of Carthage, a canon was approved that all altars without the body of a bishop or relics of a martyr should, where possible, be destroyed.[8] Locally, at Santa Maria Maggiore, fragments of the crib and grotto of the Nativity are the only relics that are known to have been there in the early Middle Ages, and may have been installed after the Arab conquest of Jerusalem in 638. This was particularly appropriate to the dedication of the church, and was clearly an evocation of Bethlehem, translating the sanctity of the martyrium to a place of safety. The development of a *confessio* in Santa Maria Maggiore *c.* 700 may have been associated with these relics, and indeed the fragments excavated in the eighteenth century were described as stone, chalk and wood from the grotto of the Nativity. By the late eleventh century, the relics of the apostle Matthias and of the Virgin, pieces from her clothing, some strands of her hair, and her milk are also listed as being in the church. There is no concrete evidence to link the *confessio* to the relics of Matthias, but the story goes that the Empress Helena brought them back with her from Jerusalem. On the other hand, St Jerome was first buried in the Church of the Nativity, then at some unknown date translated to Santa Maria Maggiore, presumably because of the association with the relics of the grotto.[9]

Pilgrimage to a shrine included touching or kissing relics, as with the wood of the True Cross at the *Anastasis* in Jerusalem, and as Egeria recorded of that relic, it was necessary to control access. Increasing pressure of numbers forced architectural solutions. A centrally important example of this was, of course, St Peter's in Rome. In the fifth century, its antiquity and prestige acted as a bulwark against iconoclastic arguments, for example when, in 406, St Jerome refuted the Gaulish Vigilantius' arguments that earthly remains were not worthy of veneration: 'So does the Bishop of Rome do evil, when he offers sacrifices to God over what to us are the hallowed bones but to you is the miserable dust of the dead men Peter and Paul, and when he treats their tombs as the altar of Christ?' Of course, the practice was extremely ancient and had already been discussed in the *Didascalia Apostolorum*, probably written *c.* 230 in Syria.[10]

The Form of the Roman Chancel and the Performance of the Liturgy

The archetype of the rebuilt parish churches of Rome is San Clemente (see Figure 4.2). The late fourth- (or early fifth-) century architects filled in the courtyard rooms of the *horreum* and built the simple basilica at first-floor level, with the nave over the court, and aisles over the side rooms. The whole was preceded by an atrium or courtyard colonnaded on all four sides. It would appear that the Mithraeum continued in use in the lower-level apartment house, perhaps as late as 395, when Mithraism was outlawed. The Church acquired that part of the site, where the apse was then built. This basilica stood until *c.* 1100, when it was replaced by the present one, reusing much of the liturgical arrangement of the screened choir and *ambo* from the early basilica (see Figure 4.3), just

---

8   Crook (2000), p. 13, and Kemp (1948), p. 15.
9   De Blaauw (1987), pp. 196–201, gives a very full discussion of the church and its relics..
10   Discussed in Crook (2000), p. 12.

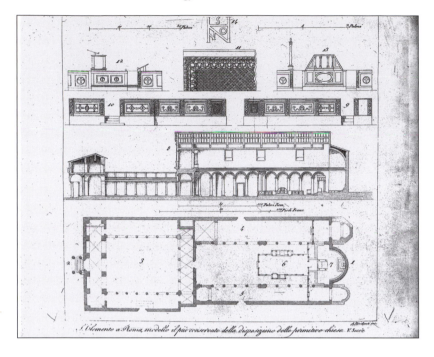

Figure 4.2   San Clemente, Rome, plan and section of the early twelfth-century church and of the reused liturgical furnishings of 533–35; Conway Library, Courtauld Institute of Art.

Figure 4.3   San Clemente, photograph showing the liturgical furnishings; photograph James Anderson, Conway Library, Courtauld Institute of Art.

as the early basilica had reused columns of high quality which may have been taken from another building of the third century on the site.[11]

The liturgical arrangement is closely related to that of the Lateran Basilica, which had a *solea* beginning either at the doors or perhaps halfway down the nave, the latter being the arrangement adopted at San Clemente itself (installed between 533 and 535), as well as San Pietro in Vincoli (dedicated 439/40), Sto Stefano in the via Latina (between 440 and 460), Santa Maria Antiqua (mid- to late-sixth century), and San Marco (some time between 550 and 650).[12] Archaeological evidence confirms that the common chancel arrangement in fifth-century Rome included a *solea* or *scola cantorum*, that is, a long passage projecting from the chancel and protected by barriers, as was the case not only in the Lateran Basilica, but in so many Byzantine churches as well. In addition, these Roman churches had further barriers that reached out laterally from the corners of the sanctuary across the side aisles. At San Clemente, the pavement of the lower church points to a similar arrangement enclosing at least the right-hand aisle. The parapets of the *scola cantorum* in the present church display the monogram of John II, who was pope during 533–35. These must have been salvaged from the earlier arrangement, and transferred when the basilica was rebuilt in the early twelfth century.

Working back from the architectural form to the liturgical function, in an early article on the archaeological data, Mathews qualifies what earlier liturgists (including Jungmann, Duchesne and Dix) had to say, by mapping the chancel arrangement (in the absence of earlier manuscript evidence) onto the rubrics of the *Ordo Romanus I*, 'which is generally accepted as a description of the stational mass in the seventh century in Rome':

> A comprehensive study of the early rubrics, of course, is not called for here. What we have selected is a number of problem areas in which the ceremony of the Mass, by its external ritual, would be liable to explain the spatial disposition of the early Roman chancel. These areas are four: 1, the ceremonies of pontifical entrance and exit; 2, the readings of Sacred Scripture; 3, the procession of the offertory; and 4, the procession of the communion.[13]

What is particularly notable, since the focus is on processions, is that whereas in the East the patriarch and the emperor led the processions, in the West the order was from the least to the greatest significance. Hence, the pontifical entrance was the climax of a series of processions beginning with representatives of the clergy of Rome processing down the length of the nave to the apse, or at Santa Maria Antiqua, to benches on either side of the apse, because it was unusually small. Meanwhile, members of the parish and a guard of honour would process through the city to meet the pope on his way from the Lateran: 'At Santa Maria Maggiore and the other great basilicas of Rome, procession through atrium and narthex, down the nave and toward the apse, was the culmination of a richly contextualised ritual of procession through the city, particularly at times such as Christmas when this basilica was the centre of papal liturgy.'[14] Over the course of the liturgical year, the urban geography was sacralized and the unity of the congregation of Rome given real expression.

It is worth pausing here to note that though Sant' Apollinare Nuovo in Ravenna is a church of very different proportions from the contemporary Roman basilica, its mosaics (dating from *c.* 550)

---

11   Claridge (1998), p. 286.

12   For background, see Krautheimer et al. (1937–77), vol. V, p. 87, Mathews (1962), pp. 73–4, and Krautheimer (1980), pp. 47ff.

13   Mathews (1962), p. 75; see also his summary of the rubrics, the analysis by Duchesne (1903), pp. 161ff, Klauser (1979), pp. 59ff., and Jungmann (1959), pp. 50–56.

14   See Kieckhefer (2004), p. 32, and in more detail, De Blaauw (1987), pp. 26ff.

give an impression of these stately processions, though what is depicted is heavenly processions of virgins and martyrs (Plate 8). Again, within the fabric and decoration of the church, the worship of heaven and earth meet.

In the papal celebration in Rome, on his arrival he retired to a vestry, from which a sub-deacon would lead an acolyte with the Gospel-book to the altar. At the altar, the sub-deacon received the book from the acolyte and placed it with due honour on the altar. Next came the cantors and boys, after receiving a papal blessing. They took up their places on either side of the *scola*, with men on the outside and boys inside. This left a route clear for the papal procession. First came a guard of honour of military standard bearers, then seven candles, a thurifer with incense (both of these were imperial honours), and the archdeacon and deacon either side; finally came the pope himself, led by the hands by two deacons (reflecting Eastern court ceremonial).[15] The guard of honour would stop at the *solea*, effectively forming an extension to it and leaving enough room to allow the papal procession to pass between them. Room would likewise be left in the *solea* between the cantors singing a psalm. The congregation answered the cantors with an antiphon. Before entering the sanctuary, the pope was met by a sub-deacon and acolytes bearing bread consecrated at the previous papal mass. This emphasized the unity of the sacrament over time; and after the consecration, some of the bread would be sent to the *tituli*, or parish churches of Rome, unifying the celebrations across space.

After entering the sanctuary, the pope gave the kiss of peace to the senior bishop, priest, and deacons. He then knelt on the apse side of the altar (or, according to Jungman, prostrated himself in prayer) while the other clergy kissed its sides. As the introit ended, the pope then rose, kissed the book of the Gospels, then the altar, and went to his throne. Standing at his throne in the centre of the apse, he faced east and the *Kyries* were sung. Turning west, he sang the introduction to the *Gloria*, then back towards the east while the rest was sung. At the end, he again turned and greeted the people with 'Pax vobis', said a prayer and a collect. All sat down, and a lection from the epistles was read from the *ambo*. Alleluias were sung, and a responsorial psalm, or gradual, by a single deacon from the *gradus*, or step of the *ambo*. The architectural elements along the axis of the church in this way became punctuation for the spatial unfolding of the text of the mass.

When the lector saw that the pope, bishops and clergy were in their places, he approached the pope for a blessing, then kissed the gospel and took it from the altar where it had been placed during the entry procession. Accompanied by candles and incense, the gospel was taken by the deacon as lector up into the *ambo*, and the gospel was sung, after which a sub-deacon would take it to all the clergy in succession for it to be kissed.

More remarkably, the sermon is not mentioned at all in *Ordo I*, and may even have fallen out of use by the middle of the fifth century, though Pope Leo's own sermons were clearly exceptional, setting the standard of orthodoxy. Rome, longer than most cities, maintained the exclusive right of the bishop to preach from the lessons.[16] In the early fifth century, Sozomen wrote that there was no preaching at Rome. Within two centuries, towards the end of the sixth, Gregory the Great was unwilling to do without a sermon even though the thrust of his reforms was to simplify the mass and reduce its length.[17] Dating of archaeological evidence suggests that the *ambo* may well have been introduced through Byzantine influence in the sixth century. In this context, where preaching may have fallen out of use, it is interesting to reflect on Foucault's notion of discourses.[18] The liturgical text, the *Ordo*, was clearly a key statement, but the rubrics along with the archaeology

---

15   See Jungmann (1959), p. 52.

16   De Blaauw (1987), p. 36.

17   See Mathews (1962), p. 86, where he refers to Duchesne (1912), p. 171, and Sozomen, *Hist. Eccl.* VII. 19; Hope (1980), p. 234; Klauser (1979), p. 64; Jungmann (1959), p. 53.

18   See especially Stringer (2005), pp. 10–14.

help to reconstruct the *praxis* or actual presentation of the liturgy, and as the transfer of bread between masses shows, its architectural, temporal, and even urban context contribute to the full significance of the larger Christian 'discourse'.

The point is that the liturgical year, with its celebrations of saints, martyrs and seasons, took the pope out from the Lateran to celebrate his stational masses at different churches according to the particular significance of the day and its association with the place. It emphasized that the Christians of Rome belonged to one congregation who inhabited a holy geography within sanctified time, the City of God. The dress of the participants indicating their roles, their hierarchical ordering, the coordinated movement of the processions, the flags, the urban and architectural routes, the connotations of the materials making up the architecture and liturgical furnishings, the vessels and works of art, which include text in the mosaics of the walls, all this forms the matrix into which the liturgical text and its performance are embedded. Together, it is an extremely complex yet clear articulation, every aspect of which could be tightly controlled, whereas preaching week by week and day by day by ordinary clergy within discrete congregations could all too easily fall into error, or even heresy.

A very significant original contribution is made by Mathews in his reconstruction of the organization of the offertory and the distribution of communion. His reconstruction is based on the archaeological evidence for the architectural arrangement of the *solea/scola cantorum* in San Marco and, partially, in San Clemente.

He suggests that for the offering, the clergy descended from the apse to the eastern ends of the aisles which appear to have been separated off with low chancel barriers at San Marco, and at San Clemente there is evidence for this arrangement at least at the end of the right-hand aisle in the lower church. In these enclosed ends of the aisles, the offerings would be made by the people, and communion would be distributed at the entrances. At the offertory, the pope, accompanied by the clergy, would descend to the enclosure at the end of the aisle on his left to receive the bread-offering from the men of rank in order, and then proceed to the other side, similarly to receive the gifts of the women. The small flasks of wine and loaves of bread offered by each were passed by the pope or his archdeacon to the assistants to fill chalices, and the bread was passed to fill linen cloths held between two acolytes.[19] Other clergy followed behind, performing a similar action with the rest of the congregation.

The gifts were then placed in order on the altar by the archdeacon, while the pope washed his hands in preparation for the eucharistic prayer. The pope was now at the altar facing the people, with the deacons behind and acolytes to either side, and the bishops and priests in their places in the apse. The sub-deacons were ranged to the west side and facing the altar. The pope again greeted the people with 'Dominus vobiscum' ('The Lord be with you') and said 'sursum corda' ('Lift up your hearts'), the people responding as now. Then he sang the special preface for that particular mass, followed by the *Sanctus*, a long passage listing those for whom the oblation is being made (corresponding to the ancient reading of the *diptyches*), and the consecration during the Canon of the Mass, at the end of which there was an elevation of the bread and wine so they could be seen by the congregation. At this point, he then placed a small piece of the bread from the last papal mass in the chalice, and broke off a piece from the newly consecrated bread for this use at the next papal mass.[20] The pope administered the consecrated bread to the clergy from his throne, and his senior assistant administered the chalice. Then, as a parallel action to the offertory, the pope and

---

19 The practice described by Klauser (1979), p. 65, is later (*c.* 700) than that described by Mathews (fifth and sixth centuries), which was extremely time-consuming. See also Jungmann (1959), pp. 53–4.

20 For the dating and composition of the Eucharistic prayer, see Duschene (1903), pp. 176–83, and Klauser (1979), pp. 65–6; for the Gregorian reforms, see *ibid.*, pp. 47ff.

archdeacon administered communion to the men of rank at the entrance to the screened end of the aisle to his left, then to the women of rank at the barrier in the opposite aisle. As at the offertory, priests and deacons followed, communicating the rest of the men, then the rest of the women. For this, they brought the wine in a large *scyphus* and administered the sacrament through a tube called a *pugilaris*. Meanwhile, back at his cathedra, the pope would communicate all his other assistants, including all the sub-deacons, cantors, and his guard of honour. Klauser describes the simplified, and shorter, later form of distribution from *c.* 700.

When all had communicated and the altar and altar-plate had been set in order, the pope gave a series of blessings, after which a deacon announced the end of the mass: 'Ite, missa est.' The congregation responded 'Deo gratias,' and the procession took the pope back to the *secretarium*. This architectural/liturgical arrangement became strongly established, and continued in Rome (with some modifications, especially limiting the movement of the people, necessitated by pressure of time and numbers) until the ninth century.

Byzantine Influence in the West

In 533, the year the chancel barriers of San Clemente were installed and John II became pope, Emperor Justinian began a series of campaigns to re-conquer the Western Empire which had been overrun by barbarians. After celebrating victory in north Africa with a spectacular triumphal parade in Constantinople, Justinian's general, Belisarius, was dispatched via Sicily to Italy in 536, and in 540 he entered Rome. In a little less than two decades, a devastated Italy had been freed from Ostrogothic rule by 554. In Italy and Africa, but not in Gaul, the Church was in a position to reassert authority and orthodoxy over Arian heresy, though the Lombards arrived in northern Italy in 568. Victory had come at a high price: there had been one of the greatest plagues in history in 542, striking Constantinople and the Eastern provinces, and throughout the period Justinian was having to buy off (not entirely successfully) attacks by Persians and Arabs on the Eastern front. The Italian campaign had been long, and had been fought with relatively small resources, with the Byzantine forces greatly outnumbered by the Goths. Italy was devastated, many of the Senatorial class fled to Constantinople, and the Roman Senate collapsed as an institution.

Gregory the Great and the Gregorian Sacramentary

Byzantine influence on the Roman Church, both positive and negative, can be seen in the person of Gregory I (the Great). His father was a senator, and Gregory became Prefect of Rome in 573. The next year he became a monk in a monastery he had founded in his own house. With wealth based on Sicily and Rome, he established monasteries in both, and supported the poor of Rome. Around the year 578, he was sent to Constantinople as a papal diplomat, and became close to the emperor and his family. After about seven years in Constantinople, he returned to Rome with a hearty dislike of Byzantine politics. As pope from 590, his name is traditionally linked with the development of the liturgy by reorganizing the *scola cantorum* for singing what we still call 'Gregorian chant'. Apart from some local practice (which Gregory encouraged), such as the Ambrosian chant of Milan, the earliest manuscripts that include musical notation are all remarkably consistent. Gregory was thought to have codified the local Roman rite in the so-called *Gregorian Sacramentary c.* 595, which would come to have enormous influence.

Notably, the *Gregorian Sacramentary* contains a Mass on the Octave of Christmas which affirms the reality of Mary's motherhood of Jesus – a liturgical refutation of Arianism. Dix notes that very few saints of the New Testament have festivals in this compilation (at least as received at the Court of Charlemagne in the 780s). These are closely related to the cult of relics, and include the feast of St Peter's Chains on 1 August, which celebrates the dedication in 461 of the Roman basilica in which the relic was kept (San Pietro in Vincoli), and the Feast of St Stephen, the Protomartyr, celebrated on 26 December from the end of the fourth century. Stephen's relics were discovered in 415, which caused a great wave of enthusiasm, and his feast was being celebrated in Rome after the middle of the century, and the discovery of his relics ('Inventio Sancti Stephani') was at one time itself kept on 3 August.[21]

During the century prior to the production of the *Gregorian Sacramentary*, other liturgical collections had been compiled: the earliest manuscript is probably the so-called *Gelasian Sacramentary* (*codex Vat. Reginensis lat. 316*), which has traditionally been associated with Pope Gelasius (492–96), though this manuscript is thought to have been written in France *c.* 750. Another has been attributed to Bishop Maximian of Ravenna (546–56). Sacramentaries were produced for use and represent the point at which that use was becoming fixed and standardized.[22] Klauser's summary of the relationships between the traditions is as follows:

> … the Roman collection which forms the basis of the Codex [Reginensis] we have been dealing with reflects the state of the liturgy as it was in Rome before the time of the Gregorian Sacramentary, but after that of the Leonine. Since, however, the Leonine Sacramentary itself takes us right into the second half of the sixth century, the Roman core of the Gelasian Sacramentary cannot have originated much before the Gregorian Sacramentary.[23]

The *Leonine Sacramentary* (more properly referred to as the *Verona Sacramentary*, *Verona Codex lxxxv*) is now thought to have been compiled from collections of prayers, some of which do appear to be associated with Pope Leo) made by the clergy of the *tituli* of Rome, but compiled (according to Hope) in Verona *c.* 600. In fact, it is more of a compendium of prayers rather than a true sacramentary meant for use.[24] The dates and relationship of the original compilations have been much studied and debated, but what is relevant here is the similarity of forces and developments at work in both architecture and liturgy. In both, local canonical forms are emerging, which shows just how varied local practice must have been, but at the same time the immense importance of what would become the standardizing Roman model is becoming evident. The long process of codification of liturgical forms and standardization of architectural form continued into the seventh century within the Italian context; in Gaul, and within the Gallican Rite, that process had a very much longer and even more complex history.

Late Antique and Merovingian Architecture and the Gallican Rite

Gaul had long been a difficult part of the Empire to govern. Christianity had taken root there in the second century, when Irenaeus was Bishop of Lyon. During the second quarter of the third century, under the Consulship of Decius, seven bishops were sent to Gaul: St Saturninus to Toulouse, Gatianus to Tours, Trophimus to Arles, Paulus to Narbonne, Dionysius to Paris, Stremonius to Clermont-Ferrand and Martialus to Limoges. Decius had been successful in campaigns against the Goths on the Danube frontier, and was proclaimed emperor by the army. Gregory of Tours relates in his *History of the Franks* how a disciple of the bishops converted a number of men at Bourges

---

21 Dix (1945), pp. 377–8.

22 *Ibid.*, p. 566.

23 Klauser (1979), p. 56.

24 For a good discussion of the manuscript tradition, see Hope (1980), pp. 222ff.; see p. 225 for the dating of the *Verona Codex*.

whom he ordained: 'They were taught how to chant psalms, and they were given instruction in building churches and in celebrating the rites due to Almighty God. As yet they had little chance of building a church, so they asked for the house of one of the townsfolk, so that they could make a church of it.' Here we have in detail a description of the creation of a *domus ecclesiae*:

> The Senators and other leading men of the place were still committed to their own heathen religion, and those who had come to believe in God were from the poorer classes … . They did not obtain the use of the house for which they had asked; and they therefore went to see a man called Leocadius, the leading Senator of Gaul, who was of the same family as that Vettius Epagatus [an ancestor of Gregory himself] who, as I have already told you, suffered martyrdom in Lyon in the name of Christ. They told him of their Christian faith and explained what they wanted. 'If my house,' he replied, 'which I possess in Bourges, were worthy of being put to such a use, I would be willing to offer it to you.' When they heard him they fell at his feet. They said that his house was indeed suitable to be used for religious ceremonies and they offered him three hundred golden pieces for it, together with a silver salver. Leocadius accepted three of the golden coins for luck and refused the rest. Up to this moment he had believed in heathen gods, but now he became a Christian and turned his house into a church. This is now the most important church in the town of Bourges, constructed with great skill and famous for the relics of Stephen, the first martyr.[25]

This is a pattern familiar from other parts of the Empire, with converts for the most part poor, but with rich and influential patrons. That is not to say, however, that this congregation did not have considerable resources of its own, offering 300 gold pieces and a silver salver, though this may have been exaggerated to enhance the generosity of the patron in refusing payment. He was, after all, a kinsman of Gregory's. The story is also an example of how these grand senatorial families not uncommonly continued their patronage and influence, often keeping bishoprics in the family for generations. The house was said to be 'suitable for religious ceremonies', presumably in its present state for the time being, but it was 'turned into a church … now the most important church in the town of Bourges, constructed with great skill', which implies that in the intervening time, careful architectural changes were carried out, just as they had been in the almost contemporary example at Dura Europos.

In the 250s, the Franks and the Alamanni crossed into imperial territory over the Rhine. In the second half of the third century, a number of Gallic emperors emerged to provide for the defence of Gaul. Late in the third century, Constantius, father of Constantine the Great, restored order in Gaul, and subsequently, under Constantine there was an imperial capital in Trier. The presence of the emperor in a city or territory was no small matter. He was the embodiment of authority, and until the confrontation between Ambrose of Milan with Valentinian II, his mother Justina (both Arians), and then with Theodosius I (the Emperor of the East), that imperial authority encompassed both the temporal and the spiritual.

The Influence of the Imperial Adventus on the Ceremonial of the Cult of Saints

In 335 or 336, when Bishop Athanasius of Alexandria was in exile in Trier, he compared the Incarnation of the Son of God with the presence of the emperor; both emperor and Godhead had to appear before the people to maintain the kingdom and prevent usurpers: 'But when the real king comes forth and is revealed, then the deceitful revolutionaries are refuted by his presence, while the citizens, seeing the real king, abandon those who formerly deceived them.'[26]

The *adventus*, or arrival of an emperor or god, had been a pagan and imperial ceremony which became invested with new Christian meanings across the whole of the Empire, both East and West.

---

25   *HF* I.31.
26   Van Dam (1985), p. 22.

In Ambrose's Milan, the emperor's *adventus* was key in the siting of the *Basilica Apostolorum*, and it became the model for the ceremony accompanying the translation of relics in the East, as shown on the Trier ivory. A traditional *adventus* was celebrated in 357 at the entry of the Emperor Constantius, son of Constantine the Great, into Rome. He rode in a golden carriage, posing as stiff as a statue, his gaze fixed straight ahead. Despite the jolts caused by the road surface, he suppressed all movement, appearing like the statue of a god. He became the very image of an emperor, and significantly, it was possible to perform an *adventus* with images or insignia of an emperor. The honour accorded corresponded to the authority embodied – to the Emperor himself, or his insignia, the citizenry would shout their requests for justice or relief from a particular tax.

As in the East, so in Gaul the *adventus* ceremony was transformed into a Christian idiom for the translation of relics. At the translation of relics to Rouen in the late fourth or early fifth century, Bishop Victricius preached a sermon in which he encouraged the people to celebrate the arrival of the saints and the building of a new church as a 'palace' to house them. As at an imperial *adventus*, the people made requests before the saints for pardon, not from taxes, but from their sins – both inevitable facts of life. Ceremonial forms can travel and be translated (or 'baptized'), and any contrast with the original meaning of the forms can even intensify their effectiveness in their new application. Victricius was explicit about the contrast in his sermon:

> If one of the emperors were to visit our city today, every street would happily be covered with garlands, women would fill the rooftops, and a wave of people would surge from the city gates. … People of every age would sing of honour and of war, and they would marvel at the flaming splendour of the emperor's cloak and at the imperial purple. … But now, instead of the royal cloak there is right here the garment of eternal light. Here is the purple, … here are diadems decorated with the splendid gems [of different Christian virtues].[27]

Reliquaries, Church Plate and the Power of Gifts

These 'gems' of Christian virtues became real gems as reliquaries became more elaborate, and gifts dedicated by the rich and powerful became more spectacular. Even the props and accoutrements of the imperial *adventus* could be transposed into the Christian context, such as the astonishing fifth-century Roman parade mask reused for the head of the reliquary of Ste Foy, with enamelled eyes and the surface overlaid with gold and jewels. Here is an image to which any emperor would aspire at an *adventus*. The forms, materials and use of reliquaries were a direct extension of the virtues and holiness of the fragments they contained. These fragments were existential connections with the hosts of heaven. Such connection was a conduit of the power and authority of the Emperor of Heaven which was more direct, and certainly more stable, than the power and authority derived from the presence of the imperial insignia, or even the emperor of Rome himself.

Although the *adventus* ceremony had been translated into a Christian idiom, it retained its imperial associations and bridged the two worlds. Clovis, King of the Franks in the late fifth and early sixth centuries, was a pagan, and Gregory of Tours records that his queen, Clotild, tried to convert her husband by doctrine, but without result: 'When she brought her son for baptism: she ordered the church to be decorated with hangings and curtains, in the hope that the King, who remained stubborn in the face of argument, might be brought to the faith by ceremony. The child was baptised; he was given the name Igomer; but no sooner had he received baptism than he died in his white robes. Clovis was extremely angry.' Despite this unpropitious encounter with Christianity, when Clovis was at war with the Alamanni in 496, the battle was going against him and he prayed to Christ, 'If you will give me victory over my enemies, and if I may have evidence

---

27 Translated in *ibid.*, p. 60.

of that miraculous power which the people dedicated to your name say that they have experienced, then I will believe in you and I will be baptized in your name.' Immediately, the Alamanni fled. When Clovis was subsequently baptized, colourful hangings lined his route to the baptistery, which had been prepared by Remigius, Bishop of Rheims, with burning incense, and 'God filled the hearts of all present with such grace that they imagined themselves to have been transported to some perfumed paradise.' This was Clovis' *adventus* into the Christian religion, and the imperial nature of the occasion was not lost on Gregory: 'Like some new Constantine, he stepped forward to the baptismal pool …'. He had driven a hard bargain with Christ in his demands for a sign, but he was baptized a Catholic, and his sister, who had become an Arian, also became a Catholic.[28] Clovis had begun the expansion of his kingdom by defeating the Roman general Siagrius. Now, as a Catholic, he had an excuse to attack the Arian Visigoths and seize the rest of Gaul.

When Clovis drove the Arian Visigoths out of Gaul across the Pyrenees in 507, he killed their king, Alaric II, and seized most of his treasure, though not the treasures from the Temple of Solomon (which had been seized in the Sack of Rome) and other symbols which had become tokens of their dynastic power. Alaric's father-in-law was Theoderic the Great, King of Italy, whose splendid mausoleum still stands in Ravenna.

The dedication of treasure at a shrine established what may be seen as the traditional patron–client relationship between the saint and the pilgrim. The patronage of the saint could be very practical indeed. Before attacking Alaric, Clovis sent gifts to St Martin's church, seeking another sign. When his messengers entered the church, 'it happened that the precentor was just beginning to intone this antiphon: "For thou hast girded me with strength unto the battle: thou hast subdued under me those that rose up against me. Thou hast also given me the necks of mine enemies: that I might destroy them that hate me." [Ps. 18:39–40] When the messengers heard this psalm they gave thanks to God. They made their vows to the saint and went happily back.'[29]

Naturally, Clovis was victorious, and when he had consolidated his power over former Gothic lands, it suited Anastasius, Emperor of the East, politically to name him Consul. Clovis assumed the title in St Martin's church at Tours, where 'he stood clad in a purple tunic and the military mantle, and he crowned himself with a diadem. He then rode out on his horse and with his own hand showered gold and silver coins among the people present all the way from the door of Saint Martin's church to Tours cathedral. From that day on he was called Consul or Augustus.'[30] By gifts, he became a 'client', so to speak, of St Martin, and St Martin his Patron Saint; then, by gifts of money showered on them, his new people became his clients in turn. These gifts, of coins, treasure and imperial titles, and the ceremonies when they were given or liturgies during which they were displayed all defined power and patronage. This was no play-acting, it was reality given physical expression. The physical objects were tangible evidence of the truth. When a royal gift was a reliquary, or became part of one, its display proclaimed to all both the wealth and power of the donor, and that however great and powerful the giver, the saint, as patron, was far greater as an intercessor in heaven. This would achieve its greatest demonstration in the Saint-Denis of Abbot Suger and in Canterbury Cathedral's shrine of St Thomas Becket.

Very little remains of reliquaries and dedicated objects of this early period due to many factors, including the nature of gift-giving and the dedication of treasures and their high value, making them susceptible to plunder and being melted down. Virtually all we have left of the treasure and altar-plate contemporary with Gregory is a sixth-century oblong paten (or perhaps it is a portable

---

28   *HF* II.29–31.
29   *HF* II.37.
30   *HF* II.38; see also Smith (2005), pp. 200–201.

altar) with its central cross and raised border in cloisonné enamel. The piece is from the treasury of Gourdon (Saône-et-Loire), and is now to be found in Paris in the Cabinet des Médailles.[31]

A particularly rich example of an abbey treasury which escaped the ravages of plunderers, including the Revolutionaries, is still to be found intact at the Abbey of Conques. The reliquary of Ste Foy in that treasury contains a fifth-century parade mask, some very ancient cameos, cabochons and other jewels, but the assemblage dates only from the ninth century, when the relics themselves, having been stolen from a monastery at Agen, first arrived at the Abbey of Conques on 14 January 866. Fixed to the throne of the reliquary, and contemporary with this, was a rock crystal engraved with the crucifixion (*c.* 870) and an Ottonian crown. This reliquary was augmented and built up, but also cut back and renewed like the throne – a process which continued up to the twelfth century. In the same treasury is a twelfth-century reliquary of the True Cross in the form of a miniature Holy Sepulchre mounted on a cube with medallions showing Sampson and the Lion, the Good Shepherd, and Christ in Majesty. Its form and the iconography declare it to be a physical and real connection with the instrument of Christ's glorification, and through him as the Shepherd of our souls, our glorification as well. Here is also a reliquary called the 'A' of Charlemagne, which holds another relic of the True Cross, and the '*châsse* of Pepin' dating partly from the eighth, but mostly from the ninth to the eleventh centuries, which is, at least in origin, one of the oldest in the treasury. It is a small, gabled and distinctly architectural reliquary of 18 cm by 18 cm. This is a form frequently seen on an altar in medieval pictures. Elements of some of the reliquaries at Conques are Carolingian, and even Merovingian (dating from the time of the previous dynasty reputedly founded by King Merovech). The relics themselves are equally diverse: a fragment of the Holy Sepulchre was given by Pope Pascal II in 1100; a relic relating to the circumcision and the umbilical cord of Christ (both now lost), bread from the Last Supper, the Holy Blood, relics of the boys in the burning fiery furnace, Daniel, hair of the Virgin, and relics of Apostles, saints and martyrs.[32]

The Architectural Setting and the Liturgy in Merovingian Gaul

Merovingian Architecture

Relics were a physical connection between the pilgrim and the reality of Holy Scripture and the continuing presence of the holy in more recent people of faith. Pilgrimage had been a growing part of private devotion since the time of Constantine and his mother, Helena. Egeria herself appears to have been a nun (or female religious of some sort) from Aquitania in Gaul on pilgrimage during 381–84. By the time of Gregory of Tours, two hundred years later, the numbers of pilgrims had swollen. In his *History of the Franks*, Gregory placed his reader before the same reality of the events of Holy Scripture and holy people by using the first book to 'cover five thousand, five hundred and ninety-six years from the beginning of the world down to the death of Saint Martin'.[33] The literary and physical connection (through relics and holy places) with the story of salvation and the power of the saints was integrated in the liturgy and its physical architectural setting, which in turn were unified with the worship of 'angels and archangels and the whole company of heaven': Gregory relates how:

---

31   The paten and a chalice, also from Gourdon, are reproduced and discussed in Vieillard-Troiekouroff (1976), p. 124 and plate v; Lasko (1971), p. 35, suggests it may be a portable altar.

32   See Renoue and Dengreville (1997), pp. 72–91.

33   Translated in Thorpe (1974), p. 99.

The wife of Namatius built the church of Saint Stephen in the suburb outside the walls of Clermont-Ferrand. She wanted it to be decorated with coloured frescoes. She used to hold in her lap a book from which she would read stories of events which happened long ago, and tell the workmen what she wanted painted on the walls.[34]

Clearly, specific narratives were of great concern to her and the dedication of her church, and a miracle and blessings ensued for the woman. It may well be that the book was an illuminated manuscript from the cathedral library, since her husband was the bishop. The architectural and spatial relationships between the frescoes on the walls of the building affected both the narrative and meaning of the paintings originating in the sourcebook.

An altogether grander setting, also frescoed,[35] was provided for the shrine of St Martin, who was highly venerated amongst the greatest of saints at Merovingian Tours. At least some of the architectural details given by Gregory in his *History* have proven to be archaeologically verifiable:

In the city of Tours Bishop Eustochius died in the seventeenth year of his episcopate. Perpetuus was consecrated in his place, being the fifth bishop after Saint Martin. When Perpetuus saw how frequently miracles were being performed at Saint Martin's tomb and when he observed how small was the chapel erected over the Saint's body, he decided that it was unworthy of these wonders. He had the chapel removed and he built in its place the great church which is still there some five hundred yards outside the city. It is one hundred and sixty feet long by sixty feet broad; and its height up to the beginning of the vaulting is forty-five feet. It has thirty-two windows in the sanctuary and twenty in the nave, with forty-one columns. In the whole building there are fifty-two windows, one hundred and twenty columns and eight doorways, three in the sanctuary and five in the nave. The great festival of the church has a threefold significance: it marks the dedication of the building, the translation of the Saint's body and his ordination as a bishop. You should observe this feast-day on 4 July; and you should remember that Saint Martin died on 11 November. If you celebrate this faithfully you will gain the protection of the saintly Bishop in this world and the next. The vault of the tiny chapel which stood there before was most elegantly designed, and so Bishop Perpetuus thought it wrong to destroy it. He built another church in honour of the blessed Apostles Peter and Paul, and he fitted this vault over it. He built many other churches which still stand firm today in the name of Christ.[36]

Already in 472, Perpetuus had elevated St Martin's body from its crypt, evidence that the number of pilgrims, as well as the number of miracles, had even then become so great as to require an architectural solution. Access had become totally inadequate. The tomb was built in the apse, and it seems that it was possible for pilgrims to enter and touch the sarcophagus in order to be healed, in the same way as Gregory himself had been relieved of headache and eye problems.[37] The liturgical festival recorded by Gregory in the extract above celebrated both the church building and the saint it honoured, and keeping the festival brought the saint's protection now and in the world to come. The original small chapel found so inadequate by Bishop Perpetuus had been built by St Brictius in the early fifth century over the tomb. Late in the fifth century, it had become commonplace to build churches over *hypogea*, underground tomb-chambers containing the body of a saint. The cult of the saints and the associated liturgy not only influenced the form and fittings of the architecture, it often dictated precisely where the churches should be built.

---

34   *HF* II.17.
35   *HF* VII.22.
36   *HF* II.14.
37   Crook (2000), p. 71.

The Merovingian Rite

The shrine of the local saint was particularly important, and so was the associated liturgy. St Saturninus of Toulouse was celebrated lavishly, even grandiloquently, on his feast-day with the proper preface:

> It is very meet and right ... . And most chiefly should we praise thine almighty power, O God in Trinity, with special devotion and the service of our words of supplication for the triumphant sufferings of all Thy saints: But especially at this time we are bound to exalt with due honour the blessed Saturninus, the most loud-thundering [*conclamantissimum*] witness of Thine awful name: whom the mob of the heathen when they thrust him from the temple thrust also into heaven. Nevertheless thine high-priest sent forth from eastern regions to the city of the Tolosatians, in this Rome of the Garonne as Vicar of Thy Peter fulfilled both his episcopate and martyrdom.[38]

The altar furnishings, the architectural setting and the liturgy were all clearly elaborate and impressive.

Another indication of how elaborate the contemporary Gallican Rite was, is given by Gregory in his story of the saintly Bishop Sidonius, of Clermont-Ferrand, who was from a leading senatorial family of Gaul and married to the daughter of the Emperor Avitus. At this time, the facility of memory was highly prized, but even then it was seen as just short of miraculous when:

> Some malicious person removed the book with which it was his habit to conduct the church service. Sidonius was so well versed in the ritual that he took them through the whole service of the festival without pausing for a moment. This was a source of wonder to everyone present and they had the impression that it must be an angel speaking rather than a man. I have described this in more detail in the preface of the book which I wrote about the Masses composed by Sidonius.[39]

It would appear that it was still not unknown for Bishops to compose, probably even extempore if the Bishop was skilful enough, the collects and preface, though it seems that these 'propers' (that is, prayers and readings appropriate to the day or particular celebration) were more usually prescribed at this date. The *Missale Gothicum* (Vat. *Reg. lat.* 493), copied in Burgundy, probably at Autun, just more than a century after Gregory completed his *History of the Franks* in 594, has a set of propers including *Prefatio, Collectio, Collectio post Nomina, Collectio ad Pacem, Immolatio, Post Secreta, Ante Orationem Dominicam*, and *Post Orationem Dominicam.*[40] If this complexity reflects an earlier complexity from the time of Sidonius, then the Bishop either had an amazing eloquence to be able to extemporize, or an even more remarkable memory, since these propers were specific to the day, and so used only once a year.[41]

It was expected that the bishop would bring his flock in every way into the divine presence; an extreme example was St Salvius, who, according to Gregory, died and went to heaven, only to return to his earthly body as he was being carried to his grave. He then revealed the glories of heaven to his people. While this was not something all bishops were able to mediate directly to their flock, they were able to integrate them with the worship of heaven especially in the liturgy, as did Bishop Sidonius, and in its architectural setting, as did his predecessor Bishop Namatius, who built the Cathedral of Clermont-Ferrand where the number of windows meant that 'one is conscious of the fear of God and of a great brightness, and those at prayer are often aware of a

---

38 Translated in Dix (1945), p. 381.
39 HF II.22; the book about the masses by Sidonius has unfortunately been lost.
40 Whitaker (2003), p. 258; for the structure of the mass, see Hen (1995), pp. 67–70.
41 For the form of the Gallican Mass, see Jungmann (1959), pp. 35–7.

most sweet and aromatic odour which is being wafted towards them'.[42] This is also reflected in the language and form of the Gallican liturgy; although no complete manuscript texts of the liturgy itself survive from this early date, contemporary with St Martin in the fourth or even Gregory in the sixth century,[43] Gregory mentions the bishop singing the canticle, the *Benedictus*,[44] with its emphasis on the people, and implying that they were the new Israel. Similarly, the *Bobbio Missal* (a Gallican missal which already integrated Roman material) from *c.* 700, in one of the collects for baptism, reads: 'O God who restores that which is lost and preserves that which is restored, God who has ordained that the reproach of Gentile birth shall be taken away by the sign of your Name, so that men may be accounted worthy to approach the fount of baptism …'.[45] Manuscripts of the late seventh or early eighth century include the *Benedictus* ('Blessed be the Lord God of Israel: for he hath visited and redeemed his people') or the *Benedicite* ('O all ye works of the Lord, bless ye the Lord') before the Gospel.[46] The people seem to have been very active in the liturgy, and were provided with many responses. The rite varied from place to place, and abounded in dedicated propers. The celebration was dramatic, colourful, long, elaborate and sensuous, with quantities of incense. The architecture, like that of Namatius' cathedral at Clermont, was expected not just to provide the setting for the drama, but to heighten it, and like Gregory's frescoes in his cathedral at Tours, to enhance the colourful ceremonial. Just as the people were more active, so was the deacon, who still conducted a good deal of the worship of the people and their movement within the space.

After the *Benedictus*, which was original to the Gallican rite, came the Gospel procession with candles and incense, and the deacon sang the Gospel, which was followed by a Latin translation of the Greek *Trisagion*. Then came a sermon, followed by a deacon's litany which was a close translation from the Eastern rite and was interspersed by the congregational response *precamur te Domine, miserere*, a paraphrase of the *Kyries*. At a later date, the Great Entrance was imported from the Eastern rite in some places (perhaps via Spain, see page 139ff.), where it seems also to have effected the architectural arrangement with the introduction of a sacristy on either side of the apse after the manner of the Eastern *prothesis* and *diaconicon*. This arrangement was to be found at the cathedral at Clermont in the middle of the fifth century, as described by Gregory:

> It has a rounded apse at the end, and two wings of elegant design on either side. The whole building is constructed in the shape of a cross. It has forty-two windows, seventy columns and eight doorways. In it one is conscious of the fear of God and of a great brightness, and those at prayer are often aware of a most sweet and aromatic odour which is being wafted to them. Round the sanctuary it has walls which are decorated with mosaic work made of many varieties of marble. When the building had been finished for a dozen years, the saintly Bishop sent priests to Bologna, the city in Italy to procure for him the relics of Saint Agricola and Saint Vitalis, who, as I have shown, were assuredly crucified in the name of Christ our Lord.[47]

---

42   The quotation is from *HF* II.14; for the story of St Salvius, see *HF* VII.1, and Van Dam (1985), pp. 62–3.

43   See the helpful summary of extant later manuscripts in Hen (1995), pp. 44–53.

44   *HF* VIII.6.

45   Whitaker (2003), p. 269.

46   Maxwell (1945), pp. 49–50.

47   *HF* II.16; and see Lavedan (1956), p. 83, for his interpretation of the architectural arrangement.

The Cult of Relics

In the middle of the sixth century, there was also a strong connection with Constantinople, and liturgical practice in Gaul shared some characteristics with the East, especially elaboration and variability, particularly of 'propers'. St Radegund, Queen of Lothar I sent to the Eastern emperor for relics for her nunnery, and Justin II and the Empress Sophia gave a relic of the True Cross to her envoys. This is still in the nunnery, in a small gold triptych (whose wings have been lost) just over 2 inches square which is possibly the original Byzantine reliquary.[48] Relics were extremely powerful diplomatic gifts, or appropriate relics could be very costly, perhaps the reason that it took twelve years before Saint Namatius could provide relics for the Cathedral at Clermont. When Gregory succeeded to the See of Tours in 573, the cathedral had been destroyed by fire, and Gregory had completely rebuilt it by 590: 'I rebuilt it, bigger and higher than before, and in the seventeenth year of my episcopate I re-dedicated it.' The culmination of his *History of the Franks*, completed in 594, is the enumeration of his building projects and furnishing them with a wealth of relics. The relics of the Legion reputedly martyred because, as Christians, they refused to take part in pagan sacrifice were found by Gregory in the Church of St Martin, and:

> As I was examining the relics with great care, the church sacristan said to me: 'there is a stone here with a lid on it. I don't know what it contains. ... He fetched the stone and I, of course, carefully opened it. Inside I found a silver reliquary which contained not only the relics of those who had actually seen the Holy Legion but also the remains of many saints, martyrs and holy men. I took charge of it, and at the same time I also took a number of other hollowed-out stones in which had been preserved the relics of other holy apostles and martyrs. I was delighted with this gift sent by God. In my gratitude to Him I kept a number of vigils and said Masses. Then I placed in the cathedral all that I had found, except that I put the relics of the martyrs Saint Cosmas and Saint Damian in Saint Martin's cell, which adjoins the cathedral.

In the whole diplomatic etiquette of giving and receiving gifts of the time, Gregory was indebted to God for the gift of these many relics, which were so powerful and so valuable as to be worth encasing in gold and silver, and which would in turn attract the gifts of kings and pilgrims. Gregory's debt was to be paid liturgically and architecturally – in vigils and masses, and buildings as reliquaries-writ-large to house the holy objects. Gregory concluded the narrative of his *History* just before beginning the epilogue:

> I found the walls of Saint Martin's church damaged by fire. I ordered my workmen to use all their skill to paint and decorate them, until they were as bright as they had previously been. I had a baptistery built adjacent to the church, and there I placed the relics of Saint John and Saint Sergius the martyr. In the old baptistery I put the relics of Saint Benignus the martyr. In many other places in Tours and its immediate neighbourhood I dedicated churches and oratories, and these I enriched with relics of the saints. It would be too long to give you a complete list.[49]

The cycle of frescoes in Gregory's Church of St Martin 'stressed the charitable behaviour and militant antipaganism of Martin', and over the sanctuary arch was written: 'How awesome is this place! This is none other than the house of God, and this is the gate of heaven.'[50] The liturgy joined in the worship of heaven, of 'angels and archangels and the whole company of heaven' (some of

---

48 *HF* IX.40; Martin Conway, 'St Radegund's Reliquary at Poitiers', *Antiquaries Journal* (1923), pp. 1–12; also illustrated in Lasko (1971), p. 74.

49 *HF* X.31.

50 Van Dam (1985), p. 137; Genesis 28:17, in McManners (1990), p. 80.

whom were physically present in the saintly relics) singing the *Sanctus*, and the architecture placed them physically on its threshold.

The cult and shrine of St Martin were the definitive Gallican answer in practice to the priest Vigilantius, at the foot of the Pyrenees in Gaul, who criticized the veneration of relics, and this physical answer was coextensive with the written answer earlier in the fifth century by Jerome from Bethlehem. The cult of St Saturninus had recently been expanded in Toulouse, and Vigilantius, who had just returned from a pilgrimage to the Holy Land, was responding to this, by now growing, practice in Gaul: 'Most significantly, Jerome now represented a version of Christianity that located its meaning and authority in specific places, tangible objects, regulated ceremonies, and a number of holy books. Vigilantius had questioned all these assumptions about the authority of Christianity.'[51] Jerome's position has profound consequences for the form and performance of the liturgy and the structure, function, and even veneration of its architectural locus. Consequently, the funeral of Bishop Martin was described by his biographer Sulpicius in terms of an imperial triumphal entry. The entry was, of course, both into the heavenly Kingdom and to the place of his permanent presence, his shrine, where his authority and power would be always available for the service of his people, in death as the patron saint, as it had been in life as their bishop.

Whether or not Gregory was exaggerating the number of his works, besides the rebuilding of the Church of St Martin, for the sake of rhetoric, he was clearly a prodigious builder, and we do know that he consecrated other churches at Petit-Pressigny and Pernay (both Indre et Loire), both with relics of his uncle St Nicetus,[52] yet nothing remains of these buildings, and moreover, there is precious little hard archaeological evidence giving us insights into the detail of Gallo-Roman ecclesiastical architecture. The only excavated church cited by Pierre Lavedan is Saint-Bertrand-de-Comminges, dated by him to the fourth century. There was an enormous narthex, a nave and a five-aisled apse. Fragments indicate that the interior was plastered and painted with white flowers on a red ground. Probably, the baptistery of Marseilles is also from late that century. Of fifth- and sixth-century work, there are the other baptisteries of Provence: Fréjus, Aix, Riez, Vénasque, Mélas and Valence. Of Merovingian work, there are fragments at Saint-Pierre in Vienne and the Cathedral of Vaison.[53]

The Merovingian Baptistery

As so often, the dating of these early baptisteries is disputed. The Baptistery of Saint-Jean, Poitiers, with its very ancient font, may date in part to the late fourth, but more likely the fifth to seventh centuries (see Figures 4.4 and 4.5). At the Council of Auxerre in 578, Canon 18 forbade baptism except at the Easter service, apart from the dying and infirm, but Canon 3 of the second Council of Macon of 585 makes it clear that baptism continued to occur popularly on saints' days, and all were enjoined to return to the custom of Easter baptism.[54] This gives an indication of the frequency of use for the baptistery (which was supposed to be shut during Lent), and by looking at the order in the *Missale Gothicum*, we can get a picture of how the building was used, perhaps in the sixth, but more certainly by the end of the seventh century.

Entry into the Baptistery of Saint-Jean, Poitiers is from the west into a half-octagon separated from the main baptistery by a pair of columns. It was presumably here in this first chamber where the vigil was kept, a candle was lit and a series of prayers said; when the service of baptism began,

---

51 Van Dam (1985), p. 138.
52 Crook (2000), p. 49.
53 See Lavedan (1956), pp. 82–4.
54 Whitaker (2003), p. 257.

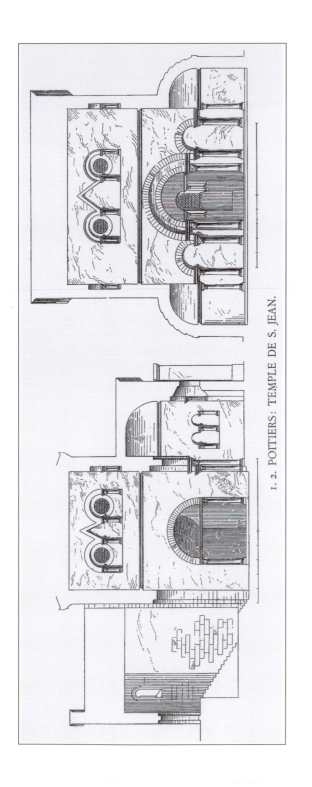

1. 2. POITIERS: TEMPLE DE S. JEAN.

Figure 4.4   Baptistery of St Jean, Poitiers, sections; from Dehio and von Bezold (1887–1901), vol. I, pl. 84, no. 2; (1736b.1&2) Bodleian Library, University of Oxford.

Figure 4.5   Baptistery of St Jean, Poitiers, view from the northeast; courtesy Allan T. Kohl/
              Art Images for College Teaching (AICT).

opening collects were said, one for the candidates, next a prayer admonishing the candidates to
'Receive the sign of Christ: accept the words of God: receive the light of the Word of God: for
this day Christ confesses you to be his own. Through Jesus Christ our Lord.' The words of this
collect all but demand actions, especially in a liturgy known to be as extravagant as the Gallican:
signing with the sign of the cross; presentation of a Bible, and presentation of a lighted candle. The
next collect would have the officiant sign the candidate: 'your eyes to see the clearness of God;
your ears to hear the voice of the Lord; your nose to savour the sweetness of Christ; your mouth
to confess the Father, the Son, and the Holy Spirit; your heart to believe the holy and undivided
Trinity ...'. The Trinitarian formula was very important in the fight against Arianism.

   Proceeding through to the second chamber, there is a very ancient font in the middle, an apse
on the north and south walls to either side, and a small sanctuary in the eastern apse. The font was
blessed, then the water, and the Holy Spirit was invoked to sanctify the water; then the sign of the
cross was made with chrism to exorcize the water. The officiant breathed three times on the water,
then the chrism was poured in, making the sign of the Cross. This was followed by baptism in the
threefold name and anointing with chrism. The new Christians now had their feet washed, and a
white robe was placed on them. The three elements of this part of the rite, chrism, footwashing and
white robe, may be the key to the two side absidioles and the apse, or the rite may have continued
straight on to the first mass of Easter after two more concluding collects. If so, the footwashing may
have taken place at the font, turning then to the apse, where mass was celebrated with references to
baptism in both the Preface and *Immolatio*:

It is meet and right, fitting and right, that here and in all places we should thank you, should sing your praises and offer sacrifices and confess your mercies, O Lord holy, Father Almighty, everlasting God ... . For this is the night which has knowledge of the saving sacraments, the night in which you offer pardon to sinners, make new men from old, from worn out old men restore full grown infants whom you bring from the sacred font renewed unto a new creature. On this night your people are new born and brought forth unto eternal day, the halls of the kingdom of heaven, by your blessed ordinance human conversation is changed to divine ... the night in which Adam was set free, the night in which the piece of *silver which had been lost was found* [Luke 15:8], the night in which the *lost sheep was carried on the shoulders of the Good Shepherd* [Luke 15:5], the night in which the devil slept and Christ the *Sun of Righteousness* [Mal. 4:15] arose, when the bonds of hell were burst and its bars broken, and *many bodies of the saints broke out from their tombs and entered the holy city* [Matt. 27:52]. ... For you Almighty God, the multitude of heavenly beings and the innumerable choir of angels unceasingly do praise, saying, Holy ... .[55]

The liturgy is very visual, and presents a potential decorative programme in itself for its own architectural setting – elements of which have already been noted in other baptisteries, such as Adam, the Good Shepherd, the Sun of Righteousness may be an interpretation for the problematical 'Christ-Helios' in the crypt of St Peter's, Rome, and the resurrection of the saints is a very common theme. The extant frescoes at the Baptistery of Saint-Jean, Poitiers are later additions, but much of the fabric is consistent with an early date, despite Romanesque changes and much restoration.

Hypogea *and Funerary Crypts*

Another important liturgical space in Poitiers is the Hypogeum of Dunes. A significant number of relics were installed at its consecration, and this has given rise to a dispute as to whether this was a place of pilgrimage or a funerary chapel. Camille de la Croix, who excavated the monument in the 1880s, maintained that it was a martyrium, but Crook believes, on the basis of inscriptions, that it was for burial *ad sanctum*, that is, in a place near saints or their relics. Besides the coffins that crowd the space, there are up to 37 burials in a cluster around the *hypogeum*.[56] Inside, there is too little room for regular access by pilgrims, but as a *cella memoriae*, it has an altar and is fully equipped for worship, including what must have been intimate memorial masses. An inscription identifies it as the tomb of Abbot Mellebaude, and archaeological details such as the intertwined plant and animal motifs of the carving place the work in the late seventh or early eighth century. One of the carved sarcophagus lids has labelled images of the Evangelists Matthew and John (the eagle), the Archangels Raphael and Raguel, and below, the names Laurentius, Varigatus, Hilary and Martin. It may be that there was another matching slab with Mark and Luke, Michael and Gabriel. These invocations of saints who were biblical, Roman and local, drew on their power for help and support in death, much as relics functioned for the living.

The example of the Church of Saint-Martial in Limoges will serve to illustrate typical developments at a site where a shrine church was built over a *hypogeum*, or funerary crypt.[57] St Martial was the Apostle of Aquitaine, one of the 'Seven Bishops' of the mid-third century, and the first Bishop of Limoges. He was buried in a vaulted *crypta* cut into the soft tufa stone in an extramural Gallo-Roman cemetery. This was excavated in 1960 and 1962, just to the north of the Romanesque basilica. It was originally the shrine of St Valerie, and was created by Martial. Probably near the turn of the fourth century, it was enlarged to accommodate St Martial and his two priests in stone sarcophagi in a corner, which is how it was seen by Gregory. In the eighth century, the relics were moved to the church above, and the funerary chapel was reordered as a church.

---

55   Translated in *ibid.*, pp. 262–3.
56   Crook (2000), p. 61.
57   The subject of funerary chapels is very extensively treated in *ibid.*, pp. 51ff.

Other examples attributed to the fourth century include Saint-Maximin-la-Sainte-Baume in Provence, reputed to be the tomb of Mary Magdalen. It does contain four Gallo-Roman sarcophagi, though these may have been introduced later. A similarly mysterious burial is found in St Victor's Church in Marseilles. Victor was a Roman soldier who was martyred in 303, but a coin deliberately inserted to the sealing-mortar of one of the two tombs is a newly minted coin of the Emperor Decius dating to 249–50. Part of the rather spacious chapel can be dated to the fifth century by the mural decoration, so the Christian cult may have begun then, at the foundation of the Monastery of St Victor *c.* 420. It was here that Bishop Theodore took up residence during a great plague, 'giving up all his time to prayers and vigils'.[58]

Other crypts are thought to be originally fourth-century or to be the very places of which Gregory wrote, including the tomb of St Maximinus at Trier, and the two burials below Saint-Seurin, Bordeaux. Eric Fernie supports the idea that the crypts at Déols were as seen by Gregory, but Crook believes them to have been rebuilt in the late tenth century.[59] The fact remains that there is enough consistency across the range of examples and a high enough level of literary and archaeological evidence to give a relatively secure picture of what they were like, their range of uses (including the liturgical), and their development, including the fact that there was a period from the end of the late sixth century when crypts ceased to be as important in the cult of saints, when the relics were moved into the church above, as seen in the example of Saint-Martial, Limoges.

A particularly important example is a mausoleum in an ancient cemetery on a hill about two kilometres outside Augustodunum, modern Autun. The city may have had one of the most ancient Christian communities in Gaul. Saint-Symphorian was said to have been martyred here *c.* 180, and Gregory records that Eufronius built the Church of St Symphorian before being elected bishop of the city.[60] Certainly Bishop Reticius of Autun, who is mentioned by both Jerome and Augustine, was one of three Gallic bishops called to the Council of 313 by Constantine. Excavations have uncovered what appears to be the first funerary basilica at Autun, which numismatic evidence proves must have existed by the middle of the fourth century at the latest.[61]

These funerary basilicas were the early nodes in the matrix of holy people and holy sites that was being spread across Merovingian Gaul and becoming the objective of pilgrimage and the source of power and wealth for many religious houses. Liturgy is very like religious drama, in that its existence as text, like the dramatic text, is vestigial at best. It only comes into full-blooded existence when enacted and embodied. The presentation of the liturgy (or a play) is interpreted through its dramatic presentation, its vestments (or costume), and the arrangement of its architectural setting (props, stagecraft and the theatre itself). The cosmic drama, enacted liturgically through the offices, the sacraments, the lectionary, the calendar, has become a Christian discourse embedded locally in the architecture, but by the end of the Merovingian dynasty it also spread as a mantle over the whole geography of Gaul.

---

58 *HF* IX.22.
59 Crook (2000), pp. 60–61.
60 *HF* II.15.
61 Young (2001), p. 171.

CHAPTER 5

Carolingian Architecture and Liturgical Reform

Royal Ritual and Court Architecture

The Royal Abbey of Saint-Denis

The Royal Abbey of Saint-Denis, like so many others mentioned in Gregory of Tours' *History of the Franks*, began as a funerary chapel in a Gallo-Roman cemetery. Gregory makes only oblique references to the abbey, not because it was lacking in interest, on the contrary, because under royal patronage and as the burial place of Merovingian royalty from the sixth century,[1] it was becoming a serious rival to his own church and shrine of St Martin. The growth of Saint-Denis is of great importance to both the history of architecture and the liturgy. St Denis, or Dionysius, was one of the missionary bishops Gregory refers to as the 'Seven Bishops'. He became the first Bishop of Paris, and was martyred in the middle of the third century. Gregory's occasional references to the Church of Saint-Denis are very negative, including an oath sworn over the altar and grave of the saint that resulted in swords drawn at the very tomb of the saint and the church being spattered with blood. The men were nobles at the court of King Chilperic, an evil tyrant, according to Gregory.[2] This particular contribution to the reputation of the patron, Chilperic, was surely intended to reflect on the reputation of the shrine, which was already rising in status relative to Saint-Martin in Tours.

Research suggests that after St Denis was buried in 251 in the pre-existing Gallo-Roman cemetery, the huge Gallo-Roman decorated stones uncovered on the site had been reused in the church of 475; this was the church of which Gregory wrote. Others maintain that those stones had formed part of an early mausoleum built over his grave.[3] Whichever is true, its origins conform to a familiar pattern. The church of 475 was used for services (which were temporarily suspended in the aftermath of the bloody brawl), but it would appear from the text to have been very small. The tradition, first documented in the ninth-century *Gesta Dagoberti*, attributes a very considerable rebuilding to Dagobert I, doubling its size in the 630s. Whether Dagobert provided these foundations and a very much larger building, or a 'foundation' in terms of lands and wealth, is a moot point. At the very least he had the existing building lavishly decorated. As a result of Crosby's excavations at the site and close consideration of the documentary evidence, he is very clear that:

> No documents of the seventh or eighth centuries refer to Dagobert's work as more than a sumptuous embellishment of the church dedicated to Saint Denis, and no text before 836 mentions any rebuilding by Dagobert. The fact that the passage in the *Gesta Dagoberti* referring to Dagobert's 'complete construction' is clearly a reworking of the charter of Clovis II, 654, and it interpolates what was not present in the earlier

---

1 Romero (1992), p. 15; *HF* V.34; Vieillard-Troiekouroff (1976), pp. 262–5.
2 *HF* V.32.
3 Crosby (1987) is of the former, Perin (1991) is of the latter view; these are discussed in Blum (1992), pp. 5–6.

document, would indicate that the whole tradition was invented by the ninth-century monks. Furthermore the explicit reference in such texts as the *Chronica Fredegarii* to a rich decoration of the church, and to nothing more, provides compelling arguments for stating that there was no rebuilding of the church at St-Denis from the end of the fifth to the middle of the eighth century. In other words Saint Genevieve's church protected the relics of Saint Denis for about three hundred years; and Dagobert I was responsible not for an entirely new building, but only for the adornment of the already existing shrine.[4]

Whatever the extent of Dagobert's work at Saint-Denis, by the time he finished, it was an impressive and rich interior with silver revetment in the apse, cloth of gold on the walls of the nave, and over the tomb of St Denis, a marble baldachin decorated with gold and gems.

There was a legend to the effect that on the eve of the consecration of this church, all had left except a leper who had tucked himself away. During the night he saw a great light, with Christ himself in the midst of the Apostles, accompanied by St Denis as well. The Saviour was dressed in pontifical robes, and together they celebrated the liturgy of consecration. He told the leper to inform the king what had happened, and as proof, he released the leper from his diseased skin and flung it against the wall. The relic remained in the abbey for centuries as proof of its very special status.[5] When King Dagobert I was alive, he gave rich endowments to the abbey, and when he died in 639, he was buried there. Almost nothing of this structure remains above ground apart from three capitals which were deliberately reused in the twelfth-century rebuilding by Abbot Suger.

Around the year 754, Pepin the Short was anointed a second time at Saint-Denis by Pope Stephen II[6] who had journeyed across the Alps during the winter of 753 to solicit the King's aid against the Lombards (see above, page 88). It was probably on his return from the campaign against the Lombard threat that Pepin began rebuilding the church to celebrate his victory.

The method of king-making amongst the Merovingian Franks is unknown, and until the conversion of Clovis, it took place in a pagan and warrior-class context. By the late seventh and early eighth centuries, the Merovingian kings had been reduced by a series of royal minorities and two assassinations to mere figureheads. Power resided with Charles Martel, the 'Mayor of the Palace' from 717. He was buried at Saint-Denis. Pepin was Charles's son, and along with his brother, succeeded to power in 741; five years later, his brother retired to a monastery. Pepin consulted the Frankish nobles in 750, and having secured their support, he sent an embassy, including Abbot Fuldrad of Saint-Denis, to Pope Zacharius to get his approval to remove the powerless Merovingian King Childeric III and assume the title himself.

Royal Ritual

With the pope's approval, the king-making ritual took place at Soissons, where he was anointed with holy oil by St Boniface and the Frankish bishops before enthronement. The anointing was an innovation. The pope, in giving his approval and later re-anointing Pepin at Saint-Denis[7] on 28 July 754 (a post-baptismal anointing which Pepin would not have received according to the Gallican rite), he also gained access to Pepin's military power. It was perhaps in token of this that

---

4   Crosby (1942), p. 67; see also Romero (1992), pp. 29–30; despite this very clear position, Blum (1992), for instance, footnotes Crosby (1942), pp. 29–50 and plan, pl. 3, when she writes: 'Excavations indicate that it was hardly more than a chapel. Then, under the patronage of Dagobert I, the chapel built on the urging of Ste. Geneviève was enlarged to the east and west to more than double the original size' (p. 6); Clark (1995), p. 98, also refers to the 'nave of Dagobert', though his real concern is the later church, and this may have been a kind of shorthand.

5   See Crosby (1942), p. 43.

6   Also referred to as Stephen III, since 'Stephen II' died only four days after his election.

7   *Clausule de unctione Pippini*, translated in Dutton (2004), p. 13.

he invested him and his sons with the title of Patrician of the Romans.[8] The linking of royal and baptismal anointing affirmed the notion of the Franks as a 'chosen race, a royal priesthood', the new Israel. Liturgical ceremonial affirmed their biblical self-understanding, but it also changed things, gave legitimacy, transformed reality. By anointing Pepin's young sons, Charles and Carloman, at the same time, first by way of confirmation, then as kings, the pope inaugurated a new dynasty, the Carolingians, enjoining the Franks 'on pain of interdict and excommunication, never to presume in future to elect a king begotten by any men other than those whom the bounty of God has seen fit to raise up and has decided to confirm and consecrate by the intercession of the holy apostles through the hands of their vicar, the most blessed pontiff'.[9] According to Crosby, it was under their rule that the Abbey of Saint-Denis was enlarged, which of course is a direct reflection of their political ambitions at least from the time of Charles Martel. Their association with Saint-Denis was an essential sign of the legitimacy of their rule.[10]

The Lombards continued to pose a very considerable threat to Rome, and they failed to return lands to the pope as agreed with Pepin, so Charles (Charlemagne) led a Frankish army against them in 773. At Easter 774, he made a ceremonial entry, an *adventus*, into Rome to celebrate the feast at St Peter's. The pope's officials met him thirty miles from Rome with the papal standard. A mile from the gates of the city, he was met by the army and the papal crosses, and in their honour the king dismounted from his horse and walked to the steps of St Peter's. He kissed each of the steps as he mounted to meet Pope Hadrian at the doors of the propylaeum. Then, in imitation of the custom in Constantinople, they exchanged the kiss of peace and entered hand in hand. *Benedictus qui venit* was sung as they processed down the nave.[11] It was an imperial entry, but it would be another quarter of a century before he received the title of Emperor in the same basilica. Not surprisingly, this radical step was accomplished by an enhanced rite:

> Pope Hadrian (772–95) seems to have added yet another ritual to the inauguration process for Frankish kings: the first such occasion on which a coronation is mentioned is 781 – the consecrations at Rome of Charlemagne's son Carloman as king of the acquired realm of Italy, and of his little brother Louis as king of Aquitaine. The pope may well have borrowed the idea of coronation from Byzantium where it was the centrepiece of the imperial inauguration. Hence in 800, the pope crowned Charlemagne emperor, in imitation of Byzantine ritual. But whereas Byzantine ritual featured coronation only, and not anointing, in the West the popes stressed a linkage between the two. In 816 a pope again crossed the Alps to anoint and crown as emperor Charlemagne's son, Louis the Pious who had succeeded his father two years before. The idea of coronation had long since been invested with Christian connotations. In the New Testament, a heavenly crown was held out as the reward of faith for all Christians. In the liturgies of the early church, baptismal anointing was presented as a symbolic coronation, and the whole initiation rite as a kind of king-making, complete with acclamations to the newly-raised. The linking of anointing with coronation was thus in itself not really a papal innovation. The application of both to a Frankish king was. And in the ninth century, it was picked up by Frankish clergy themselves.[12]

---

8   Duckett (1951), p. 57; Crosby (1942), p.76, gives the precise date.

9   See the *Clausule de unctione Pippini*, translated in Dutton (2004), pp. 13–14, and Nelson (1987), p. 152.

10   Jackson (1995), pp. 23–4, makes inferences regarding liturgical actions and texts used at the ceremonies for Pepin, Carloman and Charles, using texts from the sacramentary of Angoulême (*c.* 800) and the *Clausula de unctione Pipini regis*, Saint-Denis, 767.

11   Duckett (1951), pp. 72–73.

12   See Nelson (1987), pp. 142–3, where 'Carolingian Royal Ritual' is discussed in detail. See Thegan's *Life of Louis*, section 17, in Dutton (2004), p. 164.

Saint-Denis Rebuilt

On 24 February 775, Charlemagne attended the dedication of the newly rebuilt Abbey Church of Saint-Denis, the first of all truly Carolingian buildings. The size of the community required a large monastic choir, and with a steadily growing number of pilgrims to the shrine of St Denis, special architectural provision was necessary for access to and security of the relics. Building had probably been started by Pepin, who encouraged the use of the Roman liturgy, though it was not until the turn of the ninth century that a degree of uniformity was achieved by Charlemagne. Archaeology has provided mounting evidence that this shift to a more standardized liturgical use had a profound effect on the architecture of Carolingian churches. Crosby notes of Saint-Denis at this time that: 'the eastern end of the church was a single apse that projected about six meters beyond the walls of the transept. … This feature [the apse] identifies the edifice as belonging to the series of churches built according to the "Roman custom". And it should immediately be noted that Saint-Denis was the first church of this type to be built north of the Alps.'[13] Furthermore, the plan of the crypt, with two curved passages, strongly suggests an annular crypt (or ring-crypt) with a *confessio* behind and below the high altar. Access to the crypt was by stairs on either side of the altar. This arrangement is very similar to the earlier examples in Rome, San Pancrazio (625–38), San Crisogono (731–41), and of course, also closely related to the prototype, St Peter's, as remodelled under Gregory the Great, though there the *confessio* is in front of the altar.[14] It would appear that Abbot Fuldrad, in charge of the rebuilding at Saint-Denis, had been very observant on his visit to the pope on behalf of Pepin. Two examples of ring-crypts, at Saint-Luzius, Chur, and Saint-Maurice d'Agaune in present-day Switzerland, have been identified as possibly even earlier than that at Saint-Denis, but these too have been associated with growing contact between Pepin and the pope, who went through Saint-Maurice on his way to see Pepin in 753/54.

Bishop Chrodegang of Metz was another member of the pope's Frankish escort that winter. Together they stayed at the Abbey of Romainmôtier, where there is a remarkable survival from that period – a very beautiful *ambo* on a platform of two steps with stairs on either side. Chrodegang would repeat the form and style of that *ambo* in his future building projects at Metz.

The work begun at Saint-Denis by Pepin was a Roman type of aisled basilica. Charlemagne had his father, Pepin, buried in a western apse that was flanked by two towers – a 'westwork' of experimental form. Just as Pepin had begun the rebuilding of Saint-Denis on a Roman model which was completed by Charlemagne with the vigorously experimental westwork, so the work of ridding the pope of the Lombardic threat was also begun by Pepin and completed by Charlemagne. By the time of the election of Leo III as Pope in 795, the alliance between pope and King of the Franks was such that Charlemagne wrote to him saying:

> My duty is by Divine aid to defend everywhere with armed might the Church of Christ from inroads of pagans and from ravaging of infidels without; from within to fortify it by the learning of the Catholic Faith. It is your part, holy Father, to support our fighting by hands raised to God as those of Moses, so that, through your intercession and the guidance and the gift of God, Christian people may ever have victory over his enemies, and the Name of our Lord Jesus Christ be glorified throughout the world.[15]

Military victory over pagan Saxons and Avars was sealed symbolically by the baptism of the vanquished, and in conquered Saxony, churches were built to establish religion and order. Liturgy and architecture were being used as military and political instruments.

---

13 Crosby (1942), p. 97.
14 Crook (2000), pp. 80–85.
15 Translated in Duckett (1951), p. 87.

Charlemagne expected the same work from his own clergy, who were either with him on campaign or at home at court, as he expected from the pope:

> So we have held three days of solemn litany, beseeching the Lord for peace and health and safe return. Our priests prescribed a fast during this time from wine and meat; but those who needed wine through sickness or advanced years were allowed it on payment of one solidus a day, if they could afford it – if not, of one denarius. Everyone was bidden to give alms according to his goodwill and means. Each priest, unless he was sick, said a special Mass; each one who knew his psalter well enough chanted fifty psalms; and they all walked barefoot in procession.
>
> Now I should like you to consult the clergy at home for the same ritual there.[16]

Charlemagne wrote this letter in 791 to his queen, Fastrada, whose verse epitaph was written three years later by Theodulf, court poet, and later appointed Bishop of Orléans.

In his drive for education and reform, Charlemagne saw himself as a new Josiah, the Old Testament king who rebuilt the Temple of Jerusalem and reformed its worship.[17] In 781 Charlemagne recruited Alcuin of York to establish a school and library at Aachen. Charlemagne had already in 774 received a collection of books of Roman canon law as a gift from Pope Hadrian and with these he stepped up the reform of the Frankish Church and the Romanization of the Gallican rite, begun by his father.

Charlemagne's son, Louis the Pious, was deposed in 833, and when restored, he was crowned and reinvested in Pepin's Saint-Denis by Frankish bishops following the innovative procedures established by the pope at Louis's coronation in 816. Saint-Denis made itself indispensable to the legitimacy of the Royal line. When Abbot Suger rebuilt Saint-Denis again in the twelfth century, the royal Merovingian and Carolingian associations were so important that despite the radical nature of the rebuild, they governed the whole approach: the integration of the new with the old. The integration of different periods of architectural elements was a sign for the historical continuity reaching back from Capetians through Carolingians and Merovingians to the Patron Saint of the monarchy. As the embodiment of this historic continuity, the prestige and fortunes of the Abbey itself were also greatly enhanced.

> Thus, walking around the new crypt ambulatory at Saint-Denis, the twelfth-century viewer would have been able to see both the authentic Merovingian pieces as well as constant variations on them along the polygonal piers separating the crypt chapels. ...
>
> In the centre west bay the capitals should be read within the context of the special historicizing character of that bay. The unusual octagonal shape of the bay, resulting from the size and plan of the massive piers alternating with arched openings, was recognized by Crosby, but he did not relate it to its obvious predecessor, the polygonal bay in the westwork, thought in the twelfth century to have been constructed by Charlemagne around the burial site of Pepin. That the capitals were copied after Merovingian originals in the eighth-century nave would have confirmed for the viewer the association of the new work with its historical predecessor. In fact, this bay was part of an iconographic sequence that began with the new façade with its twin towers and crenellations, at once triumphal arch, city gate and fortress church: the visitor passed through the portals, with their oft-cited royal associations, into the westwork evoking Pepin and Charlemagne and hence into the nave of Dagobert. The experience became a royal journey back in time to the high altar above the original burial place of Denis.
>
> ... What is embodied in the physical structure of the building, the ultimate synthesis of past and present, culminated in the translation of the holy bodies, in 'the venerable shrines executed under King Dagobert', from their original burial place in the crypt up to the new *chevet*. Religious past and secular

---

16 Translated in *ibid.*, p. 97.

17 McKitterick (1977), pp. 2–3.

present were conjoined as Louis VII, the 'Most Serene King of the Franks', carried (devoutly and nobly, according to Suger) the *châsse* of Saint-Denis to its new place in the chevet.[18]

What is so beautifully brought out in this passage is how three-dimensional physical architecture manifests the same values as, and is completed in, the temporal movement of the ceremonial of the liturgy, in which not only religious, but also social and political relationships, and power, were displayed, enacted and embodied.

The Palatine Chapel at Aachen

During the 790s, Charlemagne's imperial ambitions were clearly shown by the palace chapel being built for him by Odo of Metz at Aachen (Figure 5.1). The main relic to be installed here was the cloak of St Martin.[19] Pope Hadrian permitted Charlemagne to remove columns and marble from the palace at Ravenna, the residence of the last Emperor of the Romans. These columns and the marble were reused to produce a magnificent interior with deep historical resonances. The ground-floor piers were faced with polychrome marble revetment and porphyry. The segmental vault was covered in a gleaming gold mosaic showing the 24 elders of the Apocalypse and the Lord enthroned, originally probably the Lamb.[20] The Apocalyptic iconographic programme and, it has also been suggested, the measurements of the building present it as the Heavenly Jerusalem, and the sovereign as 'a little lower than the angels'. The mosaic programme continued in the ambulatory and galleries.

The plan was modelled on San Vitale in Ravenna, built by Justinian I in the sixth century, whose liturgically based mosaics are the last known major imperial works of art before iconoclasm (see Figure 5.2). But there are also echoes of the Rotunda over the Holy Sepulchre, the classical mausoleum, and its lineal descendant, the Christian baptistery, Constantine's Golden Octagon at Antioch, SS. Sergius and Bacchus, and the imperial throne-room in Constantinople – the Chrysotriklinos. Charlemagne's throne, said to be modelled on Solomon's throne for the man known in the intimacy of the court as 'King David',[21] was indeed elevated in the western gallery opposite the altar of the Saviour below the mosaic of the Lamb, with a view of the altars of the Virgin and of St Peter below. This position gave him a clear view of the liturgy, but enthroned, he was invisible to the rest of the chapel. The liturgy was the focus of the architecture, but visible or invisible, you could hardly be unaware of the presence of the imperial throne.

Even on the exterior, the imperial bay is marked by the western tower flanked by stair towers giving access to the galleries for the Emperor and his court. On the entrance façade at gallery level was a great concave niche where, some believe, the ruler could appear to the assembled crowds in the atrium below, from which point the niche was strongly reminiscent of the Palace of the Exarchs in Ravenna. At this point it is worth noting the *palatium* mosaic in S. Apollinare Nuovo in Ravenna, which originally showed a figure under each arch of the *palatium*, the one in the middle most likely intended to be Theodoric 'appearing to his subjects surrounded by the splendours of his palace and by his court dignitaries who performed the courtly ceremonial around their king. After the Byzantine conquest of Ravenna, this mosaic was reset and the dignitaries standing in the arcades, together with Theodoric himself, were erased to be replaced by a blue and gold background.' The panegyrist Ennodius referred to Theodoric in imperial terms (though not as emperor) as *princeps et sacerdos*, and the framing of imperial, royal and holy figures within arches, or similarly under

18   Clark (1995), pp. 97–8.
19   Grodecki (1966), p. xxiii.
20   But see Heitz (1980), pp. 74–7.
21   Duckett (1951), p. 85.

Plate 1   Santa Costanza, interior, detail of the annular vault with mosaics including grape-harvesting putti; courtesy Allan T. Kohl/Art Images for College Teaching (AICT).

Plate 2   The 'Riha' Paten with the Communion of the Apostles, silver with gilding and niello, 35 cm. Early Byzantine, Constantinople (565–78); © Dumbarton Oaks, Byzantine Collection, Washington, DC.

Plate 3   Hagia Sophia, mosaic over the southwest portal, showing the Emperor Justinian
to the left offering the church to the Virgin and Child, and to the right the Emperor
Constantine offering the city he founded; tenth century; photograph by Wayne Boucher,
© Cambridge 2000.

Plate 4   San Vitale, Ravenna, mosaic of the Emperor Justinian and his retinue; courtesy Allan T. Kohl/Art Images for College Teaching (AICT).

Plate 5   San Vitale, Ravenna, mosaic of the Empress Theodora and her retinue; courtesy Allan T. Kohl/Art Images for College Teaching (AICT).

Plate 6   Sant' Apollinare in Classe, Ravenna, apse mosaic of St Apollinaris as orant; courtesy
Allan T. Kohl/Art Images for College Teaching (AICT).

Plate 7   Santa Sabina, Rome, interior towards the apse; courtesy Allan T. Kohl/Art Images for College Teaching (AICT).

Plate 8   Sant' Apollinare Nuovo, Ravenna, nave mosaic showing a procession of martyr saints; courtesy Allan T. Kohl/Art Images for College Teaching (AICT).

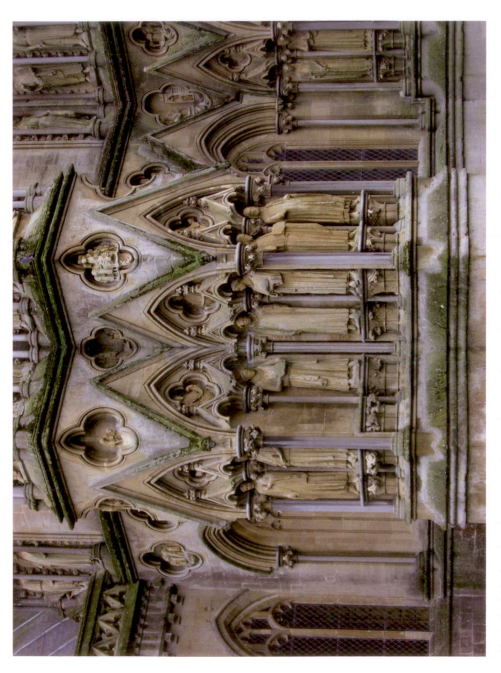

Plate 9   Wells Cathedral, showing the supposed Gospel Procession on the northeastern corner of the West Front; photograph Allan Doig.

Plate 10 Ely Cathedral, Gothic canopies and Renaissance panel with the bishop's coat of arms and those of Henry VIII above the door to Bishop West's Chantry Chapel. Below is his motto: 'Gratia dei sum id quod sum'; photograph Allan Doig.

Figure 5.1   The Palatine Chapel, Aachen, plan and sections; from Dehio and von Bezold (1887–1901), vol. I, pl. 40; (1736b.1&2) Bodleian Library, University of Oxford.

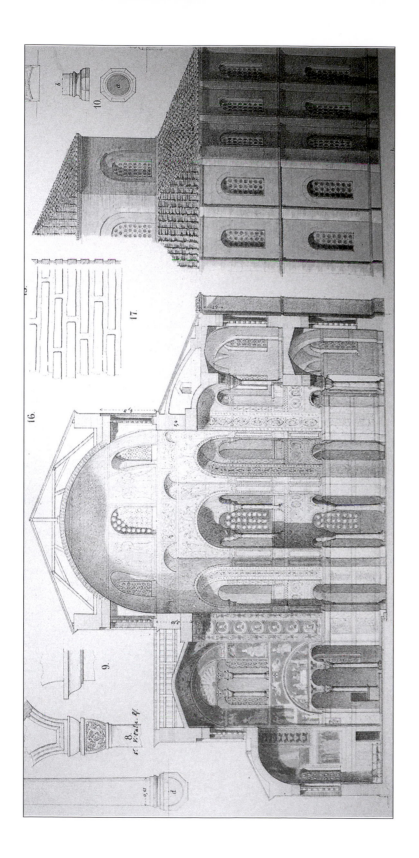

Figure 5.2   San Vitale, Ravenna; from Henri Hübsch (1866), *Monuments de l'Architecture Chrétienne depuis Constantin* (Paris, Morel), pl. XXII, nos 1 and 4; Sackler Library, University of Oxford.

a baldachin, becomes an increasingly familiar theme.[22] Charlemagne would bring the statue of Theodoric, whom he saw as the first German Emperor, from the pediment of this palace back to his own palace at Aachen.

On the cross-axis to the north and south of the palatine chapel there were entrances to aisled basilicas, which have long since disappeared. The great four-metre-high bronze doors originally at the entrance in the westwork, and the railings of the galleries, were Classical revival pieces cast in Aachen's foundry. These include a large bronze pinecone, intended as a fountain, with spouts at the ends of its spines. It would have been technically very challenging to cast, and part of its base is incomplete. This was a copy of the pinecone fountain in the atrium of Old St Peter's in Rome, recalling his own crowning as Emperor. The doors themselves have lion-headed handles, perhaps alluding to the Holy Sepulchre, since Early Christian ivories show such handles on its doors.[23] The square eastern apse housed the altar of the Virgin on the ground floor and the altar of the Saviour at gallery level, opposite the throne.

Bishop Theodulf's Oratory at Germigny-des-Prés

A common architectural language (and a will to produce a common liturgy on the Roman model) emanated from Aachen through elite court circles. Around the year 798, Charlemagne appointed Theodulf, a Visigoth, but also a highly cultivated courtier and poet, Bishop of Orléans and Abbot of Fleury at Saint-Benoit-sur-Loire. The *Libri Carolini*, now ascribed to him, is a work with an important section on icons which shows both the Frankish attitude to the iconoclastic debate and Theodulf's personal artistic erudition and taste.

Between 799 and 818, he built an oratory for himself within the nearby Gallo-Roman villa at Germigny-des-Prés. The *Catalogue des abbés de Fleury*, written about a century later, is clear about Theodulf's intention: 'He vied in this with Charlemagne, who, at this time, had built at his palace of Aachen a church of such splendour that its like could not be found in all of Gaul ... . Theodulf consecrated his oratory to God, Creator and Preserver of all things and had a master artist represent, above the altar, cherubs covering the mercy seat of Divine Glory with their wings.' This mosaic has been connected to a section of the *Libri Carolini* commenting on I Kings 6.19, and to the illustration of contemporary Jewish Bibles; one study concludes that: 'it is clear that the mosaic decoration at Germigny-des-Prés represents a form of Iconoclastic art', the only art justified by the Bible, according to Theodulf.[24] The images seem curiously to deny their own materiality, hovering as a vision on a gold ground. The inscription around the apse reads: 'Beholder, gaze upon the holy propitiatorium and cherubim: and see [how] the ark of the covenant of God shimmers. You, perceiving these things and ready to beset God with prayers, add, I implore you, Theodulf to your invocations.'[25] The argument of the *Libri Carolini*, it is true, denies that images can contain the spiritual properties of their original and should not be venerated, but they are not against images *per se*. Moreover, they cite Gregory the Great concerning the usefulness of images for teaching scripture to the illiterate.[26] With some of the extended narrative cycles, however, it would take a great deal of preaching to make them comprehensible to the populus.

---

22   MacCormack (1981), pp. 232 and 237.

23   Henderson (1994), p. 260; see also the panel of 'the Women at the Tomb', *c.* 420, in the British Museum, illustrated in Morris (2005), p. 74, and noted in Lasko (1994), p. 11.

24   The *Libri Carolini* is discussed in Eco (1986), pp. 99–100; the *Catalogue des abbés de Fleury* is translated in Barral I Altet (2002), pp. 137–8; Beckwith (1969), p. 16, makes the link with Iconoclasm.

25   Translated in Dutton (2004), p. 100.

26   See Mayr-Harting (1992), especially pp. 48–50.

His poetry painted *picturae* of the seasons, the seven liberal arts and a *mappa mundi*. John Beckwith believes that there was 'a "gallery" of paintings and that there were frescoes depicting the seven liberal arts, the four seasons and a map of the world', and others have argued that Theodulf's *mappa mundi* may well be reproduced in a manuscript from Ripoll (*Vat. Reg. 123*).[27] Mary Carruthers, however, maintains that: 'there are two pictures described in his poems, an "arbour mundi" and a "mappamundi." Neither is now accompanied by a drawing; as I will argue, there is no reason to suppose they ever were.'[28] She argues that these were mental images and maps for contemplation and the 'picturing' or 'mapping' of thought, as the poem about the *mappa mundi* says: 'A shape for the whole world is here painted, / It will give you to understand a great matter in a small body.'

While Umberto Eco refers to the aesthetics of the *Libri Carolini* as being 'of pure visibility, and at the same time an aesthetics of the autonomy of the figural arts',[29] this can surely only apply to Theodulf's formal appreciation of the arts such as metalwork and pottery, rather than these other *picturae*, and the figural arts in general. Whether or not the Ripoll *mappa mundi* reproduces one by, or belonging to, Theodulf or one on the wall of his villa, and whether the poem describes a fresco of 'the Seven Liberal Arts Painted in a Certain Picture' in the villa, the mental and physical *picturae* would all function in the same way; the poem ends:

> This tree bore both these things: leaves and pendant fruits,
> And so furnished both loveliness and many mysteries.
> Understand words in the leaves, the sense in the fruits,
> The former repeatedly grow in abundance, the latter nourish when they are well used.
> In this spreading tree our life is trained
> Always to seek greater things from smaller ones
> So that human sense may little by little climb on high,
> And may lastingly disdain to pursue the lower things.[30]

Though this foray into *memoria* would appear to be straying well outside the confines of both liturgy and architecture, the function of *memoriae*, of decorative programmes, the form and disposition of the architecture itself, and the temporal unfolding of the liturgy (particularly when in procession through architectural spaces) could all be similarly used for contemplation of the structure of knowledge of the world 'in which our life is trained', as a reflection of its Creator. The knowledge and truth to which the monk aspired was not 'encrypted' into visual forms and liturgical action, rather they were instruments of contemplation with which to draw together, focus, re-integrate and synthesize material from memory.

The oratory was built on a centralized plan, but was very much simpler than the palatine chapel at Aachen. It is a cross-in-square, originally with a lantern over the crossing, and with either domes or barrel vaults over the aisles. The horseshoe arches betray Visigothic influence, but its decoration, particularly the mosaic of the apse showing seraphim and cherubim over the Ark of God, was Byzantine in inspiration. There was an apse on the central bay of each side, and the eastern apse, which housed the altar, was flanked by absidioles. The western apse was for the bishop's throne. The oratory, its form, decoration and its liturgy reflected the erudition and imperial connections of Theodulf and the glories and reforms of the imperial court.

---

27 Beckwith (1969), p. 16, talks of a 'gallery', and in a footnote refers to Vidier (1911), who makes the connection with *Vat. Reg. 123*.

28 Carruthers (1998), p. 210.

29 Eco (1986), p. 100.

30 Translated in Carruthers (1998), p. 212.

Carolingian Liturgical Reforms

The education of the clergy and people in orthodox belief was of particular importance to Theodulf, who required in his *Statutes* that his clergy explain the liturgy to the people. In this, too, he vied with his master Charlemagne. His *Statutes* give precise instructions on the sacraments, the liturgy, religious and moral education. It is very likely, then, that sermons were in the vernacular. He further required that before baptism, all candidates must be able to recite the Lord's Prayer and the Creed, presumably in the Latin of the liturgy. Theodulf's *Statutes* were the earliest amongst the west Franks, and were influential and widely accepted in Charlemagne's dominions.[31] Bringing this education into vast numbers of isolated parishes posed huge difficulties. Few of those would possess a manuscript of the Bible or a lectionary, since they were necessarily hugely expensive to produce.

It may be surprising to the modern mind that such emphasis was placed on religious education and the liturgy in the government of Charlemagne's realms, until you consider, as Dennis Nineham points out, that: 'Charlemagne insisted that all his subjects must be Catholic Christians. Failure to be baptized meant disenfranchisement and virtual outlawry. Citizenship and being a Christian were synonymous.'[32] Building up the Church Catholic through education and building up the state were part and parcel of the same thing to Charlemagne, which is not at all surprising in a polity built on sacral kinship. The Carolingian *renovatio* was also a radically new and all-embracing vision for the structure of society. All the relationships between the individual, the Church and the state were embodied and enacted in the liturgy and frozen in the architecture, making them not just the objects, but the instruments, of education and reform. The personal life of every member of society was punctuated by liturgical rites, as was the calendar, and even the farming year by Rogation Days, with their processions through the fields, psalms and prayers for the harvest. For Charlemagne, military success also depended on prayer and the liturgy. Carolingian reform was all-encompassing, and what follows will show that two of their most effective instruments for education and reform were liturgy and architecture.

Bishop Chrodegang and the Roman Use at Metz

Romanization of the liturgy proved to be a slow process, partly because of the time and expense involved in producing the manuscripts, partly because of the independence of the bishops, and partly because of the differing needs and resources of the ecclesiastical establishments. The adoption of the papal mass would naturally have enhanced the prestige of a presiding Frankish bishop, but it is very difficult to imagine all of them being able to command the necessary resources. However, there are one or two notable exceptions. Klauser points out a sentence added to the end of *Ordo II* which, 'probably added by an editor commissioned by the Frankish court or by a Synod, states quite clearly that *Ordo I* must be followed just as faithfully in the episcopal cities of France as in Rome itself ... "The bishops who preside over congregations in towns must perform everything in the same way as the Pope."'[33] Chrodegang, Bishop of Metz from 742 to 766, did just that. He had been one of Pope Stephen's distinguished escort from Rome in 753/54, and he did in fact introduce sung stational masses modelled on papal practice in Rome.[34] This was continued by his successors, but Angilramus of Metz gradually withdrew, and appointed surrogates to perform the stational liturgies since his presence was required at Aachen as chaplain to Charlemagne from 784: 'And

---

31 See Dutton (2004), p. 112, and McKitterick (1977), especially pp. 139, 187 and 207.
32 Nineham (1993), p. 28.
33 Klauser (1979), p. 71.
34 MS *lat. 268*, Bibliothèque Nationale.

that the clergy of Metz had to be lured into taking part in the stational services by the prospect of an honorarium can only be attributed to the fact that they no longer appreciated the usefulness of the system of stational masses.'[35]

Around the year 754, Chrodegang drew up a rule for his cathedral clergy based on monastic life, and over the course of the eighth century it was widely adopted in the Frankish realms. A common life required special architectural arrangements for the chapter, including a chapter house, oratories, dormitory and refectory. He provided these at Metz, had the Cathedral of St Stephen redesigned, and also introduced Roman chant. The earliest part of the church was fifth-century, which had been enlarged in the sixth. At the west end of Chrodegang's new church was an atrium, a western tower with a first-floor chapel dedicated to St Michael; at the east there was a substantial transept and a choir over a crypt. All this is familiar, but Chrodegang's most significant changes concerned the liturgical furnishings, including an episcopal throne and a baldachin in a chancel enclosed by a low screen. Two ivory panels for the cover of the Sacramentary of Drogo (Bibliothèque Nationale *lat. 9388*), a son of Charlemagne and successor of Chrodegang as Bishop of Metz from 823 to his death in 855, are each divided into nine compartments;[36] astonishingly, these highly detailed works show, in fine miniature, Chrodegang's liturgical and architectural arrangements in use by Drogo, who is shown wearing the pallium granted to him in 844.

The front panel shows an ordination, the Baptism of Christ, the Ascension, the blessing of an altar, the Sermon on the Mount, the translation of relics and their installation in the altar, signing with chrism, blessing of the baptismal font on Holy Saturday, and a baptism (see Figure 5.3). It would seem that the sequence was mixed during a restoration. The importance of the architectural setting of these liturgical acts is very clear, and the liturgical furnishings appear in great detail. According to Heitz, the compartment showing the dedication of a church has the Bishop on the left outside knocking on the door to gain entry; in the middle, the procession bearing in the relics, and to the right, the bishop installing the relics in the altar. In the Holy Saturday compartment, the font is at the top of three steps, and is covered by a baldachin with a segmented dome. The bishop stands behind the font, gesturing over it in blessing with his right hand, and looks to his left to read from a sacramentary held by a sub-deacon. They are surrounded by other clergy, with one to the left with a bucket, and one to the right with a ewer, probably containing oil. The Sacramentary itself features prominently in the scenes of ordination, blessing the altar, and blessing the font on Holy Saturday.

The back panel shows specific moments in a mass unfolding within the liturgical setting of Chrodegang's cathedral (see Figure 5.4). Again the compartments are out of sequence, but the main points in the mass involving the bishop can be identified. In the middle at the top, the bishop, flanked by deacons and preceded by candles and incense, is bowing low, reverencing the altar. Next, top right, he gives the kiss of peace to his assistants. Here the form of the altar is revealed as a very architectural design, with columns and arcading at the side. Above it is a hanging crown. During the whole time encompassed by these two compartments, the antiphon was being sung, and here it is worth pausing to point to another ivory in the Fitzwilliam Museum, Cambridge (*M.12/1904*) showing the precise moment when the bishop is signalling to the choir that he is ready for them to stop. His book is open and the text is clearly legible: 'Ad te l[e]vavi anima[m] mea[m] deus meus in te confido non erubescam [neq]ue inrideant me inimici mei etenim universi qui te expectant non confunden[tur]' ('To you, O Lord, I lift up my soul; O my God, in you I trust; let

---

35 Klauser (1979), pp. 79–80.

36 There are illustrations and discussion in Heitz (1980), pp. 13–15 and 201–5; my analysis compares the scenes with the liturgy described in Klauser (1979), pp. 62–5, and assumes that Chrodegang would follow the papal mass as closely as possible.

Figure 5.3   Front panel of the Sacramentary of Drogo, metal with ivory plaques; Bibliothèque nationale de France.

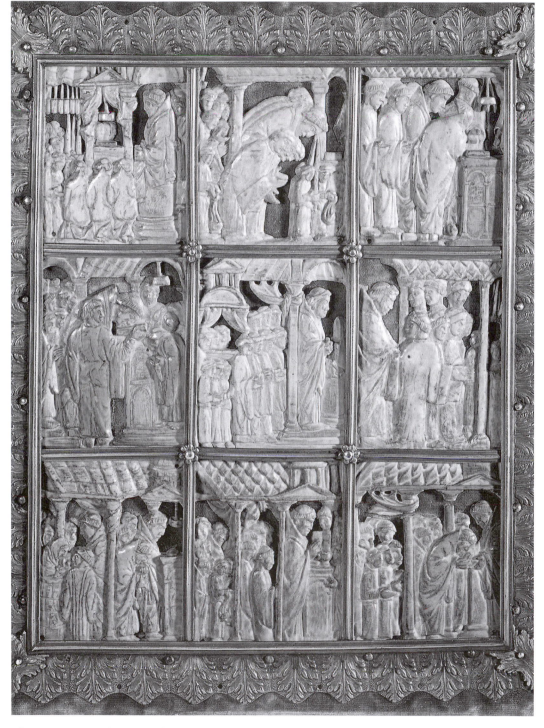

Figure 5.4   Back panel of the Sacramentary of Drogo, metal with ivory plaques; Bibliothèque nationale de France.

me not be put to shame; let not my enemies triumph over me. Let none who look to you be put to shame'), this, from Psalm 25 verses 1 and 2, is the beginning of the introit for Advent Sunday, the beginning of the liturgical year.[37] After the signal, the introit would end with the 'gloria patri', and at the 'sicut erat' he would kiss the Gospel, as in the compartment middle left in the ivory panel on the back of the Sacramentary of Drogo.

The bishop then proceeded to his throne, and facing east (central compartment), the *Kyries* were sung. When these were finished, he would face west and intone the 'Gloria in excelsis Deo', and turn to the east while the singing continued. Turning west, he would greet the people, 'Pax vobis', and again turn east for the collect. Interestingly, in the scene showing the bishop standing facing east before his throne, the canopy of the baldachin over the throne becomes visually confused with the roof of the cathedral itself, and even with what appears to be a raised reliquary above the canopy over the altar.[38] This visual 'elision' may indicate an elision of meaning, where all these coverings set their respective spaces apart, sacralizing them all within a hierarchy of holiness. Careful inspection, however, can distinguish the roof of the nave with diagonal tiles, the baldachin over the altar, with *fastigium* and reliquary, and the arched canopy over the throne. Top left, he is shown seated on his throne, very like the one that still exists. The only significant amount of time he spent on his throne was during the lections. The baldachin over the altar has curtains drawn back, and hanging reliquaries can be seen. Next – bottom right – the deacon appointed to read the Gospel would approach for a blessing, and in this compartment appears to be kissing the bishop's hand or ring; in the Roman stational liturgy, he would kiss the pope's feet, as in eastern court ceremonial.

The hierarchical separation implied in the depiction of the architecture appears to be a reflection of two things: in the first place, the fight against Arianism in Gaul and Spain had a long history, to the point where the emphasis was on the majestic divinity of Christ; and secondly, the Latin of the mass was entirely inaccessible to all but a few: 'Thus in the Carolingian Empire the Mass-liturgy, so far as understanding its language was concerned, became a clerical reserve. A new kind of discipline of the secret had developed, a concealment of things holy, not from the heathen – there were none – but from the Christian people themselves.'[39] The linguistic separation of the rite and the doctrinal exaggeration would eventually result in a growing architectural separation, with the altar moving to the eastern wall of the chancel and the separation of the rood screen, though this was very much later, with the first hard evidence dating to the eleventh century at Fleury.[40]

Three more panels show the second part of the Eucharistic celebration. The middle right-hand scene is of the bishop receiving the offertory at the entrance of the chancel by the screen. Bottom left, the bishop is seen at the altar with an attendant receiving the host, and in the left half of the panel, separated by a slender column, he is distributing the consecrated bread. In the middle at the bottom, the bishop is at the altar, lifting the chalice to consume the consecrated wine.

Around the Cathedral of Metz there were other churches in the episcopal group ranged around the chapter *claustrum*, including the mid-eighth-century St Paul built by Chrodegang, the late-eighth-century St Gorgon, and the seventh-century St Peter, for which Chrodegang built a new screened choir with an *ambo* and throne. Relief carvings from the church are very probably fragments from that screen. One shows a saint, also identified as Christ holding eucharistic bread, standing between two carved columns under a canopy. The character of the carving is similar to the contemporary *ambo* at Romainmôtier and another at Saint-Maurice, both churches on the route

---

37   Rankin (1994), pp. 274–5.

38   For one of a similar form, see the ciborium presented to King Arnulf by King Odo or Charles the Simple in about 896, see Hubert, Porcher and Volbach (1970), pp. 256–9, illustrated on p. 258.

39   Jungmann (1959), p. 62.

40   For an extended discussion, not entirely focused on England, see Spurrell (2005), *passim*.

taken by Chrodegang and the pope in 753.[41] The architectural setting of the holy figure, an aedicule or baldachin, proclaimed his status in the same way that Chrodegang's architectural changes, which included the chancel screen, baldachin throne and canopy, enhanced the position of the bishop in a very similar way to the Roman rite itself. This added prestige offered great encouragement to the independent princes of the Church to build grand new architectural settings for the liturgy and to adopt a standardized Roman order. Frankish bishops otherwise answered to no one but the emperor or the pope; they never did, and Duchesne maintains they never would.[42]

Liturgical Manuscripts and Reform

The richness and variety of the Gallican liturgy is known from the manuscripts of the *Missale Francorum* (Vatican *Reg. lat. 257*), *Missale Gallicum Vetus* (Vatican *Pal. lat. 493*), the *Missale Gothicum* (Vatican *Reg. lat. 317*) and the *Bobbio Missal* (Paris BN, *lat. 13246*). Liturgical practice was extremely varied and localized, as was belief. Orthodox belief and teaching were naturally best served by a standardized liturgy, and Pepin encouraged the re-establishment of Roman usage by conforming the text as far as possible to the Gelasian Sacramentary and adding to it all the material useful in the Frankish context. One manuscript (*MS Cambrai 159*) represents the 'Hadrianum', or form (of the Gregorianum) sent by Pope Hadrian in the later 780s to Aachen at the request of Charlemagne. The papal 'Hadrianum' needed considerable supplement for use in the Frankish kingdom. The supplement, formerly attributed to Alcuin, is now associated with Benedict of Aniane.

The result was what has been called the 'mixed eighth-century Gelasian Sacramentary' (represented by the manuscript Vat. *Reg. lat. 316*). Once this mix was accomplished with the addition of the necessary material, the Frankish rites ceased to be copied – none of the manuscripts is later than the third quarter of the eighth century. The mixed type of book was found particularly useful in the monasteries, 'and in the library catalogue of St Riquier of 831 there are listed no fewer than nineteen Gelasian Missals'.[43] Caution must be exercised when drawing conclusions from this, since it cannot be known when the missals came into the possession of the monastery. It is very probable that at least some were in use at the monastery before Angilbert became Abbot in 790, but subsequently they would also provide material for the extraordinarily elaborate liturgy he designed for the vastly enlarged abbey re-founded by Charlemagne. The manuscript *Reg. lat. 316* was produced in the middle of the eighth century near Paris, possibly at Chelles, and is illuminated with colourful architectural framing of the liturgical text, including impossible double-horseshoe Visigothic arches. The colourful and rhythmical stylistic effects may give valuable clues to the effects sought in the architecture as well.

On a basic level there had to be provision for continuing local variation because the commemoration of local saints required special masses, and many ecclesiastical establishments had very specialized functions, as was the case at the Royal Abbey of Saint-Denis. There, of all places, it was important for the authority of Rome to be visible, since royal authority and legitimacy were based on papal blessing.

Priests were to be taught the meaning of the prayers of the mass and to chant the psalms in the Roman rather than the Gallican chant: 'The clergy are to learn the Roman chant thoroughly and that it is to be employed throughout the office, night and day, in the correct form, in conformity with what our father of blessed memory, King Pippin, strove to bring to pass when he abolished the

---

41   Architectural details in Barral I Altet (2002), p. 144; the carving is discussed in Lasko (1971), pp. 80–81, Heitz (1980), pp. 13–17, and Hubert, Porcher and Volbach (1970), pp. 28–33, and illustrated on pp. 29 and 276.

42   Duchesne (1903), pp. 103–4.

43   Hen (1995), p. 60; Bishop (1918), p. 14; see also McKitterick (1977), pp. 125–7.

Gallican chant for the sake of uniformity with the Apostolic See and the peaceful harmony of God's holy Church.'[44] Pepin had already begun the Romanization in the 750s, when Pope Stephen had given him an antiphonal and responsory and Chrodegang had enthusiastically carried out liturgical reforms at Metz. In 760, Bishop Remidius of Rouen, a son of Charles Martel, was in Rome on an embassy, and obtained Pope Paul's permission to take the second master of the *scola cantorum* back with him to instruct his monks in chanting the psalms. When the master was summoned back to Rome, some of Remidius' monks went to be trained there: 'it mattered that elements of Roman culture should re-emerge; music, as a central part of the liturgical ritual, as a vehicle of poetic expression, and as one of the seven *artes liberales*, occupied a pivotal place in this cultural programme'. It also mattered that singing together became a figure for unity in the highly diverse Frankish lands. The monarch literally wanted them all to be 'singing from the same hymn-sheet'. But the programme was by no means wholly backward-looking:

> It is hardly too high a claim to state that the century between 770 and 870 was the most intensive period of musical development of the whole Middle Ages; to this age belonged the invention of a detailed system of musical notation (some of the essential elements of which have remained in the western notational system ever since), the systematisation of modal behaviour (literally the grammar of relationships between individual tones and groups of tones), the final shaping of a characteristic melodic dialect for an enormous melodic repertory (the 'Gregorian' chant), and the setting down in textual form of a theory of modes.[45]

It was *c.* 784 that Charlemagne received the mass book known as the *Sacramentarium Gregorianum* or *Hadrianum* from the pope, as noted in a letter from Pope Hadrian I.[46] Furthermore, in *scriptoria*, mature experienced monks were needed to produce accurate manuscripts of the lectionary Charlemagne commissioned from Paul the Deacon in the 780s, since many existing texts were corrupt, which prevented proper observance of the offices. Biblical reform was also undertaken during the last quarter of the eighth century at centres including Corbie, Metz, Orléans and Tours under Alcuin.[47] Education, such a strong centralizing and standardizing force (as demonstrated in the nationalist use of standardized language in schools in Germany, France and the Netherlands in the decades leading up to the Great War), was encouraged in all religious houses both for the monks and the laity. Unity was essential in Charlemagne's far-flung realms (as it was in those nation-states in the face of external threats), and unity of practice and orthodoxy of teaching was certainly not to be found in the local nature of the Gallican cult, either in its devotion to local saints or its independent liturgical practice. Such unity could only be found in appealing to the primacy of the See of Peter. In the event, the *Hadrianum* needed a very considerable supplement, traditionally written by Alcuin, now generally accepted to be by Benedict of Aniane, to cover the needs of the Gallican rite. For one thing, the *Hadrianum* was a papal mass-book, containing stational masses for the Roman basilicas, but it did not have masses for ordinary Sundays. Very considerable supplementary material was necessary, and the mixed use that resulted eventually found its way to Rome itself, ironically replacing the older Roman use from the eleventh century.[48]

However much Charlemagne had tried to standardize the liturgy, he had clearly been only partially successful, no doubt due to the stubborn independence of the Frankish bishops. When

---

44 'General Admonition', 789, c, 80, translated in King (1987), p. 218.
45 Rankin (1994), pp. 276 and 278–9.
46 McKitterick (1977), p. 123.
47 Brown (1994), pp. 21 and 23; McKitterick (1994), p. 222.
48 Duchesne (1903), p. 104.

Walahfrid Strabo wrote his *Little Book about the Origins and Development of Certain Aspects of the Liturgy* in 840, the liturgy was still subject to great local variation.[49]

Angilbert and his Liturgy at the Abbey of Saint-Riquier

Charlemagne's closest courtiers were frequently rewarded with bishoprics or abbeys, and sometimes both, like Theodulf at Orléans and Fleury. Angilbert, like Theodulf, was a highly cultivated poet, and was known in court circles as 'Homer'. He had acted as envoy for Pepin in Rome, and then often for Charlemagne too, and was clearly a key figure at court. Charlemagne introduced him to the pope as 'the counsellor of my intimate and private ear'.[50] Though Angilbert never actually married her, he had a family by Charlemagne's daughter Berthe.

In 790, Charlemagne made Angilbert Abbot of Saint-Riquier, at Centula near Abbéville in the Somme. He immediately razed the existing abbey and began a vast new building programme with magnificent funding from Charlemagne. These buildings, then, were somewhat earlier than Charlemagne's own chapel at Aachen, begun in 792. Angilbert loved the arts, was an original poet and thinker, and had an exuberant personality, all qualities which he invested in the grand new buildings of the abbey. The scale of the rebuilding, as known from the excavations, was enormous. An early seventeenth-century engraving of a now-lost drawing from an eleventh-century manuscript has been used as a basis for the reconstruction of Angilbert's work, but serious questions have been raised because it is known that there was considerable destruction by fire during a Viking raid in 881.

The great work was completed in 799, and Charlemagne and the court kept Easter 800 (19 April) with Angilbert at Saint-Riquier. As the king's special envoy to the pope, he paved the way for the events which took place at Christmas that year, when Charlemagne was crowned Emperor. Almost exactly a year before, on St Mark's Day, Pope Leo III had been attacked, blinded, had his tongue mutilated, and was imprisoned in a monastery on 25 April 799. Having recovered from his wounds, he managed to escape to the court of Charlemagne at Paderborn. There is at least circumstantial evidence that Charlemagne had consultations with many of his closest advisers and with the pope preparing for events culminating at Christmas 800. Under the protection of the Frankish king, he had returned to Rome during the previous Summer. In November Charlemagne arrived, and on 23 December Leo swore on oath that he was innocent of the crimes which were alleged to have led to the attack. Two days later, Leo crowned Charlemagne Emperor of the Romans during the Christmas Mass in St Peter's. Charlemagne claimed that it was unexpected, and some allow this enough credibility to at least pass over lightly,[51] but Charlemagne took up the role with gusto, appropriate ceremonial and symbolism. Alcuin toyed with the idea that the title should be 'of the Christians' as a way of unifying the diverse peoples of the realm.[52]

The engravings of the new buildings of Saint-Riquier[53] show round western and eastern crossing towers each about 180 feet high, with large multi-storeyed transepts and side-aisles running the length of the intervening nave (see Figure 5.5). At either end, the apses (giving the building a combined length of about 250 feet) were flanked by round turrets – an arrangement that Conant relates to the narthex of San Vitale in Ravenna, and which reappeared at the chapel at Aachen

---

49   See Harting-Corrêa (1992), especially pp. 79–81.

50   Duckett (1951), p. 104.

51   Einhard's *Vita*, section 28, gives much of this detail, translated in Dutton (2004), p. 44; see also Brown (2003), p. 435.

52   Collins (1991), pp. 270–71 and 277, and Collins (1998), 141–7.

53   Heitz (1980), Pétau, 1612, illustrated on p. 52, and Mabillon, 1673, illustrated on p. 53, both Bibliothèque nationale.

Figure 5.5   The Abbey of Saint-Riquier, engraving; Bibliothèque nationale de France.

in its westwork. It was the westwork of Saint-Riquier that was the most original and influential architectural element. Conant calls it 'the earliest really imposing and boldly articulated façade in church architecture – a historical landmark'. Recent archaeological evidence has confirmed that there was an atrium in front of the west end.[54] Angilbert himself was buried in the outer vestibule, which was flanked by circular stair-towers giving access to the chapel above. The inner vestibule had a font, an altar and the *capsa maior*, containing 25 relics of the life and Passion of the Saviour. This low vaulted space carried the lofty and galleried centralized Chapel and 'Throne' (altar) of the Saviour above, making the westwork a complete vertical church, reminding the pilgrim at the outset of his journey of the primary focus of worship. With the font's connotations of death and resurrection, this centralized space had distinct echoes of the Rotunda of the Holy Sepulchre. Liturgically, the Chapel of the Saviour could be used independently; it is even described as 'the Church of the Holy Saviour' in contemporary documents.

The Palatine Chapel at Aachen was also dedicated to the Holy Saviour, just as the main church at Saint-Riquier was dedicated to the Saviour and All Saints. Royal Chapels in westworks were often dedicated to the Saviour:

> At the time when the palace clergy of the Carolingian rulers were building a Westwerk at the entrance to their churches it was a policy to present the emperor in both imperial and Biblical terms as a Messiah, the new David destined to reunite the peoples of God, who was comparable to the Savior. It was not

---

54   Conant (1978), p. 44.

uncommon for the emperor to be designated 'the Savior of the World' and in the protocol of 877 he was called 'Salvator mundi'.[55]

If this argument is accepted, the teaching function implied in the dedication of this part of the church was double-edged, to say the least, since the throne of the emperor was to be found there, as at Aachen. The conflation of the Emperor with the Saviour would, however, be no new idea; it had been used in imperial circles from the time of Eusebius. On the other hand, Charlemagne did not take part in the liturgy in the same way as the Byzantine emperor, with the Easter liturgy focused on his own person, as did Charlemagne's grandson, Charles the Bald.[56]

The altar in the Church of the Saviour was one of a remarkable 30 altars accommodated in various chapels of the complex on different levels in this veritable 'city of God'.[57] At the crossing was a twin of the western round tower, and off that to the east was the Throne of St Riquier, a seventh-century ascetic, at the high altar. This circular architectural form at the crossing, then, was a 'martyrium', equivalent to the 'Palatine Chapel' at the west.

The *Ordo*, containing the services composed by Angilbert for use in his abbey, also describes how during solemnities, when there were four choirs singing antiphonally from different parts of the church, the boys' choir sang in the galleries of the westwork. At other times, when only three choirs were used, the boys sang as an angel choir in the galleries at the west end of the apse near the 'throne of St Riquier', while a choir of monks sang at the altar of the Holy Cross, and a third group sang under the *buticum*, which has been suggested was the baldachin.[58] At other times, the three choirs were disposed in different parts of the building, including the altar of Crispin and Crispinian, 'whom the common people adore', or of St Maurice. The architecture, the offices, the chants, the liturgical calendar, the relics, and the social and ecclesiastical structures were all closely co-ordinated. Rabe maintains that at the end of each office, a third of the choir left the church to attend to other aspects of the life of the monastery, leaving the other two to chant psalms. They would return to sing the next office together, after which another third would leave – a remarkable *laus perennis* in a continuous and highly elaborate liturgy unfolding in a complex series of architectural spaces and related buildings.[59]

Fundamental to it all was orthodox teaching. For example, vespers was celebrated by the monks at the tomb of Richarius (St Riquier) in the apse, and when that was finished, they went to a large relief of the Passion, singing psalms all the way. When prayers were complete at the Passion, they divided into two choirs, one proceeding to another large relief of the Resurrection, another to a third relief of the Ascension. Private and liturgical prayers were said at those stations, then one choir went via the altar of St John, the other past the altar of St Martin, and passing more altars, they combined again at the altar of the Holy Cross, in the middle of the nave. Naturally, when vespers and matins were held in the Holy Saviour, it was necessary to take a different but equally complicated route, ending up again at the altar of the Holy Cross. Processions often left the confines of the main church and took in the two other churches in the triangular cloister – essentially, they

---

55 See Baldwin Smith (1956), p. 89; he disagrees with Conant that Aachen derives from San Vitale, see pp. 95–6, and Conant (1978), p. 48.

56 Mayr-Harting (1992), p. 57.

57 Conant (1978), p. 468 n. 3; see Rabe (1995), p. 114, for Bernard on the atrium, and Heitz (1980), p. 54, for the number and distribution of the altars of the abbey.

58 See Bishop (1918), p. 322, where the *Ordo*, which contains the details of the services and use of the building, is reproduced in a Latin edition, and Conant (1978), p. 45.

59 Heitz (1980), p. 54; Rabe (1995), p. 123.

were credal processions, affirming orthodox belief.[60] But this is not to say that they were simply about narrowly conceived content; they were rich and varied sequences punctuated at stations: 'The processions in St.-Riquier show in a particularly rich way how a locational memory could be woven into the very fabric of monastic buildings.'[61] The altars, reliquaries and the canopies above were all decorated with gold, silver and gems.

Although the liturgy followed Roman practice, Angilbert was as original in the way he mixed in Gallican elements as he was in the design of the architectural setting. To a poet like Angilbert, the Roman rite must have been a distinct contrast, possibly as barren as Dix suggests:

> Accustomed to elaborate symbolical ceremonies and the more rhetorical and flowery style of the Gallican and 'Frankish Gelasian' prayers, the people of the north were likely to view the simplicity of Gregorian as baldness, its sobriety as dullness and the pregnant brevity of its prayers as cramping to their own exhuberant and affective devotional style. As it stood they would never bring themselves to make it the framework of their own devotion.[62]

The complexity of the architecture accommodated his own processional presentation of the liturgy. The Trinity was the basis of his theology and the reason for the threefold grouping of the architecture, and even the relics. Offices and masses were held in the three churches of the triangular group, and the triangular arrangement of the cloister provided for the complex processions between.[63] On Saturdays, the offices took place in the Church of Mary the Mother of God and the Twelve Apostles. It was a twelve-sided, centralized structure at the south-western angle of the cloister. The central altar was dedicated to Mary the Mother of God, and there was an altar for one of the Apostles on each of the walls. On Marian feasts and Maundy Thursday, all the offices were said here, and at Pentecost, mass was celebrated. The unusual triangle of the cloister was completed at the eastern angle by the Church of St Benedict and the Holy Abbots Regular.

Angilbert did not escape criticism for his highly dramatic presentation of the liturgy. Surely it was with this in mind that his friend Alcuin wrote, still rather fondly of his friend 'Homer', to Adalhard, Abbot of Corbie: 'I fear Homer will be angry at the statute forbidding shows and devilish fictions, all of which Holy scripture forbids.'[64]

Amalarius of Metz and Allegory

The elaborate celebration of the liturgy with processions through a highly symbolic architecture, not to say landscape on Rogation Days, was theologically interpretive and didactic. This strand of Carolingian liturgical understanding reached its most extreme in the writings of Amalarius of Metz (*c.* 775–*c.* 850). After 835, he administered the See of Lyon following the deposition of Archbishop Agobard. Amalarius had been a pupil of Alcuin's, and wrote the first Carolingian systematic exposition of the liturgy. At the time, most works explaining the liturgy were simple expositions of the mass, for example the monk of Corbie who began: 'Why do we celebrate the mass? For a number of reasons. In the first place …' – clearly a straightforward catechetical approach to educate the people.[65] Amalarius, on the other hand, was highly allegorical in his interpretations, especially

---

60 See the reconstruction by Bernard, reproduced in *ibid.*, fig. 7. Rabe's disposition of the dedications is useful, but speculative.

61 Carruthers (1998), p. 268.

62 Dix (1945), p. 580.

63 See Rabe (1995), pp. 122–4.

64 Translated in Hen (1995), p. 230.

65 McKitterick (1977), pp. 148–53.

in his detailed study of the offices, *De ecclesiasticis officiis*. He went to Rome in 831, and in the preface to the third edition of the work he pointed out many differences between the Gallican and Roman uses.[66] In that work he encouraged the amalgamation of the Roman and Gallican use, so the process was clearly taking a long time.

His text was very influential, but some particularly idiosyncratic sections were so extreme that they were actually declared heretical at the synod held in Quiercy in 838. Some of his ideas had surely been influenced by his presence in Constantinople on a diplomatic mission between 810 and 812, and this may go some way to explain why they were so exceptional when the norm was simple catechesis. He also introduced changes to ceremonial, especially chant, which Angobard described as 'theatrical sounds and stagey musical settings' (*theatrales soni et scenicae modulationes*). In this 'liturgical theatre', Amalarius interpreted not only the words, but every action allegorically. Though not as explicit nor as extreme as Amalarius, this must broadly have been Angilbert's intention at Saint-Riquier.

For example, on Rogation Days in early summer, the whole monastic community of Saint-Riquier, the people of the village, and of the seven neighbouring parishes, all processed in ranks of seven (for the sevenfold gifts of the Holy Spirit) through the countryside, and with antiphons, prayers and singing psalms they prayed for the harvest. Heitz has pointed out that on the ivory cover of the Sacramentary of Drogo, the deacons and sub-deacons are seen ranged three plus four, and four plus three: 'Voila! We find Angilbert and his *Institutio de diversitate officiorum* of Centula!'[67] In the Rogation procession, the boys also sang *laudes*, prayers 'for the good estate of all Christendom', and the creeds. The monks sang litanies, 'first the Gallic, then the Italic, then the Roman'. The simple responses could be sung by all, literate and illiterate alike. Rogation Days first appear in the *Gregorian Sacramentary* in Rome, but Angilbert seems literally to be taking the whole local population with him from the familiar to the new standard as an all-inclusive and elaborately co-ordinated celebration. The liturgy unfolded through time and the architectural spaces of the monastery complex which was the 'City of God', but beyond that it spilled out and animated the 'sub-urban' spaces of the town and the whole of the surrounding landscape.

Key architectural elements expressing both theological and political dimensions of the liturgy were being developed along the processional axis of the church, in the westwork, the choir, the sanctuary and the apse. Experimentation with the form of the western entrance of the church, begun at Saint-Riquier and Aachen, continued, at Charlemagne's suggestion, at the Monastery of Aniane founded in 782 by Benedict. Like Saint-Riquier, Aniane was the result of a unified conception, but one significant change at Aniane under legislation by Louis the Pious was the participation of the laity; the processions were confined to the church, the monks' choir was screened, and movement of the laity within the church was limited.[68]

The Development of the Westwork

Of all the architectural changes which affected the liturgy, none was more emblematic of the religious and political situation during the Carolingian period than the development of the westwork. The *adventus* was a ceremony originally celebrating the arrival of a god or a deified ruler. Now it had been transformed to celebrate either the arrival of the king or of relics of the saints – members of the 'heavenly court'. Its original architectural manifestation was the city gate or triumphal arch.

---

66   Jungmann (1959), p. 57.
67   Heitz (1980), p. 204.
68   Rabe (1995), p. 143.

Now this tradition would be applied to the west front of royal abbeys in particular.[69] Finally, it would also be applied to cathedrals as 'the house of God and the Gate of heaven', or the 'City of God'.

The Senate had granted Julius Caesar the honour of having a *fastigium* or gable on his house, and the *fastigium* became a common element in the sanctuaries of Byzantine churches in honour of the Emperor of Heaven. The westwork which Charlemagne built over the grave of his father Pepin at Saint-Denis may have belonged to an older tradition,[70] but its historic royal associations would be instrumental in later developments at Saint-Riquier and Aachen. The reconstruction of the façade of Saint-Denis implies a relatively modest façade relating to eastern examples especially in Syria, such as Qalb Lozeh.[71] In Rome, the image that may have exerted a direct influence was the panel on the door of Santa Sabina which has also been interpreted as showing either the Lord, or conceivably the emperor, acclaimed by an angel at the towered gate of heaven. Theologically, by extension it may be any faithful Christian who, having been anointed at baptism, is about to receive their heavenly crown. However it is interpreted in detail, architectural and liturgical symbolism meet in this image. Charlemagne's *adventus* at Rome and St Peter's at Easter 774, at the dedication of Saint-Denis in February 775, at Saint-Riquier at Easter 800 or his appearance to the crowds on the balcony or tribune of the Chapel at Aachen framed in the great niche all have powerful resonances of sacral kingship.

The Gatehouse of Lorsch

An interesting example of what is a purely honorific entrance-gate, free-standing like a triumphal arch, is the triumphal gate of the monastery of Lorsch, Germany, founded between 760 and 764 under the auspices of Chrodegang of Metz (see Figure 5.6). There was a large atrium in front of the monastic church, consecrated in 774 by Lullus, Archbishop of Mainz. This was a basilica with a forecourt, nave and aisles. Distinctively, the first square cloister appeared here, and soon became a staple of monastic building. The ceremonial gate stood unattached in the open space towards the western end of the atrium, well within the proper western entrance-gate. On the ground floor are three large open arches opening on to a clear space with a spiral staircase at either end on the cross-axis which led to a chapel above. Its prototype would appear to have been the propylaeum of Old St Peter's in Rome, and as there, the building was used to greet honoured guests and in stational liturgies such as Palm Sunday. The gate is said to commemorate Charlemagne's victory over the Saxons.[72]

In the churches of the West, the westwork itself was an invention of the eighth century as a symbol of the Carolingian monarchy:

> While some of the churches in the West are described as *in modum turris* and Apollinaris Sidonius refers to a church at Lyon with 'a bulwark of stone rising up high and strong at the west front', there is no specific evidence of there having been any churches with a two-towered façade before the end of the eighth century. Even if the builders in some instances may have been influenced by the gateway symbolism of the Bible, the figurative imagery of St Augustine's *City of God*, and the precedent of the Syrian churches, it is nevertheless true that the towered façade was uncommon, if not unknown, in the West before it became an expression of political ideas in the Carolingian period.[73]

---

69   See Baldwin Smith (1956), *passim*, the reconstructed plan is shown on p. 124; Stalley (1999), pp. 46–9, is more guarded about the imperial connections, placing greater emphasis on the liturgical use.

70   Crosby (1942), pp. 123–5.

71   See Krautheimer (1986), p. 153, and Peña (1997), pp. 144 and 147.

72   See Conant (1978), pp. 54–55, and Barral I Altet (2002), pp. 150–51.

73   Baldwin Smith (1956), p. 76.

Figure 5.6   The Gatehouse or 'Torhalle' of the Benedictine Abbey of Lorsch , view of the western
               façade; courtesy Allan T. Kohl/Art Images for College Teaching (AICT).

Pepin may have had himself buried face down at the west door of Saint-Denis as an act of penance,
but Charlemagne transformed his humility into honour by erecting the westwork over the tomb, and
the emperor had his throne in the tribune of the westwork here at Saint-Denis and at Saint-Riquier,
just as he did in the tribune of the westwork at Aachen.[74] The gatehouse at Lorsch functioned in a
very similar symbolic way within royal ritual and as a gateway to the monastic complex as 'City
of God'.

The Abbey of Corvey

The westwork at Corvey on the Weser, near Höxter, is a prime example of an imperial chapel in
a westwork, and the only Carolingian example to survive. Corvey was founded in 822 by monks
from Corbie Abbey near Saint-Riquier, and the westwork was built between 873 and 885. It had
a great central tower with a pair of smaller, but very tall, flanking towers. The tribune over the
entrance was of two storeys, consisting of the imperial chapel and a gallery above with the throne.
This elevated position placed the emperor in front of a west window, surrounding him with light – a
very different presentation of sacral kingship from Charlemagne's at Aachen. As at Saint-Riquier,
the angel choir probably sang from this upper gallery, and musical notation called 'neumes', which
uses letters of the alphabet, has been found scratched into the plaster of its walls.[75] The most
important new development at Corvey was at the east end, where wrapped around the apse was an

---

74   *Ibid.*, pp. 82–3.
75   Stalley (1999), p. 49.

aisle which opened onto three separate chapels. This is an early sign of the '*chevet*' scheme that will become increasingly important in Romanesque architecture – apse, ambulatory and radiating chapels.[76] This would be essential for the management of the crowds of pilgrims already increasing in the ninth and tenth centuries.

Despite the originality shown in the combination of elements to create a form like the westwork, it was none the less dependent on the revival of earlier Roman imperial imagery expressive of the divine authority of the emperor. Not long after being crowned emperor, Charlemagne issued a new seal with an architectural symbol of Rome and the inscription, *RENOVATIO ROMANI IMPERII* – 'the revival of the Roman Empire'.[77] That Roman revival was true both of the architecture and the liturgy, and it became of central importance for the classical revival of the Romanesque. But that new classicism was based on a new political, liturgical and cultural situation, and significantly, the westwork, as symbol of the old situation, was outdated and began to change, as at Werden and Cologne, and at Rheims in 976 it was no longer to be found. The Romanesque westwork was a dramatic architectural form that lost its specific royal liturgical function. It came to be associated with the prestige of the foundation, rather than act as an architectural language with a specific reference to imperial and liturgical meanings. This is what happened at Jumièges, an arrangement repeated at St-Etienne, Caen, and which would travel with William the Conqueror to England.

---

76 Conant (1978), p. 64.
77 Stalley (1999), p. 39.

CHAPTER 6

Monasticism, Pilgrimage and the Romanesque

The Cult of Saints and Monasticism in the West

Athanasius spent two periods of exile in the West, first in Trier from 335 to 336 and again 362 to 363; the second was of special importance for the development of monasticism and for the cult of saints. Around the year 357, he wrote a life of Antony of Egypt, a year after the death of the saint, and translated it into Latin *c.* 363. In early Christianity, those who glorified God in their death were venerated, but Saint Antony was not a martyr, he glorified God in the sanctity of his life, as demonstrated by Athanasius. The *Vita* recounts how as a young man, Antony owned a considerable amount of land and responded willingly on hearing the tale of the 'rich young man' who was told by Jesus to 'Sell what you have and give to the poor, you will have treasure in heaven; and come, follow me.' (Mark 10:21). Unlike that rich young man who 'went away sorrowful, for he had great possessions', Antony did just what Jesus asked, and became a hermit in the uninhabited desert of Egypt *c.* 285. Athanasius' *Vita Antonii* was read by Jerome in the third quarter of the fourth century when he was in Trier, and in 386 Augustine heard from his friend Pontitian about two civil servants who became monks after reading Athanasius' *Vita*. In this manner, Antony's fame spread abroad in the West, inspiring large numbers of young men to enter the religious life.

Ascetic Life and Worship: Hermits and Communities

By the end of the third century, there were already significant numbers of ascetics, but Antony was distinguished by the order and discipline of his life, and he attracted many disciples whom he formed into a community early in the fourth century. After only a few years, he again retired as a hermit, but his opinions were widely sought and he wrote a number of letters giving advice to groups of monks about the ascetic life.[1] Antony was also portrayed in the *Vita* as fiercely anti-Arian, and Athanasius used this in his uncompromisingly orthodox position maintaining the divinity of Christ in the Arian dispute. He was strongly supported in this by the Western Church, and it was highly attractive to the Gallo-Roman aristocrats who occupied the bishoprics of Gaul. Antony lived to a great age, dying *c.* 356, by which time he had a very large number of followers, so large that Athanasius described how he had turned the desert into a city of monks!

As those large groups of monks were organized more tightly and formally into communities with an ideal of unceasing prayer, so those communities developed more formal and specialized architectural arrangements. In the *Lausiac History*, written *c.* 419 and an extremely valuable document of early monasticism, Palladius claimed that there were five thousand monks on the mount of Nitria, where:

---

1   See Dunn (2000), pp. 3–6.

The Guesthouse is close to the church. Here the arriving guest is received until such time as he leaves voluntarily. He stays here all the time, even if for a period of two or three years. They allow a guest to remain at leisure for one week; from then on he must help in the garden, bakery, or kitchen. Should he be a noteworthy person, they give him a book, not allowing him to converse with anyone before the sixth hour. On this mountain there are doctors living, and also pastry cooks. They use wine, too, and wine is sold.

All these work with their hands at making linen, so that none of them is in want. And indeed, along about the ninth hour one can stand and hear the divine psalmody issuing from each cell and imagine one is high above in paradise. They occupy the church on Saturdays and Sundays only. Eight priests have charge of the church; while the senior priest lives, none of the others celebrates or gives the sermon, but they simply sit quietly by him.[2]

The numbers may be exaggerated, but were clearly large, and it is possible to see nascent specialization here in terms of function, both social and architectural.

The independent life and devotions of the hermit is one model of the monastic life (the eremetical), the other is life in community (the cœnobitic). Possibly the earliest fully communal monastery was founded by Pachomius, who died as early as 346. He originally attached himself to a hermit, but soon left to found a community of monks in Tabennese, a deserted village, in the 320s. The monks were organized into groups of about twenty, and communal worship took the form of midday and evening services with prayer, long readings from Scripture, and the singing of psalms. Though the Bordeaux pilgrim in 333 does not mention hermits or religious communities, contact with Gaul was very early. In 353, Hilary of Poitiers was exiled from his diocese, and spent four years in the East, where he probably came into contact with monastic communities. The communal model spread quickly, and in the West there were urban communities in Rome and Milan by the 370s.

When Egeria, who was probably from Gaul, went on pilgrimage between 381 and 384, her objective was not only to visit the holy sites, but the holy people too, and amongst these she was particularly interested in those leading an eremetical life. When she arrived in Jerusalem, the bishop was Basil of Caesarea, who had founded a hospice for the poor, a veritable 'new city' of buildings. Egeria could not have arrived in a more hospitable or charitable context. She addressed the account of her travels to 'my ladies and reverend sisters', which sounds like an already established religious community of some sort back home in Gaul. On her return journey, she visited Charra and a church on the site of Abraham's house. She happened to arrive on the day of commemoration of Helpidius, a holy ascetic whose martyrium was in the church: 'This is a day when all the monks of Mesopotamia have come in to Charra, including the illustrious ones called ascetics who dwell in the desert. ... So we had the unexpected pleasure of seeing there the holy and truly dedicated monks of Mesopotamia, including some of whose reputation and holy life we had heard long before we got there.'[3] In May 384, Egeria visited the martyrium of St Thecla, three staging posts from Tarsus in Cilicia. There she re-connected with someone she had known in Jerusalem, Marthana, a deaconess who was 'superior of some of the cells of apotactites or virgins. ... There are a great many cells on that hill, and in the middle a great wall round the martyrium itself, which is very beautiful. The wall was built to protect the church against the Isaurians.'[4] This was architecturally quite a sophisticated fortified monastery for women and men, and seems to have been a kind of 'federation' with a number of superiors over sub-groups.

---

2   Palladius, *The Lausiac History*, 7.4 and 7.5.
3   Egeria 20.5–6, Wilkinson (2002), p. 137.
4   Egeria, 22.3–4, Wilkinson (2002), p. 141.

Ascetics in Gaul

Somewhat earlier than Egeria's pilgrimage, St Martin had been an exorcist in the diocese of Poitiers under Bishop Hilary. Then he had himself been a monk, living in a 'hermitage' surrounded by a large group of followers in a community that would become the monastery of Ligugé, outside Tours.[5] When that See became vacant, Martin was acclaimed third Bishop of Tours by the people in 371, thus becoming the first monk-bishop in the West. His cult had enormous appeal, and he was an inspiration for a number of aristocratic Gauls to become monks, turning their villas into small monasteries. Sulpicius Severus, St Martin's biographer, founded a monastery on one of his own estates at Primuliacum, where he was entrusted with the education of young Gallo-Roman aristocrats and their preparation for monastic or clerical careers.

Likewise, Honoratus, who *c.* 407/8 founded the monastery at Lérins (on what is now the Ile Saint-Honorat near present-day Cannes), was from a consular family. He was joined by other Gallo-Roman aristocrats who would later become bishops of Arles, Lyon, Riez, Troyes, Tarantaise and Cimiez. This was a very learned society whose model of monasticism was rather different from Martin's solitary asceticism, and Lérins and its founding group did much to change the attitude of the aristocracy to monastic and clerical careers for their sons.[6] At neither the monastery of St Martin nor at Lérins did the monks do any manual labour. John Cassian (born 365, died *c.* 435), formerly a monk at Bethlehem and author of both the *Institutes* and *Conferences*, guidebooks for the ordering of monasteries, was highly critical of this aspect of Gallic monasticism, though he dedicated the *Conferences* to Leontius, Bishop of Fréjus, and Honoratus and Eucherius, founders of Lérins. The link with the Holy Land is of the greatest importance; Cassian formulated the classical statement of the spiritual meaning of Jerusalem 'in the historical sense as the city of the Jews, in allegory as the church of Christ, in anagoge as the heavenly city of God "which is mother to us all" (Gal. 4:26), in the tropological sense as the human soul'.[7] However brief his experience of monasticism in the East, his understanding of the significance of Jerusalem and account of the liturgy, doubtless at least descriptive of that at Bethlehem, will have influenced monasticism in southern Gaul, and monks of Lérins who later became bishops will have taken that influence into their dioceses. He was critical of practices in Gaul, most especially the length of the liturgy, especially in the monastic offices. An indication of the growing sense of community in Gallic monasticism is shown by the fact that until now, monks appear to have inhabited individual cells, and the first mention of a dormitory is from the beginning of the sixth century, in the *Lives of the Fathers of Jura*, when after a fire destroyed the cells, Eugendus had a communal dormitory built in their place.[8]

Gregory, a successor of Martin's as nineteenth Bishop of Tours, was an aristocrat, like most of the other bishops of Gaul. Martin, as an ascetic former soldier, had been very much an exception. Bishops did found monasteries, however, as did Eparchius, ninth Bishop of Clermont-Ferrand, 'who built the monastery on top of Mount Chantoin, where the oratory now is, and there he would go into retreat during the holy days of Lent. On the day of the Lord's Supper, he would process down to his cathedral, escorted by his clergy and the townsfolk, and accompanied by a great singing of psalms.'[9] Gregory mentions great numbers of churches and monastic houses in his *History of the Franks*. Typically, these were built over or near the graves of saints, or were furnished with suitable relics. Gregory's story of his contemporary, St Aredius, or Yrieix, is very revealing; it takes place in 591:

5　Collins (1999), p. 236.
6　Bartlett (2001), pp. 211–15.
7　John Cassian, *Collations*, 14.8, translated in Cassian (1985), p. 160.
8　See Dunn (2000), pp. 73–5, 79 and 85.
9　*HF* II.21.

Aredius' father and brother both died, and this man of God, filled, as I have said, with the Holy Ghost, went back home to console his mother Pelagia, who had no one to look after her except her one remaining son. He was by now devoting all his time to fasting and to prayers, and he asked his mother to go on being responsible for all the household duties, to be in charge of the servants, the tilling of the fields and the culture of the vines, so that nothing should come between him and his praying. There was only one commitment for which he wanted to remain responsible, and that was that he should have control of the building of churches. What more can I tell you? He built churches to the glory of God's saints, collected relics for them and tonsured as monks his own family retainers. He founded a monastery in which was observed the rule of Cassian, Basil and the other abbots who had regulated the monastic life. His saintly mother provided food and clothing for all the monks. She did not allow this heavy responsibility to interrupt her prayers to God. No matter what she was doing she continued to pray and her words rose up like fragrant incense, finding favour in God's sight.[10]

The sanctity and power of holy places, people and their relics were operative in the foundation and location of churches and monasteries. As with St Aredius, people came to the saint, and later to his tomb or relics, to be healed or helped by his intercession in heaven. Many churches and monasteries would grow rich on the offerings of pilgrims. It is impossible to know how many of these monastic houses there were, and many would not have long outlived their founders. Aredius founded his monastery the year after Gregory I was elected pope.

Gregory had himself founded a monastery in his own house on the Caelian hill, and from that monastery in 596 sent Augustine and a group of his monks to re-evangelize England. By this time there were already monastic communities in the farthest reaches of Britain, with one established in the sixth century by St Columba on the island of Iona in the Western Isles of Scotland. A century later, between 679 and 688, Adomnan, his successor as abbot, wrote an account of the holy places of Jerusalem, based on a verbal description given to him by Bishop Arculf. Adomnan 'carefully questioned holy Arculf, especially about the Lord's Sepulchre and the church built over it, and Arculf drew its shape for me on a wax tablet'.[11] Drawings and measurements by Arculf were included in the manuscript, which between 702 and 703 Bede used along with other sources to produce the most important early guide to Jerusalem. These two sources were widely available across Europe, and fed the Carolingian imagination: 'liturgical orders too, show a genuine knowledge of the Sepulchre; in one of about 800 it was observed that the vessels for the bread at the eucharist are called towers (*turres*) "because the Lord's Sepulchre (*monumentum*) was cut out of the rock like a tower, with a bed inside where the Lord's body rested"'.[12] To 'do this in remembrance of me' embedded the memory in the form of the liturgy, the vessels it employed, and the buildings and the communities in which it was celebrated. The various levels of the understanding of 'Jerusalem' became intertwined in the liturgy and its setting.

From the fifth to the eighth centuries, great monastic basilicas where monks chanted the offices were built in Gaul, first over the tomb of St Martin at Tours, next over St Denis near Paris. Although so little is known of their architectural detail, there is enough, as in the nascent westwork at Saint-Denis (see above, page 131), to encourage speculation about a formal architectural link with Syria. The Syrian Church at this date was strongly ascetic, and it may be that architectural ideas travelled hand in hand with eremetical practice and liturgical influence. Gregory of Tours, for example, describes how the deacon Vulfolaic imitated Simeon Stylites, standing on a column[13] and it is entirely possible that the church at Qal'at Si'man, built over Simeon's column a century before Gregory wrote, was also known in Gaul. At Qal'at Si'man, as at St Martin's hermitage, a monastic

---

10   *HF* X.29.
11   Adomnan, 1.2, from Morris (2005), p. 102.
12   *Ibid.*, p. 103.
13   *HF* VIII.15.

community overtook the solitary life of the saint, and a community living under a rule was much more easily controlled by the Church hierarchy. Interestingly, at this time Pachomius, seen as the founder of cœnobitic, or communal, monasticism, was wrongly identified as a Syrian in the *Lives of the Fathers of Jura*.[14] In conforming Gallic monasticism more closely to the Pachomian model, it would not be surprising to see the architecture similarly conforming to Syrian models. Again, in the Gallican liturgy of the later sixth century the *Trisagion* was imported from Syria, and the position of the preface and *Sanctus* as an introduction to the eucharistic prayer is also a Syrian practice, adopted in Gaul as early as the middle of the fifth century.[15]

The Mozarabic Rite and Cultural Exchange in Islamic Spain

Although it has little to do with monasticism, there was another route for the migration of Syrian forms, and that is via Spain. From the fourth century, pilgrimage to Jerusalem, Syria and Sinai had become increasingly common from Gaul, and possibly Spain too, and in the fifth century monasticism spread westwards along the same routes. Influence from the eastern Mediterranean naturally travelled to north Africa and the West with Byzantine imperial administration, and in architectural terms, carved details and elements including church screens and liturgical furnishings had been sent prefabricated from Justinian's imperial workshops by ship. One such ship of the sixth century has been discovered off the coast of Sicily with its cargo still on board. It is possible that such architectural kits reached Hispania, and there is a school of thought that supposes that the liturgy used there at this time was strongly influenced by the Byzantine rite. That would not be surprising, since Justinian's troops occupied part of Andalusia from 554 for about a century, and a Patriarchate dependant on Constantinople was established in Cartagena. In the sixth century, droves of Spanish pilgrims are known to have visited the pillar of Simeon Stylites at Qal'at Si'man in Syria.[16]

Before Hispania was conquered by the Arian Visigoths, it was strongly Catholic, and the faith persisted amongst the population under the new masters until 589, when King Recared converted to Catholicism. Whatever liturgy was then in use, it certainly differed from that of Rome. In the early seventh century, Isidore of Seville described the old Hispanic rite, and it was fundamentally this that in the eighth century, under Islamic rule, became known as the Mozarabic rite. It has much in common with the Gallican use in its variability, colourful ceremonial, probably also its form of chant, and in its greater emphasis on responses between the priest and congregation, which reinforces community. The relative isolation of the Mozarabic Christians under Islamic rule meant that its communal emphasis would have been important to a subject people, and such change as there was between the eighth and the eleventh centuries would make the rite seem more, rather than less, idiosyncratic. The Mozarabic liturgy was abolished in the twelfth century under Alfonso VI, who was a magnificent benefactor of the Abbey of Cluny, but it may be that both liturgical and architectural elaboration of form, characteristic of Mozarabic use, survive within the remarkably innovative Gothic synthesis.

The best example of a Visigothic church to survive is San Juan de Baños, founded in 661 by King Recceswinth. It has a nave of four bays with side-aisles, a sanctuary with a horseshoe tunnel vault, and off the transepts were side chapels either side of, but detached from, the sanctuary. These chambers either side of the chancel recall the *prothesis* and *diaconicon* of churches of the Eastern rite, reinforcing the notion that the liturgy at this time was influenced by the Byzantine rite.

---

14 Dunn (2000), p. 85.
15 See Dix (1945), pp. 466–7, 538 and 541.
16 Bevan (1938), p. 10.

A glance at the plans of churches through to the eleventh century will confirm the dominance of the tri-apsed aisled basilica, though there was quite as much variation in the architectural detail as in the Mozarabic liturgy.[17]

The seventh-century expansion of Islam had quickly absorbed Byzantine Syria. This provided a rich source of architectural forms for Western development, including the cruciform, tri-apsed, domed basilica, as at Qal'at Si'man (450–80), and the twin-towered façade, as at the sixth-century Church of Turmanin. The Muslim advance subjugated north Africa in the early years of the eighth century (that is, by 714).

Even before the whole of north Africa had been subjected, Tariq, Governor of Tangiers, made his first incursion into Visigothic Spain, or al-Andalus, in 710, and built a fortress on the rock of Jabal Tariq, which still bears his name – Gibraltar. Their forces continued to press northwards and waged a Holy War, until defeated at what they would call 'the Plain of the Martyrs' near Poitiers by Charles Martel between 25 and 31 October 732.[18] The Muslim forces continued to hold a good deal of Frankish territory in Provence, and even added territory, capturing Valence, Vienne, Burgundy and Lyon, until Narbonne was recaptured by Pepin the Short in 751.[19] It was not until 758 that the Franks pushed them back beyond the Pyrenees. Many Christians left Spain, including Theodulf, who built the oratory near his Abbey of Fleury using Visigothic horseshoe arches, a very early introduction. Charlemagne, like his father Pepin, continued to be engaged in military campaigns to contain the threat of invasion.

To build their great architectural monuments, the Muslim rulers (from the time of 'Abd al-Rahman in the middle of the eighth century onwards) brought in Syrian masons who maintained many practices and forms from their Christian Byzantine past. 'Abd al-Rahman was nostalgic for all things Syrian, as the survivor of the usurpation of the Baghdad Caliphate. At the end of that century, when Charlemagne built the westwork of the Abbey of Saint Denis over the grave of his father Pepin, it was in a form that relates closely to Syrian prototypes, especially the twin-towered façade of the Church of Turmanin. Though this Syrian influence may have come via contacts with Constantinople or from Pepin's embassy to Baghdad in 765,[20] a much more direct and practical route would have been via al-Andalus, that is, Islamic Spain. Here is a strong possibility of Muslim influence on one of the most important developments in Carolingian church architecture, the westwork.

'Abd al-Rahman built the Great Mosque of Cordoba in a unique style, reusing Visigothic and Roman columns and capitals, borrowing the stacked arches from a surviving Roman aqueduct at Mérida in the region, and the horseshoe arch from the conquered Visigoths. The architectural plan, and perhaps even some details of the form of worship, appear to have been influenced by Mozarabic architecture and liturgy. In the tenth century, the mosque was extended by 12 bays to the south, and the axis was emphasized by the addition of a domed bay at the west and a domed *maqsūra* (where the Koran was kept), which transform the space from an undifferentiated and un-hierarchical space forested with columns to a directional space strongly reminiscent of a Mozarabic Christian church. Islamic architecture was hugely enriched by the adoption of indigenous forms and the use of the finest craftsmen in the world, including Byzantine mozaicists, and all was synthesized in a distinctively Islamic and extremely beautiful new style. Cordoba during the Caliphate was a great centre of learning and culture, with a vast library said to contain 400,000 volumes, perhaps as many as 600,000 – an astonishing collection considering other European collections contained

17   See examples in Whitehill (1941).
18   Makki (1992), p. 15.
19   Glick (1979), p. 36, 2nd edition (2005), p. 26; Makki (1992), p. 16.
20   Atroshenko and Collins (1985), p. 29.

only a few hundred at best.[21] Muslims learned paper-making from the Chinese, and bound sheets as a codex. Though the most beautiful and prestigious volumes fetched huge prices, paper volumes were much less expensive to produce than volumes made from the skins of huge numbers of animals. The influence of this great centre of learning spread to the Christian lands in the north of the Iberian Peninsula, and then via Catalonia to the rest of Europe, as seen in the symbolic architecture in the carving of the lintel at Saint-Génis des Fontaines in the Pyrénées-Orientales. The Mozarab Christians who lived under Islamic domination acted as a conduit of ideas and artistic and architectural forms to Christian lands.

There is no doubt about the distinctiveness and brilliance of the art and architecture of Islamic Spain, but as Oleg Grabar has observed:

> The art of Islamic Spain can be seen in two ways. It can be part of a large body of monuments known as 'Islamic', that is to say as made by or for people who professed the Muslim faith; or else it can be seen as Spanish or Hispanic, that is the creation of a land with traditions which would have been, in part at least, independent of the religious, ethnic or cultural allegiances of rulers of the moment.[22]

Grabar points to unique qualities of the mosque of Cordoba that are continued even in the Christian chapels built so much later by King Alfonso X,[23] and the Cathedral built within the Great Mosque. Grabar is clearly referring to the characteristic stucco designs, the horseshoe arches and the geometric tile dados which echo aspects of the former mosque. The horseshoe arches were a borrowing from earlier Visigothic architecture of the Iberian peninsula. Yet Alfonso also built León Cathedral as a copy of Reims Cathedral, the place of the coronation of French kings.

This is why it is important to dwell on the Mozarab example, since it brings a particular function of both architecture style and liturgical ceremonial into sharp relief: here style and design were utilized within different contexts to express different aspects of the complex political and religious situation, and carry different messages. Messages about Alfonso's imperial aspirations were in a Romanesque language to speak to an audience in the courts of the Christian kingdoms to the north, and to his ethnically and religiously mixed subjects he used the formal structures of the regal vernacular. He embraced the ethnic and religious diversity of his realm, while sending clear signals to his European neighbours.

Is this perhaps 'collective memory', as Grabar suggests; is it cultural continuity and ethnic mix; or is it perhaps the (even triumphalist) appropriation of the signs of one culture and religion by another? Which of these, for instance, best describes what was happening in successive stages of building at the Bāb al-Mardūm mosque in Toledo? It was built on the ruins of a Visigothic church, reusing some of the materials. The articulation of the walls is a very clear reference to the entrances of the Great Mosque of Cordoba, and the dome is obviously a copy of one added to that mosque by al-Hakam II in the late tenth century. Then, in the 1190s, after the re-conquest, a large chancel with an altar was added to turn the nine-bay Bāb el-Mardūm Mosque into an axial church suited to Christian liturgical practice. During different periods, the reading of this mix of cultural signs, including the style and presentation of the architecture and ceremonial of the liturgy, may well shift between these various approaches. The situation is reminiscent of the Early Christian conversion of pagan temples into Christian churches, but the Spanish example has an added dimension of inculturation and appropriation of cultural and religious signs that are not simply triumphalist.

---

21   Battles (2004), p. 65; Hattstein (2000), p. 216: '400,000 books, indexed in 44 catalogues'; Atroshenko and Collins (1985), p. 29, 'said to contain 400,000 volumes'; Hillebrand (1992), p. 120 '400,000 volumes whose catalogue itself ran to 44 registers of 50 (some other accounts say 20) leaves apiece'.

22   Grabar (1992), p. 583.

23   See Casamar Perez (1992), p. 78.

In al-Andalus, Mozarabic art, that is to say Christian art under Islamic rule, continued to produce work with a complicated formal relationship to the dominant Islamic art. The fact remains that even after the return of Christian domination, Muslim architecture, forms, arts and artisans continued in their employ, producing what is known as Mudejar art. Mozarabic and Mudejar may not even be an entirely satisfactory description of the ethnic origin of all the artists, but a more accurate description of the religion, ethnicity and cultural situation of the patron. That is to say, while the Christian and Islamic artistic communities may have been separated and serving different masters, so much of their artistic currency was held in common that Grabar seems to be driving towards a position that this is Spanish art which has been given a particular emphasis because of the context in which it was commissioned. When other religions and cultures were not perceived as a threat, their artistic and architectural forms could be used freely in a highly creative synthesis. For example, there are two synagogues in Toledo, one from the twelfth and the other the fourteenth century, which were built in Islamic style and subsequently converted to the Christian churches of Santa Maria la Blanca and El Tránsito. In these, the plan is also remarkably similar to a mosque, as is the elevation and decoration, but that does not indicate a confluence or mixing of belief, but rather a secularization of artistic form and cultural interdependence. Was there a similar cultural interdependence at work in the ceremonial of the Mozarabic rite? Is it possible, for instance, that the (presently undecipherable) neumes in which the chants are written will one day reveal a musical interdependence?

In the secular sphere, the image of kingship was conveyed through the architecture of the palace, and the defining image remained the (Islamic) Alhambra, even much later in the fourteenth century. When Pedro the Cruel built the Alcazar Palace in Seville in its present form, he reproduced the confusing sequence of rooms and courts, the slender columns supporting elegant tracery, geometric tile dados, and even Arabic inscriptions. It is treated as a magnificent and powerful cultural heritage, and a necessary cultural setting for Spanish kingship, whether Muslim or Christian. The diversity of the *ethnic* heritage was unified in the convergent embrace of the *cultural* heritage. Aspects of that cultural heritage were used locally, nationally and internationally as dialects or languages, speaking eloquently in those different contexts, and consolidating political and religious unity and power through cultural means.

The circulation of artistic, and perhaps even religious, practice was by no means all in one direction. In the mosque of Cordoba, under the dome in the *mihrab* area, perhaps in imitation of Christian usage, the *muezzins* prayed in front of the *mihrab* before the call for prayer. There was also a huge Koran that would be carried about during prayers, preceded by a lighted candle, like the Christian Gospel procession. Later, when Christian advances under Alfonso VI threatened the fragmented *tā'ifa* kingdoms, the religiously purist north African Almoravids took over the rule of al-Andalus. Under them, the purity of Islam was expressed by a puritanical architecture rejecting interdependence with Christianity; when Islam had been politically strong, cultural interdependence could be embraced.

The Christian kingdoms that maintained a hold in north-western Spain throughout this period developed a highly characteristic style through exposure to Islamic architecture, and in turn made a considerable contribution to the development of the Romanesque. The earliest Romanesque architecture had appeared during the first half of the eleventh century in these northern kingdoms and across southern Europe to Lombardy. A splendid Spanish example is the mid-ninth-century Santa Maria de Naranco near Oviedo, where the walls are clearly articulated with piers of clustered, sculpted columns, capitals with a braided astragal, and a kind of veined early stiff-leaf decoration. This supports an elegant arcade with roundels in the spandrels and a barrel vault with heavy ribs. This kind of architectural articulation can be seen on the gates and the interiors of the Great Mosque of Cordoba, built in the late eighth century.

Pilgrimage and the Migration of Forms

Ideas and artistic forms travel with people, and during the late eleventh and early twelfth centuries there was a great flood of new building in a mature Romanesque style enlivened by Islamic forms and travelling all along the pilgrimage routes to Compostella. Examples along these pilgrimage routes show strong evidence of migration of architectural forms, for example the early-eleventh-century dome of Notre-Dame-du-Port, Clermont-Ferrand, uses squinch arches to fit the dome to the square space, which may well have been learned from the Great Mosque in Cordoba. The arches at tribune level in the nave are horseshoe arches, and decorative tiles and coloured voussoirs on the apse reinforce the sense of Arabic influence. The façade articulation of Notre-Dame, Le Puy-en-Velay likewise seems related to Cordoban examples. Further Islamic details include cusped arches, stripes in the coursed ashlar and the voussoirs, patterned panels, and wooden doors with cufic inscriptions. Conant also notes that 'in all there are nearly a hundred carved capitals of Moslem type at Le Puy'.[24] As far away as Vézelay, at the beginning of one of the most important routes, the semi-circular transverse ribs of the vault alternate the colour of the voussoirs just as in the emblematic Great Mosque of Cordoba. Collins and Atroshenko wrote of Islamic culture that:

> What flowered in Cluny, Vézeley, Autun and Fontenay came to Burgundy from Tours from Provence and Toulouse, which received along the pilgrim and trade routes the methods and techniques of the 'Islamic' architects via the abbeys of Cuxa, Canigou and Ripoll in Catalonia – a province in the north-east of Spain, strongly influenced by Mozarabic culture.'[25]

Most certainly, Cluniac architects adopted these Islamic motifs, but the precise staging posts are impossible to reconstruct in this great flood of people and ideas along the pilgrim routes.

The Carolingian Ideal: The St Gall Plan

Monastic communities, particularly those under the Rule of St Benedict, were devoted to prayer and the liturgy. Cassian had objected to the number of psalms and the length of the offices in Gaul, and at the extreme, the monks of Saint-Maurice d'Agaune were divided into relays, so to speak, to keep the liturgy forever praising God in the *laus perennis*: 'With great care and attention to detail, Sigismund [King of Burgundy] built the monastery of Saint-Maurice d'Agaune, providing it with chapels and living accommodation.'[26]

Whether worship was the brisker version of Cassian or the perpetual praise of Agaune, and later Saint-Riquier, every hour of the day, and increasingly every aspect of life, in the monastery was governed by the Rule. That ideal way of life was reflected in the architecture of the ideal City of God, which was the monastery. The clearest image of this was the St Gall plan drawn up *c.* 820, probably under the influence of Benedict of Aniane or Einhard in Charlemagne's court circle. Conant summarized the circumstances of its production: 'It is now clear that the layout was drawn up after a council of 816 at Inden, near Aachen, and this somewhat imperfect copy sent with alternative dimensions by Abbot Haito of Reichenau (806–23) to Abbot Gozbert of St Gall (816–37), who had not attended the council.' He goes on to say that it is not just a diagram, and treats it very much as a design for building. Stalley questions this point by point:

---

24   Conant (1978), p. 178.
25   Atroshenko and Collins (1985), p. 35.
26   *HF* III.5.

An inscription indicates that the plan was sent to Gozbert, abbot of St Gall (816–37), at a point when he was contemplating the reconstruction of his monastery. There is evidence (but not absolute proof) that it was composed at Reichenau under the direction of Haito, one-time abbot of Reichenau and bishop of Basle. Haito appears to have been offering advice to a colleague, though some scholars have tried to read far more into the situation. It has been claimed that the plan was a product of the reforming synods held in 816 and 817, and was intended as a model or 'paradigm' for the whole Carolingian Empire. It has also been argued that the plan is a copy of a master drawing that was made at Aachen at the time of the synods. Neither of these theories is tenable in the light of recent research, which has conclusively proved that the St Gall plan is an original drawing and not a copy.[27]

An important contribution was made by Braunfels, who wrote that 'the Plan is to promote meditation upon the meaning and worth of the monastic life'. This has been built upon by Carruthers, who traces meditation on architectural plans to exegesis of Old Testament buildings: 'In the case of the St. Gall plan, certain features seem modelled on details of the visionary Temple of Ezekiel, the subject of ten exegetical sermons by Gregory the Great that were a common part of monastic colloquia, the reading in chapter and at meal times.'[28] In the Plan of St Gall (see Figure 6.1), the disposition of functions, the liturgical nodes, the routes between, the social relationships, the biblical resonances, and comparison with other monastic houses would provide a rich source of contemplation for the abbot. What is true of a drawing could be equally true of a building, making the built 'City of God' a very suitable object for contemplation.

Drawn in red ink, at the heart of the complex the St Gall drawing shows the church with sacristy and scriptorium, dormitory, refectory and cellar ranged about the cloister, which was one hundred feet square. On the axis to the east was a chapel, with infirmary and novitiate on either side. Beside the infirmary was the physician's quarters, with a herb garden and leeching-pond either side. At the south-eastern corner was the orchard cemetery, garden and gardener's house and fowler with chickens and geese. There were barns, workshops, a brewhouse, mill, press, a cooper, and stables to the south, livestock to the west, and a guesthouse, school and Abbot's house to the north. While some scholars maintain that the plan was merely schematic, others insist that it could easily have been used for building, and actually was so used in the oldest easternmost parts of the church.[29] It is detailed enough to show an impressive western section with a pair of free-standing towers not unlike those already built (though attached to the nave) at Saint-Riquier, Aachen and Fulda. The towers at St Gall were separated from the western apse by a semicircular portico and garden which gave access left and right to the northern and southern sectors. The western entranceway aligns with the church and chapel to form the spine of the whole arrangement

The drawing shows the liturgical layout of the great church. Like Fulda after the building programme of 802–19, the church in the St Gall plan was a 'double-ended' aisled basilica with entries at the west end of the north and south aisles and from the dormitory off the south transept. Altars are shown in every other bay of the aisles, two in the nave, one elevated by three steps in the chapels in each transept, and one in the apses at the east and west ends. The design could be solely for monastic, use and would be totally inappropriate for the circulation of pilgrims. The western apse was dedicated to St Peter, and immediately to the east in the nave was the monks' choir for the offices. Next along the axis came the Chapel of John the Baptist, with a font, and in the following two bays of the nave was the Altar of the Cross in its usual place in the centre of the monastic church. The high altar was elevated over a crypt dedicated to St Gall, and the eastern apse,

27 Compare Conant (1978), p. 56, with Stalley (1999), p. 185.
28 Braunfels (1972), p. 46, and Carruthers (1998), p. 230.
29 Compare Stalley (1999), p. 184, with Conant (1978), p. 56, Heitz (1980), p. 110, and Hubert, Porcher and Volbach (1970), p. 42.

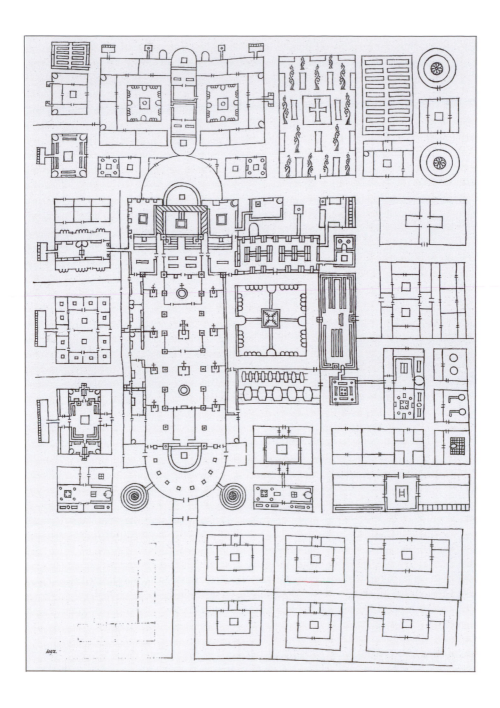

Figure 6.1   Plan of St Gall; image by The Institute for Advanced Technology in the Humanities at the University of Virginia through the St Gall Monastery Plan Digital Project (P. Geary and B. Frischer, PIs, and image processing by E. Triplett), © Board of Visitors, University of Virginia, 2007.

complementing the western, was dedicated to St Paul. The compartmentalized layout was geared to smaller services and stational liturgies, rather than huge processional celebrations. In fact, the plan is so awkward that it lends itself best to episodic reflection on aspects of liturgy, architecture and exegesis, giving weight to Braunfels' and Carruthers' arguments. A gloss on the drawing notes that the monks were to meet in the north walk of the cloister. There was no chapter house.[30]

Ninth- and Tenth-century Liturgy and Architecture

Strabo's Analysis of the Parallel Development of Liturgy and Architecture

Charlemagne's dominions were vast, and his son Louis the Pious attempted to hold them together. Like his father, he brought able churchmen to his court in Aachen, including Walahfrid Strabo from his monastery of Reichenau in 829 as tutor to his son Charles. Nine years later, when Charles reached his majority, Louis appointed Strabo Abbot of his old monastery. Between 840 and 842 he completed a sage and balanced history of the liturgy which 'views the liturgy as a kind of rhetoric in action'.[31] In the *Libellus*, he further draws a parallel between the development of the liturgy and architecture:

> What we do today in a complex liturgy of prayers, readings, chants and consecrations, we believe the apostles and their immediate successors did simply with prayers and the commemoration of the Lord's Passion as He Himself taught. ...
>
> Subsequently, the Faith gained more ground, and Christians elaborated the liturgy of the Mass because either the stability which peace brought further spread the Church's limits, or the growing Christian practice multiplied the number of saints. We have already said that the same sort of development also took place in the construction and embellishments of sacred buildings.[32]

The book has a masterful rhetorical structure, laying out the liturgy as 'rhetoric in action', and architecture, by extrapolation, unfolds similarly for the action of the liturgy as a spatial rhetoric.

Strabo was naturally an advocate of standard Roman use, but he recognized the continuing variety of use without condemning it, so long as it was consistent with, and communicated, orthodox belief within the specific context. In support of this, he refers to Gregory the Great on baptism:

> ... within one faith the Church's diversity of practice does no harm. We immerse three times to signify the sacraments of the burial of three days. When a child is brought up three times from the waters, the resurrection after three day's time is represented.
>
> But in case anyone thinks that this is also done to venerate the supreme Trinity, by the same token nothing prevents the baptizand from being immersed once in the waters. While there is one being in three substances, there can be nothing wrong in immersing an infant at its baptism either three times or once, because the Trinity of Persons can be represented by three immersions and the Unity of the Divinity by one.[33]

Diversity was acceptable, but conformity to Rome was recommended because of the authority of the Apostolic See and because it had throughout history remained free of heretical tendencies

---

30 Stalley (1999), pp. 185–9.

31 Harting-Corrêa (1996), p. 18; the book contains a complete translation and commentary on Strabo's *Libellus de Exordiis et Incrementis Quarundam in Observationibus Ecclesiasticis Rerum*.

32 *Libellus* 23, Harting-Corrêa (1996), p. 127.

33 *Libellus* 27, Harting-Corrêa (1996), p. 177.

(ch. 23). Orthodoxy was the constant test in the way all liturgical actions were interpreted and in the adoption of Gallican prayers:

> Because there is really such great diversity in the liturgy not only in racial and linguistic variety but also in just one race and language because of change over the years or the teachers' zealous instruction, if I wished to reveal everything we read now about this profusion, I would be more irksome than productive to those who will listen to me. I shall pass over these endless matters and affirm only that the complete arrangement of the liturgy, which is now observed throughout the Roman world, was established long after antiquity elapsed; it was then disseminated to every prominent Christian centre. For when the faithful grew and the pestilence of heresies stained the orthodox peace in a greater variety of ways, the liturgy of true observance had to be enlarged: a more intelligible religion might attract the souls of those approaching the faith, and a more enhanced liturgy of Truth might show the consistency of the catholics against the foes.[34]

This section is embedded in a discussion of 'hymns', especially *Gloria Patri et Filio et Spiritui Sancto sicut in principio et nunc et semper et in saecula saeculorum, amen* ('Glory be to the Father and to the Son and to the Holy Ghost; as it was in the beginning, is now and ever shall be, world without end. Amen'). Hymns were introduced to encourage and teach the faithful, as used by Ambrose in his fight against the Empress Justina and the Arians of the court. Paintings were useful in the same way, and he refers to Gregory the Great, for whom 'painting is a kind of literature for the illiterate'.

Strabo typically rehearses a measured argument concerning images and the dangers of idolatry in ch. 8. The controversy about images and iconoclasm was supposed to have been definitively settled at the Synod of Paris in 825, but was clearly still enough of an issue to require a long and careful argument setting out the usual Gallican position that mere paint was not worthy of veneration and worship, but images were educationally useful, and iconographic programmes which were architecturally deployed could be highly subtle and complex teaching aids, not just for the illiterate. Excesses in either the proliferation and veneration of images or their denigration and destruction were both to be condemned: 'The villain in this case appears to be the difficult Claudius of Turin, an early-ninth-century protester against pilgrimages, the intercession of saints and the worship of both images and the cross, but did not achieve the results Luther did several centuries later.'[35]

Even at this date, the expectations of pilgrims that they would see a grand, not to say lavish, setting for the display of relics were very high. In Germany, at the monastery of Prüm, not long after the translation of new relics:

> a certain woman arrived with a wagon full of food and drink and precious things which she proposed to offer to God and to the holy martyrs. But, seeing that the saint's tomb did not glitter with gold and silver, she uttered a contemptuous guffaw, as is wont of foolish and irreligious minds. Then, rushing back home, she bade her friends retrace their steps saying 'you won't find anything holy in that place'.[36]

All these practices were on the increase, and they would drive, and fund, the ecclesiastical, liturgical and architectural developments over the coming centuries, and the reaction, when it came, would split the Church.

Gradually, attacks from without and from within, and the tendency towards independent action, so long displayed, for instance, by the Frankish bishops, fractured the empire into three. Stability

---

34 *Libellus* 26, Harting-Corrêa (1996), pp. 161–3.
35 *Ibid.*, p. 228.
36 In Sumption (1975), p. 153.

was threatened from within, and even more dangerously, from without, by attacks by Normans in the west and Magyars in the east. Henry, Duke of Saxony, became King of the East Franks in 919. His son, Otto I, succeeded him in 936 and began to rebuild the empire. He emulated Charlemagne in his political ambition and in architecture. Given that there was no real dividing line between religious and secular, great churchmen naturally had power in the political sphere. By the turn of the millennium, many Sees and monasteries had built great new churches characterized by powerful and unified architectural form – the message was loud and clear.

Otto invaded Italy in 951, and in 955 he was victorious over the Magyars at Lechfeld, and fortified the church at Magdeburg served by Benedictine monks from Trier. In 962, he was crowned Holy Roman Emperor by the Pope in St Peter's. In 968, the church at Magdeburg became the cathedral for the newly established Archbishopric, focusing ecclesiastical power. Nothing remains of this church, and the other cathedrals it spawned have also been changed beyond recognition.

The Church of St Cyriakus at Gernrode (see Figure 6.2), begun by Margrave Gero the year before Otto I was crowned Emperor, still gives a clear picture of early Ottonian architecture, though there were thorough (but archaeologically well-founded) nineteenth- and twentieth-century restorations, and the rest of the conventual buildings have been destroyed. The western apse is a later addition, as is the exterior arcading above the aisles, but the interior, including the flat wooden ceiling, is essentially as built (see Figure 6.3). The arcading of the aisles alternates between columns with carved capitals and very plain square piers. The rhythms of the arcading above are broken into sets of five columns supporting six arches, with three double relieving arches above those. Square piers separate the arcades above and align with those in the arcading below, dividing the nave into two equal parts just where the altar of the Holy Cross might have stood. Mayr-Harting asks whether the nuns in their liturgy 'would not sometimes have tested their musical possibilities', presumably singing the psalms antiphonally.[37] The rhythm established by the arcading of the nave walls is much more sophisticated than any corresponding Carolingian work. Just below the ceiling is an unarticulated range of clerestory windows. The square crossing, perhaps a twelfth-century insertion, is emphasized by strong square piers, and beyond at the east end is an elevated sanctuary in a half-round apse. Under this is a hall-crypt. The exterior, with round towers clasping the west end and one remaining at the east, strongly echoes Saint-Riquier, though without the great round lanterns.

In 972, Otto the Great arranged the marriage of his son to the Byzantine Princess Theophanu, and the next year he succeeded as Otto II. The Empress is said to have contributed to the completion of St Cyriakus. Is there some Byzantine influence to be seen in the arcading that was imported during diplomatic exchanges preceding their betrothal?

The westwork continued to be an important element of the Ottonian repertoire, as can still be seen at St Pantaleon, Cologne, built between 966 and 980 (see Figure 6.4). The church is known to have had a chapel dedicated to St Michael, and the western gallery would have been the most usual location. Another west end of note is at Essen Minster, where the western apse was modelled on the Palatine Chapel at Aachen, an extremely interesting example of iconography and function in the agglomerative build-up of Ottonian architecture.

Within this additive approach to architecture, painted decorative schemes and narrative sequences of wall-paintings played an important part. Such schemes had been described by Gregory of Tours, and were also to be found in the rather iconoclastic Carolingian form at Germigny-des-Prés. A remarkable overall fresco cycle still survives at the Church of St John the Baptist in the Italian Alps at Müstair, in the Grisons. The work has not been securely dated, but the church was probably founded at the end of the eighth century, and the monastery is first mentioned in 805. Some maintain that the Carolingian Court's misgivings about images, particularly of the Godhead,

---

37   Mayr-Harting (1999), p. 215.

Figure 6.2   St Cyriakus, Gernrode, Saxony-Anhalt, exterior view from the south; courtesy Allan
              T. Kohl/Art Images for College Teaching (AICT).

make a mid-ninth-century dating for the frescoes safer, but then again the style of the work does
not look toward court art, but rather towards Rome, but Birchler argued at length that they must
have been executed when the church was first built.[38] New Testament narrative scenes are arranged
in four tiers from floor, originally culminating in a tier of scenes from the life of King David just
below the ceiling (now in the Landesmuseum, Zurich). The walls are uninterrupted by architectural

---

38   Beckwith (1969), p. 25; see also Hubert, Porcher and Volbach (1970), pp. 23–7, as against Birchler
(1954).

Figure 6.3   St Cyriakus, Gernrode, Saxony-Anhalt, interior view towards the east; courtesy
               Allan T. Kohl/Art Images for College Teaching (AICT).

mouldings and only provided with narrow windows. The church was originally a large hall with a
span of about 41 feet, and in the fifteenth century, columns were added to support ribbed vaulting,
dividing the hall into nave and aisles. On the west wall was a Last Judgement and Christ enthroned
in the apse. It is very possible that a processional liturgy related to that of Saint-Riquier, but on a
much-reduced (not to say vestigial) scale, was celebrated in this large open monastic hall-church,
with processional routes determined by the relationship between the narrative cycle, the offices and
the liturgical year.

Figure 6.4   St Panteleon, Cologne, Nordrhein-Westfalen, exterior view of the west end; courtesy
Allan T. Kohl/Art Images for College Teaching (AICT).

As with preceding dynasties, royal iconography made a very considerable impact on contemporary ecclesiastical architecture and liturgy. Henry II, successor to Emperor Otto III, in 1002 made an *Umritt*, travelling round his kingdom seeking public acceptance for his rule,[39] essentially staging a traditional *adventus* in the cities of his realm, to establish his power by his personal presence. He laid the cornerstone of Bamberg Cathedral on 6 May 1007, his own thirty-fourth birthday. The Cathedral was consecrated on the same date five years later, in the presence of most of the bishops of the realm. The contents of the treasury he created were used, and the manuscripts used in the service (Pericopes giving selected readings for services, Gospels and Sacramentary) in their imperial iconography reinforced a very particular vision of his rule. The Sacramentary especially presented an iconography aligned with Henry's imperial ambitions. The presence and participation of the bishops of Henry's realm was (willingly or not) a sign of their recognition of the ecclesiastical and temporal reorganization represented by the foundation of the new cathedral, See and royal capital.[40] Art, liturgy and architecture were marshalled as powerful instruments of a new political contract and the consolidation of political power.

39   Mayr-Harting (1999), p. 228.
40   See the detailed study of Bamberg by Garrison (2003).

Monasticism in England

There is some evidence that early in the tenth century, after the death of Alfred the Great in 899, his daughter built 'new St Peter's' in Gloucester with an apse at the western end and a square chancel, influenced, it would seem, by Continental examples, including the St Gall plan, and by about 1020 a very large western apse and an altogether Ottonian west end, described by Eadmer, was added to Canterbury Cathedral.[41] There was a revival of the religious life of England from the middle of the century, led by Dunstan, Æthelwold and Oswald. Dunstan was active in founding and re-founding monasteries, and Oswald was professed a monk at Fleury. Æthelwold was a monk under Dunstan at Glastonbury, and first became Abbot of Abingdon in 954, and then was Bishop of Winchester during 963–84. As bishop, he presided over the Council of Winchester summoned by King Edgar in the early 970s to consolidate the recent reforms. Dunstan, by that time Archbishop of Canterbury, also attended. The Council drew up the *Regularis Concordia*, which codified the liturgy and was accepted for use by all the heads of the monastic houses. Fernie comments that:

> One might expect that churches built to fulfil a particular function would take their form at least in part from that function, but attempts to link liturgical practice and permanent architectural arrangement (as opposed to screens and barriers) have proved notoriously difficult. The architecture of the English monastic reform movement should stand a better chance than most of showing a correspondence because the reforming of the monasteries, the drawing up of the liturgical formulae, and the patronage of the buildings were all so heavily concentrated in the hands of a small group of individuals. Even given this set of circumstances the results are disappointingly meagre, yet cannot be ignored. (p. 94)

It is very true that permanent architectural arrangement is by nature very resistant to changes in liturgical function, and even in newly built structures, changes in use tend to be accommodated through the placement of screens, pulpit, *ambo*, *solea*, altar, ciborium and other liturgical furniture. Fernie notes that the *Regularis Concordia* mentions three liturgical sections of the church, the *oratorium*, *ecclesia* and *chorus*, each with its own altar. With only one per section, he deduces that they would likely have been axial. This would place the altars of the choir and the body of the church in the familiar Carolingian positions, but the westernmost altar would create an obstruction, so he concludes that the one in the *oratorium* would be likely to be in a gallery – again, a usual Carolingian arrangement. The rubrics of the celebration of the night office of *Tenebrae* on the *Cena Domini* specifies responses of the *Kyries* to be sung by pairs of boys on either side of the choir and to the west, before the whole choir sings the awful words: 'Christus Dominus factus est obediens usque ad mortem' ('Christ our Lord was made obedient even unto death').

The pair to the west could stand either in the nave or the *oratorium*, but those on either side, 'unless they were to stand hidden behind the choir stalls, would need upper chambers looking into the choir from above flanking porticus'. The rubrics specifically state that this is not a compulsory practice,[42] but the implication is that it would, in general, be possible to replicate for most, so either most monastic churches had such upper chambers (provided by the design of this small coterie of clerics?) or there was a much simpler (and probably non-architectural) solution.

Interestingly, William of Malmesbury describes Dunstan adding aisles or *porticus* either side of SS. Peter and Paul at Glastonbury, as well as a tower. It may be that these provided just the upper chambers, and potentially even the *oratorium* needed for this liturgy, but the archaeological

---

41   Fernie (1983), pp. 93 and 108, however, believes only Gloucester was a double-ender; information supplied by John Blair.

42   Bedingfield (2002), p. 118, reproduces the relevant section of the *Regularis Concordia*, in both Latin and English, using Kornexl (1993), and also Symons (1953); see Bedingfield (2002), p. 2 n. 5.

excavations so far provide some evidence for a tower at the east (rather than the west) end.[43] The physical evidence is inconclusive, but consistent with the textual evidence. At any rate, *porticus* either side of a nave is a not uncommon arrangement, and was found as early as the seventh century at Old Minster, Winchester. At Deerhurst, Gloucestershire, there were openings at first-floor level between the *porticus* and the nave, and its architectural arrangement has been related directly to the *Regularis Concordia*, though this has been strongly disputed.[44] In the late tenth and eleventh centuries, western galleries were also to be found, as at Dover.[45]

Corroborative evidence for the office of *Tenebrae* is to be found in Ælfric's *Letter*, dated to about 1005, to the monks of Eynsham Abbey. There are also significant differences in the performance, in that the boys standing to either side are described as standing in the north and south porches, while to the west there is a pair of men. Gittos also notes that 'the partial Old English translation of the *Regularis Concordia* in Cambridge, Corpus Christi College, MS 201 (s.xi 1) also specifies the south and north *porticus*'.[46]

A more general link between the architecture and its liturgical function is shown by the example of the office of *Tenebrae* and further ceremonies of the *Regularis Concordia* – that is, that the whole building and its iconography was to be used in the dramatic presentation of the liturgy:

> This manner of arousing religious compunction was, I think devised by catholic men so that the terror of the darkness which struck the tripartite world with unusual fear, as well as the consolation of the apostolic preaching which revealed to the whole world Christ obedient to His Father even unto death for the salvation of the human race, may be signified most manifestly.

This is to bring alive the biblical events of the Passion, Crucifixion and Resurrection in the manner of Amalarius of Metz, and much that appears in the *Regularis Concordia* was drawn from the Cluniac tradition, but liberally mixed with local English tradition, in the way that Gregory the Great commanded Augustine for his mission.

Tenebrae, with the declaration of the death of the Saviour, was to be performed each of the three days before Easter, on Good Friday there was the *Adoratio Crucis*, when the Passion according to John was read as in the *Ordo Romanus I*. At the words 'and they parted my garments among them', two deacons stripped the altar-cloth as though stripping Christ's robe, a shocking and distressing, if rather abstract, action which, after all, is violence against an element of the architecture rather than an actor, or even an image of Christ. After solemn prayers, the Cross was addressed and venerated. Two deacons held the Cross before the altar and sang the Reproaches, 'Popule meus …' – Christ himself addressing and accusing the people present. After further reproaches, antiphons, prayers, psalms and a collect, the abbot, followed by others in order, kissed the Cross. The Cross was then 'buried':

---

43   Gittos (2003), p. 93, and William of Malmesbury, 'Vita Dunstani', in Winterbottom and Thomson (2002), p. 205.

44   Klukas (1984), pp. 81–98, as against Spurrell (2005), p. 18.

45   Gittos (2003), p. 96.

46   *Ibid.*, p. 98.

On one part of the altar, where there is space for it, there shall be as it were a likeness of a sepulchre, with a curtain stretched around it, into which the holy cross, when it has been adored, shall be placed according to the following arrangement: the deacons who previously carried the Cross shall come forward and wrap it in a cloth in the place where it was venerated. Then they shall carry it, singing the antiphons *In Pace in idipsum*, *Habitabit*, and *Caro mea in requiescet in spe*, until they come to the place of the sepulchre. When they have laid the cross inside, as if for the burial of the body of our Lord Jesus Christ, they shall sing the antiphon *Sepulto Domino signatum est monumentum, ponentes milites qui custodirent eum*. In that same place the holy cross shall be guarded with all reverence until the night of the resurrection of the Lord.[47]

The climax of the Gospel story unfolds in real time before the witnesses of this generation. In the *Concordia*, the new fire is brought at None, in the late afternoon, to light the Paschal candle, which is then blessed and prayers are said. Litanies are sung in procession to the font. The master of the *scola* shouts *Accendite!*, 'and now all of the candles in the church shall be lit and, with the abbot beginning the *Gloria in excelsis Deo*, all of the bells shall be rung'. The collect of Easter was sung and the Gospel book, having been preceded by incense only, in imitation of the holy women at the tomb, is opened for the singing of the same account as the mass continues.

That reading provides a delicious anticipation of the *Visitatio Sepulchri* during the first mass of Easter day:

As the third lesson is being read, four of the brethren shall dress, one of whom, dressed in an alb as if for some other purpose, shall enter and go secretly to the place of the sepulchre and, holding a palm in his hand, shall sit there quietly. Then, as the third respond is being sung, the other three shall enter, all of them dressed in copes and holding thuribles with incense in their hands, and step by step, in the likeness of those seeking something, they should come before the place of the sepulchre. Now truly these things are done in imitation of the angel sitting on the tomb and of the women coming with perfumes so that they might anoint the body of Jesus. When, therefore, the one seated shall see these three draw near, acting just like those wandering and seeking something, he shall begin to sing in a moderate and sweet voice, *Quem quaeritis?* As soon as this has been sung completely, the three shall answer with one mouth: *Ihesum Nazarenum*. Then the seated one shall say: *Non est hic. Surrexit sicut praedixerat. Ite nuntiate, quia surrexit a mortis*. At this command the three shall turn to the choir saying: *Alleluia. Resurrexit Dominus*. When this has been said the seated one, as though calling them back, shall say the antiphon: *Venite et videte locum*. Saying this truly, he should rise, lift the veil, and show them the place void of the Cross, with only the linen in which the Cross was wrapped. When this has been seen, the three shall lay down the thuribles, which they were carrying, in that same sepulchre and shall take up the linen and show it to the clergy and, as if showing that the Lord had risen and is not now wrapped in it, they shall sing this antiphon: *Surrexit Dominus de sepulchro* and they shall place the linen on the altar.

This liturgical drama incorporates an understanding of the eucharist itself in terms of the Passion, as presented by Amalarius of Metz. Liturgy is notorious for the way it varies from place to place, and the *Regularis Concordia* does not describe the liturgy as it was practised, but rather the way the Council thought it should be practised. Nevertheless, this was a key moment in the Passion narrative, as evidenced by the space allotted to it in the frescoes of the third-century church at Dura Europos, and the power of the dramatic presentation of the *Visitatio Sepulchri* and the fact that it was widely performed in the liturgy is demonstrated by small ivories from Metz, now in the Victoria and Albert Museum (Inv. nos 380-1871 and 266-1867). They both depict the Marys at the Tomb, but showing them not carrying spices, but thuribles, as do the monks in the *Visitatio*. Experience of the liturgy has changed the detail of the depiction of a key Gospel scene.

Importantly, music for the *Visitatio Sepulchri* is contained in the two manuscripts of the Winchester Troper, which 'gives tropes and certain other elements of the liturgy at the Old Minster

---

47   The whole ceremony is described in detail in Bedingfield (2002), pp. 126–31.

Cathedral at around 1000, probably to a certain extent preserving liturgical uses from before 980'. William of Malmesbury also records Dunstan giving bells and an organ to Malmesbury Abbey, 'to rouse the people to joy on festive days by its harmony'. Aethelwold made an organ himself, installing it first at Abingdon, then taking it with him to Winchester, where Alphege as his successor added another.[48] These must have been used liturgically, and when they were, the effect would have been sensational.

The props are few, and those there are have been abstracted, or 'spiritualized'. The architectural setting, being the same as for the daily celebration of the liturgy, strengthens the association of the *Visitatio* as a figure of the eucharist. The architecture functions for the dramatic presentation in the same way as a theatre functions for drama itself, and it is all the more powerful for its abstract, 'spiritualized' character.

From Anglo-Saxon to Norman: Ely

Æthelwold had been consecrated Bishop of Winchester in 963, after which the *Anglo-Saxon Chronicles* present him as having 'made many monasteries' and restoring others that had been ravaged by the Vikings. In 970, about a century after its destruction by the Vikings, he re-established Ely, introducing the Rule of St Benedict and sending Byrhtnoth, formerly Prior of Winchester, to be abbot. King Edgar was the sponsor of this monastic reform, and his original endowment of Ely grew to make the abbey one of the greatest in the land. The *Liber Eliensis* describes how Byrhtnoth was able to rebuild the church more magnificently than before:

> those parts of it which were so much decayed by time as to have fallen down he rebuilt; and by constant application and much labour and expense, he finished all the stonework, in less time than could be expected; and afterwards completing the roof, which had been quite destroyed by the fire; the church was so thoroughly repaired in all parts that it appeared on the whole more splendid than when it was first built.[49]

The church had at least one western tower and a south *porticus*, but as Fernie has demonstrated, for any more detailed reconstruction the documents can be read in different ways, either as a fore-runner of the twin-towered Norman west end (as Clapham did), or 'more like the west end of Deerhurst or Brixworth as remodelled in the tenth or eleventh centuries'. It is not entirely certain whether Deerhurst was monastic at this time, or whether it had a community of secular clergy.[50] In either case, it is likely to have been well suited to the liturgical practices recommended by the Council of Winchester under Æthelwold. Maddison draws attention to a description in the *Liber Eliensis* of what appears to be the east end: 'In the tower, to be sure, Etheldreda, Queen and famous virgin, was resplendent, entombed on the south side at her own altar, and her glorious sister, Sexburga, shone forth, buried to the north in the same place. These two olive trees of celestial mercy remained ... these two columns in the house of God.' Crook further notes that Etheldreda had been elevated, and that her sister Withburga, and later St Wendreda, were translated to Ely, the latter 'in a shrine, suitably adorned with gold and precious stones'.[51] Of course, this raises further questions about

---

48   Petersen (2003), p. 108; details of the organs are found in Bicknell (1996), pp. 13–14; the quotation from William of Malmesbury is from the translation in Winterbottom and Thomson (2002), p. 259.

49   Quoted in Maddison (2000), p. 7.

50   Fernie (1983), p. 115, referring also to the more definite reading of Clapham (1930), pp. 90, 94 and 98; further comments on Deerhurst supplied by John Blair.

51   Maddison (2000), p. 10, as in *LE ii, 146*; Crook (2000), p. 167, as in *LE* ii, 52, 53 and 76. See also Keynes (2003), pp. 23–5.

the nature of the 'tower' and whether there was a third High Altar placed centrally and forward of the saints' altars back against the walls. The arrangement remained until the newly built Norman church, or at least the monastic choir, was ready in 1106 for the saints to be translated.

In any case, the resources were certainly available to provide a splendid setting for the saints and the liturgy. Byrhtnoth provided wooden statues of the local saints covered with silver and overlaid with gold and precious stones. Leo, Byrhtnoth's sub-prior, gave a silver crucifix containing relics of St Vedast and St Amand, and King Edgar gave a golden crucifix containing relics for the altar of St Etheldreda. The king also gave a robe embroidered with gold and a Gospel book. Æthelwold gave a number of rich copes. Already in the 990s, Abbot Ælfsige had carried out some building works, extending the church and adding an altar to the Virgin, and over this a life-size enthroned Virgin and Child 'superbly made with gold and silver and gems'. He is also recorded as having had decorated silver gilt covers made for five of the Gospel books and left stoles, albs, gold-fringed vestments and copes to the abbey.[52]

The Normans reformed the English monasteries, and the rebuilding of Ely was begun in 1081 by Abbot Simeon, who had been Prior of Winchester. Together with his brother Bishop Walkelin, Simeon had begun the rebuilding of the new Cathedral at Winchester in 1079. Both new buildings were certainly very grand, not surprisingly their form was closely related, but the west end of Ely is quite distinctive (see Figure 6.5). Fernie points out that the differences between Continental and Anglo-Norman architecture are attributable to the influence of Anglo-Saxon work, and (though he himself remains sceptical) that Clapham specifically thought it possible for the remarkable western towers of Norman Ely to have been derived from the earlier Anglo-Saxon arrangement.[53]

The interior arrangement has side-aisles that may have been blocked to some extent, at least later in the Middle Ages, indicating that they probably were not used as processional ways. Maddison has speculated on the richness of the interior of the Norman western transept: 'It is almost as though we were stepping into a different church and it is quite conceivable that these architectural fireworks underline the significance of a new liturgical focus at the west end.'[54] He goes on to suggest that the use of the *Regularis Concordia* may have persisted even after Archbishop Lanfranc's *Constitutions* were being introduced elsewhere, and it is easy to see that the earlier liturgical use would be consistent with a western tribune, nave and original bridges at the ends of the crossing transepts. Fernie confirms that there were aisles on all three sides of the transepts, with the end aisles supporting a platform or bridge much wider than the present walkways and able to accommodate liturgical processions at gallery level.[55] They would have provided for the division of singers for *Tenebrae* in the Easter season, and even high-level processions. Furthermore, a great number of chapels for the individual masses of the priest-monks could be accommodated at tribune level. The demolition of the transept bridges was a major step that indicates that the use of the tribune changed radically, or had even ceased because of a change to the observance of the rite described in Lanfranc's *Constitutions*. The new church was ready for the translation of the bodies of Ely's saints on 17 October 1106. About a quarter of a century later, a very detailed description of the twelfth-century shrine was written:

---

52 *Ibid.*, pp. 29–30.
53 Fernie (1983), p. 172, and Fernie (2003), pp. 108–10.
54 Maddison (2000), pp. 27–9.
55 Fernie (2003), pp. 97 and 110; Klukas (1978), p. 312.

Figure 6.5   Ely Cathedral, view of the extant western towers from the southeast; photograph Allan Doig.

> The side of the shrine which faces the altar is of silver with embossed figures well worked in gold. Around the 'Christ in Majesty' are 7 beryls and crystals, 2 onyxes, 2 garnets and 26 pearls, and in the crown of this 'Christ in Majesty' are an amethyst, 2 carnelians, 6 pearls, and eight translucent stones; and in the four corners, 4 large crystals; and around it 9 crystals. And in the southern corner of this side, a golden collar affixed with a topaz, 3 emeralds and 3 sardonyxes. In the crown of the upper figure are 7 precious stones and 11 pearls. There is a knob bearing a cross of well gilded copper, with 12 crystals.

The description continues with each side described with equal care and delight in the precious materials, as is the antependium of the altar, an older work of the 1070s made by Abbot Theodwine. This provided a magnificent setting for pilgrim prayer and monastic liturgy. On the antependium, however, the text includes an enumeration of missing stones and pearls. They were fabulous pieces that most likely included earlier work, perhaps from the earlier shrine, as was so common with shrines and reliquaries. The missing stones and pearls may have been lost or stolen, but more likely they had been removed for other purposes. Perhaps it was part of the treasure given to King William which included the gold and jewels that covered Ælfsige's life-size sculpture of the Virgin and Child.[56]

The clerestory of the west front was completed some time after 1174 by Bishop Ridel in a characteristic Gothic form with pointed arches. The great period of the Norman Romanesque was drawing to a close in England.

---

56   The quotation is from Keynes (2003), pp. 54–5, the payment to William, p. 44.

Figure 6.6   The Abbey of Cluny, axonometric; from Dehio and von Bezold (1892), vol. II, pl. 212, no. 2; courtesy the Warden and Fellows of All Souls College, Oxford.

The Rise of the Cluniac Order

The reformed Abbey of Cluny was founded in 909, and from 910 was housed in a Frankish villa. As an 'exempt house', independent of episcopal power and subject only to the pope, its constitution made its abbots extremely powerful, and their prestige was greatly enhanced when the first six of their number were canonized. Very soon daughter-houses were being founded, and monks of Cluny were being brought in to reform other abbeys. The first church at Cluny was dedicated in 927, but the growth of the power of the order soon required a grander abbey-church, and Cluny II was built over the course of nearly a century from 955. Conant has suggested (though without strong evidence) that the basilica was tunnel-vaulted[57] with a tower at the crossing, two at the west end, apses at the ends of the aisles and the transepts, and an extended choir that culminated in an apse-echelon. In any event, tunnel vaulting did indeed come to be preferred by Cluniacs because of its fine acoustic, which so enhanced Gregorian chant. The sung liturgy was of such importance that the technical capabilities of Romanesque engineering were stretched to their limits to provide vaulting of the necessary span for the larger churches. The layout of the huge monastic complex was strongly reminiscent of the St Gall drawing, but with the inclusion of a chapter house as a significant innovation.

The liturgical arrangement of the church saw important developments in the sanctuary area. There were three altars to provide sequentially for the three main masses of the day, the morrow mass, the high mass, and at this later period, the Lady mass. The chancel gave on to side-aisles, and all three of these sections were provided with apses, producing a variant of the apse-echelon scheme, which allowed for elaborate processions. On Sundays, the procession moved round the cloister, stopped in the Galilee porch at the entrance to the church for a station, and entered the

---

57   Conant (1978), p. 148.

church. On the eastern side of the cloister, beyond the chapter-house, was the Lady Chapel which also was the site of a station in many liturgies, since there was a special devotion to the Virgin at Cluny.

When the number of monks had increased to more than two hundred, Cluny III was begun on an adjacent site in 1086 (see Figure 6.6). The church of Cluny II was dwarfed by the new building, and though the nave was cleared away to extend the cloister, the choir and *chevet* remained as a chapel about the size of one of the new transepts. The plan of the new church was a logical development of the old, gaining necessary width with double aisles, wrapping the inner aisle around the chancel as a semicircular ambulatory with radiating apsidal chapels in the *chevet*, and more apsidal chapels on the eastern sides of the transepts, as in the previous building.

By the time the great new church was completed in 1121, there were well over three hundred monks, and the order was approaching the peak of its power. By the middle of the twelfth century, there would be a thousand dependant houses across Europe. The architecture and the liturgy of Cluny III was a direct reflection of the size and magnificence of the order, not simply to accommodate increased numbers and function in that rather prosaic and narrow sense, but to function as a transcendent image of the heavenly Jerusalem such as the world had never seen. Such a building programme required huge resources, and these came from a somewhat surprising direction. Abbot Hugh gave spiritual support to King Alfonso VI of Spain, who gave 10,000 talents as a thank-offering for his survival during the bloody dynastic struggle and for the capture of Toledo from the Muslim rulers of al-Andalus on 25 May 1085. Alfonso's queen, Constance, was Hugh's niece, and the French clergy who reformed and strengthened the Spanish Church came from Cluny.

Figure 6.7 The Abbey of Cluny, view of the south transept from the northwest; courtesy Allan T. Kohl/Art Images for College Teaching (AICT).

All that remains of this great building campaign of Cluny III is the south arm of the transept, which challenges the imagination to envisage the stupendous scale of the whole (see Figure 6.7).

The designers were two monks of Cluny – Gunzo, a musician and formerly Abbot of Baume, and Hézelon, who is said to have been a mathematician. Conant analyses the complex proportional system 'from copious and exact measurements taken in the excavations':

> In the superstructure the 600-foot length was so divided that the various parts made up 400, 300, 250, 200, 150, 100, 50, and 25-foot sections. Again, the high vault of the nave, 100 feet to the point, was systematically related to the interior impost levels (at 80, 66 2/3, 40, and 25 feet). Vitruvian *symmetria postulates a minor unit, repeated in building up the design.* Cluny III, in this sense, had modules of 5, 7 (symbolic), 8 1/3, 25, and 31 feet. Tolerances never exceed 4 inches.[58]

Precision and harmony governed both the physical design and the musical use of the building, firmly interlocking the liturgy and architecture. The musical numbers of the Pythagorean series, which were believed to be the source of all beauty and harmony, were also employed, and 'the capitals of the choir, still preserved, represent the "tones" of medieval music'.[59] The vast sanctuary and double transept could hold the Chapter General of the order, which numbered 1212 monks in 1132, and the church could conceivably have held a general assembly of the whole order, if that were ever to have taken place. The abbey was the largest church in medieval Europe. In many ways, the building stood for the order and was the measure of its spiritual dimension, certainly for the period when it rang to the chant of the *laus perennis*. In the sanctuary were two altars embraced by a half-circle of columns. On the north side was a capital representing the Fall, and on the south, one of the Sacrifice of Isaac – a prefiguring of the Crucifixion and the eucharistic sacrifice. The capitals of the other columns screening the surrounding ambulatory had carved allegories of the monastic life. Above in the semi-dome was Christ in Majesty. The liturgy celebrated below was the focus of the monastic life idealized in the register of the capitals above, supporting the vision of the Saviour on his heavenly throne.

The co-ordinated movement of the processions through the hierarchically ordered spaces which gave physical scale and dimension to the music was astonishing. In 1682, before the destruction of the church, the Benedictine scholar Mabillon wrote that 'Even when one sees its majesty a hundred times, each time one is overwhelmed.' St Hugh had been elected Abbot at the age of 25 in 1048, and ruled over the order until he died in 1109. He did not live to see the completion of Cluny III, but the antiphon for his festival on 29 April most appropriately runs: 'Quomodo amplificemus illum, qui in diebus suis aedeficavit domum et exaltavit templum sanctum Domino'[60] ('How shall we praise him, who in his own day built a house and raised up a holy temple to the Lord?').

At Cluny III, as at so many other Cluniac establishments such as Paray-le-Moniale, Saint-Philibert at Tournus, and Romainmôtier, there was a large Galilee porch at the western entrance. This arrangement had first appeared at Saint-Riquier, where the Church of the Saviour was to be found above the narthex, but recent research indicates that at Cluny, the chapel above the narthex served a very different purpose. At Saint-Riquier, the Church of the Saviour had been fully integrated into the liturgy celebrated by the whole monastic community, whereas in Cluniac establishments, the chapel above the narthex, known as the Galilee, seems to have been used separately to celebrate the masses for the commemoration of the dead. The association of Galilee (and the 'Galilee') with the resurrection of Jesus and his entrance to eternal life, in combination with the monastic custom of holding a station before the western portal during the Sunday procession commemorating the

---

58   *Ibid.*, p. 200.
59   Sutton (1999), p. 52.
60   Conant (1978), pp. 187–8.

resurrection, is a strong argument for commemorative masses to have been held here.[61] A total of 30 masses were said for each deceased during the 30 days following his death, and again each year on the anniversary of his death. In an abbey of over three hundred monks, the chapel would be under considerable pressure and would be in use during the offices, so it would have to be an independent space, separate enough not to interfere with other celebrations.

Latterly, as though to underline the significance of this part of the church, the central portal below the chapel was characteristically surmounted by a *Majestas* depicting Christ in Majesty exercising judgment on the Last Day. There was clearly going to be growing pressure, eventually unsustainable, on the use of the Galilee, and after about a century the requirements began to be relaxed. The arrangement continued in Burgundian examples until the mid-thirteenth century, but elsewhere there was a reduction of the narthex chapel to a small chapel within the depth of the wall.

The extended commemoration of the dead for their salvation encouraged vocations to the monastic life and rich patronage. Such a demanding function would require a very significant architectural solution, and the Galilee would meet those needs, both practically and symbolically.

Pilgrimage and Pilgrimage Churches

The Church of Saint-Martin at Tours had itself long been a place of pilgrimage, since the death of St Martin in 397, and its popularity spurred Bishop Perpetuus to build a larger basilica in 472. The many miracles there had been the spur to Gregory's restoration of the shrine at the beginning of his own episcopate. Even before that, he records that it was evidence of miracles there that had helped to draw Clovis to the faith. The building history is widely disputed, and dates assigned to rebuilding range from the tenth or early eleventh centuries to the late eleventh century. Conant has reconstructed events as follows. After a terrible fire, the church was rebuilt from 903 to 918. In any event, the popularity of Saint-Martin as a place of pilgrimage is shown by the sermon Abbot Odo preached there about the importance of building churches with wide naves and aisles, so that the great crowds would not overturn the stalls and spill into the choir. This church was in turn destroyed by fire at the end of the century in 997, to be rebuilt under Hervé, who was Treasurer between 1003 and 1014.[62]

Saint-Martin proved to be the ideal pilgrimage church, with a long nave, large transept, an enclosed choir and an apse with ambulatory. The ambulatory made a complete circuit of the church, enabling the monastic offices to continue uninterrupted while pilgrims continued to circulate. The radiating chapels of the *chevet* have been widely accepted as having been part of this earlier scheme which were then reconstructed in the eleventh-century church, but recently Crook has maintained that 'it has yet to be satisfactorily proved'.[63] In any case, the fully developed scheme was present after the eleventh-century work, and in the middle of that century the transept was rebuilt with a ribbed tunnel vault and groined vaulting in the aisles as a precaution against fire. There were large towers over the transept porches and the crossing, and finally, another pair of towers was built at the west end.

The double aisles of the nave, the commodious transepts and the complete circuit of the ambulatory around the transept and choir turned out to be perfectly suited for the circulation of the large crowds of pilgrims, but the function of the radiating chapels is less certain. Crook concludes his study of 'Architecture and the Cult of Saints, from the Ninth to the Early Eleventh Century' by saying that:

---

61 Krüger (2003), pp. 151–3.
62 See Crook (2000), pp. 70–71, and Conant (1978), pp. 68 and 162.
63 *Ibid.* (1978), pp. 66 and 162, as compared with Crook (2000), pp. 158–9.

These few examples suggest that the link between radiating chapels and the veneration of saintly relics must be regarded as unproven. The notion that radiating chambers at crypt level might have accommodated secondary relics is an attractive one, but there is no certain evidence to this effect. The growth of radiating chapels at main level might simply be related to the need in monastic cathedrals to provide a greater number of altars.[64]

Despite the lack of conclusive evidence, the existence of a highly appropriate architectural form and a collection of important relics, combined with the number of priests and the need for commemorative masses, all press towards the conclusion that at Tours, the earliest of the type, radiating chapels housing the many relics were subsidiary spaces as secondary objectives of pilgrimage. It would seem natural that a pilgrim would want to enlist the help of as many saints as possible as a matter of simple spiritual economy.

By the time the apse-échelon arrangement existed at Tours, Saint-Martin was already the main shrine on the Paris–Bordeaux pilgrim route to Santiago de Compostella. Churches of a very similar type were built on the other pilgrimage routes through France: at Saint-Martial, Limoges, on the Vézelay–Périgueux route; Sainte-Foi, Conques, on the Le Puy–Moissac road (see Figure 6.8), and Saint-Sernin, Toulouse, on the Trier–Arles–Jaca road. Finally, there was the great Church of Santiago itself. Of these, the last three still exist, and it is Sante-Foi that gives the best impression of the original form, though it was the smallest and least grand of the group. Its treasury is a remarkably rich survival, and when on display in the church itself, must have been an awe-inspiring sight. Even though it was built between *c.* 1050 and 1130 with only a crossing-tower and a stair-tower on the south transept, it still has a lively silhouette in its largely unchanged wooded valley. The others of the type were at least twice its size, and bristled with many more towers, making an exciting and inspiring distant prospect for pilgrims.

Figure 6.8   The Abbey of Ste-Foi, Conques, view from the northeast; courtesy Allan T. Kohl/ Art Images for College Teaching (AICT).

---

64   *Ibid.*, p. 159.

Above the west door is a very beautiful carved tympanum dating from *c.* 1124 (see Figure 6.9). It was originally polychromed, and there are still traces of red, yellow, blue and black. It would have been an arresting sight, and the narrative graphically depicts the reason for pilgrimage. In the centre is Christ in Majesty with angels above exalting the Cross. Below, to his left, are souls being tormented and driven into the jaws of hell by devils, and to his right are the blessed being drawn towards the gates of heaven by a nimbed saint. The Virgin and St Peter lead the blessed in procession, including Abbot Begon of Conques and a crowned Charlemagne, who was a great benefactor of the Abbey. Ste Foi is shown praying for the faithful, and the chains of those released by her intercession hang beside her. Balancing the scenes of hell, on the other side below the procession is the heavenly Jerusalem. The message is abundantly clear, and fixes the path, and the hope, of the approaching pilgrim – make your prayers to the saint for her intercession to release you from the chains of your sins, make your personal offering for the salvation of your soul, and continue on your pilgrimage in the hope that you will ultimately arrive in the heavenly Jerusalem, which lies open to you beyond these doors. In the mean time, take your repose in the worship of this church as an earthly figure of that heavenly place.

Conques was never Cluniac, but Saint-Martial in Limoges became affiliated to Cluny round about the late 930s, at the end of Odo's abbacy, and it later withdrew. A decade after fire destroyed the church in 1053, it was transferred again to Cluny against the will of the monks, but when the community was settled, Cluny built them a great new church on the pattern of Tours. It was dedicated in 1095.

Saint-Sernin, Toulouse had originally been founded over the grave of the first Bishop of Toulouse, St Saturninus, one of the 'Seven Bishops' mentioned by Gregory of Tours.[65] He was martyred in the middle of the third century, a church was built over his tomb outside the city, and a

Figure 6.9   The Abbey of Ste-Foi, Conques, tympanum above the west door; courtesy Allan T. Kohl/Art Images for College Teaching (AICT).

---

65   See pages 95 and 109.

pilgrimage soon began. As the route to Compostella became established, Saint-Sernin became one of the major stopping points. It became an Augustinian house, and the Romanesque church was probably begun in the late 1070s or early 1080s, with the *chevet* completed before the end of the century, but the building programme continued well into the twelfth century. The high altar was consecrated in 1096 by Pope Urban II, and was signed by its carver, Bernardus Gilduinus. There are very few signed works of art from this period, but it is finely carved with birds and angels in the foliage around its edges. The theme unites the music of this world with that of the next, as its use unites the worship of men and angels.

In the north transept, there are some recently uncovered mural paintings, including a 'Noli me tangere' and one of the three Marys at the sepulchre, which was the most important of the images at Dura Europos and became a very common theme in ivories, manuscripts and liturgical 'drama' for Easter morning. From this transept, pilgrims had access to the ambulatory and to the crypt, where now, at any rate, there are reliquaries in the chapels, including a twelfth-century Limoges *châsse* of the True Cross and one of the early thirteenth in silver-gilt of St Saturninus, showing scenes of his martyrdom.

The end of the pilgrimage, the Church of Santiago de Compostella, in the twelfth century appears to have been the first cathedral to have had a walled-in choir, only relatively recently destroyed. Like Toulouse, Santiago was under the Augustinian rule. King Alfonso VI, the great benefactor of Cluny, also financed a good deal of the building here. Under the influence of Cluny, Alfonso outlawed the Mozarabic liturgy, and as his conquests advanced towards the south, senior French ecclesiastics from the Cluniac Order were given key positions in the hierarchy to reform and build up the Spanish Church.[66]

Religious wandering, particularly among the Irish, occurred between the seventh and eleventh centuries, but still the liturgical structure held: Bede tells of a wandering monk, Egbert, who even during his journeying, 'in addition to the solemn psalmody of the canonical offices, ... would recite the entire psalter in praise of God, unless prevented by illness. Every week he would fast for a day and a night'.[67] From at least the early eleventh century, when the first known formulary appeared, pilgrimage began liturgically. For the year 1099, Ekkehard wrote in the *Chronicon universale*: 'among these peoples, massing at the churches in greater hordes than can be believed, a priestly blessing bestowed, according to a new rite, swords with staffs and wallets'.[68] Later, a cross was added to the list.

During the eleventh century, the end of the journey was marked by a final stage to the sea, where a scallop shell was collected as a token of completion. By the early twelfth century, these shells, or later one of lead, would simply be purchased at the shrine. The pilgrimage to Compostella allowed the individual to participate in a long 'stational liturgy', so to speak, across the sacred geography of Europe – with a healthy added dose of carnival during the travelling. But attendant dangers were very real; a blessing on pilgrims ran: 'O Lord, heavenly Father, let the Angels watch over thy servants that they may reach their destination in safety ... that no enemy may attack them on the road, nor evil overcome them. Protect them from the perils of fast rivers, thieves or wild beasts.' A range of emotional needs was met, from fellowship to adventure to the unburdening of sin and the amendment of life unto salvation, with prayers said for you at each church along the way (after an appropriate offering was made), and collecting a whole choir of saints and angels to intercede on your behalf. Langland described a pilgrim with his collection of badges:

---

66   Conant (1978), p. 173.
67   Sumption (1975), p. 96.
68   Morris (2005), p. 202.

An hundreth of ampulles on his hatt seten,
Signes of Synay and shells of Galice
And many a cruche on his cloke and keyes of Rome
And the vernicle before; for men shulde knowe
And se by his signes whom he soughte had.[69]

Pilgrimage became highly formalized during this period, at least partly because it gave very real legal privileges, such as exemption from tolls, though not surprisingly, this was not always observed, at least in crossing the Pyrenees.

Cistercian Protest

In 1098, the same year that worship was transferred from the choir of Cluny II to the vast space of Cluny III, a pair of monks, Stephen Harding and Alberic, convinced Robert, their abbot at Molesme in Burgundy (founded by Robert in 1075, and not itself a Cluniac house) to leave with them and begin a new community which would follow the Benedictine rule more strictly. Along with 18 others, they settled at Cîteaux. There and in the daughter houses, of which there were 694 only about a century later in 1200, there was an austerity and simplification of both the liturgy and architecture.[70] Rather than the breath-taking grandeur of Cluniac liturgy in its setting, the Cistercian reforms pared both back to essentials, emphasizing abstract architectural qualities and spiritual depth in the structure of the liturgy.

Like Abbot Hugh who built Cluny III, the Cistercian Bernard of Clairvaux (1090–1153) also had a vision of his monastery as an image of the Heavenly Jerusalem, but the two were totally different. In a letter to Alexander, Bishop of Lincoln, St Bernard wrote of a pilgrim known to Alexander:

> Your beloved Philip, who wished to go to Jerusalem, has found a short-cut and has reached his goal much sooner than expected. ... His feet already tread the soil of Jerusalem and that city, which he had heard spoken of as on the banks of the Euphrates, he found in the clearings of a forest and of himself adores the place where he has halted his step. He has entered the holy city and taken his place among those about whom it is rightly said: 'From now on you are no longer strangers and sojourners, you are fellow citizens with the saints and servants of God.' But I do not speak of the earthly Jerusalem which is next to Mount Sinai in Arabia, the one which has fallen into slavery like all her sons; I speak of the one which is free, our celestial mother.
>
> And if you want to know, this is about Clairvaux. Clairvaux is connected ... by a kind of spiritual sonship with the celestial Jerusalem.[71]

This was an inward Jerusalem, as opposed to what the Cistercians saw as the outward show, wealth, liturgical pomp and architectural excesses of the Cluniacs. The opposition made for very public rows, and within the Cistercian Order, for constant vigilance against such vanities.

The differences are best characterized by the two famous twelfth-century texts by Abbot Suger of Saint-Denis and Bernard of Clairvaux. Suger described the work he has carried out at the Abbey of Saint-Denis, clearly stung by Cistercian criticism: 'The detractors ... object that a saintly mind, a pure heart, a faithful intention ought to suffice [for the administration of the Holy Eucharist] ... [But] we profess that we must do homage also through the outward ornaments of sacred vessels

---

69 Both quotations are from Sumption (1975), pp. 174–5.
70 Conant (1978), p. 223.
71 Pressouyre (1990), p. 102.

… with all inner purity and with all outward splendour.' Bernard's riposte to such an argument is in his *Apologia* to William of Saint-Thierry: 'The church is resplendent in her walls, beggarly in her poor; she clothes her stones in gold, and leaves her sons naked.' Suger protested: 'Bright is the noble work; but being nobly bright, the work should brighten the minds, so that they may travel through the true lights to the True Light where Christ is the true door.' What was true of the respective liturgical settings was also true of the liturgical books, with Cistercian legislation dating from the early twelfth to the early thirteenth centuries against the elaborate decoration of books.

The New Monastery originally used liturgical books from Molesme, and committed itself to keep rigorously to St Benedict's Rule. For the reform of the liturgy, they went to the Rite of Milan for the Office hymn of Vigil, Lauds and Vespers. They stripped away the accretions to the liturgy that destroyed the balance of prayer, work and study in the monastic life:

> In the liturgy these include the Psalmi Familiares, the Trina Oratio, the Offices for the Dead and for All Saints, the recitation of the Penitential Psalms, the visits to altars. These additions to the fundamental structure came to be associated in many Cistercian minds with the supposed ceremonial excesses of Cluny, where, according to the Cistercian in Idung of Pröfening's *Dialogue* of the mid 1150s, the monks kept their voices shrill with licorice juice and costly cordials, and the bells were so heavy that those ringing them ruptured themselves.[72]

Their return to original sources took them to the reforms of Gregory the Great, but posed the very real problem of where these reforms were best preserved. Initially, they looked to Metz, but on receiving a copy, found it corrupt, despite the high reputation of its *scola cantorum*. It would appear that they made do with amended versions of this until complete revision was achieved at the turn of the thirteenth century.

What is very remarkable is that in their rigorous application of the Rule, they required uniformity of use throughout the, by then very large, international order. Bernard retained central and personal control of the constitution of new foundations. In 1133, the year after the foundation of Fountains Abbey, Bernard sent the trusted choir monk Geoffrey to ensure their liturgical and musical use conformed, and also to supervise the building project. The nave now standing is thought to date from after the fire of 1147.[73] Such exceptions to the liturgical discipline as can be seen in surviving manuscripts only reinforce the sense of uniformity of practice despite the wide spread of geography and time. Deviations from the strict norms seem for the most part to be explained by local and national devotion to particular saints. The same uniformity is to be found in the architecture of the order. The General Chapter legislated for everything, and paid special attention to architecture and the liturgy.

Because there was such conformity between Cistercian houses, the architectural form and planning of the monastery buildings can be seen through a few examples. The basic plan is a simple version of St Gall or Cluny without ornamentation (forbidden in 1124), coloured glass (directed to be removed in 1182), crypts or towers (forbidden in 1157), with the arrangement of the elements adjusted to the particular site. A connecting stair gave the monks access from the dormitory to the transept in order to say the night offices. Lay brothers worshipped in the western end of the nave, and outsiders were provided with a chapel near the entrance gate. The simplified and (relatively) shortened liturgy gave time for the manual labour that made each abbey self-sufficient, and the design (and, ideally at least, some of the building) was carried out *proprio labore* by the brothers themselves, though lay brothers contributed much skill, craftsmanship and hard graft.[74]

---

72 Chadd (1986), pp. 300–301.
73 Brooke (1986), p. 16; Chadd (1986), p. 304; Fernie (2000), p. 190.
74 See Brooke (1986), pp. 17–18, concerning *proprio labore*.

The earliest and most complete survival, and surely the most faithful to Cistercian ideals, is Fontenay, built between 1139 and 1147. With pointed arches in the vaulting of the nave and aisles, and ribbed vaulting in the chapter house, it has a very Gothic feel. Repetition of architectural elements is a hallmark of the style; it was in every sense 'regular'. The tunnel vaulting is ideal for the sung liturgy, though that singing distinguished itself from the music of Cluny.

The churches did show considerable development, with chapels later added to the simple plans. The earliest had square chancels, but when the vast new monastery was built at Clairvaux in the late twelfth century, the church was given a polygonal apse with nine chapels. Clairvaux was a victim of its own success, and the scale of the new buildings gave them not just a little grandeur, even stern pride. At Cîteaux, the double aisles in the chancel allowed 11 chapels. It was not elaboration of the liturgy that required the elaboration of the architectural form of the chancel, but it was the result of liturgical requirements. All that had changed in the liturgy was the addition of a few feasts, but by the later mediaeval period, most of the choir monks were also priests, and needed separate altars to say their daily mass and the growing number of masses for the dead. England remained dedicated to the square-ended apse, giving room for five extra altars at the east end, or in the extraordinary case of Fountains Abbey, an eastern transept creating a Chapel of the Nine Altars, built soon after 1203.[75]

Cistercian houses throughout Europe were as far as possible uniform in plan, style and liturgical use, at times enforced by hand-picked envoys. There was, however, allowance for some variation in local building practices and peculiarities of site, but Cistercian architectural and liturgical uniformity in combination with their early use of the technical engineering advances of the pointed arch and ribbed vault, signature forms for the Gothic style, resulted in their playing a crucial role in the international spread and character of the Gothic and a tradition of sobriety of liturgical use.

---

75 Coldstream (1986), pp. 147–9.

CHAPTER 7

Gothic Architecture and the Latin Rite: From Origins to the Close of the Middle Ages

Gothic Architecture and Liturgical Use

The Gothic style has everything and nothing to do with liturgy. It has been approached as a kind of visual 'Scholastic argument' (Panofsky), an elaborate theological code (Mâle) or as feats of engineering (Viollet-le-Duc, Kidson and Wilson): 'The ritual and devotional use of mediaeval churches is a subject of great intrinsic interest but … the functions and architectural forms of the Gothic great churches showed remarkably little interaction.'[1] It was by no means changes in the liturgical functions that resulted in the development of the architectural forms of the Gothic from those of the Romanesque. New structural techniques involving the pointed arch, rib-vaulting and flying buttresses produced an architectural aesthetic based on linear definition of space rather than on mass and weight. On the other hand, churches are not just technical feats of architectural engineering, but were built as a solution to a diverse set of problems, including the provision of a range of spaces for the adequate performance of the contemporary liturgy, presented to highly skilled and widely experienced mason/architects by the ecclesiastical patron. Liturgy is the worship of the Church aligned with the worship of heaven, and a renewed conception of the Heavenly Jerusalem, along with new technical developments, tempted architects and their patrons towards a realization of its image on earth as a fitting setting for the liturgy. The contemporary vision of heaven was grounded in the biblical use of light imagery, epitomized by the Revelation of John the Divine, with precious stones, pearls, jasper and gold, crystal, music, incense, and above all, light. A theological aesthetics was developed from this strand by Augustine, Pseudo-Dionysius, Hugh and Richard of St Victor.

The enactment and ceremonial of the rite interprets the liturgy and its theology, and the whole history of the interaction of liturgy and architecture demonstrates that the setting also has its role to play in that interpretation and articulation of the vision. Recent studies, most particularly by Binski, emphasize that, as he writes, 'to see such buildings in terms of theology and belief more generally is … to see them poetically and imaginatively'.[2] As far back as the fourth century, Eusebius wrote that the Cathedral at Tyre 'is a marvel of beauty, utterly breathtaking, especially to those who have eyes only for the appearance of material things. But all marvels pale before the archetypes, the metaphysical prototypes and heavenly pattern of material things – I mean the re-establishment of the divine spiritual edifice in our souls. This edifice the Son of God himself created in his own image.'[3] A great many churches housed the bodies of saints, or had relics placed in or beneath, or at the very least near, the altar. While an altar is a symbolic link, the bodies of the saints and other relics are existential links with heaven itself. Such existential and physical links encouraged churchmen and their architects to create appropriate surroundings as an image of the Heavenly

---

1   Wilson (1990), p. 9.
2   Binski (2007), p. 2.
3   Eusebius 10.4, translated in Louth (1989), p. 318.

City built of precious stones – not a new aspiration by any means, stretching as it does back to Eusebius at least, but there were new technical means to produce the dazzling scale and brightness of already familiar descriptions of heaven with its 'sea of glass' and 'radiance'.

Imagery is extremely powerful in both architecture and liturgy, but it needs renewal, as happened with the immediacy and identification provided by the liturgical enactment of relevant biblical scenes during Easter week in the Palm Sunday procession and the *Visitatio Sepulchri* in particular. But even small changes in ceremonial and its allegorical interpretation could have architectonic ramifications: for example, as early as Ivo of Chartres (d. 1117), it became customary to keep the book at the altar and move it from the left, or 'epistle side', to the right or 'Gospel side' (liturgical north) of the altar, which led to the re-allegorizing of the mass and the considerable lengthening of the altar itself.[4] The Cistercians achieved their image of the Heavenly City by an inward regularity and discipline that could be repeated endlessly and everywhere by anyone following the strict religious life. This they did throughout Europe, taking with them, as a kind of architectural vanguard, the technical means which were the basis for the development of the Gothic – the pointed arch and the ribbed vault. Ironically, their inward vision contrasted sharply with the outward expression that was the full flowering of the style for which they acted as unwitting missionaries.[5]

During the Gothic period, there is a vast amount of both architectural and liturgical material spread over a huge geographical area for consideration. Many volumes could be devoted to this era alone. In order to maintain a degree of comparability, it will be useful to consider a relatively restricted geographical area, and for a reasonable balance it will be necessary to characterize some of the main issues at stake in the relationship between the liturgy and Gothic architecture. There are, then, four main themes to be explored here in the development of Gothic architecture as it relates to the liturgy. In the first place, there is the new vision of the Kingdom that stirred Abbot Suger when rebuilding Saint-Denis, the *locus classicus* of the Gothic. Secondly, there is the metaphorical dimension of architecture used in the rebuilding of the choir of Canterbury Cathedral around the tomb of the martyred Becket. Thirdly, there are elements of architecture that are retained but utterly transformed both formally and liturgically, such as the west end singers' gallery, quintessentially at Wells, also at Salisbury and Lichfield. Finally, there is the unified, single-build new cathedral at Salisbury related to the rational, codified Sarum Use. In looking at these different kinds of relationship between liturgy and architecture, particular care must be exercised. As Binski cautions: 'Becket is embodied in the Church, and the Church in him. Such interpretation is inevitably a delicate matter. Canterbury's new architecture is not so fully propositional as to allow "Becket" to be deduced from it alone, any more than "scholasticism" can be deduced from Amiens or "Use of Sarum" from Salisbury.'[6]

Saint-Denis and Abbot Suger's Vision of the Kingdom

Significantly, the first thing Abbot Suger did on his appointment to Saint-Denis was to commission new reliquaries from the abbey's in-house jewellers, who were pre-eminent in Europe. They were given fabulous material for their task: crystal and gold for the arm of St James, and for the sarcophagus of the patron, St Denis, there were 42 marks of gold, which the jewellers studded with pearls, topaz, sapphires, emeralds, rubies and diamonds. Impressive reliquaries were essential in attracting further offerings at the shrine, and Suger would need vast sums to achieve his ultimate

---

4   Jungmann (1959), pp. 81–2.
5   See Wilson (1990), p. 73, and Wilson (1986), p. 86, referring to Schnaase (1843–64).
6   Binski (2004), p. 9.

end – the creation of a great new church to provide a transcendental vision of the heavenly home of Denis and the other saints whose relics provided points of contact with the heavenly realm. In 1124, because of its support of the pope in the Investiture Controversy, France was being threatened by the English King, Henry I, and the Holy Roman Emperor, Henry V. This was a struggle of control of the Church through the power to invest the higher clergy with their ring of office and pastoral staff during the liturgy. When the investiture was carried out by a layman, in the person of the king or emperor, the bishop became their feudal vassal, compromising the autonomy of the Church. The French King, Louis VI, had to unite the powerful and factious regional nobility, and during a special ceremony at a royal assembly at Saint-Denis, he swore an oath before the relics of the saint that if he was victorious, he would make great gifts to him. The king was given the saint's banner, the *oriflamme*, to rally the nobility and carry into battle. The combined French forces gathered at Reims to await the emperor's attack, but it never came, and miraculously, the emperor withdrew. When the king fulfilled his vow with his offerings to the saint, St Denis himself had the resources to rebuild the abbey. The king also returned the Crown of Thorns and the sacred Nail of the Crucifixion, important objects of pilgrimage, and the revenues from, and jurisdiction over, the *Lendit* fair. The French king, Louis the Fat, was a vassal of the Church as a 'client' of St Denis, from whom he held the Vexin in fief.

Suger's high sacramentalism made him a natural 'Ambrosian' in matters of art, architecture and worship.[7] He had an extremely long abbacy, from 1122 to 1151, during which time he totally transformed the old abbey, consolidating 'the old walls and their impending ruin in some places', painting and gilding the structure of the old nave. At the beginning of his work *De Administratione*, he records that in the twenty-third year of his abbacy, the general chapter of the abbey pressed him to record the works accomplished during his administration.[8] For the Patronal Festival of Saint-Denis in particular, the Royal Abbey Church was too small, and it took some temerity to begin by tearing down the towered western entrance built by Charlemagne over the grave of his father Pepin and consecrated in 775. Even more remarkably, he carried out radical building and rebuilding programmes on a structure he believed to have been consecrated by Christ himself, but Suger's vision required that the building provide a fitting stage for the grandeur of the liturgy. Work began on the west end in 1137:

> In the front part, towards the north, at the main entrance with the main doors, the narrow hall was squeezed in on either side by twin towers neither high nor very sturdy but threatening ruin, we began, with the help of God, strenuously to work on this part, having made very strong material foundations for a straight nave and twin towers, and most strong spiritual ones of which it is said: 'For other foundation can no man lay than that is laid, which is Jesus Christ.'[9]

Throughout his writings, Suger, like Eusebius, laced the text with biblical quotations and references, and by playing on words dissolved the boundaries between biblical metaphor and sanctuaries built with and without hands, and hard labour and hard stone. He repeatedly stressed the role and lavish gifts of divine Providence: 'Solomon's riches could not have sufficed for his Temple any more than did ours for this work had not the same Author of the same work abundantly supplied His attendants. The identity of the author and the work provides a sufficiency for the worker.' There could hardly be a better defence against his critics than to say that it was a direct response to the richness of God's Providence, sometimes through miraculous assistance and divine intervention.

---

7   Grant (1998), pp. 24–6, and the Vexin, and the *oriflamme*, pp. 115–17.
8   Suger, *De Admin.*, I, translated in Panofsky (1946), p. 41; the quotation is from XXIV, p. 43.
9   *De Consecratione*, translated in Panofsky (1946), p. 89.

The consecration of the extended nave, the new West Front and its Chapel of St Romanus took place on 9 June 1140, and gave a foretaste of what was intended at the east end. The procession left the east end by the door of the south transept, and went right along the south side of the nave past the great west doors and in by the north door of the new work. The venerable old door from the cemetery had been carefully preserved and replaced in the new work. Though Suger and his architect swept away important sections of the old, they were clearly sensitive to elements of the architecture that would have historical and symbolic resonance within the new. The chapels were dedicated by Archbishop Hugues of Rouen, Manasseh Bishop of Meaux and Peter Bishop of Senlis, 'and very many other bishops'. Of the Chapel of St Romanus, Suger wrote: 'How secluded this place is, how hallowed, how convenient for those celebrating the divine rites has come to be known to those who serve God there as though they were already dwelling, in a degree, in Heaven while they sacrifice.' This chapel, elevated at tribune level, was out of sight from the nave while enjoying the open space of the church. Suger's master mason formed the chapel in two bays of the western block, but the architectural elements such as the bevelled piers were treated in a way that visually integrated the two.[10] It was clearly carefully designed to accommodate the action of the liturgy, and the whole intention was to create in the worship in this world an intimation and parallel of the next.

Light is a very common biblical image for the divine, and was clearly of utmost importance in the aesthetic of Saint-Denis. Panofsky made a much bigger claim that the same Neoplatonic theological approach that governed the liturgy and its setting also governed the other architectural and artistic elements.[11] The corrupted and contingent forms in this world can serve as a bridge to an understanding of the true forms that exist in the transcendent heavenly Kingdom. Suger's ninth-century predecessor, Abbot Helduin, had conflated the third-century St Denis of whom Gregory of Tours had written with the first-century Greek mystical theologian Dionysius the Areopagite. His writings associated God with Light, and 'a ninth-century Latin translation of the original Greek Pseudo-Dionysian corpus (which we now know was written in Syria in the early sixth century) was housed in the library of Suger's abbey and lent further credibility to this legend.'[12] The great west doors were of gilt bronze, depicting the Passion and Ascension and inscribed with verses ending:

> Bright is the noble work; but being nobly bright the work
> Should brighten the minds so that they may travel,
>   Through the true lights,
> To the True Light where Christ is the true door.
> In what manner it be inherent in this world the golden door defines:
> The dull mind rises to truth through that which is material
> And, seeing this light, is resurrected from its former submersion.[13]

No sooner was the west end complete than work began at the east. Suger records that it was completed in three years and three months, and consecrated in 1144. This new east end *chevet* was to be a regular and unified design, with a double ambulatory providing nine altars sheltered

---

10   *De Admin.*, XXVI, p. 45; the chapel is discussed in Radding and Clark (1992), pp. 66–7.

11   See also Kidson (1987), pp. 1–17, and for an extensive discussion of the controversy surrounding the interpretation of Saint-Denis by various authors, see Raguin, Brush and Draper (1995), especially the chapters by McGinn (1995), Fernie (1995) and Clark (1995).

12   Thibodeau (2006), p. 221; Von Simson (1989), especially pp. 120–23, agrees concerning the influence of Dionysius the Pseudo-Areopagite, as does Brown (2004), pp. 274–6, but he also notes those who disagree.

13   *De Admin.* XXVII, pp. 47–9.

in semicircular recesses under large windows: 'a circular string of chapels, by virtue of which the whole [church] would shine with the wonderful and uninterrupted light of most sacred windows, pervading the interior beauty'.[14] The gold and jewelled *châsses* of the Patron Saints were behind the altar at the centre of this 'circular string of chapels', and would have caught, refracted and reflected the light from the great windows. In order to achieve this revolutionary new form, Suger had to destroy the whole of the most sacred part of the edifice believed to have been consecrated in a pontifical ceremony performed by Christ himself. But, writes Suger in his own defence: 'Deliberating under God's inspiration, chose – in view of that blessing which, by the testimony of venerable writings, Divine action had bestowed upon the ancient consecration of the church by the extension of [Christ's] own hand – to respect the very stones, sacred as they are, as though they were relics.'[15] There was a similar tale of the miraculous consecration of a royal abbey in England, where St Peter himself was said to have consecrated Westminster Abbey.[16]

The west end had been consecrated on 'the fifth day before the ides of June', and only a month later, 'on Sunday, the day before the Ides of July', a very remarkable architectural liturgy took place which interpreted to those present Suger's vision of the architecture and the role of the abbey itself: 'St Augustine describes … the basilica as an image of heaven and goes on to relate the manual labor of its construction to the spiritual process of edification. For Augustine, as for Suger, the two are inseparable.'[17] Liturgy, architectural construction and spiritual edification were assembled by Suger in the most extraordinary way: a great number of bishops and abbots were brought together 'in the presence of our Lord, the Most Serene King of the Franks, Louis'. The procession to the excavations was led by relics of immense importance, the Nail from the Crucifixion and the Crown of Thorns, the arm of St Simeon who held the infant Jesus at the Presentation in the Temple, and many other relics. In the presence of this great cloud of witnesses, holy water from the consecration of the west end was used by the bishops present to prepare mortar; as Amalarius wrote: 'mortar is made from lime, sand and water. … Water is the Holy Ghost. … For in the same way that the stones in a wall cannot be linked without mortar, nor can people be brought together in the building of the New Jerusalem without the love of the Holy Ghost.'[18] Chanting the psalm 'His foundation is in the holy mountains' (Psalm 87), the dignitaries laid stones in the foundation of the *chevet*. King Louis VII himself joined them to lay his stone, as did many others in their turn: 'Certain persons also [deposited] gems out of love and reverence for Jesus Christ: chanting *Lapides presiosi omnes muri tui* ["All thy walls are precious stones"].' The ambiguity makes it seem that the gems were also pressed into the mortar, which is very unlikely, but that reinforces the symbolism of both actions. Eusebius' sermon at the consecration of the Cathedral at Tyre comes strongly to mind:

> An acute and discriminating judge of other matters, he [Bishop Paulinus of Tyre] is well able to appreciate and evaluate the character of the souls entrusted to his care; and from almost the first day he has never ceased to build, finding the right place, now for the shining gold, now for the tested pure silver and the precious, costly stones among you all. So once more a sacred, mystic prophecy is fulfilled in what he has done for you – the prophecy that says: 'Lo, I prepare for you the carbuncle for your stone, and for your foundations the sapphire…'.[19]

---

14   *De Consec.* IV, Panofsky (1946), p. 101.

15   *Ibid.*

16   See *The Life of King Edward the Confessor*, Cambridge University Library MS Ee.3.59, fo. 18r, where the scene is illustrated.

17   See Von Simson (1989), pp. 128–30, for his analysis of the relationship between the architecture and liturgy; the quotation is from p. 129.

18   Amalarius of Metz, *Liber officialis*, quoted in Binding (2002), p. 48.

19   Eusebius 10.4, in Louth (1989), p. 319.

At Saint-Denis, the living stones laid their own stones in the foundation of the chief architectural element of the Royal Abbey, whose prayers and banner (the *Oriflamme*) protected and unified the realm under King Louis VI in 1124; they also gave precious stones, which would most likely have been pressed into the walls of the *châsses*, or architectural cases of the relics as scaled versions of the *chevet* and its jewel-like windows. At both scales, these are vessels of holiness. Ever practical, Suger didn't neglect to provide a foundation in the form of perpetual revenues to ensure the completion of the architectural project, its maintenance and function.

It is easy to see how this imagery would appeal to the king. All these dignitaries had literally joined themselves to one another and to him in one fabric – a much-needed political act in his fragmented kingdom. In *De Consecratione*, Suger continues his description of the architectural symbolism with references in the Psalms (46 and 48) to Zion and the 'City of the Great King', then to the superstructure of the *chevet*, with the 12 inner columns:

> representing the number of the Twelve Apostles and, secondarily, by as many columns in the side-aisles signifying the number of the [minor] Prophets, according to the Apostle who buildeth spiritually. *Now therefore ye are no more strangers and foreigners, says he, but fellow citizens with the saints and of the household of God; and are built upon the foundation of the apostles and prophets, Jesus Christ himself being the chief cornerstone* which joins one wall to the other; *in Whom all the building* – whether spiritual or material – *groweth unto one holy temple of the Lord. In Whom we, too,* are taught *to be builded together for an habitation of God through the* Holy *Spirit* by ourselves in a spiritual way, the more loftily and fitly we strive to build in a material way.[20]

None of this imagery is at all new, standing in the tradition stretching back through Amalarius to Eusebius, but Suger had given it a new and powerful architectural and liturgical expression that served the purposes of both the abbey and the king. The architectural and liturgical synthesis of already existing elements renewed both the architectural and liturgical language in a Gothic synthesis which could be used with local inflection to convey local concerns, whether royal ambition, the cult of saints, ecclesiastical order, or local or national politics.[21] It was not by any means Suger's (nor his architect's) invention, but he was undoubtedly one of its earliest and greatest poets.

Three years later, on 11 June 1144, at the consecration of the new *chevet* and translation of relics, there was, if anything, an even greater gathering of hierarchy and nobility of the realm, lovingly enumerated by the abbot. The archbishops and bishops, in white pontifical robes, with mitres and carrying crosiers, were stationed around the vat of holy water placed centrally between the new High Altar and the Altar of the Saviour near the chord of the *chevet*. They exorcized the water and 'celebrated the wedding of the Eternal Bridegroom so piously that the King and the attending nobility believed themselves to behold a chorus celestial rather than terrestrial, a ceremony divine rather than human.'[22] The liturgy was one with the cosmic music, and those harmonies were also embodied in the design of the architecture 'by means of geometrical and arithmetical instruments … with the wonderful and uninterrupted light of most sacred windows, pervading the interior beauty'.[23]

After the consecration of the building, the translation began with the prostration of the archbishops and bishops before the relics, and then the king himself led the procession of relics with the *châsse* of St Denis, his patron and patron of the abbey and all France. Kings and emperors had long been problematic figures within the liturgy, from Constantine to Charlemagne, but here

---

20 *De Consec.* V, p. 105, quoting Ephesians 2:19–22.
21 For the early debate about the first fully Gothic building, see Von Simson (1989), p. 156 n. 49.
22 *De Consec.* VI, p. 115.
23 *De Consec.* IV, p. 101, and see Von Simson (1989), pp. 132–3, for his discussion of medieval music.

the king both retains their quality of being the image of Christ and is seen in ecclesiastical terms as being of Episcopal rank through his anointing at the coronation. By virtue of the coronation liturgy, he embodies both Church and state in his own person. Physical reality and 'symbolism', but not mere symbolism, were conjoined in the architecture and the liturgy: 'What appears to us as no more than festive pageantry was, in point of fact, an act of sacramental as well as constitutional significance. It was precisely his anointment as *Christus Domini* that raised the king above even the most powerful dukes.'[24] These liturgies lent much-needed legitimacy and authority to the king in his struggle with the regional nobility of France and their courts.

Suger proudly claimed that a procession of such grandeur had not been seen since Christ himself consecrated the original church. The route took them from the narrow crypt through the cloister, and the other relics were taken from temporary resting-places in tents near the entrance to the Monks' Choir to the door to meet the Patron's relics and accompany them to the steps leading to the elevated choir. The other relics were placed on the old altar, while the king placed his *châsse* on the new altar in front of the new tomb of the Patron and his Companions.

The main altar was consecrated by the Archbishop of Reims, and the Altar of the Saviour and the Holy Cross near the chord of the *chevet* was consecrated by Theobald, Archbishop of Canterbury, and a further 19 altars were consecrated by the many other bishops present. After the consecrations of the altars, the bishops proceeded to celebrate masses 'so festively, so solemnly, so different and yet so concordantly'. Suger clearly values the unity in diversity of practice. *De Consecratione* ends with what could well be the Collect for those masses:

> Blessed be the glory of the Lord from His place.
> Blessed and worthy of praise and exalted above all
>   be Thy name, Lord Jesus Christ,
> Whom God Thy Father hast anointed the Highest Priest
>   With oil of exaltation above Thy fellows.
> By this sacramental unction with the most holy chrism
> And by the susception of the most holy Eucharist,
> Thou uniformly conjoinest the material with the immaterial,
>   The corporeal with the spiritual,
>   The human with the Divine,
> And sacramentally reformest the purer ones to their original condition.
> By these and similar visible blessings, Thou invisibly restorest
>   and miraculously transformest the present
>   Into the heavenly Kingdom.
> Thus, when Thou shalt have delivered up the Kingdom to God,
>   even the Father,
> Mayest Thou powerfully and mercifully make us
>   and the nature of the angels,
>   Heaven and Earth, into one State;
> Thou Who livest and reignest as God for ever and ever. Amen.[25]

The consecration of the altars of the *chevet* had been co-ordinated at a single ceremony, and thereafter the liturgy would incorporate 'in a specific way, Suger's new *chevet*, integrating it into the daily, weekly, and yearly cycles'. For example, there were daily processions round the *chevet*

---

24 *Ibid.*, p. 138.
25 *De Consec.* VII, p. 121.

at the end of matins and after vespers. As might be expected, there was also a procession after the festal celebration if there was an altar in the *chevet* dedicated to that saint.[26]

By now, the old nave, though it had been consolidated and redecorated, itself needed to be harmonized with the splendour of the east and west ends: 'We would retain, however, as much of the old walls on which, by the testimony of the ancient writers, the Highest Priest, our Lord Jesus Christ, had laid His hand; so that the reverence for the ancient consecration might be safeguarded, and yet congruous consistency [might be assured] to the modern work.' When the nave was consecrated, Bernard himself was probably there, and never criticized what he found.[27]

By the time the restoration of Saint-Denis was complete, the fabric had been enlarged and integrated within a new, logical architectural language (see Figure 7.1). As Suger used it, the rich and glittering materials spoke in a matching register to the elaboration of the ceremonial

Figure 7.1   The Abbey of Saint-Denis, interior of the nave towards the apse; courtesy Allan T. Kohl/Art Images for College Teaching (AICT).

---

26   Rasmussen (1986), p. 43.
27   *De Admin.* XXIX, pp. 51–3; and for Bernard, see Grant (1998), pp. 25–6.

of the liturgy, where 'the kingdom of this world is become the Kingdom of our Lord, and of his Christ'. His detailed writings on his *Administration* and the *Consecration* of his splendid abbey were not written solely as record; they were apologetic. He was defending his theological position against the criticism of friends such as Bernard of Clairvaux, who saw such extravagance as the sin of pride. The Gothic, spread by his Cistercians, was in a register of utter simplicity, stripped to the deeper level of its architectonic power. The Cistercian dialect was hugely successful in its reach, but the growing wealth and power of the Cistercians drew even them away from Bernard's austerity. Bishops and kings, on the other hand, had few qualms about using Suger's higher register of liturgical and architectural language.

Built from *c.* 1130 to 1164, the Cathedral of Sens was contemporary with Suger's work at Saint-Denis, and it is also very successful in transforming Romanesque elements into a convincing Gothic style, though light was not so crucial to the design. But it was neither as complex nor as radically innovative as Saint-Denis; it was cooler and simpler, as would be expected of a cathedral which (through its archbishop, Henry) was under the influence of Clairvaux. Bernard wrote *On the Conduct of and Office of a Bishop* at Henry of Sens' request, and in that text he enjoins modesty in building.[28] Though it was the seat of the premier archbishop of France, Sens bears little comparison to Saint-Denis in national, theological or liturgical terms. Both the Archbishop of Sens and the Bishop of Chartres, Geoffrey, were under the influence of Bernard of Clairvaux. Geoffrey was also a friend of Suger, and was present at the consecration of the new *chevet* of Saint-Denis, himself consecrating the altar of St Stephen, Protomartyr, in the crypt.

The second half of the twelfth century experienced a fever of building, especially in the Île de France. After the fire of 1134 at Chartres Cathedral, Geoffrey began rebuilding the west end, and the façade and towers, though sculpturally more sophisticated, bear a strong resemblance to Saint-Denis.[29] On the night of 10 June 1194, the Cathedral of Chartres was destroyed in a great fire. Only the west façade survived. The miraculous survival of their greatest relic, the Virgin's Tunic, encouraged the chapter and townsfolk to build an even grander cathedral to house this sign of divine favour. This relic, and an even earlier legendary tradition, made Chartres the centre of Marian devotion in France, not to say Europe: 'Before the end of the Middle Ages [these beliefs] had been embodied even in the authoritative and solemn language of its liturgy.'[30] Within about forty years, this new paradigm of the High Gothic was complete, and was soon applied in the choir at Soissons, and the plans of Reims, Amiens and Beauvais.[31]

Canterbury Cathedral: Architectural and Liturgical Imagery of Martyrdom

In December of 1170, four of King Henry II's knights entered Canterbury Cathedral, drew their swords and struck down Thomas Becket, Archbishop of Canterbury, before his own altar. Hugh Mauclerk, one of the knights, when the crown of Becket's head was struck off by a blow, scooped out his brains and dashed them to the floor. The whole of Christendom was appalled, England held its breath, and the community in Canterbury struggled to realize the meaning of the catastrophe:

> The insistence of early iconographers of the saint that he was martyred sacrilegiously before an altar implied that Christ was crucified again in Thomas's martyrdom. ... The gruesome facts of St Thomas's

---

28   Von Simson (1989), pp. 144–5.
29   For a thorough discussion of the sculpture of Sant-Denis, see Blum (1992).
30   Von Simson (1989), p. 160.
31   See Grodecki (1986), pp. 58–68.

martyrdom illustrate the way in which allegory helped those nearest to Thomas to comprehend and assimilate horror, and also the extent to which such narratives were premised on liturgical and allegorical thinking.[32]

The king was not immediately penitent, and when the monks were finally allowed to elect a successor, he disputed the result. Richard, the new archbishop, had to go to Rome to have his election confirmed. He arrived back in Canterbury on 4 September 1174. The following day, a second catastrophe ironically presented an opportunity for a monumental realization of the full meaning of Becket's life and death in these liturgical and allegorical modes. On 5 September 1174, fire in nearby cottages sent sparks flying onto the roof of the choir of Canterbury Cathedral, and 'being driven by the fury of the wind between the joints of the lead, remaining there amongst the half rotten planks ... . For the well-painted ceiling below, and the sheet-lead covering above, concealed between them the fire that had arisen within.'[33] Gervase, a monk of Canterbury, gave this eye-witness account, and continued with a detailed description of the rebuilding of the cathedral. The monks had managed to save the relics and moved them and the bodies of the saints to the nave where services were temporarily held at the altar of the Holy Cross. In the nave, they were shielded from the laity and pilgrims only by a low screen, and there, in their grief, they 'wail and howl, rather than sing, the diurnal and nocturnal services'.[34] Underlying popular politics determined Canterbury's future. Becket's resting place was the crypt beneath the now-ruined 'Glorious Choir', begun at the turn of the twelfth century and consecrated in only 1130. Following the death of Becket, the destruction of the choir was a devastating loss. It had been one of the greatest buildings of England, as William of Malmsbury wrote: 'Nothing like it could be seen in England either for the light of its glass windows, the gleaming of its marble pavements, or the many coloured paintings which led the wondering eyes to the panelled ceiling above.'[35] Miracles began to take place soon after the martyrdom, and when the choir of the Cathedral was gutted by fire, it soon became obvious that there was an opportunity to provide a splendid new architectural context for Becket's shrine. There was, after all, a great new narrative of a Christ-like figure to be told in the glass of new windows for the benefit of spiralling numbers of pilgrims attracted by the increasing number of miracles. The finance would be provided by these waves of pilgrims, and by the time Becket's body was translated to a new shrine in the Trinity Chapel in 1220, the offerings of pilgrims amounted to £1142, almost two-thirds of the total revenues of the monastery.[36]

To begin rebuilding, the monks took advice from a number of master masons, and appointed William of Sens to rebuild the choir. Until then, there had been no 'full-dress' Gothic work in England; the new choir and corona at Canterbury would be the first, though there was significant Cistercian Gothic work in the north at Ripon and York. French sources are immediately obvious in the magnificent capitals, which are similar to examples at Saint-Denis and Sens. At the beginning of the fifth year of construction, William had a serious fall from the scaffolding, and he was replaced by William the Englishman, who immediately began the preparatory work for Becket's chapel at the east end:

For this was the place assigned to him; namely the chapel of the Holy Trinity, where he celebrated his first mass, where he was wont to prostrate himself with tears and prayers, under whose crypt for so many years

32 Binski (2004), p. 8.
33 Gervase of Canterbury, translated in Holt (1957), pp. 52–3.
34 Gervase, in Holt (1957), p. 54.
35 William of Malmesbury, *De Gestis Pontificum Anglorum*, quoted in Tatton-Brown (1989), p. 67.
36 Sumption (1975), p. 160.

he was buried, where God for his merits had performed so many miracles, where poor and rich, kings and princes, had worshipped him, and whence the sound of his praises had gone forth into all lands.[37]

At the beginning of the next season of building, 'the sixth year from the fire', the new master was pressed by the monks to bring the new choir into use by the next Easter. He completed the enclosing wall, and built a temporary wooden wall across the unfinished east end. 'He erected the three altars of the presbytery. He carefully prepared a resting-place for St Dunstan and St Alphege.' Oddly, the translation of the relics of these patrons of the cathedral back into the choir was carried out, much to the annoyance of the monks, almost as unceremoniously as they had been removed on the night of the fire. Gervase explained about the complications of Easter eve:

> As all that was required could not be fully performed on the Saturday because of the solemnities of that sacred day, it became necessary that our holy fathers and patrons, St Dunstan and St Alphege, the co-exiles of the monks, should be transferred to the new choir beforehand. Prior Alan, therefore, taking with him nine of the brethren of the church in whom he could trust, went by night to the tombs of the saints, that he might not be incommoded by a crowd, and having locked the doors of the church, he commanded that the stone-work that enclosed them be taken down.
> The monks and servants of the church therefore, in obedience to the Prior's commands, took the structure to pieces, opened the stone coffins of the saints, and bore their relics to the *vestiarium*. Then having removed the cloths in which they had been wrapped, and which were half consumed from age and rottenness, they covered them with other and more handsome palls, and bound them with linen bands. They bore the saints, thus prepared, to their altars, and deposited them in wooden chests, covered within and without with lead; which chests, thus lead-covered, and strongly bound with iron, were enclosed in stone-work that was consolidated with lead.

That was an astonishing amount to achieve in one night's work, but the translation of patron saints was an act of such liturgical importance that the angry monks had clearly expected it to take place on Easter eve with great ceremonial. The actions of the prior and his associates, however, were accepted by the archbishop 'after due apology and repentance'. In effect, the solemnities of Easter had been given liturgical precedence even above the return of the patrons to their permanent resting-places. They should be in place for the liturgies, but they should not impinge on the celebration of 'that sacred day'. The contingencies introduced by the state of the building (see Figure 7.2), the fact that they were moving into the new choir for its first use, and the particular liturgical requirements of Easter eve all required that the liturgy follow a rather unusual progression:

> The service of Holy Saturday was performed in the chapter-house, because the station of the monks and the altar which had been in the nave of the church were removed to prepare for the solemnities of the following Easter Sunday. About the sixth hour the archbishop in cope and mitre, and the convent in albs, according to the custom of the church, went in procession to the new fire, and having consecrated it, proceeded towards the new choir with the appointed hymn. At the door of the church which opens to the martyrium of St Thomas, the archbishop reverently received from a monk the pyx, with the Eucharist, which was usually suspended over the great Altar. This he carried to the great Altar of the new choir. Thus our Lord went before us into Galilee, that is, in our transmigration to the new church. The remainder of the offices that appertain to the day were celebrated. And then the pontiff, standing at the Altar and vested with the *infula*, began the *Te Deum laudamus*.[38]

In the next phase in the building of the Trinity Chapel, to the east of the new choir, allegory, made concrete in coloured materials, linked Becket's martyrdom, the liturgy and the architectural

---

37 Gervase, in Holt (1957), p. 59, also in Woodman (1981), pp. 93–4.
38 Translated in *ibid.*, p. 95.

Figure 7.2   Canterbury Cathedral, interior view towards the Trinity Chapel and corona; courtesy
Allan T. Kohl/Art Images for College Teaching (AICT).

setting. Becket's blood and water, given out at his passion, was diluted and drunk as a cure, as a parallel to wine mixed with water at the eucharist as a memorial of the blood and water flowing from the side of Christ at the Passion; the columns of rose-pink Tournai marble and white limestone from Caen of the Trinity Chapel above Becket's tomb-space also commemorate the way in which he died, with his blood shed and brains spilt before the altar. Fragments preserved in the cathedral library and said to be from the shrine itself are also of this unusual pink marble. Binski has recently speculated that since there had been salvage of some of the high-quality surviving materials such as stained glass from the destruction of the choir, perhaps some of the old pavement before the old high altar where Becket's body rested before burial was also reused in front of the great new shrine in the Trinity Chapel. They would virtually be contact relics of his martyrdom:[39]

> Colour allegory was also becoming part of the universal language of the Church. In the 1190s Lotario de' Conti, the future Pope Innocent III, a schoolman from the same circle as [Archbishop Stephen] Langton, and a devotee of Becket, volunteered one of the first and most important codifications on colour symbolism in his thoughts on liturgical colours in *De missarum mysteriis* which recorded contemporary Roman practice understood within a broadly Victorine framework of allegory. Drawing on Exodus 28, Canticles 2:1 and Canticles 5:10, Innocent states that of the five colours used in the Church (white, red, green, black and violet) white is the colour for the feasts of confessors and virgins, red for the apostles and martyrs.[40]

---

39   Binski (2004), p. 24.
40   *Ibid.*, p. 9; and see Jungmann (1959), p. 84.

Colour symbolism and allegory inform the liturgy, and especially the architecture surrounding the commemoration of the martyr. Both serve to interpret his life and the horrific manner of his death. The lower parts of the outer walls were all that was left of the 'Glorious Choir' (begun in 1096 and dedicated in 1130) of Becket's own cathedral, but their presence was a fitting *memento mori* showing the determination to rebuild the community on the basis of Becket's life and death. The saint clearly wanted a more exalted setting for his shrine than the lower crypt. The high windows of the choir have biblical scenes, and the walls of the corona virtually dissolve in glass painted with scenes of Becket's posthumous miracles. The encircling twin columns of the choir arcade bear a clear resemblance to the imperial mausoleum, Santa Costanza, in Rome. Christopher Wilson notes that 'the presence of the shrine determines … the materials of the inner columns, rare cream and pink stones symbolising Becket's virginity and martyrdom and also the brains and blood spilt at his death'.[41]

With his tomb as the architectural focus of the new Trinity Chapel, the narrative of his life and death emblazoned in the windows of the corona giving light to the surrounding space, reused materials possibly treated as contact relics, and architectural form and materials chosen for their allegorical potential (the pink columns and the 'corona', built to house the reliquary of Becket's crown, at the *caput* or head of the cathedral), the building comes to embody the saint and the spiritual meaning of his martyrdom (see Figure 7.3).

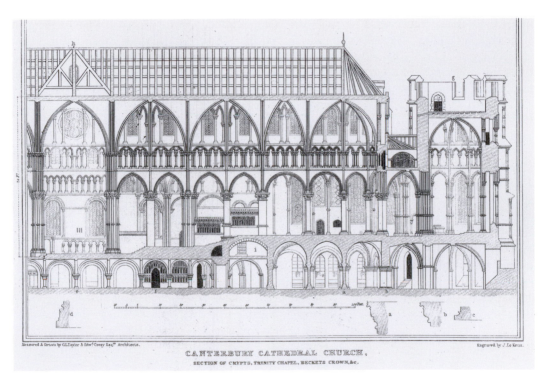

CANTERBURY CATHEDRAL CHURCH.
SECTION OF CRYPTS, TRINITY CHAPEL, BECKETS CROWN, &c.

Figure 7.3   Canterbury Cathedral, longitudinal section of the Choir, Trinity Chapel and corona; Conway Library, Courtauld Institute of Art.

41   Wilson (1990), p. 90.

Architectural, biblical and liturgical hermeneutic all function similarly in the way they unfold and interlink, without precise one-to-one mapping of references; they suffuse and illuminate each other rather than correspond directly: 'The same pattern of allegorical reading of columns and other parts of the Church can be recognized in the *De gemma animae* of Honorius of Autun and in Peter of Roissy's later treatise on the liturgy, the *Manuale de mysteriis ecclesiae*. Columnar and lapidary images are used pointedly with reference to Becket himself.'[42] These commentators on the liturgy were in the tradition of the Carolingian liturgist Bishop Amalarius of Metz, who interpreted the liturgy allegorically. Contemporary with the building of the new choir at Canterbury and Becket's Crown, Bishop William Durandus of Mende wrote the *Rationale for the Divine Offices* (*c.* 1292–96) in the tradition of Amalarius. In it, he describes the four levels of exegesis:

History is when the words describe an actual event, when, for example, whatever is being described exactly as it occurred. ... Allegory is when what is said literally has another meaning spiritually, or when something else can be understood from a simple deed. ... Tropology means the conversion of manners or moral exhortation for the foundation or correction of morals, speaking either mystically or plainly. ... Anagogy comes from the words *ana*, meaning 'elevated', and *goge*, meaning 'lead', as if to say 'leading upwards'. Thus the anagogical sense leads us from the visible to the invisible realm.[43]

Suger used anagogical argument when writing *De Administratione* from 1145 to justify the lavishness of his works at Saint-Denis. The method of exegesis can equally be applied to scripture, liturgy and architecture; in fact, the first chapter of Durandus' *Rationale* is devoted to the symbolism of the church building. Durandus opens his first chapter with a common idea: 'First of all, let us consider a church ... as the material church is constructed from the joining together of various stones, so is the spiritual Church by that of various men.' Hugh of St Victor similarly opens the first chapter of his *Mystical Mirror of the Church* by saying: 'The material church in which the people come together to praise God, signifieth the Holy Catholic Church, which is builded in the heavens of living stones. ... All the stones be polished and squared: that is, all the saints be pure and firm.'[44]

It is hardly to be wondered at that such a 'high doctrine' of representation of personal qualities in material substance, to the point that there should be a sense of their actual presence, should be current at this historical period, since it was then, at the end of the twelfth century in France, that the practice of elevating the host at the consecration was introduced. As the theology of this simple action was developed, it came to be seen as sacramentally effective in itself. The host was thus reverenced and adored as more than just a relic, as the very body of Christ himself. This high devotion ironically led to a great reduction in lay communion at mass, where seeing became a substitute for receiving.[45] Less than half a century after the translation of Becket into the new Trinity Chapel, the feast of Corpus Christi was made universal in the West. Carrying the consecrated host, as the very Body of Christ, in a monstrance through towns and villages in great processions to allow the laity to see and worship became a substitute for receiving the sacrament.

---

42 Binski (2004), p. 10.

43 *Rationale*, Pro. CCCM 140:9–12, quoted in Thibodeau (2006), p. 238; Mâle (1972), 'Introduction', explores the 'symbolic code' of mediaeval art and liturgy, especially as presented by Durandus.

44 Durandus, translated in Neale and Webb (1906), p. 10; Hugh, in *ibid.*, p. 153.

45 Rubin (1991), pp. 63ff.

Wells Cathedral and the West Front as a Renewed Liturgical Element

The Anglo-Saxon Church at Wells lost its cathedral status *c.* 1090. Its apse has been excavated, and foundations of what appears to have been an atrium at the west end have been uncovered. Towards the end of its early period as a cathedral, Bishop Giso (1061–88) introduced the Rule of Chrodegang to the college of secular canons.[46] On 23 June 1174, Reginald FitzJocelin de Bohun was consecrated in Savoy as Bishop of Bath, and on his return journey he was in Canterbury on the night of 4/5 September, witnessing the awful fire.[47] Later in the 1170s, he decided to rebuild the collegiate church to the north of the Saxon structure, and he will have kept in close touch with the magnificent developments at Canterbury, though it is difficult to identify any borrowings. Wells perfectly preserves the whole range of buildings necessary for a college of secular canons, with its cloister, library, chapter house, houses for the senior clergy and for the vicars choral, fortified precinct with gateways, and a moated bishop's palace. Tatton-Brown has heralded Wells Cathedral as 'the first cathedral to have pointed arches everywhere, and in every way can be considered the first truly "English Gothic" building in Britain', but it was to be Canterbury that exerted the greatest architectural influence in the thirteenth century.[48]

Documentary evidence is poor for the progress of works at Wells, but most recent archaeological evidence suggests that Bishop Reginald's builders first set about providing a self-contained eastern chapel for the celebration of the liturgy while work progressed on the three bays of the choir, which was completed in 1184.[49] The western arch was then temporarily blocked up to allow the choir to be used while construction continued on the transepts, in turn finished early in the thirteenth century, perhaps in 1206. The next phase consisted of the eastern bays of the nave, to *c.* 1210. There was a hiatus in the works at this point, caused by the papal interdict of 1208–13 and excommunication of the king. The bishop was in exile, and work on the choir did not begin again until 1215 at the earliest. Finally, there was the great West Front, begun in 1220. The plan is extremely well suited to the Use of Sarum, and it appears that the square east end, the double-aisled transepts and the towered West Front were taken from the work carried out by Bishop Roger at Old Sarum.[50] Phased construction had meant that at each stage there was the maximum provision for the liturgy while allowing for changes to the design or plan, and for the phasing and allocation of resources, but it is in the design of the West Front that the liturgical masterstroke is to be found.

When the central portion of the West Front had closed the nave (see Figure 7.4), and the whole of the lower tier was completed as far as the string course below the west windows, the Cathedral of St Andrew, Wells was consecrated on St Romanus Day, 23 October 1239. The whole of the West Front was completed by 1250, and its vast sculptural programme was carved between *c.* 1235 and 1243, a remarkably short time considering its extent. The use of sculpture was on an even grander scale than its probable source in the portal sculpture in French Gothic as at Chartres, and the decorative treatment of the reredos, architectural shrines, reliquaries and even manuscript illumination and seals may have been re-imported to the full-scale architectural façade.[51]

---

46   Sampson (1998), p. 12.
47   Tatton-Brown (1989), p. 89.
48   Tatton-Brown (1989), p. 97, agrees with Harvey (1974), p. 119, and Clifton-Taylor (1986), p. 74; but for a more detailed discussion of Wells's position in stylistic developments, see Wilson (1990), pp. 78–82, and also Draper (1995).
49   The results of the most recent archaeological study are published in Sampson (1998), which is concentrated on the West Front; p. 13.
50   Draper (1995), p. 122.
51   Sampson (1998), p. 135, and see also Binski (2004), pp. 109–10.

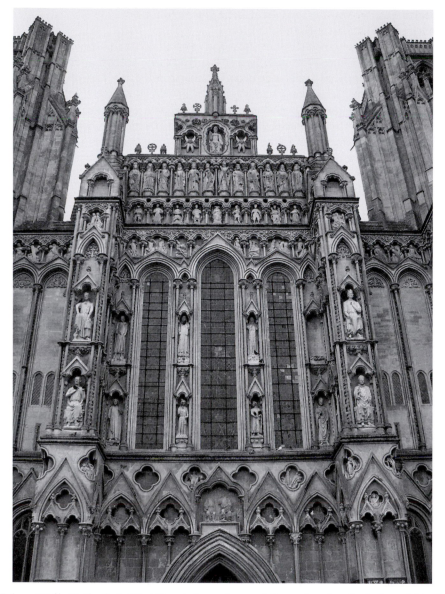

Figure 7.4   Wells Cathedral, West Front above the west door, showing the holes within the lower range of quatrefoils opening from the singers' gallery; photograph Allan Doig

    In repair and conservation work during the late nineteenth and early twentieth centuries, traces of paint were found on the figure-sculpture and some of the architectural elements of the façade. During the major conservation of the West Front between 1974 and 1986, the archaeologist Jerry Sampson gradually built up a picture of the original decorative programme, including ghostly traces of texts in Lombardic letters in the sheltered mouldings of three of the niches and one of the quatrefoils above right of the west door.[52] This lower tier of niches has been empty since the iconoclasm of the seventeenth century, but some identifiable figures (from the Gospels) remain on

---

52   Sampson (1998), p. 123.

the north-east return face of the front. The labelled quatrefoil is from the biblical range just below the string-course below the windows.

The evidence together points to there having been Old Testament figures filling the lowest tier towards the south, and New Testament towards the north. At least some of the figures were glossed by texts, presumably allowing identification, and probably also contributing more broadly to theological interpretation. Only a few of the individual sculptures can be securely identified by their attributes, including Thomas Becket holding his severed crown, so a full reconstruction of the iconographic programme is no longer possible, but the fact that there are deliberate groupings of figures (including a possible Gospel Procession; Plate 9) and some figures have had attributes re-carved to maintain the order, suggests a carefully worked out scheme. The sculptural programme was unfinished, and most probably the painting was too, though all completed figures bear traces of paint and were probably fully polychromed. The best and most extensive evidence exists for the area around the west door, which is also the liturgical focus as the entry point for the Palm Sunday procession. From what remains, Sampson summarizes the interpretation of the lower tier as follows:

> The association of the Four Maries with the figures on the north tower suggests that they are New Testament personages, an association that is amplified by the biblical quatrefoils above them. There are no such defining characteristics on the south side, and only the implication of the biblical quatrefoils above suggests an Old Testament origin for the two surviving sculptures. These narrative quatrefoils divide at the centre of the west elevation, radiating out to north and south: on the south they begin with the creation and continue through the fall and the flood, probably up to the time of the prophets; on the north they begin with St Matthew and follow the New Testament narrative from the nativity to the ascension. This division between the Old Testament to the south and the New Testament to the north must almost certainly have been perpetuated in the life-size sculptures beneath.[53]

Above this range, at the level of the west windows, the niches are peopled by saints, ecclesiastics and historical figures, and in the narrow strip above the windows are the dead rising at the end of time. The third and final group, carved in the third quarter of the fifteenth century, is contained in the central gable, with angels, above them apostles must be intended in the 12 aedicules, and the culmination of the design is the seated Christ of the Second Coming. All the figures were brightly coloured and gilded, with their tiered niches held within an architectural matrix defined by a grid of polished black lias stone. What Mâle wrote of Chartres could as well apply to Wells:

> The cathedral recounts the history of the world after a plan which is in entire agreement with the scheme developed by Vincent of Beauvais. At Chartres, as in the *Speculum historiale*, the story of humanity is entirely reduced to the history of the elect people of God. The Old and the New Testament and the Acts of the Saints furnish the subject-matter, for they contain all that is necessary for man to know of those who lived before him. They are the three acts in the story of the world, and there can be but three. The Old Testament shows humanity awaiting the Law, the New Testament shows the Law incarnate, and the Acts of the Saints shows man's endeavour to conform to the Law.[54]

Just as the text of the liturgy itself is an interweaving of scriptural quotations and references recounting salvation history, so is the cathedral, and most especially this façade. The architecture does not just provide a series of spaces shaped for a series of actions, the architectural setting plays an active role in the interpretation of those actions, and here is the masterstroke: within the depth of the façade below the west windows and above the vaults are two passages with holes that

---

53 *Ibid.*, p. 157; see also p. 164 for the procession, and p. 155 on the reconstruction.
54 Mâle (1972), p. 131.

open in quatrefoils which formerly had sculptures of singing angels in the lower range, and above trumpeting angels in the higher. These were singers' and musicians' galleries respectively, used to animate the façade for processions beginning in the burial ground in front of the west doors. The faithful, living and departed, were gathered up within that salvation history awaiting the promised resurrection at the last day before the Great High Priest who had gone before into the heavenly sanctuary: 'For Christ has entered, not into a sanctuary made with hands, a copy of the true one, but into heaven itself' (Heb. 9:24), 'and since we have a great high priest over the house of God, let us draw near with a true heart in full assurance of faith' (Heb. 10:21–2). The *Golden Legend*, the *Te Deum*, Anglo-Saxon liturgical sources, Augustine's *City of God*, the *Revelation* of St John the Divine, and Hugh of St Victor have all been suggested as sources for the sculptural programme, and Binski sees it primarily as a political statement in the dispute over primacy in the See between Bath and Wells, in combination with conventional imagery of the New Jerusalem coming down adorned as the bride of Christ.[55] All are surely relevant, but the most telling consideration in the interpretation of the architecture is its liturgical function.

Liturgy and architecture are inextricably bound up together in a single matrix of meaning, and so interpret one another. Durandus' *Rationale* (*c.* 1292–96) again comes to mind. It opens:

> All things associated with the services, furnishings and vestments of the Church are full of signs and symbols of the divine, and they all overflow with a celestial sweetness when they are scrutinised by a diligent observer who can extract 'honey from a rock and oil from the stoniest ground [Deut. 32:13] 'Who knows the order of the heavens and can apply its rules to the earth?' … A reason cannot always be given for everything which has been handed down to us by our predecessors … therefore, I, William, Bishop of the holy church of Mende by the indulgence of God alone, knocking at the door, will continue to knock, until the key of David deigns to open it for me [cf. Rev. 3:20] so that the 'king might bring me into his cellar where he stores his wine' [Cant. 2:4]. Here the celestial model which was shown to Moses on the mountaintop will be revealed to me [cf. Ex. 20 and Heb. 8:5], so that I can unveil and explain clearly and openly each furnishing or ornament which pertains to the ecclesiastical services, what each of these signifies or represents figuratively and to set forth their rationale, according to that which has been revealed to me by Him 'who makes the tongues of infants speak eloquently' [Wis. 10:21], 'whose Spirit blows where it wishes' [John 3:8], and gives to each one as it deserves' [1 Cor. 12:11], to the praise and glory of the Trinity.[56]

The balance of opinion suggests that the liturgy of the earliest Wells Consuetudinary of c. 1273–98, contemporary with Durandus' *Rationale*, followed the Sarum Use very closely, with changes adapted to the specific circumstances of Wells. As elsewhere in England since the reforms of St Dunstan c. 870, there was a well-established tradition of vivifying the biblical narrative with processions and theatrical presentations such as the *visitatio sepulchri*.[57] Dunstan's Rule describes the procession on Palm Sunday starting in front of the west door of the church with the singing of the Carolingian hymn *Gloria, laus et honor*, written by Bishop Theodulf of Orleans. The procession described in the Consuetudinary began after the office of Terce around 9 a.m., proceeding from the choir into the north aisle, round the east end, then round the cloister, passing the old Lady Chapel which had been the east end of the old cathedral,[58] and out into the cemetery opposite the west door. Here

---

55 Sampson (1998), pp. 152–53, and see Binski (2004), pp. 112–21, who uses a sermon by St Bernard particularly poetically to explore the richness of the imagery of empty niches as 'clefts in the wall'.

56 Quoted in Thibodeau (2006), p. 242; see also Neale and Webb (1906), pp. 1–2.

57 Concerning the Wells Consuetudinary, see Sampson (1998), p. 168, following Watkin (1941) and Klukas (1981). For the debate concerning the liturgy as drama, see Hardison (1965), who accepts, and Young (1933) who rejects the mass as drama; and see more recently Bedingfield (2002) and Swanson (1992).

58 Draper (1995), p. 121.

branches had been blessed and passed amongst the waiting crowd. A consecrated host specifically referred to as 'the body of the Lord' in a pyx was placed in a shrine with relics and, preceded by a light, was taken directly into the cemetery to meet the procession. Considering this high doctrine of the host being the very 'body of the Lord', it is interesting to note that the earliest English mandate for the feast of Corpus Christi is from 4 June 1318 (only a couple of decades later than the Consuetudinary) by Bishop John Droxford of Bath and Wells. In the fourteenth century, Corpus Christi fraternities were highly involved in the dramatic liturgies of Easter.[59] Levels of reality were revealed in the shifting perceptions made possible through the liturgy and its architectural setting.

The Palm Sunday procession was the re-enactment of the entry of Christ into Jerusalem,[60] and the account from Matthew 21 of Christ's triumphal entry was read at the first station. The procession then made its way to the second station at the west door, where the choir sang *Gloria, laus et honor* from the singing gallery behind the painted angels, holding golden crowns for the just on either side of the Coronation of the Virgin over the west door. The gathered throng would answer with the hymn's refrain:

> The façade thus worked as an *organum*, the generic expression for concerted chanting or, more literally, organ playing. The Passage at Wells is too small literally to have accommodated an organ of any consequence or profundity. But the analogy with organs is not entirely idle, since the ecclesiastical use of such instruments in England had been encouraged during the pre-Conquest Church reforms of St Dunstan and St Ethelwold, and one possible location of early organs as siren-like sources of clamour, rather than for liturgy, may have been the type of atrium or *westwerk* that existed at Winchester and, possibly, Wells itself.[61]

The next station was at an aisle door where three priests sang *Unus autem* facing the people. Probably with the blast of trumpets or perhaps the clamour of an organ from the top gallery or at the east end of the nave, all returned to the west door, and it is worth remembering that the cantor Wulfstan as early as 993–94 recorded of the Winchester Organ that 'the melody of the pipes is heard everywhere in the city'.[62] The procession next entered 'Jerusalem' with Jesus, and the 'New Jerusalem' where Christ has gone before, by passing under the shrine and pyx held aloft by its two bearers. Progress to the next station was also probably accompanied by music; material had been set aside in 1310 for building an organ at Wells, and it was most likely positioned above the otherwise inexplicable large stone corbels below the triforium on the south side of the nave, though such an organ may have been removed when the pulpitum was built in about 1335.[63] The next station of the procession was before the rood screen, where the president sang *Ave rex noster*. Until at least the eighteenth century, there were still 'station stones' in the pavement marking the places for members of the choir and clergy (as was also the case at York, Fountains and Lincoln, and there were other forms of processional pavements at Canterbury, Old St Paul's, Westminster Abbey and St George's Windsor).[64] After this station, they would enter the choir itself.

Starting with a blast of angelic music above sculptures of the rising dead and the singing of angels above the heads of the assembly who were in the midst of death, they had entered into the sanctuary made with hands as a figure of the one made without hands, and there they would celebrate the eschatological banquet in the eucharist.

---

59 Rubin (1991), pp. 199 and 236.

60 See Brieger (1957), p. 30.

61 Binski (2004), p. 112.

62 For a discussion of the use of early organs, see Bicknell (1996), p. 11.

63 Bowers, Colchester and Crossland (2006), pp. 1–2.

64 Detail of the stations is given in Sampson (1998), pp. 168-69; see also Vallance (1947), pp. 16–19, for a general discussion of processional pavements.

Salisbury Cathedral and the Use of Sarum

The ancient See founded by St Birinus at Dorchester in Oxfordshire was divided into the Sees of Winchester, Ramsbury and Sherborne. Ramsbury and Sherborne were united by Bishop Herman of Ramsbury in 1058, and transferred to Old Sarum in 1075. In 1078, St Osmund was made Bishop of Salisbury by William the Conqueror. Like his king, Osmund was a great administrator, giving the cathedral its constitution and ordering its services. Considering the high regard for his sanctity, it would be surprising if much of that constitution and liturgical use did not survive in the classic formulation in the Consuetudinary of Richard Poore, appointed dean *c.* 1198. Not much more than a century later, by the early fourteenth century, the Use of Sarum had been adopted by most of the dioceses of the southern province, except Hereford.

The cathedral on the hill at Old Sarum was hemmed in by the fortifications and the garrison was oppressively thrown together with the chapter, and at the very beginning of his appointment Richard Poore and his brother Herbert, who was Bishop of Salisbury (1194–1217), petitioned the king for permission to move the cathedral a few miles to the south down to the water-meadows. Richard was appointed Bishop of Chichester in 1214 and translated to Salisbury in 1217, the year a petition finally went to the pope to move the See from Old Sarum. The petition was granted in 1218, and on 14 April 1219 a temporary wooden chapel was erected within the new precincts. By Trinity Sunday that year, the chapel, dedicated to the Virgin, was ready for use, and the bishop celebrated the liturgy there and dedicated the burial ground. On 28 April 1220, St Vitalis' Day, after the service there was a litany in procession, a sermon, and foundation stones were laid at the east end. The bishop laid a stone for himself, and as proxy, laid one on behalf of the pope and the Archbishop of Canterbury; the Earl and Countess of Salisbury laid stones as patrons and benefactors, and then came the dean, archdeacon and members of the chapter. 'Still more stones were laid at a later date by distinguished laymen who had been with the king to fight the Welsh at the time of the original ceremony.' This was on a smaller scale than Suger's great ceremony at Saint-Denis, but was building a similar metaphorical fabric. Five years later, work had progressed to the extent that three altars were consecrated on Michaelmas Eve to the Trinity and All Saints, St Peter and the Apostles, and St Stephen and the Martyrs.[65] Archbishops, including Langton, and bishops gathered during the ensuing days, and on 21 October King Henry III 'heard a mass in state ('*gloriose*': or does it mean 'Mass of the Glorious Virgin', which Bishop Poore had started, and for which that bishop presented a pair of candlesticks which had been provided by a legacy?)'.[66] The King gave a silk cloth and ten marks of silver, to be followed by a golden cup and a ring with a ruby, which he intended should be inserted into the golden cover of a gospel book already containing relics.

There is a Sarum inventory compiled by Abraham de Winton, Treasurer between 1214 and 1222. It is an impressive list of the altar-plate, vestments including scores of copes, banners and other 'props' for the theatrical presentation of the liturgy. Many gifts are recorded along with the donors, including a silver flabellum (liturgical fan) given by Bishop Herbert Poore, an ampulla (small flask for oil) decorated with precious stones from Richard Poore when Bishop of Chichester, and a morse, or clasp set with precious stones and pearls for a cope, given by Archbishop Langton. The inventory details the ornaments included in the Treasurer's audit of 30 March 1214 which the chapter brought with them when they moved from Old Sarum to their new cathedral. At the end of the inventory is recorded what was allocated by the Treasurer before 1222 (when he was succeeded as Treasurer by Edmund Rich, now known as St Edmund of Abingdon) to the altars of St Peter, All

---

65   Tatton-Brown (1989), p. 94; Wordsworth (1901), p. 189; Binski (2004), p. 65; the quotation is from Harvey (1974), pp. 61–2.

66   Wordsworth (1901), p. 190.

Saints, St Stephen, St Nicholas, Mary Magdalen and St Thomas the Martyr, and it is supposed that lost leaves of the manuscript contained lists for further altars.[67] The contents of the respective lists give a general impression of the type and level of ceremonial used at each of the altars.

In 1220, a whole series of remarkable liturgical events took place in England: there was the second coronation of Henry III at Westminster Abbey on 17 May (Whit Monday), Hugh of Lincoln was canonized, and on 7 July Becket was translated to the new Trinity Chapel of Canterbury Cathedral.[68] In 1226, Osmund's body was moved to the centre of the eastern Trinity Chapel, doubtless in the hope of establishing a local pilgrimage cult, though the petition for the canonization of Osmund would not be successful for another 230 years.

Salisbury was the first cathedral to be built after the hiatus caused by the interdict. The Archbishop of Canterbury was then Stephen Langton, who taught theology at Paris and had been a prebendal Canon of Notre-Dame. At Paris, one of his students had been Richard Poore, who assisted at the translation of Becket in 1220.[69] Elias de Dereham, Canon of Salisbury, was named by Matthew Paris as one of the two designers of Becket's tomb. He may also have overseen the design of the area surrounding the shrine of Osmund at Salisbury, and he probably worked closely with the master mason Nicholas of Ely on the planning and perhaps even the design of the complex eastern half of the cathedral, since he is described as 'Rector of the new fabric' from 1220 until 1245, when he died. He had been steward to Bishop Reginald FitzJocelin of Wells, where he was also a canon, and through Elias came influences from both Canterbury (especially in the tall shafting of the two Trinity Chapels) and Winchester.[70] The West Front of Salisbury is of a similar form to Wells, though most of its sculpture has been destroyed, only nine remaining in 120 niches. Presumably, the iconography was broadly similar, as the gate of (the New) Jerusalem, though any specific sources and political overtones will naturally have been a matter of local historical circumstances.

The façade certainly functioned in a similar way to Wells in the liturgy, especially the great procession of Palm Sunday, with a singers' gallery below the west windows. At Salisbury, this gallery opened both outwards and into the nave, indicating an enhanced liturgical function, perhaps including drama. The holes to the exterior are much higher, and would have required that a temporary wooden platform be erected for use in the Palm Sunday liturgy, so it would seem that the most common use was for liturgical events inside the cathedral. Sampson suggests that the dimensions of the passages at Salisbury and Wells are so closely related that Nicholas of Ely, master mason at Salisbury, may well have visited the Wells master mason, Thomas Norreys, and taken the dimensions back to his drawing board for setting out his new design.[71] Here was another entrance-gate to the New Jerusalem, and in his letter congratulating his fellow members of the chapter on their decision to move, Peter of Blois refers to Ezekiel's vision of the Temple (Ez. 40–48) and Solomon.[72]

Richard Poore was translated to Durham in 1228, and pre-deceased Elias in 1237 (by which time the east transepts and choir were complete), so neither saw the consecration of the cathedral in 1258, but they were almost certainly responsible for the general planning of the whole cathedral and its huge precinct at the centre of a new cathedral city (see Figure 7.5). The building programme was remarkably short, 38 years, and its conception and detail remarkably unified and consistent with the clarity and order of the Use of Sarum.

---

67 'Register of St Osmund', lxxxiiii–lxxxv, in ibid., pp. 169–82 and 170–71.
68 *Ibid.*, p. 190, and Binski (2004), p. 64.
69 *Ibid.*, p. 65.
70 Tatton-Brown (1989), p. 95, and Binski (2004), p. 73.
71 Sampson (1998), pp. 171–2.
72 Binski (2004), p. 72.

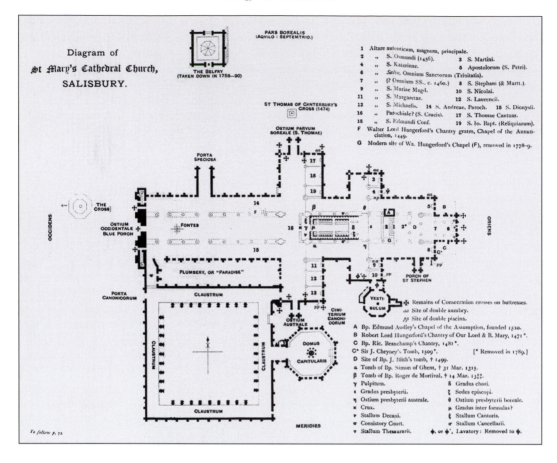

Figure 7.5   Salisbury Cathedral, plan; from Wordsworth (1901).

Although the Use of Sarum was essentially the Roman Rite, it was performed very differently. The Curial liturgy was progressively simplified, while the Use of Sarum was orderly, but highly elaborate, with many ministers allocated specific tasks. Processions of groups of these ministers were an extremely important part of the use, often taking place between the office and the liturgy, and in the Sarum Breviary there is a rubric directing that, during the Magnificat, the altars from St Martins in the north-eastern transept right round the east end should be censed in procession.[73] Significantly, the square-ended presbytery and two pairs of transepts provided that all the altars should be properly orientated, which the French *chevet* scheme with radiating chapels did not. Clearly, this was important in the Sarum rite. The architectural and liturgical preferences go hand in hand. To the west, the podium on which the side-aisle columns sit physically reinforces the notion that the aisles were to accommodate the elaborate processions of the Sarum rite, as were the unusual width and length of the passages of the cloister – the largest, and earliest, surviving in England.[74]

---

73   Wordsworth (1901), p. 194.

74   Harvey (1974), pp. 143–5, calls these cloisters 'non-functional', and goes on to say that 'It became a point of honour to rebuild cloisters in the latest fashion, and much ingenuity was expended on them.' Their

Processions were not always confined to the cathedral: for example, the Palm Sunday procession (see Figure 7.6) that began in the choir, went out the door to the north aisle of the presbytery, round the ambulatory and out the door in the great western transept into the cloister, round the cloister to the door giving access to the area before the West Front. On Rogation Days, the procession left the cathedral, and the close, and made its way to a church in the town for mass, a replication of Roman practice.[75]

The cathedral grew from the east end, and the choir, eastern transepts and presbytery functioned as a self-contained cruciform church for the 50 canons, each of whom had a designated stall according to rank. The eastern transepts marked the division of the choir and presbytery as they did at Canterbury and Cluny, which is where the arrangement probably originated. Their stalls were arranged 'collegiate-wise', that is, in banks north and south facing one another, with return stalls at the west end against the pulpitum which closed the entry to the choir and supported the great rood. The choir and presbytery were enclosed by screens to allow them to carry out the complex array

DOMINICA IN RAMIS PALMARUM.

[*Statio dum benedicuntur rami in dominica Ramis Palmarum.* Ex Procession-
alibus 1502, 1508, 1528, 1530 Regnault.

1 cruciferarius.   2, 2 ceroferarii duo.   3 thuribularius.   4 rami
pro clericis.   5 frondes, et cetera, pro laicis.   6 librum portans.   7 sub-
diaconus.   8 diaconus.   9 sacerdos benedicens ramos.   9ᵇ puer,
deferens aquam benedictam.   (9ᵇ* locus aquebajuli *in edd.* 1519—1558.
10 locus uirgae *in edd.* 1519—1558.)]

Figure 7.6   Salisbury Cathedral, 'Dominica in Ramis' from the *Sarum Processionale* of 1502, showing the order of the procession for Palm Sunday; from Wordsworth (1901).

---

function was to provide for the extremely important processions of the Use of Sarum, which spread and took the need for cloisters with it, for example at Wells.

75 Harper (1991), p. 128.

of services undisturbed by the parochial use of the nave and the private liturgies, many of which were supported by endowments, at the altars of the many chapels and, later, chantries. As these benefactions multiplied, even with so many altars, the timing in relation to other services which might require access to a succession of altars, and the provision of spaces, celebrants and servers, was a complicated logistical task. At Salisbury, certainly by the fifteenth century when there were up to 13 chantries, annual lists were drawn up detailing which chaplains would say which mass, for whom and at what time between the early morning 'Morrow Mass' and the High Mass at 11a.m.[76]

When Salisbury was being built, the arrangement of the altars had changed since the monastic reforms of Dunstan which provided altars at tribune level. Now altars had to be accessible for them to be taken in during the great processions, and 'this probably accounts for the demise of the Anglo-Norman gallery with its altars at an upper level to which the only access was by a narrow winding staircase'.[77] A prime example of this was the 'Washing of the Altars' on Maundy Thursday, when all the altars were visited in turn, beginning with the High Altar, and progressing according to the numbering in the plan, ending with the Altar of St John Baptist, or Reliquaries. Salisbury had a very significant collection of relics. By the fifteenth century:

> Besides our Lord, and the Blessed Virgin, 14 Disciples and two of the Holy Innocents were said to have their relicks preserved at Salisbury, and out of the other Saints (Martyrs, Confessors, and Virgins) which made up a total of 331 no less than 207 had reputed relicks there. In 1538 Bp Shaxton ordered his clergy to send all the relicks, with any writings attesting them, to Ramsbury to be examined, so that any which were vain, paltry, or counterfeit, might be eliminated.

The end of the glories of Salisbury Cathedral and the Sarum Use was approaching. In 1550, the Privy Council ordered 'that all the altars … be taken away, and instead of them a table to be set up in some convenient part of the chancel'.[78] By this date, Sarum Use had become the dominant rite of the English Church, and it would provide most of the material for the Prayer Book of Edward VI. The text of the liturgy changed little in the translation for the 1549 Prayer Book, but the rubrics and the ceremonial were stripped away, along with the altars and most of their ornaments and relics. Needless to say, opposition and resentment were strong in Salisbury,[79] the *locus classicus* of English mediaeval practice – many in Salisbury will have had their own understanding of the damaging lightning-strike to the spire in 1560.

What we see now at Salisbury in the architecture and liturgy is the result of a series of transformations. At the Suppression, there were still nine active chantry foundations at the cathedral (at Wells, by comparison, there were 16).[80] In 1789, James Wyatt, 'the Destroyer', began work at Salisbury. A by no means unbiased (but fair) account was given by the Roman Catholic Dr John Milner in 1798:

> First the altar-screen has been entirely taken away, in order to lengthen the choir by admitting into it the Lady Chapel and the other low aisles behind it. Secondly, two beautiful chapels, on each side of the Lady Chapel … which could not be brought in to form part of the choir have been destroyed, and their carved ornaments in the style of the 15th century, are stuck up in different parts of the church … the workmanship of the 13th century. Thirdly, a diminutive communion table, without rails or other fence, is placed at the [extreme east end] where so far from commanding respect, it is hardly perceptible. Fourthly, to make these

---

76 Wordsworth (1901), pp. 198–9.
77 Draper (1987), pp. 85 and 86; Wordsworth (1901), pp. 199–202.
78 Quotations from Wordsworth (1901), p. 302.
79 Duffy (1992), p. 406.
80 Cook (1947), pp. 118 and 120.

alterations it has been necessary to remove the monuments and disturb the ashes of an incredible number of [illustrious] personages.[81]

The impression of purity and simplicity in the nave of Salisbury is the result of James Wyatt's eighteenth-century destructive clearance of chantry chapels and many other altars and elaborations associated with the Use of Sarum.

Conclusion

Reform began even earlier at Canterbury than at Salisbury. In 1534, the monks of Canterbury acknowledged the royal supremacy, and four years later St Thomas was 'tried' as a traitor, with charges read at his tomb (see Figure 7.7) for 30 days. When no miraculous sign came in his defence, he was found guilty, and the sentence was that his bones should be burned and his personal property forfeit; the gifts at his shrine had been given to the saint himself. Thomas Cromwell sent commissioners to carry out the sentence, and in September 1538 one of the greatest cults of the

Figure 7.7   Pilgrim Badge depicting the Shrine of St Thomas; The Metropolitan Museum of Art, Gift of Dr and Mrs W. Conte, 2001 (2001.310); image © The Metropolitan Museum of Art.

---

81   John Milner (1798), *Dissertation on the Modern Style of Altering Ancient Cathedrals*, quoted in Cobb (1980), p. 111.

medieval period was destroyed, signalling the end of the liturgical and architectural focus of the Church, and its financial base.

In 1513, the great humanist Erasmus had visited Thomas's shrine at Canterbury, and he recorded the event:

> As we enter, the spacious majesty of the building displays itself. ... In ['the North part'] is shown a wooden altar dedicated to the Blessed Virgin, of small size, and not worth notice, except as an ancient monument reproaching the excessive luxury of our own days. In the altar is the point of the sword by which the crown of the best of prelates was [pierced] and his brain scattered, the instrument of his death. For the love of the sacred Martyr we religiously kissed the sacred rust of this fragment of steel. ... We went into the choir. On the north side are displayed the choice treasures; marvellous it is to tell of the store of bones brought out; skulls, jaws, teeth, hands, fingers, entire arms, upon all of which we, adoring, applied our kisses. ... After these sights we were led still farther up the church; farther upwards, for behind the high Altar there is an ascent into, what one may call, still another Church. There, in a shrine, is shown the entire face of the saintly man, overlaid with gold, and made precious by jewels. ... A wooden cover enclosed a golden one, which being drawn up by ropes, treasures beyond all calculation are displayed. The most worthless thing there was gold, every part glowed, sparkled and flashed with rare and large gems, some of which were bigger than a goose egg. Sundry monks stood reverently by, and when the other cover was withdrawn, we knelt in worship. The Prior pointed out several jewels, touching them one by one with a white rod; and, naming each in French, added the value and title of the giver, the chief of them having been bestowed by kings.[82]

It is rather surprising to witness Erasmus' devotion, considering he had already in 1509 written a biting satire on monasticism and ecclesiastical corruption, preparing the way for the Reformation. Even if a hint of irony could be detected, it was not great enough for him to cause offence to the prior. In the end, Erasmus was a peacemaker, and in 1516 he was made a royal councillor by the future Emperor Charles V. Henry VIII brought Catherine of Aragon and Charles, by that time Emperor, to the shrine three years later in 1519, and assuming the prior could not resist a similar show of pride, Henry will not simply have been inspired to generosity to match other royal visitors. In the 1530s, when he did away with this queen, he would also do away with the shrine and the practices it represented.

At Wells, an architectural change of the sixteenth century indicates a significant change in patterns of liturgical use. Bishop Knight (1540–47) built a stone pulpit in the nave with its entry through the chantry chapel of Treasurer Hugh Sugar, built only half a century earlier, between *c.* 1485 and 1490.[83] Preaching to the lay congregation was by then central to the life of the cathedral, rather than masses for the dead.

At Ely, Nicholas West, who had found favour with Henry VIII and Cardinal Wolsey through a diplomatic coup which sealed an alliance with France and the repayment of an old debt of a million crowns to the King, was given the bishopric in 1515. In the 1520s, he began building a chantry for himself with remarkable Renaissance classical detailing in pilaster strips within the elaborate Gothic canopies, and a vaulted ceiling in which the ribs create coffers containing Renaissance grotesques, urns and seraphim. Above the entrance, Gothic canopies sit in stark contrast to a Renaissance panel showing cavorting putti amongst arabesques (Plate 10). To the right are the arms of Bishop West, to the left those of the king. Below the panel is West's motto: 'Gratia dei sum id quod sum' ('By the grace of God, I am what I am'). The chapel was finished in 1534 in the twilight of this monastic house, and though replete with the visual signs of the new learning, a now-lost inscription in English still proclaimed an indulgence:

---

82 Quoted in Woodman (1981), pp. 222–3.
83 Cobb (1980), p. 19; Cook (1947), p. 121.

Of your charitie pray for the soule of Richard West, sometime Bishop of this See, and for all Christian soules; in the which prayer he hath granted to every person so doing 40 days of pardon for every time they shall so pray.

Only five years later, on 18 November 1539, the last prior co-operated in the surrender of Ely to the king. As at Canterbury, the shrine of St Etheldreda was destroyed and the gold and jewels confiscated. [84]

King's College, a few miles away in Cambridge, was magnificently founded by Henry VI, but its fortunes suffered with his. It was re-founded by Henry VIII, enabling the completion of the chapel, the apogee of late Perpendicular Gothic with its magnificent fan vault. Henry paid for its glazing and great wooden screen, both strongly Renaissance works, which in their dates bracket the most tumultuous events of the Reformation. The screen (as the end bracket) was set up between June 1533 and May 1536 (the year of Erasmus' death),[85] and has lovers' knots with the initials of Henry and Anne Boleyn. The glazing (as the earlier bracket) was begun in 1515, the year the pope, in his struggle to move on the project to rebuild St Peter's (see Figure 7.8), issued the bull *Sacrosanctis* with indulgences for contributions to his great work. There was nothing new about that; church building had long been financed by those seeking the patronage of saints through gifts, or through the endowment of prayers or masses, or through the sale of indulgences, which was a similar thing, but in a currency of specified salvific value. However, this papal architectural project was vastly ambitious, and the bull covered a prodigious amount of politics, not to say simony. Albrecht, Archbishop of Magdeburg, struck an arrangement in 1514 whereby he would become Archbishop of Mainz as well, making him also an Ecclesiastical Elector, Imperial Chancellor and Primate of Germany, naturally providing a package of financial support for the completion of St Peter's. Within the logic of the system, indulgences all had been duly regulated, but the scale of the finances, and of the advantage sought, was staggering.

Protest came quietly, but ignited a fast-burning fuse. Whether or not Luther actually nailed his 95 theses for public dispute to the door of the Castle Church at Wittenburg on 31 October 1517,

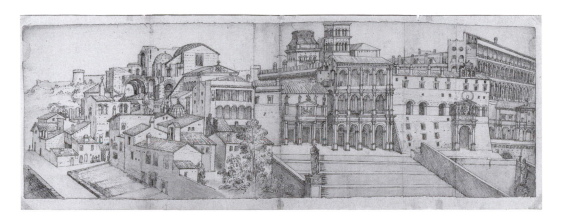

Figure 7.8   St Peter's Basilica, Rome, sixteenth-century view of the entrance before rebuilding, drawing in graphite, chalk, pen, ink and watercolour on paper; Courtauld Institute of Art Gallery, London.

---

84   Maddison (2000), p. 103, and the quotation is on p. 101.
85   Royal Commission on Historical Monuments (1959), vol. I, p. 115.

his current theological debates about justification by faith would become a significant challenge to the whole system of indulgences. Luther drew from Erasmus: 'When our Lord and Master, Jesus Christ, said "Repent", he meant that the whole life of believers should be one of penitence.' And, however angrily, he revealed his basic faith in the system: 'Christians should be taught that, if the Pope knew the exactions of the preachers of indulgences, he would rather have the basilica of St Peter reduced to ashes than built with the skin, flesh and bones of his sheep.'[86]

Erasmus, Luther and Henry VIII were not radicals in the 1520s, but events they put in train were overtaking them. Erasmus was deeply saddened by the destruction of the images of the saints in Basle Cathedral, where his own memorial came to stand. Henry tried to temper the 'Bishops' Book' and its incitement to iconoclasm with the 'King's Book', but to no avail. Henry also burned Luther's books in 1521, and aided by his bishops, wrote *The Assertion of the Seven Sacraments*, earning him the title of 'Defender of the Faith' from the pope. Luther's own position on images was very temperate: they were for 'recognition, for witness, for commemoration, for a sign'.[87] But though the forces at work were theological, to be sure, they were also political. The old opposition of Church and state, played out in the Investiture Controversy in 1124 between Henry I of England, Emperor Henry V and Louis VI of France to the benefit of Suger at Saint-Denis, and later between Henry II and Becket in 1170 to the eventual benefit of Canterbury, was still abroad. Other lands had their crises, and in England the result was Henry VIII's Act of Supremacy of 1534.

Still other forces were at work. As divisions deepened, war and the threat of war exerted huge economic pressures. Finally, the new learning of the humanists brought new cultural pressures and an attendant visual language of the Renaissance of Classicism, ironically epitomized in the design for the new St Peter's.

The new vision of the Renaissance was suddenly sweeping away the Gothic Vision. Erasmus' humanism had no truck with the allegorical interpretation of scripture by Amalarius of Metz and Durandus of Mende (or, presumably, of the liturgy and architecture), the attack on indulgences struck at the very root of the financial basis of the Church and its building programmes, and relics and shrines were being swept away. In the wake of the destruction of the driving force of medieval pilgrimage, architecture and liturgy, the rubrics of 'seeing the mass' were replaced by those of hearing the word, and in Reformation Europe, 'building the City of God' began to look more like building the city-states of God.

---

86   MacCulloch (2003), pp. 121–4; the quotations are from pp. 123–4.
87   Quoted in *ibid.*, p. 144.

Bibliography

Atroshenko, V.I. and Judith Collins (1985), *The Origins of the Romanesque: Near Eastern Influences on European Art, Fourth to Twelfth Centuries*, London, Lund Humphries.

Augustine, *Confessions*, trans. Henry Chadwick (1991), Oxford, Oxford University Press.

Baldwin Smith, E. (1956), *Architectural Symbolism of Imperial Rome and the Middle Ages*, Princeton, NJ, Princeton University Press.

Barnes, T.D. (1981), *Constantine and Eusebius*, Cambridge, MA and London, Harvard University Press.

Barral I Altet, Xavier (2002), *The Early Middle Ages: From Late Antiquity to A.D. 1000*, Cologne, Taschen.

Bartlett, Richard (2001), 'Aristocracy and Asceticism: The Letters of Ennodius and the Gallic and Italian Churches', in *Society and Culture in Late Antique Gaul: Revising the Sources*, ed. Ralph W. Mathisen and Danuta Shanzer, Aldershot, Ashgate, pp. 201–16.

Battles, Matthew (2004), *Library: An Unquiet History*, London, Vintage.

Beard, Mary, John North and Simon Price (1998), *Religions of Rome*, 2 vols, vol. I, *A History*, vol. II, *A Sourcebook*, Cambridge, Cambridge University Press.

Beckwith, John (1969), *Early Medieval Art: Carolingian, Ottonian, Romanesque*, London, Thames and Hudson.

—— (1979), *Early Christian and Byzantine Art*, 2nd edn, New Haven, CT and London, Yale University Press; first published 1970.

Bedingfield, M. Bradford (2002), *The Dramatic Liturgy of Anglo-Saxon England*, Anglo-Saxon Studies series, Woodbridge, Suffolk, Boydell Press.

Bettenson, Henry (1943), *Documents of the Christian Church*, Oxford, Oxford University Press; 2nd edn, 1963.

Bevan, Bernard (1938), *History of Spanish Architecture*, London, Batsford.

Bicknell, Stephen (1996), *The History of the English Organ*, Cambridge, Cambridge University Press.

Biddle, Martin (1999), *The Tomb of Christ*, Stroud, Sutton Publishing.

Bijlsma, T. et al. (1990), *De Tempel van Jeruzalem: beelvorming door de eewen heen*, Haarlem, Nederlands Bijbelgenootschap.

Binding, Gunter (2002), *High Gothic: The Age of the Great Cathedrals*, Cologne, Taschen.

Binski, Paul (2004), *Becket's Crown: Art and Imagination in Gothic England, 1170–1300*, New Haven, CT and London, Yale University Press.

—— (2007), 'Liturgy and Local Knowledge: English Perspectives on Trondheim Cathedral', in *The Medieval Cathedral of Trondheim: Architectural and Ritual Considerations in their European Context*, ed. M.S. Andås, Ø. Ekroll, A. Haug and N.H. Petersen, Turnhout, Brepols, pp. 21–46.

Birchler, L. (1954), 'Zur karolingischen Architektur und Malerei in Münster-Müstair', *Akten zum III. Internationalen Kongress für Frühmittelalterforschung*, Lausanne, Olten, pp. 167–252.

Bishop, Edmund (1918), *Liturgica Historia: Papers on the Liturgy and Religious Life of the Western Church*, Oxford, Clarendon Press.

Blaauw, Sible Lambertus de (1987), *Cultus et Decor: Liturgie en architectuur in laatantiek en middeleeuws Rome: Basilica Salvatoris, Santae Mariae, Sancti Petri*, Doctoral dissertation, Leiden University, Eburon, Delft.

Black, E.W. (1986), 'Christians and Pagan Hopes of Salvation in Romano-British Mosaics', in *Pagan Gods and Shrines of the Roman Empire*, ed. M. Henig and A. King, Oxford, Oxford University Press.

Blum, Pamela Z. (1992), *Early Gothic Saint-Denis: Restorations and Survivals*, Berkeley, CA, University of California Press.

Bouyer, Louis (1967), *Liturgy and Architecture*, Notre Dame, IN, University of Notre Dame Press.

Bowers, Roger, L.S. Colchester, and Anthony Crossland (2006), *The Organs and Organists of Wells Cathedral*, Wells, The Friends of Wells Cathedral.

Boyd, Susan A. (1998), 'Art in the Service of the Liturgy: Byzantine Silver Plate' in *Heaven on Earth: Art and the Church in Byzantium*, ed. Linda Safran, University Park, PA, Pennsylvania University Press, pp. 152–85.

Boyle, Leonard (1960), *St Clements Rome*, Rome, Collegio San Clemente (reprinted 1989).

Bradshaw, Paul F. (1996), *Early Christian Worship: A Basic Introduction to Ideas and Practice*, London, SPCK.

—— (2002), *The Search for the Origins of Christian Worship; Sources and Models for the Study of Early Liturgy*, revised edn, London, SPCK.

—— (2004), *Eucharistic Origins*, Alcuin Club Collections 80, London, SPCK.

Braunfels, Wolfgang (1972), *Monasteries of Western Europe: The Architecture of the Orders*, London, Thames and Hudson.

Brieger, Peter (1957), *English Art, 1216–1307*, Oxford History of English Art, vol. IV, Oxford, Oxford University Press.

Brightman, F.E. (1908), 'The *Historia Mystagogica* attributed to Germanus I', *Journal of Theological Studies*, IX, pp. 248ff and 387ff.

Brooke, Christopher (1986), 'St Bernard, the Patrons and Monastic Planning', in *Cistercian Art and Architecture in the British Isles*, ed. Christopher Norton and David Park, Cambridge, Cambridge University Press, pp. 11–23.

Brown, David (2004), *God and the Enchantment of Place: Reclaiming Human Experience*, Oxford, Oxford University Press.

Brown, Giles (1994), 'Introduction: the Carolingian Renaissance', in *Carolingian Culture: Emulation and Innovation*, ed. Rosamond McKitterick, Cambridge, Cambridge University Press, pp. 1–51.

Brown, Peter (2003), *The Rise of Western Christendom: Triumph and Diversity A.D. 200–1000*, 2nd edition, Oxford, Blackwell.

Buchwald, Hans (1999), 'Retrofit – Hallmark of Byzantine Architecture?', in *Form, Style and Meaning in Byzantine Church Architecture*, Variorum Collected series, Aldershot, Ashgate.

Bussby, Frederick (1979), *Winchester Cathedral, 1079–1979*, London, Paul Cave Publications.

Cameron, Averil (1987), 'The Construction of Court Ritual: The Byzantine *Book of Ceremonies*', in *Rituals of Royalty: Power and Ceremonial in Traditional Societies*, ed. David Cannadine and Simon Price, Cambridge, Cambridge University Press.

—— (1993a), *The Later Roman Empire AD 284–430*, London, Fontana.

—— (1993b), *The Mediterranean World in Late Antiquity AD 395–600*, London and New York, Routledge.

—— and Stuart G. Hall (1999), *Eusebius: Life of Constantine*, Oxford, Clarendon Press.

Carruthers, Mary (1998), *The Craft of Thought: Meditation, Rhetoric, and the Making of Images, 400–1200*, Cambridge, Cambridge University Press.

Cassian, John (1985), *Conferences*, trans. and Preface by Colm Luibheid, Introduction by Owen Chadwick, New York, Paulist Press.

Chadd, D.F.L. (1986), 'Liturgy and Liturgical Music: The Limits of Uniformity', in *Cistercian Art and Architecture in the British Isles*, ed. Christopher Norton and David Park, Cambridge, Cambridge University Press, pp. 299–314.

Clapham, A.W. (1930), *English Romanesque Architecture before the Conquest*, Oxford, Clarendon Press.

Claridge, Amanda (1998), *Rome*, Oxford Archaeological Guides series, Oxford and New York, Oxford University Press.

Clark, William W. (1995), '"The Recollection of the Past Is the Promise of the Future." Continuity and Contextuality: Saint-Denis, Merovingians, Capetians, and Paris', in Virginia Chieffo Raguin, Kathryn Brush and Peter Draper, ed., *Artistic Integration in Gothic Buildings*, Toronto, University of Toronto Press, pp. 92–113.

Clifton-Taylor, Alec (1986), *The Cathedrals of England*, World of Art series, London, Thames and Hudson.

Cobb, Gerald (1980), *English Cathedrals, the Forgotten Centuries: Restoration and Change from 1530 to the Present Day*, London, Thames and Hudson.

Coldstream, Nicola, (1986), 'Cistercian Architecture from Beaulieu to the Dissolution', in *Cistercian Art and Architecture in the British Isles*, ed. Christopher Norton and David Park, Cambridge, Cambridge University Press, pp. 139–59.

Collins, Roger (1998), *Charlemagne*, London, Macmillan.

—— (1999), *Early Medieval Europe, 300–1000*, London, Macmillan.

Conant, Kenneth John (1978), *Carolingian and Romanesque Architecture 800 to 1200*, 4th edn, New Haven, CT and London, Yale University Press.

Cook, G.H. (1947), *Mediaeval Chantries and Chantry Chapels*, London, Phoenix House.

Cormack, Robin (1990), 'The Temple as the Cathedral', Aphrodisias Papers, *Journal of Roman Archaeology*, Supplementary Series 1, pp. 75–8.

—— (2000), *Byzantine Art*, Oxford, Oxford University Press.

Corney, Mark (2004), 'The Roman Villa at Bradford-on-Avon: Investigations at St Lawrence School', *ARA, The Bulletin of the Association for Roman Archaeology*, 16 March.

Creed, J.L. (1984), ed. and trans., *Lactantius, De Mortibus Persecutorum*, Oxford, Clarendon Press.

Crook, John (2000), *The Architectural Setting of the Cult of the Saints in the Early Christian West c.300–1200*, Oxford, Clarendon Press.

Crosby, Sumner McKnight (1942), *The Abbey of St.-Denis, 475–1122*, vol. I, New Haven, CT, Yale University Press; London, Oxford University Press.

—— (1987), *The Royal Abbey of Saint-Denis from its Beginnings to the Death of Suger, 475–1151*, ed. Pamela Z. Blum, New Haven, CT, Yale University Press.

Crowfoot, J.W. (1941), *Early Churches in Palestine*, The Schweich Lectures of the British Academy, Oxford, Oxford University Press.

Curran, John (2000), *Pagan City and Christian Capital: Rome in the Fourth Century*, Oxford, Clarendon Press.

Dagron, Gilbert (2003), *Emperor and Priest: The Imperial Office in Byzantium*, trans. Jean Birrell, Cambridge, Cambridge University Press.

Dam, Raymond van (1985), *Leadership and Community in Late Antique Gaul*, Berkeley, CA, University of California Press.

Davies J.G. (1962), *The Architectural Setting of Baptism*, London, Barrie and Rockliff.

—— (1982), *Temples, Churches and Mosques*, New York, Pilgrim Press.

Dix, Gregory (1945), *The Shape of the Liturgy*, London, A. & C. Black (reprinted 1986).

Dehio, G. (1882), *Die Genesis der christlichen Basilika*, Sitzungsbericht der k. bayerische Akademie der Wissenschaften, phil.-historische Klasse XII, Munich.

——— and G. von Bezold (1887–1901), *Die Kirchliche Baukunst des Abendlandes: historisch und systematisch dargestelt*, 2 vols of text and 6 of plates, Stuttgart, Verlag der J.G. Cotta'shen Buchhandlung.

Draper, Peter (1987), 'Architecture and Liturgy', in *Age of Chivalry: Art in Plantagenet England, 1200–1400*, ed. Jonathan Alexander and Paul Binsky, London, Royal Academy of Arts, Weidenfeld and Nicholson.

——— (1995), 'Interpreting the Architecture of Wells Cathedral', in *Artistic Integration in Gothic Buildings*, ed. Virginia Chieffo Raguin, Kathryn Brush and Peter Draper, Toronto, University of Toronto Press.

Duchesne, L. (1886–92), *Le Liber Pontificalis*, Paris; facsimile edn, Paris, 1955–57.

——— (1903), *Christian Worship: Its Origin and Evolution, a Study of the Latin Liturgy up to the Time of Charlemagne*, trans. M.L. McClure, London, SPCK.

——— (1912), *Christian Worship: Its Origins and Evolution*, London, SPCK.

Duckett, Eleanor Shipley, (1951), *Alcuin, Friend of Charlemagne: His World and His Work*, New York, Macmillan.

Duffy, Eamon (1992), *The Stripping of the Altars: Traditional Religion in England, 1400–1580*, New Haven, CT and London, Yale University Press.

Dunbabin, K.M.D. (1999), *Mosaics of the Greek and Roman World*, Cambridge, Cambridge University Press.

Dunn, Marilyn (2000), *The Emergence of Monasticism: From the Desert Fathers to the Early Middle Ages*, Oxford, Blackwell.

Dutton, Paul Edward (2004), *Carolingian Civilization: A Reader*, 2nd edn, Peterborough, Ontario, Broadview Press.

Eco, Umberto (1986), *Art and Beauty in the Middle Ages*, trans. Hugh Bredin, New Haven, CT and London, Yale University Press (reprinted with corrections 1988).

Einhard, *The Life of Charlemagne* [*Vita Caroli*], trans. Lewis Thorpe (1969), London, Folio Society (first published 1969, London, Penguin).

Elsner, Jás (1998), *Imperial Rome and Christian Triumph*, Oxford and New York, Oxford University Press.

——— (2000), 'The *Itinerarium Burdigalense*: Politics and Salvation in the Geography of Constantine's Empire', *The Journal of Roman Studies*, XC, pp. 181–95.

Eusebius, *The History of the Church from Christ to Constantine*, trans. G.A. Williamson (1965), revised and ed. Andrew Louth (1989), London, Penguin.

Fernie, Eric (1983), *The Architecture of the Anglo-Saxons*, London, Batsford.

——— (1995), 'Suger's "Completion" of Saint-Denis', in *Artistic Integration in Gothic Buildings*, ed. Virginia Chieffo Raguin, Kathryn Brush and Peter Draper, Toronto, University of Toronto Press, pp. 84–91.

——— (2000), *The Architecture of Norman England*, Oxford, Oxford University Press.

——— (2003), 'The Architecture and Sculpture of Ely Cathedral in the Norman Period', in *A History of Ely Cathedral*, ed. Peter Meadows and Nigel Ramsay, Woodbridge, The Boydell Press, pp. 94–111.

Frend, W.H.C. (1997), '*Altare subnixus*: A cult of relics in the Romano-British Church?', *Journal of Theological Studies*, 48, part I, pp. 125–8.

Garrison, Eliza (2003), 'Henry II's *Renovatio* in the Pericope Book and Regensburg Sacramentary', in *The White Mantle of Churches: Architecture, Liturgy, and Art around the Millennium*, ed. Nigel Hiscock, International Medieval Research series, vol. 10, Turnhout, Brepols, pp. 57–79.

Gittos, Helen (2003), 'Architecture and Liturgy in England c. 1000: Problems and Possibilities', in *The White Mantle of Churches: Architecture, Liturgy, and Art around the Millennium*, ed. Nigel Hiscock, International Medieval Research series, vol. 10, Turnhout, Brepols, pp. 91–106.

Glick, Thomas F. (1979), *Islamic and Christian Spain in the Early Middle Ages*, 2nd edn (2005), Princeton, NJ, Princeton University Press.

Grabar, André (1936), *L'Empéreur dans l'art Byzantin; Recherches sur l'art officiel de l'Empire d'Orient*, Paris, Les belles Lettres.

—— (1947), 'Le témoinage d'un hymne syriaque sur l'architecture de la Cathédrale d'Edesse au Ve siècle et sur la symbolique de l'édifice chrétien', *Cahiers d'Architecture*, 2, pp. 29–67.

Grabar, Oleg (1992), 'Two Paradoxes in the Islamic Art of the Spanish Peninsula', in *The Legacy of Muslim Spain*, ed. Salma Khadra Jayyusi, New York, Brill, pp. 583–91.

Grant, Lindy (1998), *Abbot Suger of Saint-Denis: Church and State in Early Twelfth-century France*, London and New York, Longman.

Gregory of Tours, *The History of the Franks*, trans. Lewis Thorpe (1974), London, Penguin.

Grierson, P. (1962), 'Tombs and Obits of Byzantine Emperors', *Dumbarton Oaks Papers*, XVI, pp. 3ff.

Grodecki, Louis (1966), *Pre-Romanesque Art*, edited by Harald Busch and Bernd Lohse with commentaries on the illustrations by Eva-Maria Wagner, London, Batsford

—— (1986), *Gothic Architecture*, London, Faber and Faber.

Guarducci, M. (1978), *La Capella eburnea di Samagher*, Società Istriana di Archeologica e Storia Patria, Atti e Memorie, n.s. 26, Trieste.

Guidobaldi, Frederico, Claudia Barsante, Alessandra Guiglia Guidobaldi (1992), *San Clemente: La Scultura del VI Secolo con un catalogo delle sculture altomedievali*, ed. Alessandro Bonanni, San Clemente Miscellany series, IV, 2, Rome, at San Clemente.

Gwatkin, Henry Melville (1937), *Selections from Early Writers Illustrative of Church History to the time of Constantine*, London, Macmillan.

Hardison, O.B. (1965), *Christian Rite and Christian Drama in the Middle Ages: Essays in the Origin and Early History of Modern Drama*, Baltimore, MD, Johns Hopkins Press.

Harland, Philip A. (2003), *Associations, Synagogues, and Congregations; Claiming a Place in Ancient Mediterranean Society*, Minneapolis, MN, Fortress Press.

Harper, John (1991), *The Forms and Orders of Western Liturgy: From the Tenth to the Eighteenth Century*, Oxford, Clarendon Press.

Harting-Corrêa, Alice L. (1992), 'Make a Merry Noise! A Ninth-century Teacher Looks at Hymns', in *The Church and the Arts*, ed. Diana Wood, Oxford, Blackwell, pp. 79–86.

—— (1996), *Walahfrid Strabo's* Libellus de Exordiis et Incrementis Quarundam in Observationibus Ecclesiasticis Rerum*: A Translation and Liturgical Commentary*, New York, E.J. Brill.

Harvey, John (1974), *Cathedrals of England and Wales*, London, Batsford.

Hattstein, Markus (2000), *Islam: Art and Architecture*, Cologne, Könemann.

Heitz, Carol (1980), *L'Architecture religieuse carolingienne: les Formes et leurs functions*, Paris, Picard.

Hen, Yitzhak (1995), *Culture and Religion in Merovingian Gaul, A.D. 481–751*, Cultures, Beliefs and Traditions: Medieval and Early Modern Peoples series, New York, Brill.

Henderson, George (1994), 'Emulation and Invention in Carolingian Art', in *Carolingian Culture: Emulation and Innovation*, ed. Rosamond McKitterick, Cambridge, Cambridge University Press, pp. 248–73.

Henig, Martin (2004), 'Remaining Roman in Britain AD 300–700: The Evidence of Portable Art', in *Debating Late Antiquity in Roman Britain AD 300–700*, ed. Rob Collins and James Gerrard, in *British Archaeological Reports*, British Series 365, Oxford, Archaeopress.

Hillebrand, Robert (1992), 'Medieval Cordoba as a Cultural Centre', in *The Legacy of Muslim Spain*, ed. Salma Khadra Jayyusi, New York, Brill, pp. 112–35.

Hiscock, Nigel (2003a), 'The Ottonian Revival: Church Expansion and Monastic Reform', in *The White Mantle of Churches: Architecture, Liturgy, and Art around the Millennium*, Turnhout, Brepols, pp. 1–28.

——— (2003b), ed., *The White Mantle of Churches: Architecture, Liturgy, and Art around the Millennium*, Turnhout, Brepols.

Hodges, Richard and David Whitehouse (1983), *Mohammed, Charlemagne and the Origins of Europe*, London, Duckworth.

Holloway, R. Ross (2004), *Constantine and Rome*, New Haven, CT and London, Yale University Press.

Holt, Elizabeth Gilmore (1957), ed., *A Documentary History of Art*, vol. I, *The Middle Ages and the Renaissance*, Garden City, NY, Doubleday Anchor Books.

Homes Dudden, F. (1935), *The Life and Times of St Ambrose*, 2 vols, Oxford, Clarendon Press.

Hope, D.M. (1980), 'The Medieval Western Rites', in *The Study of the Liturgy*, ed. Cheslyn Jones, Geoffrey Wainwright and Edward Yarnold, London, SPCK, pp. 220–40.

Hopkins, Clark (1984), *The Discovery of Dura-Europos*, New Haven, CT, Yale University Press.

Hubert, Jean, J. Porcher and W.F. Volbach (1970), *Carolingian Art*, The Arts of Mankind series, ed. André Malraux and André Parrot, London, Thames and Hudson.

Jackson, Richard A. (1995), ed., *Ordines Coronationis Franciae: Texts and Ordines for the Coronations of Frankish and French Kings and Queens in the Middle Ages*, 2 vols, Philadelphia, PA, University of Pennsylvania Press.

Jensen, Robin Margaret (2000), *Understanding Early Christian Art*, London and New York, Routledge.

Johnson, Maxwell E. (2000), 'Worship, Practice and Belief', in *The Early Christian World*, ed. Philip F. Esler, London and New York, Routledge, 2 vols, vol. I, pp. 475–99.

Jongkees, J.H. (1966), *Studies in Old St Peter's*, Archaeologica Traiectina series, Edita AB, Academiae Rheno-Traiectinae Instituto Archaeologico, VIII, Groningen, J.B. Wolters.

Josephus, 9 vols, with trans. by H.S. Thackeray (1979), Cambridge, MA, Harvard University Press, and London, Heineman.

Jungmann, Joseph (1959), *The Mass of the Roman Rite: Its Origins and Development (Missarum Sollemnia)*, trans. Francis A. Brunner, revised Charles K. Riepe, London, Burns and Oates.

Kartsonis, Anna (1998), 'The Responding Icon', in *Heaven on Earth: Art and the Church in Byzantium*, ed. Linda Safran, University Park, PA, Pennsylvania University Press, pp. 58–80.

Kemp, E.W. (1948), *Canonization and Authority in the Western Church*, Oxford, Oxford University Press.

Keynes, Simon (2003), 'Ely Abbey 672–1109', in *A History of Ely Cathedral*, ed. Peter Meadows and Nigel Ramsay, Woodbridge, The Boydell Press, pp. 2–58.

Kidson, Peter (1987), 'Panofsky, Suger and St Denis', *Journal of the Warburg and Courtauld Institutes*, vol. 50, pp. 1–17.

Kieckhefer, Richard (2004), *Theology in Stone*, Oxford, Oxford University Press.

King, Edmund (1987), *Charlemagne: Translated Sources*, Kendal, Lambrigg.

Klauser, Theodor (1979), *A Short History of the Western Liturgy: An Account and Some Reflections*, trans. John Halliburton, 2nd edn, Oxford, Oxford University Press.

Kleinbauer, W. Eugene, Antony White and Henry Matthews, *Hagia Sophia*, London, Scala.

Klukas, Arnold W. (1978), '*Altaria superiora*: The Function and Significance of the Tribune in Anglo-Norman Romanesque', PhD thesis, University of Pittsburgh.

—— (1981), 'The Liber Ruber and the Rebuilding of the East End at Wells', *British Archaeological Association Conference Transactions*, IV, pp. 30–35.

—— (1984), 'Liturgy and Architecture: Deerhurst Priory as an Expression of the *Regularis Concordia*', *Viator*, 15, pp. 81–98.

Koch, Guntrum (1996), *Early Christian Art and Architecture*, London, SCM.

Kornexl, Lucia (1993), *Die Regularis Concordia und ihre altenglische Interlinearversion*, Munich, Wilhelm Fink.

Kraeling, Carl H. (*c.* 1935), *A Greek Fragment of Tatian's Diatesseron from Dura*, London, Christophers.

—— (1967), *The Excavations at Dura-Europos*, Final Report VIII, Part II, *The Christian Building*, New Haven, CT, Dura-Europos Publications, and New York, J.J. Augustin.

Krautheimer, Richard (1965), *Early Christian and Byzantine Architecture*, London, Penguin.

—— (1980), *Rome: Profile of a City, 312–1308*, Princeton, NJ, Princeton University Press.

—— (1983), *Three Christian Capitals: Topography and Politics*, Berkeley, CA, University of California Press.

—— (1986), *Early Christian and Byzantine Architecture*, 4th edn, London, Penguin.

—— et al. (1937–77), *Corpus Basilicarum Christianarum Romae*, vols I–V, Vatican City, Rome, Pontificio Instituto di Archeologia Cristiana, and New York, Institute of Fine Arts, New York University.

Krüger, Kristina (2003), 'Architecture and Liturgical Practice: The Cluniac *Galilaea*', in *The White Mantle of Churches: Architecture, Liturgy, and Art around the Millennium*, ed. Nigel Hiscock, International Medieval Research series, vol. 10, Turnhout, Brepols, pp. 139–59.

Lane Fox, Robin (1986), *Pagan and Christians*, London, Penguin.

Lasko, Peter (1971), *The Kingdom of the Franks: North-west Europe before Charlemagne*, London, Thames and Hudson.

—— (1994), *Ars Sacra, 800–1200*, 2nd edn, New Haven, CT and London, Yale University Press.

Lavedan, Pierre (1956), *French Architecture*, London, Penguin.

Leadbetter, Bill (2000), 'Constantine', in *The Early Christian World*, ed. Philip F. Esler, London and New York, Routledge, , 2 vols, vol. II, pp. 1069–984.

Leader-Newby, Ruth E. (2004), *Silver and Society in Late Antiquity: Functions and Meanings of Silver Plate in the Fourth to Seventh Centuries*, Aldershot, Ashgate.

Leyerle, Blake (2000), 'Communication and Travel', in *The Early Christian World*, ed. Philip F. Esler, London and New York, Routledge, 2 vols, vol. I, pp. 452–74.

Louth, Andrew (1969), ed., *Eusebius: The History of the Church from Christ to Constantine*, trans. G.A. Williamson (1965), London, Penguin.

Lowden, John (1997), *Early Christian and Byzantine Art*, London, Phaidon.

MacCormack, Sabine G. (1981), *Art and Ceremony in Late Antiquity*, Berkeley, CA, California University Press.

MacCulloch, Diarmaid (2003), *Reformation: Europe's House Divided, 1490–1700*, London, Penguin.

Maddison, John (2000), *Ely Cathedral: Design and Meaning*, Ely, Cathedral Publications.

Mainstone, Rowland J. (1988), *Hagia Sophia: Architecture, Structure and Liturgy of Justinian's Great Church*, London, Thames and Hudson.

Makki, Mahmoud (1992), 'The Political History of al-Andalus (92/711–897/1492)', in *The Legacy of Muslim Spain*, ed. Salma Khadra Jayyusi, New York, Brill, pp. 3–87.

Mâle, Emile (1960), *The Early Churches of Rome*, London, Ernest Benn.

—— (1972), *The Gothic Image: Religious Architecture in France of the Thirteenth Century*, trans. Dora Nussey, New York, Icon; translation first published New York, Harper and Row, 1958.

Mango, Cyril (1986), *The Art of the Byzantine Empire, 312–1453: Sources and Documents*, Toronto, University of Toronto Press; first published 1972 in the series Sources and Documents in the History of Art, ed. H.W. Janson, New York, Prentice-Hall.

Manuel, Casamar Perez (1992), 'The Almoravids and Almohads: An Introduction', in the exhibition catalogue *Al-Andalus: The Art of Islamic Spain*, New York, The Metropolitan Museum of Art, pp. 75–83.

Masurillo, H.A. (1972), *The Acts of the Christian Martyrs*, Oxford, Oxford University Press.

Mathews, Thomas F. (1962), 'An Early Roman Chancel Arrangement and its Liturgical Uses', *Revista di Archeologia Cristiana*, 38, Rome, Pontificio Instituto di Archeologia Christiana; reprinted in *Art and Architecture in Byzantium and Armenia: Liturgical and Exegetical Approaches*, Variorum Collected Studies series, Aldershot, Ashgate, 1995.

—— (1971), *The Early Churches of Constantinople: Architecture and Liturgy*, University Park, PA and London, University of Pennsylvania Press.

—— (1982), Private Liturgy in Byzantine Architecture: Toward a Reappraisal', *Cahiers Archéologiques*, 30, Paris, Editions Picard; reprinted in *Art and Architecture in Byzantium and Armenia: Liturgical and Exegetical Approaches*, Variorum Collected Studies series, Aldershot, Ashgate, 1995.

Maxwell, William D. (1945), *An Outline of Christian Worship: Its Development and Forms*, London, Oxford University Press; first published 1936.

Mayr-Harting, Henry (1992), 'Charlemagne as a Patron of Art', in *The Church and the Arts*, ed. Diana Wood, Oxford, Blackwell, pp. 43–77.

—— (1999), 'Artists and Patrons', in *The New Cambridge Medieval History*, vol. III, *c.900– c.1024*, ed. Timothy Reuter, Cambridge, Cambridge University Press, pp. 212–30.

McGinn, Bernard (1995), 'From Admirable Tabernacle to the House of God', in *Artistic Integration in Gothic Buildings*, ed. Virginia Chieffo Raguin, Kathryn Brush and Peter Draper, Toronto, University of Toronto Press, pp. 41–56.

McKitterick, Rosamond (1977), *The Frankish Church and the Carolingian Reforms, 789–895*, London, Royal Historical Society.

—— (1994), 'Script and Book Production', in *Carolingian Culture: Emulation and Innovation*, ed. Rosamond McKitterick, Cambridge, Cambridge University Press, pp. 221–47.

McLynn, Neil B. (1994), *Ambrose of Milan: Church and Court in a Christian Capital*, Berkeley, CA, University of California Press.

—— (2004), 'Imperial Churchgoing', in *Approaching Late Antiquity: The Transformation from Early to Late Empire*, ed. Simon Swain and Mark Edwards, Oxford, Oxford University Press.

McVey, Kathleen E. (1984), 'The Domed Church as Microcosm: Literary Roots of an Architectural Symbol', *Dumbarton Oaks Papers*, 37, pp. 91–121; reprinted in *Art, Archaeology, and Architecture of Early Christianity*, ed. Paul Corby Finney (1993), Studies in Early Christianity series, vol. XVIII, New York and London, Garland.

Meadows, Peter and Nigel Ramsay (2003), ed., *A History of Ely Cathedral*, Woodbridge, The Boydell Press.

Meates, G.W., E. Greenfield and Edwyn Birchenough (1951), 'The Lullingstone Roman Villa', in *Archaeologia Cantiana*, (1951) vol. LXIII, pp. 1–49; 'Second Interim Report' (1952), vol. LXV, pp. 26–78; 'Third Interim Report' (1953), vol. LXVI, pp. 15–36.

—— (1955), *Lullingstone Roman Villa*, London, Heinemann.

—— (1963), *Lullingstone Roman Villa, Kent*, London, HMSO.

—— (1987), *The Roman Villa at Lullingstone, Kent*, vol. II, *The Wall Paintings and Finds*, Monograph Series of the Kent Archaeological Society, no. III, Maidstone, Kent Archaeological Society.

Meeks, Wayne A. (1983), *The First Urban Christians: The Social World of the Apostle Paul*, New Haven, CT and London, Yale University Press.

Meer, F. van der, (1967), *Early Christian Art*, trans. from the German edn Peter and Friedl Brown, London, Faber and Faber; originally published in Dutch as *Oudchristelijke Kunst*, Zeist, W. de Haan, 1959.

Meyendorff, John (1989), *Imperial Unity and Christian Divisions: The Church 450–680*, Crestwood, NY, St Vladimir's Seminary Press.

Millingen, Alexander van (1912), *Byzantine Churches in Constantinople: Their History and Architecture*, London, Macmillan.

Morris, Colin (2005), *The Sepulchre of Christ and the Medieval West: From the Beginning to 1600*, Oxford, Oxford University Press.

Morris, Richard (1989), *Churches in the Landscape*, London, J.M. Dent.

Neale, John Mason and Benjamin Webb (1906), *The Symbolism of Churches and Church Ornaments: A Translation of the First Book of the Rationale Divinorum Officiorum, Written by William Durandus, Sometime Bishop of Mende*, 3rd edn, London, Gibbings.

Nelson, Janet L. (1987), 'The Lord's Anointed and the People's Choice: Carolingian Royal Ritual', in *Rituals of Royalty: Power and Ceremonial in Traditional Societies*, ed. David Cannadine and Simon Price, Cambridge, Cambridge University Press, pp. 137–80.

Nineham, Denis (1993), *Christianity, Mediaeval and Modern: A Study in Religious Change*, London, SCM.

Ousterhout, Robert (1998), 'The Holy Space: Architecture and the Liturgy', in *Heaven on Earth: Art and the Church in Byzantium*, ed. Linda Safran, University Park, PA, Pennsylvania University Press, pp. 81–120.

Painter, Kenneth (1999), 'The Water Newton Silver: Votive or Liturgical?', *Journal of the British Archaeological Association*, CLII, pp. 1–23.

Palladius, *The Lausiac History*, trans. and annotated Robert T. Meyer (1965), Westminster, MD, The Newman Press; London, Longman and Green.

Parker, D.C., D.G.K. Taylor and M.S. Goodacre (1999), 'The Dura-Europos Gospel Harmony', in D.G.K. Taylor, ed., *Studies in the Early Texts of the Gospels and Acts: The Papers of the First Birmingham Colloquium on the Textual Criticism of the New Testament*, Birmingham, Birmingham University Press, pp. 193–228.

Peeters, C.J.A.C. (1969), *De Liturgische dispositie van het vroegchristelijk kerkbouw: Plaats en samenhang van de cathedra, de leesplaats en het altar in de basiliek van de vierde tot de zevende eeuw*, Assen, Van Gorcum.

Peña, Ignacio (1997), *The Christian Art of Byzantine Syria*, trans. Eileen Brophy and Francisco Reina, Reading, Garnet.

Percival, John (1976), *The Roman Villa*, London, Batsford.

Perin, Patrick (1991), 'Quelques considerations sur la basilique de Saint-Denis et sa nécropole à lépoque mérovingienne', in J.-M. Duvosquel and A. Dierkens, ed., *Villes et campagnes au moyen âge*, Liège, pp. 599–624.

Perkins, Ann (1973), *The Art of Dura-Europos*, Oxford, Clarendon Press.

Petersen, Nils Holger (2003), 'The Representational Liturgy of the *Regularis Concordia*', in *The White Mantle of Churches: Architecture, Liturgy, and Art around the Millennium*, ed. Nigel Hiscock, International Medieval Research series, vol. 10, Turnhout, Brepols, pp. 107–17.

Petts, David (2003), *Christianity in Roman Britain*, Stroud and Charleston, SC, Tempus.

Plant, Richard (2003), 'Architectural Developments in the Empire North of the Alps: the Patronage of the Imperial Court', in *The White Mantle of Churches: Architecture, Liturgy, and Art around the Millennium*, ed. Nigel Hiscock, International Medieval Research series, vol. 10, Turnhout, Brepols, pp. 29–56.

Pocknee, Cyril E. (1963*), The Christian Altar*, London, Mowbray.

Pressouyre, Léon (1990), *Le Rêve Cistercien*, Paris, Gallimard.

Price, Simon (1987), 'From Noble Funerals to Divine Cult: The Consecration of Roman Emperors', in *Rituals of Royalty: Power and Ceremonial in Traditional Societies*, ed. David Canadine and Simon Price, Cambridge, Cambridge University Press, pp. 56–105.

Rabe, Susan A. (1995), *Faith, Art, and Politics at Saint-Riquier: The Symbolic Vision of Angilbert*, Philadelphia, PA, University of Pennsylvania Press.

Radding, Charles M. and William W. Clark (1992), *Medieval Architecture, Medieval Learning: Builders and Masters in the Age of Romanesque and Gothic*, New Haven, CT and London, Yale University Press.

Raguin, Virginia Chieffo, Kathryn Brush and Peter Draper (1995), ed., *Artistic Integration in Gothic Buildings*, Toronto, University of Toronto Press.

Rahner, H. (1963), *Greek Myths and Christian Mystery*, London, Burns Oates.

Rankin, Susan (1994), 'Carolingian Music', in *Carolingian Culture: Emulation and Innovation*, ed. Rosamond McKitterick, Cambridge, Cambridge University Press, pp. 274–316.

Rasmussen, Neils Krogh (1986), in *Abbot Suger and Saint-Denis: A Symposium*, ed. Paul Lieber Gierson, New York, Metropolitan Museum of Art/Abrams, pp. 42–47.

Renoue, Marie and Renaud Dengreville (1997), *Conques: moyenâgeuse, mystique, contemporaine*, Paris, Editions du Rouergue.

Roberts, Alexander and Donaldson, James (1884), ed., *The Ante-Nicene Fathers; Translations of the Writings of the Fathers down to A.D. 325*, US reprint 1973, revised by A. Cleveland Coxe, vol. I, Grand Rapids MI, Eerdmans.

Romero, Anne-Marie (1992), *Saint-Denis: Emerging Powers*, translated by Azizeh Azodi, Paris, Caisse nationale des Monuments.

Rostovtzeff, M. (1938), *Dura-Europos and its Art*, Oxford, Clarendon Press.

Royal Commission on Historical Monuments (1959), *City of Cambridge: A Survey and Inventory by the Royal Commission on Historical Monuments*, in two parts with a box of plans and maps, London, RCHM.

Rubin, Miri (1991), *Corpus Christi: The Eucharist in Late Medieval Culture*, Cambridge, Cambridge University Press.

Sampson, Jerry (1998), *Wells Cathedral West Front: Construction, Sculpture and Conservation*, Stroud, Sutton Publishing.

Schnaase, Karl Julius Ferdinand (1843–64), *Geschichte der Bildenden Künste*, Düsseldorf, J. Buddeus.

Sherrard, P. (1965), *Constantinople: Iconography of a Sacred City*, London, Oxford University Press.

Simson, Otto von (1989), *The Gothic Cathedral: Origins of Gothic Architecture and the Medieval Concept of Order*, Bollingen Series XLVIII, Princeton, NJ, Princeton University Press; first published 1956.

Sutton, Ian (1999), *Western Architecture: A Survey from Ancient Greece to the Present*, London, Thames and Hudson.

Smith, Dennis E. (2003), *From Symposium to Eucharist: the Banquet in the Early Christian World*, Minneapolis, MN, Fortress Press.

Smith, Julia M.H. (2005), *Europe after Rome: A New Cultural History, 500–1000*, Oxford, Oxford University Press.

Snyder, Graydon F. (1985), *Ante Pacem: Archaeological Evidence of Church Life before Constantine*, Macon, GA, Mercer University Press.

Spurrell, Mark (2005), 'The Development of the English Mediaeval Chancel and its Use by the Laity', D.Phil. thesis, University of Oxford, Bodleian Library.

Stalley, Roger (1999), *Early Medieval Architecture*, Oxford History of Art series, Oxford, Oxford University Press.

Stringer, Martin D. (2005), *A Sociological History of Christian Worship*, Cambridge, Cambridge University Press.

Suger, *On the Abbey Church of St-Denis and its Art Treasures*, ed. and trans. Erwin Panofsky (1946), Princeton, NJ, Princeton University Press.

Sumption, Jonathan (1975), *Pilgrimage: an Image of Mediaeval Religion*, London, Faber.

Swanson, R.N. (1992), 'Medieval Liturgy as Theatre: The Props', in *The Church and the Arts*, ed. Diana Wood, Oxford, Blackwell, pp. 239–53.

Symons, T. (1953), ed. and trans., *Regularis concordia Anglicae nationis monachorum sanctimonialiumque: The Monastic Agreement of the Monks and Nuns of the English Nation*, London.

Taft, Robert (1975), *The Great Entrance*, Orientalia Christiana Analecta 200, Rome, Pontifical Institute of Oriental Studies.

Tatton-Brown, Tim (1989), *Great Cathedrals of Britain*, London, BBC.

Taylor, D.G.K. (1999), ed., *Studies in the Early Texts of the Gospels and Acts: The Papers of the First Birmingham Colloquium on the Textual Criticism of the New Testament*, Birmingham, Birmingham University Press.

Taylor, Joan E. (1993), *Christians and Holy Places: The Myth of Jewish-Christian Origins*, Oxford, Clarendon Press.

Tertullian, *Apology*, trans. S. Thelwall, in *The Ante-Nicene Fathers*, ed. Alexander Roberts and James Donaldson, vol. III, *Latin Christianity: Its Founder, Tertullian*; US edn, ed. A. Cleveland Coxe (1978), Eerdmans, Grand Rapids, Michigan.

Teteriatnikov, Natalia B. (1996), *The Liturgical Planning of Byzantine Churches in Cappadocia*, Orientalia Christiana Analecta 252, Rome, Pontificio Instituto Orientale.

Theissen, Gerd (1999), *A Theory of Primitive Christian Religion*, trans. John Bowden, London: SCM Press.

Thibodeau, Timothy (2006), *The Oxford History of Christian Worship*, ed. Geoffrey Wainwright and Karen B. Westerfield Tucker, Oxford, Oxford University Press.

Thomas, Charles (1981), *Christianity in Roman Britain to AD 500*, London, Batsford.

Toynbee, Jocelyn and John Ward-Perkins (1956), *The Shrine of St Peter and the Vatican Excavations*, London, Longmans Green.

Vallance, Aymer (1947), *Greater English Church Screens: Being Great Roods, Screenwork and Roodlofts in Cathedral, Monastic and Collegiate Churches in England and Wales*, London, New York and Toronto, Batsford.

Vasiliev, A. (1948), 'Imperial Porphyry Sarcophagi in Constantinople', *Dumbarton Oaks Papers*, IV, pp. 1ff.

Vidier, M.A. (1911), 'La mappemonde de Théodulphe et la mappemonde de Ripoll', *Bulletin de Géographie historique et descriptive*, pp. 285ff

Vieillard-Troiekouroff, May (1976), *Les Monuments religieux de la Gaule d'après les oeuvres de Grégoire de Tours*, Paris, Honoré Champion.

Wallace-Hadrill, Andrew (1994), *Houses and Society in Pompeii and Herculaneum*, Princeton, NJ, Princeton University Press.

Ward-Perkins, Bryan (2005), *The Fall of Rome and the End of Civilization*, Oxford, Oxford University Press.

Ward-Perkins, J.B. (1966), 'Memoria, Martyr's Tomb and Martyr's Church', *Journal of Theological Studies*, XVII, part I, April, pp. 386–403; reprinted in *Art, Archaeology and Architecture of Early Christianity*, ed. Paul Corby Finney (1993), Studies in Early Christianity series, vol. XVIII, New York and London, Garland Publishing.

Watkin, Aelred (1941), 'Dean Cosyn and Wells Cathedral Miscellanea', Somerset Record Society LVI.

Wharton, Annabel Jane (1995), *Refiguring the Post-Classical City: Dura Europos, Jerash, Jerusalem and Ravenna*, Cambridge, Cambridge University Press.

Whitaker, E.C. (1970), ed., *Documents of the Baptismal Liturgy*, 2nd edn, London, SPCK.

—— (2003), *Documents of the Baptismal Liturgy*, 3rd edn, revised and expanded Maxwell E. Johnson, London, SPCK.

White, L. Michael (1990), *Building God's House in the Roman World: Architectural Adaptation among Pagans, Jews, and Christians*, Baltimore, MD and London, Johns Hopkins University Press.

—— (1996–97), *The Social Origins of Christian Architecture*, vol. I: *Building God's House in the Roman World: Architectural Adaptation among Pagans, Jews, and Christians*, vol. II: *Texts and Monuments of the Christian Domus Ecclesiae in its Environment*, Harvard Theological Studies 42, Valley Forge, PA, Trinity Press International.

—— (2000), 'Architecture: The First Five Centuries', in *The Early Christian World*, ed. Philip F. Esler, 2 vols, vol. II, London and New York, Routledge, pp. 693–746.

Whitehill, Walter Muir (1941), *Spanish Romanesque Architecture of the Eleventh Century*, Oxford, Oxford University Press.

Wiles, Maurice and Mark Santer (1975), *Documents in Early Christian Thought*, Cambridge, Cambridge University Press.

Wilkinson, John (2002), *Egeria's Travels: Newly Translated with Supporting Documents and Notes*, 3rd edn, Warminster, Aris and Phillips.

William of Malmesbury, *see* Winterbottom and Thomson (2002) .

Wilson, Christopher (1986), 'The Cistercians as "Missionaries of Gothic" in Northern England', in *Cistercian Art and Architecture in the British Isles*, ed. C. Norton and D. Park, Cambridge, Cambridge University Press, pp. 86–116.

—— (1990), *The Gothic Cathedral: The Architecture of the Great Church, 1130–1530*, London, Thames and Hudson.

Wilson-Dickson, Andrew (1997), *A Brief History of Christian Music: From Biblical Times to the Present*, Oxford, Lion (1st edn, 1992).

Winkler, Gabriele (1978), 'The Original Meaning of the Prebaptismal Anointing and its Implications', *Worship*, vol. 52, p. 36.

Winterbottom, M. and R.M. Thomson (2002), *William of Malmesbury, Saints' Lives: Lives of SS. Wulfstan, Dunstan, Patrick, Benignus and Indract*, Oxford, Clarendon Press.

Woodman, Francis (1981), *The Architectural History of Canterbury Cathedral*, London, Routledge and Kegan Paul.

Wordsworth, Christopher (1901), ed., *Ceremonies and Processions of the Cathedral Church of Salisbury: From the Fifteenth-century MS. No 148 with Additions from the Cathedral Records and Woodcuts from the Sarum Processionale of 1502*, Cambridge, Cambridge University Press.

Wybrew, Hugh (1989), *The Orthodox Liturgy: The Development of the Eucharistic Liturgy in the Byzantine Rite*, London, SPCK.

Yarnold, Edward (1978), 'Initiation: The Fourth and Fifth Centuries', in *The Study of Liturgy*, ed. Cheslyn Jones, Geoffrey Wainwright and Edward Yarnold, London, SPCK.

—— (2000), *Cyril of Jerusalem*, London and New York, Routledge.

Young, Bailey (2001), 'Sacred Topography: The Impact of the Funerary Basilica in Late Antique Gaul', in *Society and Culture in Late Antique Gaul: Revising the Sources*, ed. Ralph W. Mathisen and Danuta Shanzer, Aldershot, Ashgate, pp. 169–86.

Young, Karl (1933), *The Drama of the Medieval Church*, 2 vols, Oxford, Clarendon Press.

Index